To Marion
with love

THE MASTER MUSICIANS

SCHUBERT

Series edited by Stanley Sadie

THE MASTER MUSICIANS

SCHUBERT

John Reed

OXFORD UNIVERSITY PRESS

OXFORD
UNIVERSITY PRESS

Oxford University Press, Great Clarendon Street, Oxford OX2 6DP

Oxford University Press is a department of the University of Oxford.
It furthers the University's objective of excellence in research, scholarship,
and education by publishing worldwide in

Oxford New York

Athens Auckland Bangkok Bogotá Buenos Aires Calcutta
Cape Town Chennai Dar es Salaam Delhi Florence Hong Kong Istanbul
Karachi Kuala Lumpur Madrid Melbourne Mexico City Mumbai
Nairobi Paris São Paulo Shanghai Singapore Taipei Tokyo Toronto Warsaw

and associated companies in Berlin Ibadan

Oxford is a registered trade mark of Oxford University Press
in the UK and in certain other countries

First published 1987 by J. M. Dent & Sons Ltd

First paperback edition 1988
First published by Oxford University Press 1997

British Library Cataloguing in Publication Data

Data available

Library of Congress Cataloging in Publication Data
Reed, John, 1909– .
Schubert / John Reed.—[2nd ed.]
p. cm.—(The Master musicians)
Includes bibliographical references (p.) and index.
1. Schubert Franz, 1797–1828. 2. Composers—Austria—Biography.
I. Title. II. Series: Master musicians series.
ML410.S3R26 1997 780'.92—dc20 [B] 96–34211
ISBN 0–19–816630–3
ISBN 0–19–816494–7 (Pbk)

3 5 7 9 10 8 6 4

Printed in Great Britain
on acid-free paper by
J.W. Arrowsmith Ltd., Bristol,

Contents

List of illustrations   ix
List of abbreviations   x
Preface to the first edition   xi
Preface to the second edition   xv

1 Early life   1
2 The schoolhouse years (1813–16)   14
3 The origins of the Lied   26
4 Instrumental, liturgical, and dramatic works (1813–16)   37
5 New perspectives (1817–March 1821)   50
6 The opera years (1821–3)   73
7 Poetry and disillusion (1824)   98
8 Grand symphony (1825–6)   114
9 The winter journey (1827)   140
10 The final phase (1828)   158

Appendices
A Calendar   183
B Classified list of works   201
C Personalia   234
D Select bibliography   253

Index   261

List of illustrations

Between pages 144 and 145

1 Franz Theodor Schubert. Oil painting by Carl Schubert
2 Ferdinand Schubert. Oil painting (unfinished) by his nephew Ferdinand
3 Therese Grob. Oil painting by Heinrich Hollpein
4 Joseph von Spaun. Pencil drawing by Moritz von Schwind
5 Franz von Schober. Oil painting by Leopold Kupelwieser
6 Johann Mayrhofer. Crayon sketch by Ludwig Michalek after Moritz von Schwind
7 Moritz von Schwind. Self-portrait
8 Franz von Bruchmann. Etching from the original drawing by Leopold Kupelwieser
9 The Kärntnertor Theatre
10 Schubert's room at Zseliz
11 Schubert. Pencil drawing by Leopold Kupelwieser (1821)
12 Autograph of 'Das Lied im Grünen'
13 Wilhelm Müller, author of Die schöne Müllerin and of Winterreise. From an unsigned original
14 Johann Michael Vogl. Original drawing by Franz von Schober
15 Karl Freiherr von Schönstein. Lithograph by Josef Kriehuber
16 Anna Fröhlich. Crayon sketch by Heinrich Thugut
17 View of Gmunden. Pen-and-ink drawing by Carl Schubert
18 View of Gastein, 1820. Etching by Ernst Wölcker after a drawing by Karl Ludwig Viehbeck
19 Excursion of the Schubertians from Atzenbrugg to Aumühl. From the water-colour by Leopold Kupelwieser.

Nos 1–10, 13–16 and 19 are reproduced by permission of the Historical Museum, Vienna; no. 11 is privately owned; no 12, Stanford University, California; no. 17, the Albertina Graphic Collection, Vienna; and no. 18, the Austrian National Library, Vienna.

Abbreviations

AmZ	*Allgemeine musikalische Zeitung*
Brille	*Schubert durch die Brille* (Journal of the *Internationales Franz Schubert Institut* in Vienna)
Docs	O. E. Deutsch, *Schubert: A Documentary Biography* (London, 1946)
ed., eds.	edited by
f.p.	first performance
Memoirs	O. E. Deutsch, *Schubert: Memoirs by his Friends* (London, 1958)
ML	*Music & Letters*
MQ	*The Musical Quarterly*
MR	*The Music Review*
MT	*The Musical Times*
mvmt.	movement
NCM	*19th-Century Music*
Phil. Soc.	The Vienna Philharmonic Society (*Gesellschaft der Musikfreunde*)
r/p	reprinted
SATB, etc.	soprano, alto, tenor, bass
sop.	soprano
ten.	tenor
trans.	translated by
ZfK	*Wiener Zeitschrift für Kunst, Literatur, Theater und Mode*

Preface to the first edition

The posthumous reputations of great composers seem to fall into three distinct phases. First comes what A. N. Whitehead has called, in another context, the age of romance. Based on the vivid but fallible recollections of the great man's contemporaries, this thrives on legend and anecdotes and tends to emphasize the magical properties of genius. In time it gives way to the patient documentation of events in a spirit of scientific enquiry, to what might be called the phase of definitive biography, represented in the nineteenth century, for instance, by the work of Thayer on Beethoven, Jahn on Mozart, and Pohl on Haydn. Finally, a period of critical evaluation and synthesis ensues, in which the stature of the artist is looked at afresh in the context of his age, and man and artist are brought into meaningful relationship.

Schubert biography conforms to this pattern closely, except in one curious respect. Whereas the definitive work on his illustrious predecessors was done in the 1860s and '70s, it was not till 1912 that Otto Erich Deutsch, the Austrian art historian and musicologist, drew up plans for his monumental work on Schubert.[1] As originally conceived, this was to consist of four volumes: (I) A reprint of Grove's biographical article on the composer, newly edited and translated, together with a comprehensive bibliography; (II) The documents themselves in two parts, the first covering the life and the second the obituary notices, posthumous memoirs, and recollections of his friends and contemporaries; (III) An iconographical volume, the material for which Deutsch had already assembled, and which was published in 1913 under the title *Sein Leben in Bildern* ('His Life in Pictures'); and (IV) The Thematic Catalogue of his complete works.

The reasons for this late start on the documentation of Schubert's life have never been fully explained. Doubtless it owed something to the fact that only a small part of his total *œuvre* was published during his short lifetime, and even more to the shadow cast on his reputation during the

---

[1] *Franz Schubert: die Dokumente seines Lebens und Schaffens* ('Franz Schubert: the Documents of his Life and Work').

nineteenth century by the general adulation of Beethoven and Mendelssohn. A certain amount of deliberate mystification, however, seems also to have been involved. It is known that many contemporary documents, including the diaries kept by his close friends Anselm Hüttenbrenner, Leopold Sonnleithner and Johann Jenger, have disappeared. Other leading actors in the drama, such as Schwind and Schober, never found time during their long lives to write down in any systematic way their recollections of events. Even the biographical material collected in the 1850s and '60s by Ferdinand Luib and others is markedly restrained in its references to Schubert's private life, and particularly to the illness which struck him down in 1823 and plagued him for the rest of his life. It was Deutsch, in 1907, who first raised publicly in print the possibility that the illness was syphilitic.[2] No doubt this reticence showed a well-intentioned desire to protect the memory of a great artist, but like all such attempts to conceal the true facts, it has in the end proved counter-productive.

The impact of two world wars, and of the totalitarian revolution which occurred between them, delayed the completion of O. E. Deutsch's grand design for a further fifty years after 1914. At that time only the iconographical volume and the German edition of the first part of the Documents, without commentary, had been published. In 1939 Deutsch took up residence in England, and generously put all his research papers and documents at the disposal of Arthur Hutchings, who undertook to write the last volume on Schubert in the 'Master Musicians' series. This was published in 1945. But the much expanded complete edition of the Documents in English, with Deutsch's own extensive commentaries, which followed a year later, proved to be only the beginning of the modern renaissance of Schubert scholarship. The Thematic Catalogue, the source of those indispensable D numbers, appeared in 1951, and the 'Memoirs by his Friends' (part two of the documentary volume projected in 1914) was published in the original German in 1957, and in an English translation in 1958. Finally, a much enlarged and revised version of the Thematic Catalogue in German, for which the editorial team of the *Neue Schubert Ausgabe* was responsible, came out in 1978 to mark the one hundred and fiftieth anniversary of the composer's death.

These books are the working tools of all Schubert scholars, and have made possible a vigorous efflorescence of critical and biographical studies. New research techniques have given us new insights into old problems. The scientific study of watermarks and other paper characteristics, for instance, has resulted in a reordering of the various symphonic sketches Schubert left behind, and disposed finally of Grove's attractive, but ill-conceived, hypothesis of a missing symphony of 1825. Patient exploration of the archives of the *Gesellschaft der Musikfreunde*, the

---

[2] In an article in *Bühne und Welt*, vol. ix, 1907, p. 227.

Männergesangverein, and other institutions in and beyond Vienna, has brought to light many new autographs and documents. A revival of interest in the cultural and political background to Schubert's life now enables us to see many problems, from his generally assumed penury to his relations with the *Gesellschaft*, in a fresh light. Even old mysteries such as the provenance of the 'Unfinished' Symphony, and the date of the B flat major Piano Trio, do not seem quite so impenetrable as they did. Schubert scholarship has moved faster, and further, in the last forty years than it did in the whole of the previous century.

My aim in this book, however, goes a little beyond the need to make the findings of modern scholarship available in a modest and accessible compass to the student and the music-lover. Schubert is something of a special case, because the relationship between the man and the artist is so baffling. What connection can there be between the little man in glasses who made only a slight impression on his contemporaries, and the composer of the song cycles, of the D minor Quartet, and the B flat Sonata D 960? Many good critics have said, 'None'. The dramatist Eduard von Bauernfeld, who was close to Schubert in the last years of his life, thought his life showed 'so few tangible signs' that only 'a kind of poetic outline' could be given of it. Grove, in the course of his justly famous article, affirmed that 'no memoir of Schubert can ever be satisfactory, because no relation can be established between his life and his work; or rather, properly speaking, because there is no life to establish a relation with'. How far these sentiments reflect a wish to protect the composer from the prying eyes of future biographers it is impossible to say. But at least we are now free from the obligation to be discreet. Schubert's reputation as a great composer, constantly challenged in the nineteenth century, is now beyond question; and if genius must always remain a mystery, the biographer's job is to keep his eye firmly focussed on the relationship between life and work. For that reason I decided to abandon the procedure usually adopted in this series, and to deal critically with all the major works so far as possible in the course of the main narrative. My hope and belief is that by presenting a credible picture of the man against the background of his age it is possible to enhance the achievement of the great universal artist who transcends it.

A word of explanation about the footnotes may be helpful. References to the standard sources and commentaries are normally given in full on their first appearance, and thereafter in abbreviated form. Full details of publication and dates are also given in the Bibliography at Appendix D.

D numbers are given for every entry in the Classified List of Works at Appendix B, but in the main text I have used them sparingly and only where some doubt may arise about the work or works in question. No useful purpose seems to be served by attaching D numbers invariably to well-known works such as the song cycles or the mature symphonies.

Of the many friends who have helped me while this book was in preparation, I owe a special debt to Rhys Williams for advice on medical questions, and to Roger Fiske and Elizabeth Norman McKay, who read the main chapters in typescript and made valuable suggestions.

October 1985   J.R.

Preface to the second edition

The reception history of great composers, and especially that of Schubert, is best thought of as a gradual process of discovery, as a full and complete disclosure of the range of the composer's genius. Hence the importance of complete editions and performances. This was recognized even in the nineteenth century by the missionary work of such Schubert enthusiasts as Charles Hallé, who in 1868 played all the eleven then available piano sonatas of Schubert in a series of London recitals; and August Manns, the conductor of the Crystal Palace Orchestra, who in 1881 performed all eight symphonies in chronological order. Manns followed this up two years later by performing the E major symphonic sketch of 1821 in John Barnett's completed orchestration. The same urge to present Schubert whole and complete must have inspired Nicolaus Dumba and Eusebius Mandyczewski, the chief architects of the first complete critical edition in 1884–97. Little progress was made in this direction between the wars. In recent years, however, and especially in the decade which has elapsed since the first edition of this book was published, we have become accustomed not only to complete recordings and performances of the sonatas and symphonies, but also to recordings and serial performances of that rich store-house of good music, the four-hand piano duet works. Even Schubert's more than 600 songs are now available in recorded editions, a far cry from the days when he was represented in the catalogues by, say, thirty songs.

Another symptom of the growing public interest in Schubert's music is the proliferation of Schubert societies and associations throughout the world. Again, we have to look back to the 1860s for the beginning of the story. The *Musical Times* of June 1866 carried the following announcement: SCHUBERT SOCIETY 'The first *Soirée Musicale* of this recently formed Society took place on Thursday evening April 25th, at the Beethoven Rooms, Harley Street. With a view to spreading still wider a taste for the works of the renowned Franz Schubert, Mr. E. Schubert has set on foot the above Society.' It is good to know that the evening began with a performance of the E flat Piano Trio Op. 100, 'admirably rendered by Miss

Fanny Beher of the London Academy, with Messrs. Geoffrie and Schubert'. Since then, many Schubert societies have come and gone. But since the foundation of the *Internationales Franz Schubert Institut (IFSI)* in Vienna on a more permanent basis in 1987 the movement has spread throughout the five continents, so that the organization of Schubert enthusiasts literally encircles the globe.

In the Preface to the first edition of this work I spoke of the relationship between the man and the creative artist as baffling in Schubert's case. It remains baffling, in spite of serious efforts to solve the mystery of his sexuality. Of the many critical articles and books published in the intervening years, none has faced the problem more directly, and none has prompted more interest and controversy, than Maynard Solomon's essay 'Franz Schubert and the Peacocks of Benevenuto Cellini' in 1989 (*19th-Century Music*, vol. 12 no. 3). Solomon's thesis, that Schubert and some of his circle of friends were practising homosexuals, fits so neatly with some of the comments quoted in the Memoirs, and throws fresh light on so many of the problems which confront the biographer, that it cannot be ignored. I have therefore decided to refer to it at various points in the narrative where it is clearly relevant. It must be taken into account, for instance, in Schubert's relationship with Mayrhofer, and with Platen, with the musical establishment of Vienna, and the various women in his life. In the summer of 1993 *19th-Century Music* devoted a whole issue to the subject, in which Rita Steblin vigorously opposed Solomon's views, and Susan McClary and James Webster discussed how far the thesis, even if true, could be said to be important and relevant to our assessment of Schubert's music. For it is clear that it does not affect our judgement of the music in a direct and observable way as, for instance, Beethoven's influence, which is everywhere apparent.

The text has been thoroughly revised to take account of recent research, and I am grateful to Paul Reid for agreeing to bring the appendices up to date. A table of abbreviations has been added on page x.

1

Early life

Of all the great composers, Schubert is the one most often associated with Vienna. Yet he was only a first generation Viennese. His parents came from the provinces of Moravia and Silesia, from those parts of the vast Habsburg empire which are now in the Czech Republic. As the music of Dvořák, Smetana, and Janáček reminds us, the people of these lands show a deep native feeling for the joy and sadness of life; and the poetry of Schubert's music, its love of dance rhythms and emotional ambiguity, owes more to the home of his forefathers than it does to Vienna. His paternal grandfather was a successful peasant farmer from Neudorf in Moravia, and his father, Franz Theodor Schubert, was a schoolmaster who moved to Vienna about the year 1783 to become an assistant at the Carmelite School in the suburb of Leopoldstadt, where his brother Karl was headmaster. The Schuberts were able and conscientious, a little rigid perhaps in their principles, but loyal and united in their family life.

Soon after arriving in Vienna, Franz Theodor met Elisabeth Vietz, a young woman in domestic service living nearby, and they were married in January 1785. Elisabeth was also an immigrant, from Zuckmantel in Silesia. Her father was a locksmith and local official, who had got into financial difficulties and was put in prison. On being released he decided to try his luck in Vienna rather than face further legal proceedings. His family followed him to the capital, and when he died were left to fend for themselves. The Vietz family were more artistic than the Schuberts, with musicians and artists among their number. Elisabeth's first child, Ignaz, was born two months after the wedding, no unusual circumstance in those days.

Of the fourteen children of the marriage, only five survived to adulthood, the composer Franz Peter Schubert being the fourth. The infant mortality figures in the Schubert family, by the way, show clearly enough that in those days a child had only a one in three chance of reaching maturity, a fact which has to be taken into account when we consider the preoccupation with death which so absorbed many of the writers whose work Schubert set.

The composer was born on 31 January 1797 at the house called 'The

Red Crayfish' on the Himmelpfortgrund—literally 'the ground of the heavenly gate'. The house, carefully restored by the city authorities, is now maintained as a museum. It probably served both as home and as school, in circumstances which were cramped almost beyond belief. It housed several households, and the two larger rooms had to serve both as living rooms and as classrooms. The schoolmaster lived on the weekly dues he collected from his pupils, who attended in two separate shifts, one in the morning and one in the afternoon. By dint of hard work, Franz Theodor had much improved the school's reputation, so that in 1801, when Franz was four, he was able to take out a lease of more commodious premises nearby in the Säulengasse, in a house called 'The Black Horse'. Here Franz spent his childhood and youth. Here he tried out his first compositions in the family circle; and it is this house, often referred to simply as 'the schoolroom on the Himmelpfortgrund', which is often mentioned in the memoirs of his friends.

Franz Theodor is often portrayed in those memoirs as the heavy father, unimaginative and slow to make allowances for the claims of genius. He was certainly a devout Catholic of a conservative mould, and he looked to his family for obedience and support. All his sons were expected to serve as assistants in the school, but since the master had to provide for any necessary assistance out of his own pocket, this could be regarded as in the common interest of the family. The Schuberts presented a solid front to the world; Franz Theodor provided a home for his sister-in-law and her children when his brother died, and it is remarkable how close Schubert remained to his family in later life, in spite of tensions and disasters. The boy's affections, however, were focussed on his mother. From her Schubert seems to have inherited his imagination, his contemplative disposition, and easy-going ways. Franz Theodor was fond of music, and played the cello to his own modest standards. His sons all learnt a stringed instrument as well as the piano, so that from about 1810 onwards the family could muster a string quartet, with Ferdinand and Ignaz playing violin, Franz viola, and Franz Theodor cello.

Ferdinand, who followed in his father's footsteps and became a schoolmaster, was devoted to his brother Franz, and was to play an important part in his life. It was Ferdinand, in fact, who took over the responsibility of head of the family after the death of Franz Theodor, in spite of the fact that Ignaz was nine years older. The reason for this is not clear, though it probably had something to do with Ignaz's radical views. He seems to have been what we should now call a freethinker, but in those days he might more probably have called himself a Josephinian, that is a supporter of the liberal reforms and the anticlerical legislation of the Emperor Joseph II (1780–90), then still fresh in the memory of the older generation, and still widely professed and practised, though only at the risk of official disapproval and punishment.

Relations between Franz and Ignaz were also close, and there is little doubt that Ignaz influenced his younger brother's attitude towards the orthodox religious views of Franz Theodor. Ferdinand's pride in his brother's musical achievements did not stop short of getting him to compose works for his own, that is for Ferdinand's, purposes, and later passing them off as his own. But it was all done in the name of family affection and mutual help, and certainly Franz was always happy to oblige.

Schubert learned to play the piano under the tuition of Ignaz, and later his father gave him his first instruction on the violin. There were, however, two centres of musical activity, the home and the parish church of Liechtental, where various members of the family sang in the choir and took part in the services, under the supervision of the choirmaster Michael Holzer. Holzer, whom Anton Holzapfel described many years later as 'a bibulous but competent contrapuntist',[1] became Schubert's first official teacher, and initiated him into the mysteries of thorough-bass and counterpoint. Soon the boy was leading the treble line in the choir and playing violin solos from the organ loft. As for more formal instruction, Holzer was later to deny modestly that he taught his young pupil anything. 'I merely talked with him and looked at him with mute astonishment', he is reported to have said.[2]

The turning point of these early years, however, came in 1808, when Schubert won a free place in open competition as a choirboy at the Imperial and Royal Chapel. The tests were conducted by the choirmaster, Philipp Korner, and by the Kapellmeister himself, Anton Salieri. This success provided Schubert not only with the best musical training available in Vienna; it also carried with it the privilege of a free place at the Imperial and Royal Seminary, the *Konvikt*, where the teachers were brethren of the Piarist[3] order, and where scholars from various parts of the empire lived while they pursued their studies. The Director of the *Konvikt*, Dr Innocenz Lang, was a keen musician, and music played a most important role in the life of the students, with regular times set aside for practice and for chamber music, as well as daily rehearsals of the school orchestra. The seminarists wore a special uniform, a brown tunic with gilt epaulettes and three-cornered hat, just as the boys of Christ's Hospital did in London, and for much the same reason, as a guarantee of good behaviour in the city streets.

Admission to the *Konvikt* meant that Schubert's general education would be well looked after, while his musical gifts would have every opportunity to develop. Equally important, it opened up for him a social environment much more sophisticated than that of the schoolroom in

---

[1] *Schubert: Memoirs by his Friends*, collected and edited by Otto Erich Deutsch (London, 1958), hereinafter referred to as Memoirs, p. 62.

[2] Memoirs, p. 212.

[3] A religious order founded in 1617 for the education of the poor.

the Säulengasse. Here his gifts inevitably attracted attention. The Schubert circle had its roots in the *Konvikt*; the founder of it was a young law student from Linz, Josef von Spaun, who has himself described what a profound impression the shy newcomer to the school orchestra made on him when he first appeared among the second violins.[4] Many others of his fellow students later wrote down their recollections of those days. Franz Eckel, later to become Director of the Vienna Veterinary Institution, is most worth quoting because of the insight his words give into Schubert's introspective disposition.

> Even in his boyhood and youth Schubert's life was one of inner, spiritual thought, and was seldom expressed in words but, I would say, almost entirely in music . . . Even with us he was silent and uncommunicative, except in matters which concerned the divinity to which he dedicated his entire life, and whose darling he was. A measure of innate seriousness and calm, friendliness and good nature in him admitted neither friendship nor animosity of the kind usually to be found among boys and youths in educational establishments . . . Even on the walks which the pupils took together he mostly kept apart, walking pensively along with lowered eyes and with his hands behind his back, playing with his fingers (as though on keys), completely lost in his own thoughts.[5]

In this brave new world, though a rather spartan one, and with the stimulus of daily contact with musicians of the calibre of the court organist Wenzel Ruzicka and Kapellmeister Salieri, his creative gifts soon began to blossom. But he was an adolescent, rather than an infant, prodigy. The earliest autographs of his to survive probably date from 1810, that is from his thirteenth year, a stage by which Mozart and Mendelssohn had many finished works to their credit. Perhaps the earliest of them all, appropriately enough, are two fragmentary song sketches, his first essays in the extended cantata form. Both appear to be settings of a long allegorical poem called *Lebenstraum* (Dream of Life) D39, an ambitious theme for a boy of 13! Schubert wrote out the voice line and the accompaniment for nearly 400 bars before giving up. Even here familiar motifs like the running octaves and the stepwise descent in diminished fourths and fifths play a prominent part. More interesting is his very first keyboard composition, a Fantasie in G for piano duet D1. This extraordinary effusion covers some thirty-six pages, the first of three such works written during his schooldays. It was to be followed by the duet Fantasie in G minor of September 1811, D9, and the C minor Fantasie D48 of early 1813. These works represent the first stage of Schubert's lifelong preoccupation with the problem of giving organic unity to a form which is by definition improvisatory. His native predilection for monothematic structures led him in these early works to rely on the transformation of a single basic theme in distinct but linked sections. The method reaches a surprising degree of sophistication in the C minor

---

[4] Memoirs, p. 126.   [5] Memoirs, p. 50.

Fantasie for piano duet, in which the chromatic descending line of Ex. 1 is adapted to serve as the basis for the introductory Adagio, the Allegro agitato, and the final Fugue. Schubert had already evolved a method which was to serve greater ends in the 'Wanderer Fantasie' nine years later.

Schubert's career as a composer began in earnest in 1811. To that year belong the first complete songs, his first orchestral work (a sketch for the first movement of a symphony in D), an overture for strings in C minor D8, a set of minuets for wind band, and a Fantasie in C minor for piano D2 E. The wide variety of form and invention in these compositions is impressive. But so, too, is the fact that certain musical ideas constantly recur in them. These favourite motifs throw some light on the origins of Schubert's musical language, for they go much further back than is usually supposed. One harmonic sequence, for instance, which turns up frequently both in the songs and in the instrumental works, can be represented thus:

Ex. 1

The chromatically descending bass line, which is also used as an independent motif in, for instance, the C major Fugue D24 D and the C major String Quartet of March 1813, derives from the familiar ground bass of baroque composers, sometimes referred to as the 'Lamento' topos.[6] Its sombre connotations are obvious enough from its use in such works as Purcell's *Dido and Aeneas* ('When I am laid in earth'), Pergolesi's *Stabat Mater*, and Bach's B minor Mass (Crucifixus). It is significant, then, that Ex. 1 appears frequently, and in various forms and tempos, in four long and episodic songs, all of which are concerned with death, grief, or crime in macabre circumstances.

The last quarter of the eighteenth century had seen a great revival of song-writing in German lands, sparked off by the enthusiasm of Herder and Goethe for folksong. Most of these songs were strophic, and attempted to emulate the simplicity of the folksong. Schubert, however, began at the opposite, more sophisticated end of the scale, with the *Gesang*. In his memoirs Spaun tells us how, on his return to the *Konvikt* in March 1811 after an absence of eighteen months, he found Schubert engrossed in the songs of J. R. Zumsteeg (1760–1802), who had made a

[6] Ellen Rosand, 'The Descending Tetrachrod, an Emblem of Lament', *MQ*, vol. lxv, 1979, pp. 346–59.

name for himself with his long and episodic settings of Schiller's ballads.[7] Schubert followed Zumsteeg's example closely in his very first song, 'Hagars Klage' (Hagar's Lament) D5, written in March 1811, though he contrived to give the song more dramatic immediacy by the use of motifs based on Ex. 1. The structural problem raised by these cantata-like songs is similar to that posed by the Fantasie: how to give unity and progressive effect to the succession of loosely linked episodes, in different keys and rhythms. Schubert's answer is a primitive form of leitmotif. The most impressive of these 1811 songs, for instance, is the setting of Schiller's 'Leichenfantasie' (A Corpse Fantasy) D7, a vivid evocation of a father's grief, which portrays a moonlit funeral procession with the ghastly clarity of a nightmare. Schubert finds an expressive leading motif to convey a sense of mystery and foreboding, and adapts it at later points in the story to give the song emotional unity and cumulative effect (see Ex. 2).

Ex. 2

The naïve sensationalism of this song, and of others like 'Der Vatermörder' (The Parricide), D10, was a fashionable aspect of early Romanticism. Modern methods of making the flesh creep are more violent and sophisticated, so that these early essays in the macabre can easily seem to us faintly comic. In time, however, Schubert was to bring to the horror story an unprecedented dramatic force, as he did in 'Erlkönig' and 'Der Zwerg' (The Dwarf).

One further example of these thematic figures must suffice. Ex. 2

[7] Memoirs, p. 127.

reminds us of the power of an insistent pulse in the minor key to convey the idea of a nameless fear or threat. It is a time-honoured device which Schubert was to use in some of his greatest songs. His instinctive feeling for the emotional associations of a particular pulse or *Bewegung* was to enable him to build up a kind of rhythmical vocabulary to match the infinite complexity of mood and situation to be found in the songs. Much of this is already foreshadowed in the songs of 1811. In 'Der Vatermörder' he combines the harmonic sequence of Ex. 1 with a syncopated rhythm to produce a powerful image of flight.

Ex. 3

A careful analysis of these early songs, moreover, will show how skilfully the rhythm is varied to match the mood and the sense.

While Schubert's mind was filled with his own and other men's music, the fate of empires trembled in the balance. Spaun has described how, when Napoleon's army stood at the gates of Vienna in May 1809, a wave of patriotic fervour spread through the *Konvikt*. Some of the students attempted to enrol, only to be peremptorily ordered back to their lessons.[8] It is unlikely that the routine of Schubert's daily life was much disturbed by these epoch-making events. The impression we get from the memoirs of his friends, and from the only letter of his which survives from these times, is that his chief concern apart from his music was to keep warm in winter and save a little pocket money with which to mitigate the rigours of life at school. The letter is dated 24 November 1812, and is a good-humoured request for a sub. 'The few pence I get from Father go to the devil in the first few days; what am I to do for the rest of the time? ("Whosoever believeth in him shall not be ashamed"), Matthew, chapter 3, v.4. So what I thought was: what about letting me have a few shillings a month? You would never notice it, while I in my

---

[8] Memoirs, p. 353.

cell would think myself lucky, and be satisfied.'[9] The letter may have been addressed to his brother Ignaz, now chief assistant in the Liechtental school, who would appreciate the fake biblical reference.

The events of the summer of 1812 seem to mark the end of his boyhood. In May his mother, Elisabeth, died. The cause of death was certified as 'nervous fever', a common term in those days which covered a variety of conditions. (The same term was to be used many years later on Schubert's own death certificate.) In April 1813 Franz Theodor married again, this time the daughter of a local silk manufacturer, who did her best to fill the vacant space in the affections of the family, while producing five children of her own.

About this time, too, Schubert's voice broke, an event which signalled the end of his career as a choirboy, and raised the question of his future. The precise date of his departure from the services of the Imperial Chapel can be pinpointed, for a copy of the alto part in Peter Winter's first Mass has survived, which bears an inscription in his own hand: 'Schubert, Franz, crowed for the last time, 26 July 1812'. This did not necessarily mean, however, forfeiture of his place at the *Konvikt*, for endowments were provided to enable 'retired' choirboys to continue their education, provided they maintained a satisfactory standard of work. Schubert's annual marks and reports had so far been uniformly good, but in 1812 and 1813 his increasing devotion to composition began to affect his other work, so that he failed to maintain the highest standard, particularly in Latin and mathematics.

Meanwhile, however, the school authorities had come to realize the nature of his musical gifts. Ruzicka, who had been entrusted with the supervision of his work, soon came to the same decision as his predecessors, and recommended that his pupil should be passed on to the first Kapellmeister himself. Schubert began a course of lessons with Salieri in June 1812, and the two were in regular contact over the next five years at least. Salieri was indeed the only teacher Schubert ever acknowledged, so something should be said about the importance of the association and its effect upon Schubert's development.

Salieri spent more than fifty years in the service of the Imperial Court, having arrived in Vienna in 1766 as a youth of sixteen. He became the close friend of Florian Gassmann, the director of Italian opera in Vienna who had brought him from Italy, and of Gluck and Metastasio, with whom he studied the art of declamation. Most of his own 40 operas were written in Italian, though he also spent some years in Paris, so that he was closely in touch with the reforms of Gluck and Grétry. The fact that Beethoven, when he was contemplating the composition of an opera, went to Salieri for guidance suggests that he was regarded as an authority on the fashionable new French opera. Certainly he was the

[9] Otto Erich Deutsch, *Schubert: A Documentary Biography* (London, 1946), hereinafter referred to in footnotes as Docs, p. 28.

acknowledged expert on the art of declamation and word-setting. Schubert's conservative notation, his reverence for Gluck and his thoroughly traditional approach to formal and structural problems must owe a great deal to Salieri. Equally certainly, Salieri was entirely out of sympathy with Schubert's enthusiasm for German song, and indeed for the ideas and ideals of the Romantics generally. Contemporary opinion played down Salieri's importance. He was 'incapable of teaching a youth who was inspired and permeated by Beethoven's genius', said Sonnleithner.[10]

There is some evidence, however, that the series of exercises in word-setting which Schubert undertook for Salieri played a part in turning his attention away from Zumsteeg and the academic *Gesang* to more Italian melodic forms. By September Schubert was hard at work setting texts by Metastasio. He made several versions of an aria, D17, from Metastasio's oratorio *Isacco*, the first of which bears an unmistakable resemblance to the song 'Der Jüngling am Bache' (The Youth by the Brook), also written in September 1912 (see Ex. 4). This song (D30) shows a fresh feeling for the expressive power of the voice. It is an important milestone along the road to the Romantic Lied.

Ex. 4

One might suppose that Salieri would also have stimulated the young composer's interest in opera, but in fact the Kapellmeister, exasperated by the trend of public taste, had given up composing operas long before Schubert arrived at the *Konvikt*, and it was Spaun who introduced his friend to the delights of opera. Probably early in 1811 they went to hear two of the most successful folk operas of the court composer Josef Weigl, *Das Waisenhaus* (The Orphanage) and *Die Schweizer Familie*, based on the famous 'Swiss Family Robinson'. These tuneful sentimental pieces

[10] Memoirs, p. 112.

were in the German *Singspiel* tradition, with spoken dialogue and musical numbers to highlight the situations. When Schubert came to make his own first attempt at opera he copied this operetta style, basing his work on a magic play by the most popular dramatist of the day, August von Kotzebue. But *Der Spiegelritter* (The Looking Glass Knight) D11 failed to get beyond the first act. The music is tuneful and lively, witness the opening chorus (Ex. 5), but undramatic, and the piece altogether misses the satirical intention of Kotzebue's play. An experience of a quite different order came later, when the two friends went to the Court Theatre to see a performance of Gluck's *Iphigénie en Tauride*. Schubert was moved to tears, and began to study all the Gluck scores he could lay his hands on.[11]

Though his days as a choirboy were over, Schubert was allowed to

Ex. 5

[11] Memoirs, p. 129.

continue his education at the *Konvikt*, and his studies with Salieri. The tacit understanding seems to have been that the position would be reviewed after a further year. In the autumn of 1812, however, and throughout the following year, compositions began to flow from his pen in an ever broadening stream; not only songs, but liturgical pieces, string quartets, vocal exercises for Salieri, piano pieces, dances, pieces for wind band and for strings. The surviving act of 'The Looking Glass Knight' dates from the end of 1811, but soon Schubert was contemplating another opera based on a Kotzebue play; he also confided to Spaun that he intended to write a Mass. Not surprisingly, the level of his work in Latin and mathematics failed to improve, and in the summer of 1813 the question of his free place at the seminary once again came up for discussion.

The Royal and Imperial Court was a curious mixture of impersonal bureaucracy and paternal involvement. Though the Emperor was busily engaged in Bohemia in operations against Napoleon, he still expected to be kept informed about such matters as the education of the Imperial choristers. When Schubert's name was formally proposed, therefore, for the award of an endowment which would enable him to stay at the *Konvikt*, the recommendation proceeded 'through the appropriate channels', and in due course arrived at the Emperor's headquarters in the field. A few days after the battle of Leipzig, that decisive encounter which marked the beginning of the end for Napoleon, Franz I initialled the proposal to safeguard Schubert's future. However, there was an important proviso. 'Since music and singing are but a subsidiary matter' —so ran the official minute—Schubert was to take a further examination after the holidays to demonstrate his ability to maintain his position in the first grade. But music was not a subsidiary matter to Schubert. In October 1813 he decided to refuse the offer of an endowment, and renounced his position as a seminarist.

To the guardians of the conventional wisdom this unexpected decision must have seemed imprudent, to say the least, and it has given rise to some wild speculation. There is little doubt that it was Schubert's own decision. In his memoirs of the composer, Mayrhofer says simply, 'He was confronted with the alternatives of giving up either music or the endowment'.[12] This may seem to be an oversimplification, but it is probably how Schubert saw the matter himself. He had already decided that his destiny was to be a composer, and his single-minded belief in his own genius made him wary of the claims of a career, even a career as a Kapellmeister, and of the responsibilities of public life. Besides, the decision did not mean making a clean break with his friends in the *Konvikt*; he was to play an active part in the musical life of that institution for several years after his departure. Nor did it mean an end

[12] Memoirs, p. 13.

to his association with Salieri and Ruzicka, for that was to continue on an informal basis for as long as Schubert wanted. It is said that his First Symphony, which he completed on 28 October, was given its first performance by the student orchestra at the *Konvikt* in honour of the Director, Innocenz Lang. This and his close and continuing friendship with many of his old colleagues suggest that his decision was a matter of mutual agreement rather than a cause of contention. At all events, the die was cast. That autumn he registered his name for a course of training at the Normal High School of St Anna in the inner city, with a view to gaining a certificate as a qualified primary school teacher.

The most substantial achievement of his boyhood was the series of string quartets which he wrote during his last years at school. The chronology of these, and of the two earlier and more juvenile quartets, is confused. The autographs are not all dated, and the original publishers were sometimes wildly adrift in their ideas of chronology. Only in our own century has it been possible, with new techniques for dating the manuscripts, to present a more convincing picture. It may be useful, therefore, to set them out in chronological order.

No.	D	Key	Date	Remarks
1	18	Mixed	(?) 1810 or 1811	
2	94	D major	Probably 1811	Previously attributed to 1814
3	32	C major	Sept./Oct. 1812	Published in complete form 1954
4	36	B flat	Nov. 1812/Feb. 1813	The Menuetto was added later
5	46	C major	March 1813	Score has inner movements reversed
6	68	B flat	June/Aug. 1813	Two movements only
7	74	D major	Aug./Sept. 1813	'For my father's nameday'

All these quartets were intended for performance within the family circle. In spite of some structural uncertainty and occasional clumsiness, especially in the first two works, their unfailing fluency and inventiveness keep them alive, so that all of them have now been recorded and the best of them are sometimes heard in the concert hall. Like the piano duet fantasies, they display a marked leaning towards monothematic procedures. No. 1, for instance, speeds up the theme of the introductory Andante to provide the main subject of the Presto vivace. In no. 5, in C major, Schubert takes as a kind of motto theme the chromatically descending fourth of the bass line of Ex. 1, exploits it in the introduction in a manner strongly reminiscent of Mozart's 'Dissonance' Quartet, and then neatly enlists it as a counterpart to the dancing triplets of the Allegro con moto. Where there is a recognizable second subject, as in the Finale of No. 4, it is a near relation of the first.

The best of these early quartets is the fourth on the list above, in B flat, the Andante of which is perhaps the first clear sign of that light/dark polarity which was to become such a feature of Schubert's mature style. It opens with a serene Mozartian tune, but halfway through shudders to a halt on a diminished seventh, pausing before it ventures forward, pianissimo, in the remote key of C flat major. The Trio switches from D major to the flattened sixth, B flat, pivoting on a repeated octave D quite in Schubert's mature manner. The outer movements are less impressive, and it is interesting that a few months after completing the quartet he wrote two further movements in B flat, an opening Allegro and a Finale. They are usually regarded as a separate work, but the possibility that they were intended to replace the corresponding movements of D36 cannot be excluded.

The last in the list, D74 in D major, was written for the celebration of Franz Theodor's nameday on 4 October 1813. A first violin part preserved in the Spaun family's collection is proudly inscribed in French, 'Trois Quatuors composés par François Schubert, écolier de M. de Salieri', and on the next sheet, 'Zur Namensfeyer meines Vaters. Franz, Sohn'. There is a touch of bravado about it, a kind of declaration of confidence in his own genius. None of these early quartets was published until the 1890s, in the collected edition of his works.

One other aspect of Schubert's output in his schooldays deserves mention, and not only because it has generally been neglected. His declared intention to write a mass was not to be realized until 1814, but in the meantime, in September 1812, and again in the following spring, he wrote two ambitious settings of the Kyrie for soloists, chorus and orchestra, both in D minor, both urgent and dark-toned, marked Allegro. The second (D49) is perhaps the grander of the two; it is scored for trombones as well as trumpets and drums. But both are reminiscent of Haydn's 'Sturm und Drang' manner, and remarkable achievements for a youth of sixteen. Clearly Schubert intended to begin with a full-scale ceremonial mass; in these early works he seems to be experimenting, as though aware of the difficulty of finding the right tone for the first movement of the sacred rite. At the other end of the stylistic scale is a short, a cappella setting of the Kyrie in B flat D45, reflective in tone (Andante con expressione) and with something of the profound simplicity which Mozart was able to call upon. Another setting for chorus and orchestra in F major (D66 of May 1813) is less successful.

It is not only the technical mastery of these early liturgical works which seems astonishing, but their conviction, a quality not always apparent in Schubert's later masses. Here at least there is no hint of *Gemütlichkeit*. There is no record of contemporary performances, but it must not be assumed that none took place. The parish church of Liechtental could call upon a wide circle of singers and instrumentalists, and the a cappella settings at any rate were almost certainly performed there.

2

The schoolhouse years (1813–16)

For the next three years, while the long war moved on to its dramatic concluding stages and the map of Europe was redrawn, Schubert lived quietly at home in the schoolhouse on the Säulengasse. In 1814 he attended the teachers training school of St Anna, and in August passed the examination to qualify as a primary teacher. Thereafter he took over responsibility for the infants' class in the Liechtental school, teaching the youngest children their letters. According to family tradition he made an impatient schoolmaster, not above administering an occasional slap in the interest of good discipline.

For this period at any rate Grove's dictum is true: 'his life is all summed up in his music.' The biographical details can all be recounted in few words. Schubert fell in love, and like many another found that there was no future in the affair. His first complete mass was performed, and made an impression. His circle of friends and admirers grew, and his genius as a songwriter of exceptional power and originality began to be recognized. For the rest he taught, and he composed. For his services in school he received eighty florins a year. As for the compositions, the statistics are formidable. Nearly half of the works listed in the thematic catalogue compiled by Otto Erich Deutsch belong to the three years which followed his leaving school. They include five symphonies, four masses, six operas, four string quartets, not to mention a vast number of smaller pieces and about 270 songs!

This creative explosion could only have been possible if his school duties left him with a great deal of spare time and energy. The probable explanation is that the youngest children attended only for a few hours each day, so that Schubert could devote the major part of the day to composing. The point needs to be borne in mind before we dismiss his stipend of eighty florins a year as an outrageous insult. The myth of Schubert's lifelong poverty dies hard. The true value of historical incomes is indeed difficult to assess; but if we remember that the annual salary of a qualified teacher or junior civil servant in those days was only about 450 florins, we may concede that a youth of seventeen, not yet fully qualified and living at home, was not perhaps doing too badly with eighty.

Not a note of all the music written in these years was published or given a public performance (with the single exception of the Mass in F, which was a special case); but it would be a great mistake to assume that it was all put away in a drawer for posterity. Quite the reverse is true. All these works were written in the hope of performance, and most of them were in fact performed. To understand this, however, we have to make allowance for the social and cultural conditions of the time. Commercial music publishing was still in its infancy, copyright laws hardly existed, there was no clearly defined and separately organized musical profession, and public concerts represented only the 'tip of the iceberg' in the musical scene as a whole. In Schubert's lifetime Vienna was at the centre of a vast expansion of domestic music-making, linked with the decline of the aristocracy, the growing supremacy of the professional and commercial classes, and the invention and exploitation of the new pianos. A visitor to Vienna in 1808 had commented: 'There are few cities where the passion for music is so general as here. During the winter there are countless so-called "private academies"—music in distinguished houses. No nameday or birthday takes place without music-making. Every young lady must learn to sing and play the piano whether or not she is talented, first because it is the fashion and secondly because it is the most agreeable way to appear in society.'[1]

This revolutionary change in the social status of music-making received official recognition in 1814 with the establishment of the *Gesellschaft der Österreichischen Musikfreunde*, or Austrian Philharmonic Society. It grew out of the monster performances of Handel oratorios which took place in the Imperial Riding School in 1812 and 1813, at the peak of the patriotic ferment which accompanied the wars of liberation, and was given its official sanction by Emperor Franz I soon after the monarchs and the diplomats assembled for the Congress of Vienna in September 1814. Unlike earlier associations of musicians, the Philharmonic Society was a society of dilettanti. Professional artists were not excluded, but the organization was in the hands of distinguished amateurs like Ignaz Sonnleithner, Raphael Kiesewetter, and Hofrat von Mosel, all of whom were to play a significant part in the career of Franz Schubert. In its early days it organized an annual oratorio performance and occasional concerts; more importantly it provided a kind of social framework within which the network of private concerts and practices could take place. At the apex of the organization were the regular musical evenings at the houses of Sonnleithner, Kiesewetter, and others, at which chamber music, cantatas, and even whole oratorios and operas were sometimes performed. At the base of the social triangle were countless more modest groups, not the least important of which was the group which met in the schoolroom in the Säulengasse.

[1] Cited in Hanslick, *Geschichte des Concertwesens in Wien* (Vienna, 1869). Reprinted, Gregg International, 1971, vol. 1, pp. 66–7.

15

As we have seen, quartet practices had for some years been a feature of Schubert's family life. When Josef Doppler, a boyhood friend of Schubert's who lived long enough to tell his story to Grove in the 1860s, returned home from active service in 1814, he found that the family quartet had been augmented, so that it was now capable of playing Haydn symphonies in four-part arrangements. Schubert's compositions for this slimmed down orchestra are easy to identify. They include the two overtures (D8 and D20) and the delightful series of minuets and trios for string quartet of November 1813 (D89), which are not to be regarded as single movements from unwritten quartets, but rather as the orchestral equivalent of the hundreds of dances for piano which Schubert wrote throughout his life. The little group of string players prospered, so that it soon outgrew the schoolroom and was obliged to accept the offer of accommodation in the house of a city merchant, by name Franz Frischling. At the end of 1815, having now been equipped with a wind section and drums, it moved again, this time to the house of a professional violinist, Otto Hatwig, who agreed to act as leader. In its heyday this private orchestra could muster about twenty strings with double woodwind and percussion, and was capable of acquitting itself creditably in the early Beethoven symphonies. Schubert's first six symphonies, and various overtures, were written for, and almost certainly performed by, this group, in which he himself played viola.[2]

Another centre of Schubert's activity was Liechtental church. The amateur musicians who met and took part in the services there included the soprano Therese Grob and her brother Heinrich, a good pianist. All Schubert's early masses were probably first performed at Liechtental, and many of the other liturgical works as well. Long before they were published, these works were passed round from one church to another in manuscript copies. Much the same is true of his early chamber music, and it is even possible that performances of his operas, or parts of them, may have taken place in private houses, though no record of such performances has survived.

In September 1814 the parish church at Liechtental celebrated its centenary. Schubert's first mass, in F, was written in honour of the occasion, and the first performance took place there on 16 October. Schubert himself directed, Kapellmeister Salieri graced the occasion with his presence, and the celebrated violinist Josef Mayseder is said to have been enlisted to lead the orchestra. The event attracted public attention to the young composer, so that a repeat performance was arranged a fortnight later in the Augustiner church in the inner city. The soprano role was sung by Therese Grob, with whom Schubert fell in love. She was two years younger than he, and the two families had grown up side by side. During Schubert's absence at the *Konvikt*, however, Therese had grown

---

[2] Memoirs, pp. 338–41 for Sonnleithner's more detailed account.

from a child to a young woman with an attractive high soprano voice. The affair developed over the next two years and raised serious hopes of marriage. But that never became a practical possibility. Therese's father was dead, and her mother, who ran the family textile business, evidently had reservations about Schubert's eligibility as a son-in-law. First love cuts deep, and there is no doubt that strong feelings were involved, on Schubert's side at any rate. Early in 1815 he wrote a long letter to his friend, Anton Holzapfel, about his love for Therese (unfortunately it has not survived), and he spoke to Anselm Hüttenbrenner in later years in terms which leave no doubt of the seriousness of his intentions. The crisis came in 1816, towards the end of which Schubert left home, and the affair faded slowly into a wistful memory. Thereafter Schubert's feelings with regard to the opposite sex seem to have become polarized. Therese was the only woman in his life, so far as we can judge, with whom he seriously contemplated marriage.

During these schoolhouse years Schubert continued to go to Salieri regularly for lessons, taking his completed compositions to the Kapellmeister for advice, and he kept in close touch also with Ruzicka and with old colleagues at the *Konvikt*. Josef Kenner, who was at the school from 1811 to 1816, tells us that Schubert used often to attend the musical evenings after he had left,[3] and his relations with friends such as Albert Stadler, who made a valuable collection of Schubert songs in manuscript between 1813 and 1817, Anton Holzapfel, Spaun, and Kenner himself were certainly closer after his departure from the *Konvikt* than before. It is important to realize also that the links which bound the Schubert circle together were political as well as musical. As the liberal idealism which the wars of liberation had engendered came face to face with the unyielding authoritarianism of the Metternich system, the political climate rapidly deteriorated. There were student riots in Vienna, and the unrest spread to the *Konvikt* in the winter of 1814/15. (It was at this time that Anton Schindler, arriving in Brünn to take up a teaching appointment, found himself suddenly arrested and imprisoned without charge on suspicion of having been in touch with riotous students in Vienna.[4]) One of Schubert's friends, a brave young man of radical views called Johann Senn, lost his free place at the *Konvikt* for taking part in an attempt to free a colleague who had been imprisoned for some misdemeanour. There is no doubt at all where Schubert's sympathies lay in all this. Political views in the circle were decidedly liberal, and Senn was respected for his courage and leadership. For the time being, however, the rumblings of discontent were held in check by the mood of euphoria which gripped the Viennese while the great men of Europe played out the tragi-comedy of the Congress of Vienna. On 29 November and 2 December huge Beethoven concerts were held in the

[3] Memoirs, pp. 81–2.
[4] Schindler, *Beethoven as I knew him* (London, 1966), pp. 203–4.

Imperial Riding School, at which 6000 people were said to have been present. No doubt Schubert was among them to hear the performance of the cantata 'The Glorious Moment', the A major Symphony, and the 'Battle Symphony', all received in reverential silence. The event marks the highwater mark of Beethoven's reputation, though not of his genius. It is not surprising that Schubert's own Second Symphony, in B flat, which he began in this same month of December 1814, bears the marks of his admiration for his great contemporary.

Echoes of these events penetrated even to the schoolhouse on the Säulengasse. In May Schubert wrote a little song (D104) to celebrate the entry of Franz I and the allies into Paris. The cantata *Wer ist gross?* (Who is great?) D110 for bass solo, male-voice quartet and orchestra, written in July, was probably intended for some special scholastic occasion held in honour of the Emperor. But the first half of the year 1814 was not noticeably productive. Apart from Matthisson songs, and the Mass in F, about which we shall have more to say later, his chief concern was with his opera *Des Teufels Lustschloss* (The Devil's Pleasure Palace) D84, which was begun in October 1813 and not finished till a year later. This was another spine-chiller from the fertile pen of August von Kotzebue, a tale of enchantment in which the hero suffers various trials and indignities at the hands of a devilish father-in-law in a magic castle. In the end, of course, it turns out to have been just a well-meant test of the hero's loyalty and fortitude.

Schubert completed the first version in May. Salieri, to whom he submitted the draft, suggested radical alterations, and Schubert thereupon began work on a revised version, in which the last act was reshaped and extended. The trouble he took over the piece is evidence at least of his serious intentions. Perhaps they were too serious in a sense; for one may pay Kotzebue the compliment of assuming that his catalogue of horrors is meant as a 'send-up'. There is no trace of irony, however, in Schubert's score. Of all this music, nothing is heard today except the overture, a fine dark-toned piece with an extraordinary brass chorale at the end of the development section, which serves as an unconventional link with the reprise. This twenty-eight-bar episode is introduced and led by a chorale of three trombones, traditionally associated with funerals and with death. Presumably the episode is meant here to refer to the horrific fate which overhangs the hero in the opera. There is a curiously similar episode, however, in the symphonic sketch D936A which Schubert failed to complete in 1828, also led by three trombones, and also placed unexpectedly at the end of the exposition. Almost certainly this refers to Beethoven's death, and is perhaps the most striking example of Schubert's self-borrowings towards the end of his life.[5]

[5] See Daniel Jacobson and Andrew Glendening, 'Schuberts D936A: eine sinfonische Hommage an Beethoven?' in *Brille* 15, pp. 113–26.

In the autumn, as Schubert took up his duties as a teacher, the flow of compositions gathered strength. A new world opened up in October, when he discovered *Faust*. 'Gretchen am Spinnrade' (Gretchen at the Spinning-Wheel), which followed on 19 October, deserves its reputation as the first great Romantic song; it was both a culmination and a new beginning, and Schubert's first unchallengeable lyrical masterpiece. The 'Scene from Faust' D126, of December, already suggests, with its hints of choral and orchestral forces in the autograph, that his mind was turning to a dramatic presentation of the work. About the same time Spaun brought him a Mayrhofer poem ('Am See', By the Lake) to set, thus introducing him to a man who was to play a crucial part in the development of his lyrical gifts.

The entries for 1814 and 1815 in O. E. Deutsch's *Documentary Biography* are meagre indeed. For 1815 he can muster only nine, and two of those, the ones which concern the love affair with Therese Grob, are missing. In terms of creative power, however, 1815 was an *annus mirabilis*. Fortunately it was Schubert's habit at this time to date his autographs at the beginning, and sometimes also at the end, so that it is possible to study the work-pattern in some detail. Unlike Beethoven, who could keep several large-scale works germinating in his mind simultaneously, Schubert almost always preferred to concentrate on one major work at a time. As soon as one was finished he would start on another. On 24 March, for instance, he completed the score of his Second Symphony, and on the following day began work on the G minor String Quartet D173. After sketching the first 65 bars of a new symphony, no. 3 in D, in May, he set it aside to write Goethe and Ossian songs. The full score of *Fernando*, a one-act *Singspiel*, was completed on 9 July, and two days later he returned to the Third Symphony, which was finished on 19 July. Before the end of the month he had started on a new opera, *Claudine von Villa Bella*. At this springtime of his lyrical genius he was able to write songs at any time, though even in 1815 the productive peaks in spring and later summer which are traceable throughout his life can be observed. August and October are the most prolific months, with a total of fifty-two songs, and May and July (thirty-five songs) are not far behind. Already, too, the cyclical pattern of his song production, based on his changing literary enthusiasms, is plain enough. Goethe kept him busy from October 1814 to February 1815, and again in the summer months from May to August. Nine Klopstock songs date from September to October, and almost all the Kosegarten songs from June to October.

Schubert's dated autographs, however, can prove misleading. They do not preclude the existence of earlier drafts, for even where the surviving autograph is dated, sketches may prove that the dates refer only to the final stage of writing out the finished work. This will explain the sometimes surprising claims made in the composer's annotations: 'Finished in

4½ hours', for instance, at the end of the first movement of the B flat String Quartet (D112) need not necessarily be taken literally. The sketches which do survive, however, are nothing like Beethoven's tentative adumbrations of a musical idea, but more like outline drafts of a complete movement or of a song. So even in his early symphonies it seems to have been his habit to make an outline first, consisting of the leading voices; while a song sketch, where he found it necessary to make one, normally showed the whole of the voice line, with the piano prelude and postlude, and brief indications of the accompaniment.

Many reliable anecdotes testify to Schubert's speed and assurance in seizing the seminal idea of a work and committing it to paper. But it is possible to suspect that stories of his infallible gifts were sometimes allowed to proliferate unchecked. The controversial case of 'Erlkönig', the famous setting of Goethe's ballad, written almost certainly in October 1815, is very much to the point. Spaun has left us a circumstantial account, according to which Schubert composed the song one afternoon in a single transport of inspiration, one moment pacing the room with the poem in his hands, the next dashing it down on paper 'just as quickly as he could write'.[6] It is easy enough to believe that the commanding idea for the song—the headlong forward drive of the octave triplets, and the muted sweetness of the boy's questions—did come to the composer in a sudden flash. But there is something wrong with Spaun's account. It would take longer than an hour or two to write out a fair copy clear enough for Ruzicka to try out that evening in the *Konvikt*, let alone to compose the song *currente calamo*. Did Spaun, writing years after the event, confuse two separate occasions here? Or did he perhaps express in narrative form what he knew, or had inferred, about the manner in which it had come to birth?

In the autumn of 1815 we hear for the first time of Franz von Schober, a young man of brilliant gifts but unstable temperament whom Spaun introduced into the circle and who was destined to play a leading part in the story of Schubert's life. Born in Sweden of a German father and an Austrian mother, he arrived in Vienna to study law after his schooling at Kremsmünster. Schober lived with his mother (his father was dead) in some style, and his charm and *savoir-faire* soon gave him a natural authority in the circle. He, Spaun, and Mayrhofer were all pupils of Professor Watteroth, a freethinking liberal with a strong student following who had been an active supporter of political reform. Watteroth gave authority and intellectual respectability to radical opinion, and became an important influence on the Schubert circle. Spaun's friend, Josef Witteczek (1787–1859), who was to become one of Schubert's most staunch supporters and a collector of his works, was a tenant in Watteroth's house, and in 1819 married his daughter Wilhelmine. In

---

[6] Memoirs, p. 131.

May 1816 Spaun went to live with Witteczek, and for a few weeks Schubert himself moved in to share rooms with Spaun. A plan emerged to honour the professor, and doubtless also to make an oblique gesture of political support for him, by staging a musical celebration of his nameday in the garden of his house. For this celebration Schubert agreed to write a cantata, for which Philipp Dräxler wrote the words, on that revolutionary hero, Prometheus. The performance duly took place on 24 July 1816, with Schubert conducting. The score disappeared in 1828, and has never been recovered. It is clear, however, from contemporary reports, and from the fact that *Prometheus* was given a second private performance (with piano accompaniment) in January 1819, that it made a considerable impression. Schubert received a fee of 100 florins for the composition, and proudly noted in his diary, 'Today I composed for money for the first time'.[7]

Among the chorus at the first performance of *Prometheus* was a young law student called Leopold Sonnleithner, whose father Ignaz had taken the lead in founding the Philharmonic Society. The Sonnleithner family was part of the musical establishment of Vienna, and the musical evenings held at their house from 1817 onward were important occasions. The repeat performance of *Prometheus*, which took place on one of them, was due to the enthusiasm of Leopold for the work. While Schubert was still immured in the classroom, the *dramatis personae* who were to play their part in his life-story were being assembled. Another member of the student group who paid homage to Watteroth was a young man from Graz, Anselm Hüttenbrenner, who came to Vienna in 1815 to pursue his musical studies with Salieri. He and Schubert became close friends, and his reminiscences, though notoriously unreliable, sometimes throw an interesting light on Schubert's attitude to his art, and on his indifference to formal convention. 'Dress was a thing in which he took no interest whatever. Sometimes he could not bring himself to change his everyday coat for a black frock coat. He disliked bowing and scraping, and listening to flattering talk about himself he found down-right nauseating.'[8]

The performance of *Prometheus* was one of several public events which helped to bring Schubert's name before the public in 1816. In June Salieri celebrated the fiftieth anniversary of his arrival in Vienna. The occasion was marked by a public service in the cathedral, by the award of a gold medal, and in the evening by a grand party at which Salieri's pupils, old and young, each made a contribution to the performance. Schubert wrote a three-part cantata (D407), concluding with a canon in three voices, on a text of his own composition, a work more interesting, as Kreissle judiciously affirms, 'from the circumstances of its origin than from its intrinsic value as a work of art'. Another such occasion came

[7] Docs, p. 65.   [8] Memoirs, pp. 178–9.

about through the good offices of Schubert's brother, Ferdinand, who had for several years been employed at the Imperial and Royal Orphanage. There he was brought into close contact with Josef Spendou, a founder-governor of the school and a friend of the Schubert family. Spendou was another liberal churchman with a secret allegiance to the anti-clerical reforms of the Emperor Joseph II. In January 1817, on the twentieth anniversary of the founding of the Orphanage, a concert was held in honour of Spendou, at which Schubert's specially written cantata (D472) was performed. It is a substantial work in four numbers, for soloists, choir, and orchestra.

The few pages which survive of a diary which he kept in the summer of 1816 give us an insight into the introspective musings of the nineteen-year-old composer. On 13 June, for instance, he records his impressions of a private concert, one of those formal occasions for which, according to Anselm Hüttenbrenner, he had an antipathy. 'As from afar, the magic notes of Mozart's music still gently haunt me. So these fair impressions, which neither time nor circumstance can efface, linger in the soul and lighten our existence. They show us in the darkness of this life a light, clear, lovely, for which we confidently hope. O Mozart, immortal Mozart, how many, how endlessly many such beneficent intimations of a better life have you imprinted on our souls!' The passage refers to a performance of one of Mozart's string quintets. Schubert goes on to describe his own part in the entertainment, a performance of variations by Beethoven, and of two songs, Goethe's 'Rastlose Liebe' (Love without Respite) and Schiller's 'Amalia'. 'Unanimous applause for the former. Less for the latter', he notes; and he goes on to pay his tribute to Goethe's genius as a musical poet.[9]

Two days later he recorded his impressions of the reception for Salieri, praising the 'expression of pure nature, free of all eccentricity', in the compositions of his pupils, and deprecating the extravagance and disregard of conventional forms for which 'one of our greatest German artists' was to be held responsible. This is not the only evidence we have that in 1816 a reaction against the influence of Beethoven can be traced both in Schubert's music and in his sympathies. Temporarily at any rate, Mozart had replaced Beethoven as the god to be worshipped. It must be the highest pleasure for an artist, he continues, to be guided by such a one as Gluck, and by 'pure, holy Nature'.[10] These sentiments must owe something to the occasion; they were not to survive his escape from the classroom and from the influence of Salieri, which was soon to follow.

Schubert's career seemed to have reached a turning-point in his twentieth year. On the one hand there was his love for Therese Grob, and the claims of regular employment and financial security which the prospect of marriage implied. On the other hand lay the claims of his

---

[9] Docs, p. 60.   [10] Docs, p. 64.

art, and his temperamental dislike of all routine employment other than composing. In the end, as so often happens, events conspired to solve the problem for him. In February applications were invited for a new post as music teacher at the training school of Laibach (now Llubjana), a provincial capital some 200 miles south of Vienna. It is safe to assume that the prospect did not much appeal to Schubert, but the job description appeared to leave spare time available for composing, and the salary of 450 florins promised independence. In April, belatedly and reluctantly, he sent in his application, buttressed by testimonials from Salieri and from Spendou. The authorities, however, were in no hurry. The procedure went on at a leisurely pace through the summer months until finally in August they decided to appoint somebody else. Doubtless Schubert was relieved at the news.

Meanwhile Spaun had taken the lead in a scheme of a quite different kind to promote Schubert's interests. This was no less than a proposal to publish his songs in a series of volumes, each based on the work of a particular poet or poets. As Spaun himself explained in suitably reverential phrases in a letter to Goethe of 17 April 1816: 'A beginning is now to be made with a selection of German songs . . . to be followed by instrumental works. It is to comprise eight books. The first two (of which the first is enclosed as a specimen) contain poems by Your Excellency, the third contains poems by Schiller, the fourth and fifth by Klopstock, the sixth by Matthisson, Hölty, Salis etc., and the seventh and eighth contain songs from Ossian, these last excelling all the others.'[11] There is something touchingly loyal and optimistic about this ambitious plan. But alas, Spaun's request for permission to dedicate the first two volumes to the great man himself met with no response. The sage of Weimar was too busy with other matters even to look at the enclosed songs, which Schubert had carefully copied, and which are now in the *Staatsbibliothek*, Berlin. But it is unlikely that the outcome would have been any different even if he had examined them, for his widely publicised views on the primacy of the strophic song and the limited function of the composer would surely have blinded him to the merits of 'Gretchen' and 'Erlkönig'.

In spite of this setback, Schubert made fair copies over the next few months of twelve more Goethe songs, and continued to set poems by Hölty, Uz, Claudius, Jacobi, and Salis, usually concentrating on one poet at a time. In September he returned to Goethe once more, with his settings of the Mignon and Harper songs from *Wilhelm Meister*, showing an instinctive understanding of those lonely and alienated characters. In fact Schubert was to wait five more years before any of his songs reached publication in permanent form. What is striking, however, is that his friends should, even at this early date, consider so ambitious a

[11] Docs, p. 56.

plan to publish the works of a nineteen-year-old composer, and that it should be based on a recognition of the essential link in Schubert's work between the poet and the composer.

In the autumn a timely offer of hospitality from the Schober family resolved Schubert's personal problem for the time being. With the failure of his bid for a permanent post marriage was clearly not in prospect; but after the success of *Prometheus* a return to the schoolroom was not to be contemplated. The move to the inner city, he must have realized in his heart, meant in effect the end of his affair with Therese. In November he copied out seventeen songs for her, songs which had special association perhaps with their love for each other, and presented them to her as a keepsake. The songs were later bound in an album, and remained in Therese's family until recent years, steadfastly guarded from the prying eyes of musicologists. When ultimately the contents of the album became known it was realized that three of the songs in it had never previously been published.[12]

The autumn of 1816 thus marks the effective end of schoolmastering, and the beginning of his career as a free-lance composer. It initiates also a new phase in the development of his art. Hitherto he had been content to work within the limits of the classical language and (songs apart) with classical forms. Even the cornucopian facility and versatility of these early years has something of an eighteenth-century character about it, reminding us of the serviceable industry of a Dittersdorf or a Kozeluch, and contrasting sharply with his cautious and experimental approach to the sonata and the symphony over the next few years. Henceforth the flood of new compositions begins to abate, until in 1818 it almost comes to a halt. At the same time his work shows a new philosophical depth, and recognisably Romantic themes and attitudes begin to influence not only his songs but also the instrumental works.

Just when Schubert moved to the inner city is not clear. Schober spent the second half of the year in Sweden attending to family business, and did not return till December, when the move may have taken place. The mood of the Schubert circle in these last months of the year was sombre. The political situation went from bad to worse, as 'the system' gradually re-established its tight hold on free movement and free expression, and it became clear that hopes of a more liberal regime were doomed to disappointment. Johann Mayrhofer, with whom Schubert seems to have been on close terms at this time, believed that the only policy for the artist was to find what consolation he could in his art. On 7 September he wrote to Schober: 'Today Schubert is coming to me and several friends; the mists of the present time, which are somewhat leaden, must be lifted by his melodies'.[13] Later that month, while away on a walking

[12] Maurice J. E. Brown, 'The Therese Grob Collection of Songs by Schubert', *ML*, April 1968, pp. 122–34.
[13] Docs, p. 70.

holiday with Watteroth's son Hermann, he wrote a poem for Schubert which again speaks of his friend's ability to 'summon a heaven from the troubles of the present time'. Schubert gracefully accepted the compliment by setting the text to music ('Geheimnis', A Secret, D491). In his diary Schubert noted, a trifle selfconsciously, that 'happy moments brighten this gloomy life, and happier ones give glimpses of happier worlds'.[14] It must have been in one of those happier moments that he began his Symphony No. 5 in B flat, which was finished on 3 October. It is the sunniest and most lyrical of all the symphonies, and was given its first performance that autumn at the regular rehearsals of the orchestra which met in Otto Hatwig's house.

[14] Docs, p. 71.

3

The origins of the Lied

The establishment of the Lied as an autonomous musical form was by far the greatest achievement of Schubert's early years. In three years of unparalleled lyrical activity he laid the foundation of both his own greatness and a vast literature of Romantic song from Schumann to Richard Strauss. With hindsight it is tempting to see this development as the inevitable result of historic tendencies, as a kind of fusion of the new poetry, with its emphasis on subjective feeling, and the growth of domestic music-making. These things no doubt played their part: in the last resort, however, music history is made not by impersonal tendencies, but by individual composers; when all is said, it was Schubert's genius, under the stimulus of Goethe's poetry, which created 'Gretchen am Spinnrade', and which was responsible for the great outpouring of song which followed.

As we have seen, his first essays in the art of song were modelled on the extended ballads of Zumsteeg (1760–1802). Their appeal rested on the literary taste of the age, on the fascination which the macabre and the horrific held for poets like Bürger and Schiller; and they owed more to sophisticated operatic forms than to the vernacular Lied, for they relied upon alternating sections of recitative and arioso. With this essentially episodic form Schubert managed to achieve much more than Zumsteeg had done. At its best, as in 'Leichenfantasie', it can reveal an impressive power and unity of mood. The organic unity of 'Gretchen', however, is of a quite different order.

The earliest attempts at pure song, as distinct from the sophisticated *Gesang*, belong to 1812. The first strophic song, 'Klaglied' (Lament) D23, may have been written in the spring of that year. Significantly perhaps, its text, by the Leipzig critic and poet J. F. Rochlitz, expressed the sadness of the rejected lover in terms strongly reminiscent of Gretchen's monologue. In September of the same year Schubert set Schiller's 'Der Jüngling am Bache', which we have already noticed (see Ex. 4). It is the first modified strophic song; the outer verses are set to the same Italianate tune, but at the emotional heart of the song, at the words which express the depth of the lover's grief, the rhythmic flow is interrupted by a kind of declamation, neither true recitative nor true arioso.

The heavily accented dotted rhythm of the first of these interruptions was to become a favourite Schubert motif expressive of grief and despair (Ex. 6).

This attempt to break down the rigid barriers of recitative and arioso, and so to bring to domestic song the dramatic force of opera without its formal restrictions, is very much a feature of the Matthisson songs of 1814. Friedrich von Matthisson (1761–1831) was a fashionable poet whose elegant verses caught the imagination of both Schubert and

Ex. 6

A - ber tau - send Stim - men der er - wa - chen - den Na-

- tur __ we - cken in dem tief - en Bu - sen mir den schwe - ren

Kum - mer nur

27

Beethoven. In the spring and summer of 1814 Schubert set thirteen of his poems. The only one of the Matthisson songs to achieve popularity is 'Der Geistertanz' (The Ghost Dance) D116, in the version composed in October 1814. But all of them are of interest because of their preoccupation with the problem of embodying direct speech within the strophic song. In this regard they pave the way for 'Gretchen'. 'Trost, an Elisa' (Consolation, for Eliza) D97 is a bold, expressive, and surprisingly convincing attempt to write a dramatic scena almost entirely in recitative; only twice does it briefly assume the regular pulse of arioso. In 'Andenken' (Remembrance) D99 Schubert brings the voice of the narrator into close-up at the end of each verse by means of a linking motto phrase. This ability to bring the narrator's voice suddenly into focus was something Schubert was later to exploit in the song cycles.

'Gretchen am Spinnrade' is the first Schubert song to show a complete fusion of the lyrical and dramatic elements. The key to the solution of the problem was the invention of the tonal image which both unifies and defines the song. 'Gretchen' is still text-dominated, in the sense that it faithfully re-creates the great arc of passion implicit in the unhappy girl's thoughts as she sits at her spinning-wheel; but the running semiquavers in the pianist's right hand are a sensuous image derived, not directly from the words, but from the physical movement of the spinning-wheel; and it is that tonal image which frees the song to take its own autonomous musical form. So strong is the forward momentum that the eloquent pause after the words 'Ah . . . his kiss!'—at the first of the two great climaxes in the song—carries recitative to the logical extreme of silence, to the point where feeling lies beyond the reach of words. If 'Hagars Klage' can be seen as a kind of musical commentary on a story in verse, and the Matthisson songs as a compromise between the lyrical and dramatic aspects of a text, 'Gretchen' is the poem-in-music.

The great outpouring of song which followed over the next twelve months is most remarkable not for its sheer quantity and facility, but for its astonishing range of form, style, and poetic tone. Surprising as it may seem, Schubert's facility is not without precedent. He wrote well over 600 songs, but J. F. Reichardt (1752–1814) wrote 1500, and Zumsteeg over 300. Statistically speaking, the great age of German song was not the first half of the nineteenth century but the last forty years of the eighteenth. (For the evidence see the tables in Friedländer's monumental study, *German Song in the Eighteenth Century*.[1]) The variety of Schubert's 1815 songs is, however, quite without precedent. The authors, more than 30 of them, range from cult figures such as Ossian to personal friends like Kenner, from the most famous (Goethe, Schiller, Klopstock) to unknown versifiers like Bertrand and Bobrik. The musical terms of reference are equally wide-ranging. Three-part canons in pure baroque style sit along-

---

[1] *Das deutsche Lied im 18. Jahrhundert* (Stuttgart and Berlin, 1902). Reprinted, George Olms Verlag, 1970, vol. I(1).

side predictive songs which could easily masquerade as late Romantic compositions. Almost every song-form is represented in the list: strophic and through-composed songs, dramatic monologues, songs wholly in recitative, and songs in the folksong tradition.

It is not surprising that Schubert's voracious appetite for a songtext during this *annus mirabilis* led him sometimes to the banal as well as to the sublime. Sometimes he seems to have worked from a source book like an almanac or other anthology, setting one poem after another just as he happened upon them. But when he discovered a poet whose work appealed to him, it was already his established practice to go on setting his verses until he felt the urge to look elsewhere. In this way he was able to find an appropriate musical style to suit not only each poem, but each poet, so that his Ossian style, for instance, is entirely different from his Hölty or his Baumberg style. Indeed, the only sensible approach to the profusion of songs which flowed from his pen in 1815 is by authors. Schubert's friends were not wrong in planning an edition of his songs under authors.

Goethe inspired the greatest songs of the year—'Nähe des Geliebten' (Nearness of the Beloved), 'Erster Verlust' (First Loss), 'Heidenröslein' (The Wild Rose), 'Erlkönig' (The Erlking), and many others. But the twenty-seven Goethe settings of 1815 are by no means all masterpieces. With Goethe's dark and subtle parable 'Der Gott und die Bajadere' (The god and the dancing-girl) the eighteen-year-old composer is out of his depth, and the first setting of 'An den Mond' (To the Moon) D259 tries to confine a richly evocative poem within the frame of a strophic setting entirely eighteenth-century in style. Neither does Schubert make as much as Loewe does of that enigmatic poem 'Der Schatzgräber' (The Treasure Seeker). In October, however, came the masterpiece which caught the imagination of the age, and was to play an important part in his fame. 'Erlkönig' at last brought the Romantic spine-chilling ballad to the level of great art: and as with 'Gretchen', the key to its success is the unifying piano figure, the galloping triplets which give to the song its irresistible forward thrust. The theme is a near relation of the 'flight motif' in 'Der Vatermörder' (see Ex. 3). Within a single dynamic pulse Schubert is able to accommodate the words of all three protagonists in the drama. Only in the final bars do the insistent repetitive quavers pause, so that the narrator's brief recitative, when it comes, is a kind of *coup de théâtre*: 'And in his arms the child lay dead!'

The most important poets of the spring were Theodor Körner, the Rupert Brooke of his generation, and Ludwig Hölty (1748–76), an early romantic whose sense of beauty is coloured by the awareness of transience and mortality. Of the ten Körner songs of the year, perhaps the most impressive are 'Gebet während der Schlacht' (Prayer during Battle) D171, a strophic song with introductory recitative, and 'Liebesrausch' (Ecstasy of Love) D179, in which the repeated triplet chords grow in a single span of feeling and break like a wave at the end, in a way which foreshadows dozens of later romantic songs. The best known Hölty songs, 'An den Mond' D193 and 'An die Nachtigall' (To the Nightingale) D196, are remarkable for their freshness of feeling and poignancy. Schubert's own sense of emotional ambiguity, of the complementarity of sadness and happiness, was immensely stimulated by Hölty.

The twenty songs of Ludwig Kosegarten (1758–1818), written between June and October, are strophic, and for the most part too slight for the concert hall, but they are well worth exploring. Many of them, like 'Nachtgesang' (Night Song) for instance, convey an intensity of feeling which belies their small scale. 'Die Erscheinung' (The Apparition) D229 is an interesting forerunner of 'Die Forelle' (The Trout), a much more famous song, while 'Die Mondnacht' (Moonlit Night) D238 might belong to the last quarter of the nineteenth century, so precisely does it foreshadow the idiom of later Romantic song (see Ex. 7). It is astonishing that this fine and predictive song had to wait till 1894 for publication in the collected edition.

The Schiller settings of 1815 do not represent Schubert at his best, but the nine Klopstock songs of September and October are full of interest.

Ex. 7

The three songs addressed to the poet's wife ('Cidli') are all fine, and the best of the three—'Das Rosenband' (The Rose Garland) D280—is a miniature masterpiece. 'Dem Unendlichen' (To the Infinite One) D291 is an eloquent song of praise to the pantheistic God of the eighteenth century: 'Thunder forth, you worlds, in solemn measure, to the chorus of trumpets! Make a loud noise, all you suns along the shining way, to the chorus of trumpets!' The song anticipates the sublimity of 'Die Allmacht', to be written ten years later.

Finally, something must be said about Schubert's Ossian songs, if only because they were so highly regarded in their day. The story begins in June, when his friend, Anton Holzapfel, presented him with an old and tattered copy of Macpherson's prose poems, translated into German by Edmund von Harold.[2] Since the 1760s, when they first appeared, these ballads of the Celtic twilight had enjoyed an enormous vogue in Germany. The enthusiasm of Herder, Goethe, and others had given them a cult status, and this must account in part for the exaggerated rating given to Schubert's settings among his friends. In the letter to Goethe already mentioned Spaun referred to them as 'excelling all the others'; and after Schubert's death they were the first songs to be published by Diabelli in the *Nachlass*.[3] The ten Ossian settings begin with 'Kolmas

---

[2] Memoirs, p. 59.

[3] i.e. *Franz Schuberts Nachgelassene musikalische Dichtungen für Gesang und Pianoforte* (Vienna, 1830–50), 50 vols.

Klage' (Colma's Lament) in June 1815, and end in February 1817 with 'Die Nacht' (The Night). Three of them, 'Shilrik und Vinvela', 'Cronnan', and 'Lodas Gespenst' (The Ghost of Loda), come from the same poem, the *Carric-Thura*; this, and the fact that some of them are written in sections which would fit together without much difficulty, suggest that Schubert's intention was to link them all together in a kind of Ossian cantata.

Several of them do, moreover, show a certain uniformity of style, characterized by moving adjacent thirds and sixths, minor keys, ostinato keyboard figures and stepwise bass lines. This style looks back to the baroque, and has obvious affinities with the early masses. For instance, the passage from 'Die Nacht' shown in Ex. 8 closely resembles the Agnus Dei of the Mass in G, of March 1815.

Ex. 8

At its best this archaic style can achieve an impressive grandeur and sonority, as it does at the beginning of 'Kolmas Klage'. But in the main Schubert's imagination seems in the Ossian songs to be reaching out beyond his means. They are rarely heard today, though Roger Fiske has suggested[4] that some of the best music might be salvaged by returning

---

[4] Roger Fiske, *Scotland in Music* (Cambridge, 1983), pp. 84–7.

to Schubert's original idea and linking together the three songs from the *Carric-Thura* in a cantata for three solo voices.

If it is impossible to characterize the songs of 1815 except in terms of their endless variety and unpredictability, there does seem to be a more consistent tone in the songs of 1816. The spare, epigraphic idiom is well represented by the many songs in 6/8 tempo and in A minor, and by the frequency with which the word 'Klage' (Lament) occurs in the title. The note of plaintive melancholy is aptly caught in the setting of 'Ins stille Land' (The Land of Peace) D403, lines by J. G. von Salis-Seewis which express a deep longing for a better world beyond the grave (see Ex. 9). Schubert was to adapt the tune many years later for his final setting of Mignon's song, 'Nur wer die Sehnsucht kennt' (Only he who knows longing) D877. Another song in similar pessimistic vein is 'Der Leidende' (The Suffering One) D432. Here the key is B minor, Schubert's key of loneliness and alienation. This tune was also to recur, in the B flat Entr'acte of the *Rosamunde* music.

Ex. 9

In quantitative terms 1816, with well over 100 songs, is almost as remarkable as 1815, but in the first eight months, at any rate, there are few really great songs. 'Seligkeit' (Happiness), another Hölty setting, has a well-deserved reputation as the perfect encore, and Matthisson's 'Stimme der Liebe' (The Voice of Love) D418 anticipates later master-pieces in its tonal freedom and impressive climax. Of the new poets rep-resented the most important are Salis-Seewis in March, J. P. Uz (1720–96) in June, and J. G. Jacobi (1740–1814) in August and September. The last-named inspired several fine songs and one great one, 'Litanei' (Litany on the Feast of All-souls Day) D343. All these songs remind us of Mozart in their formal perfection and transparency, but then both the songs and the instrumental works of the nineteen-year-old composer seem to be inspired by the Apollonian spirit of his great pre-decessor. The introduction to the Schiller song 'Laura am Klavier' (Laura at the Piano) D388 might well pass as the beginning of a Mozart piano sonata.

In September, however, a deeper, more philosophical note begins to sound. The setting of Jacobi's 'Orpheus' D474 is a song in the grand manner, looking forward to the sublimity of Mayrhofer's Orestes mono-logues. In the same month Schubert returned to Goethe with his songs of the Harper, the apathetic victim of fate in *Wilhelm Meister*, the pro-totype of the Romantic figure of the outcast and alienated artist, and the forerunner of the homeless wanderer in *Winterreise*. In their tonal monotony (all the Harper settings are in A minor), and rhythmic insis-tence, these songs foreshadow 'Der Leiermann', and they provide us with a kind of *locus classicus* for Schubert's tonal images of spiritual iso-lation and despair. Significantly, the first of them (D478 No. 1) bases its final verse and postlude on the descending chromatic bass line of Ex. 1, while the third, 'An die Türen will ich schleichen' (I will steal from door to door), carries the same tempo indication as the first song of *Winterreise* in Schubert's autograph: *Mässig: In gehender Bewegung* ('At a moderate walking pace').

A month later came a song which was to prove as popular as 'Erlkönig'. 'Der Wanderer' was Schubert's own title for a poem by G. P. Schmidt of Lübeck which neatly encapsulates in its last verse that romantic longing for the unattainable which the Germans call *Sehnsucht*. 'I wander silent and unhappy, and sighing constantly ask "Whither?" The answer comes in a ghostly whisper: "There, where you are not, only there is happiness".' In verse 2, where the Wanderer laments that the world is old, the sun is cold and the flowers faded, we hear for the first time in its definitive form the motif which was there-after to be associated with *Sehnsucht* (see Ex. 10). The first half of this famous 'Wanderer' sequence is an obvious derivative of the descent from tonic minor to dominant major, the original form of which is given in Ex. 1. The second half is a return journey.

In November, and again in February 1817, Schubert was much occu-pied with the poetry of Matthias Claudius (1740–1815), whose sense of the kinship of life and death, of the ambivalence of joy and sorrow,

Ex. 10

[Sehr langsam]

Die Son - ne dünkt — mich hier so — kalt, die
Blü - te welk, — das Le - ben alt, (und)

made a strong appeal to the composer's imagination. The best known of the Claudius songs is 'Der Tod und das Mädchen' (Death and the Maiden) D531, but perhaps the finest of them is 'An die Nachtigall' (To the Nightingale) D497, which evokes a new world of subjective feeling in its forty-one bars. The song begins off-key, borrowing a device already exploited a year earlier in 'An die Geliebte' (To the Beloved) D303. At bar 22 the notes begin to dance with joy, and then to yearn

Ex. 11

[Mässig]

und ich kann fröh - lich sein und

with passionate longing. (See Ex. 11: 'Ah, nightingale, do not wake my darling with your song!') The major/minor exchanges here are much more than a traditional device. They seem to sum up the essence of the poetic experience of life. Perhaps here, for the first time, we become aware of the *Innigkeit*, the subjective feeling for the fragility of life and joy, which was to sustain a century of Romantic song.

4

Instrumental, liturgical, and dramatic works (1813–16)

Of the thousand works, and more, recorded in the Thematic Catalogue of Schubert's works, half were completed before January 1817, when he celebrated his twentieth birthday. They include every type of composition then known, and in a book of this size it is hardly possible to deal in detail with them all. Something must be said, however, of the major achievements of these schoolhouse years, both because many of them continue to hold their place in the repertory on their own merits, and because they represent what may be called Schubert's first-stage maturity, displaying his mastery of the classical language which he inherited. This is especially important in the case of the symphonies, for there is a striking contrast between the facility of his early years (six symphonies in a little more than four years) and the slow gestation of his two mature masterpieces in the 1820s.

The first three symphonies may conveniently be considered together, since they share the same formal and stylistic characteristics. They are No. 1 in D major of October 1813; No. 2 in B flat of December 1814–March 1815; and No. 3 in D major of May–July 1815. Schubert took as his model in these early works the symphony as it emerged in the mature public works of Haydn and Mozart. Among the most popular keys for such works were D major and B flat.[1] They usually began with a slow introduction, were in four movements, with the slow movement coming second, and the outer movements were quick and sustained by a strong forward impetus. Schubert's first three symphonies conform closely to these conventions, though he put his own stamp on them. The third movements are still called Menuets, though those of No. 2 and No. 3 are scherzos in all but name. The Trios are distinguished by Schubert's expressive writing for woodwind, and the slow movements are based on Haydnesque themes, often bland in character, though such is Schubert's gift for melodic invention and variation that they seldom outstay their welcome. He obviously made conscious efforts to extend the monothe-

---

[1] In his book, *Schubert and the Symphony. A New Perspective* (London, 1992), Brian Newbould stresses the technical advantages of these keys for the composer in the days of valveless trumpets and horns.

matic procedures by which Haydn had attempted, in the 'Drumroll' symphony and elsewhere, to underpin the organic unity of a movement. In the First Symphony, for instance, the theme of the slow introduction reappears at the end of the development (Schubert was to use the same device years later in the Octet for Strings and Wind, and in the 'Great' C major Symphony). Something similar happens towards the end of the first movement of No. 3. The finales, too, are noteworthy for their monothematic structures and cumulative tension. In the Second Symphony the four strong accents of the main theme are slimmed down at the end to an insistent beat, much in the manner of the finale of the 'Great' C major. Nor is this the only pre-echo of that much later and greater work. As has often been noticed, the main themes of the opening movement of the Third Symphony and of the 'Great' C major are virtually the same. (See pp. 133–4.)

The most popular of the first three symphonies nowadays is probably the Third in D, but the most impressive is the Second, which shows signs of Schubert's growing interest in Beethoven. The Allegro vivace is based on two splendidly contrasted themes (see Ex. 12), the first of which pays its tribute to Beethoven's *Prometheus* Overture,[2] while the second looks forward to the lyrical second subject of the *Quartettsatz* of December 1820.

Ex. 12

In 1816 Schubert wrote two more symphonies, strongly contrasted in mood, but each showing a marked advance on its predecessors. The C minor Symphony, called the 'Tragic', was so named by Schubert himself, though the sobriquet seems to have been added to the autograph later. A copy in the possession of Ferdinand Schubert, however, is dated April 1816. There is an earlier sketch of the theme for the finale, suggesting that the work was started some months earlier, possibly at the

---

[2] See Docs, p. 265, for evidence of Schubert's familiarity with Beethoven's *Prometheus* Overture.

end of 1815. This is Schubert's first symphony in a minor key, and the first to move away from the ceremonial public style to a more personal, elegiac tone. Again, the stepwise build of the themes, and the dynamic Scherzo (still anachronistically called 'Menuetto'), bring Beethoven to mind, and the main theme of the Allegro vivace has a certain affinity with the corresponding tune in the first movement of Beethoven's String Quartet in the same key, Op. 18 No. 4. However, the main ideas all derive from Schubert's own earlier works. The introductory Adagio molto is a reworking on a symphonic scale of Ex. 1, and the themes of the other movements bear a family resemblance to it, so that the Symphony appears to represent a quite new approach to the problem of organic unity in the four-movement work. Instead of the cyclical devices which are such a feature of the first three symphonies, Schubert seems here to adopt a more genuinely monothematic approach, so that all the thematic material derives, more or less obviously, from the same cell. The inner movements are impressive, but elsewhere the shadow of Beethoven seems to lie somewhat heavily over the work. This, and the generally sombre tone, make it perhaps the least popular of all Schubert's symphonies.

In the autumn, however, Schubert wrote a work which bears in every bar the stamp of his own lyrical genius, while the spirit of Mozart seems also to brood benignly over it. The Symphony in B flat, No. 5, sometimes called the symphony 'without trumpets and drums' (there are no clarinets either), was written for the semi-professional orchestra which met at Otto Hatwig's house, and it was first performed there. The usual slow introduction is missing, and there are no declamatory gestures; all is sweetness and light. The themes are handled with masterly wit and high spirits, a salutary reminder that great composers are not the slaves of circumstance, for all the signs are that in the autumn of 1816 the fortunes of the Schubert circle were at a low ebb. The main tune of the Andante con moto may well seem to some a trifle over-sweet but if so, Schubert disarms criticism by bold tonal excursions into the remote keys of C flat and G flat, set off by his unfailing ear for effective woodwind writing.

It is a sad comment on the indifference of the nineteenth century to Schubert's orchestral works that none of these early symphonies was published until the 1880s, when they appeared in the collected edition of the composer's works published by Breitkopf & Härtel. By that time such pioneers as Grove and Manns in London, and Hallé in Manchester, had given them a public hearing, but it was not until this century that they were able to command a regular place in the repertory.

In Schubert's day the church was still the most important patron of music. His own musical training was that of a choirboy, and he wrote liturgical works throughout his life. There is ample evidence, however, that his own religious views as an adult were far from orthodox; and since any composer's setting of religious texts, and especially of the Mass, must be influenced by his own attitude towards the sacred rite, it seems important to say something here about the vexed question of the deviations from the usual text in Schubert's masses.

It is well known that the words 'Et in unam sanctam catholicam ecclesiam' are omitted from the Credo in all the masses; but this is by no means the only variation from the norm. The phrases 'Et expecto resurrectionem', and 'Genitum non factum', are also sometimes omitted, and there are other less significant variants. These omissions are much too consistent to be accidental, and there can hardly have been any musical reason for them. The only explanation must be that these articles of faith were not acceptable to Schubert, and that he left them out as a matter of conscience. This explanation is quite consistent also with what we know about his religious beliefs from his letters and from the comments of his friends. But, it may be asked, if this was Schubert's attitude, how was it that his liturgical works were much in demand, and that his masses were performed in his lifetime not only at Liechtental church but elsewhere? The answer to this question is to be found in the intellectual climate of the age, which still retained much of the sceptical and tolerant temper of the Enlightenment. In particular the liberal demythologized Christianity which had found expression in the anti-clerical reforms of Joseph II was still very much alive, though officially frowned on. Many of Schubert's friends, some of them prominent churchmen such as Josef Spendou and Ladislaus Pyrker, openly professed it. There was a tradition of tolerance in such matters in Austria, and in England too, if we are to judge by Samuel Wesley's remark about his Catholic friend Vincent Novello, who was said to believe 'not a word of Purgatory, Priestly Absolution, Transubstantiation, Extreme Unction, or any other such nonsense'.[3] It seems that such variations in the text of the Mass were then by no means rare.[4]

The truth is that Schubert was a man of deep religious instincts who rejected, as did his brother Ignaz, the supernatural aspects of the Christian faith, while retaining what may be called a religious attitude to life. It should not surprise us, then, that his liturgical works lack the deep-rooted faith of a Haydn, and the philosophical depth of a Beethoven. But if his settings of the Credo and the Sanctus sometimes reflect a lack of commitment, his humanity and lyrical power give to the Benedictus and the Agnus Dei a special tenderness and poetry.

Schubert wrote four masses during his schoolhouse years, of which the first, the Mass in F of 1814, is a ceremonial mass for soloists, chorus, and full orchestra with trombones. It is a remarkable achievement for a youth of seventeen, and the first of his compositions to bring him to pub-

---

[3] Quoted by Lightwood, *Samuel Wesley, Musician* (London, 1937), p. 181.
[4] Reinhard van Hoorickx, 'Textänderungen in Schuberts Messen', *Schubert-Kongress Wien, 1978 Bericht* (Graz, 1979), pp. 249–54.

lic notice. The Kyrie (Larghetto 6/8) is set in a mood of gentle intercession, and in the original version this music returns for the concluding 'Dona nobis pacem'. The sentences of the Gloria are set separately, the 'Gratias agimus' as a trio (STB) and the Agnus Dei in D minor; here Schubert's feeling for the text and part-writing are impressive, but the concluding fugue ('Cum sancto Spiritu') does not sustain the same level. The most effective section is the Benedictus, set as a quartet in which each voice takes the melody in turn, giving a feeling of cumulative elaboration and expression. This (basically baroque) device was to provide a pattern for future settings. A few months after the mass was finished, in April 1815, Schubert wrote a fugal setting of the 'Dona nobis', presumably in the hope that this would make the work more acceptable in conventional court circles. The change, however, is not an improvement.

It cannot be denied that the fugues are often the weakest part of his liturgical works. His friends often regretted that he never found an established composer who could give him a thorough grounding in the art; not one, at any rate, who won his full confidence. His instinctive grasp of counterpoint in his own orchestral and instrumental masterpieces speaks for itself. But fugue is a different matter; he never seems to handle the form with commanding ease. If his fugues often have a mechanical feel to them, this may be due to the fact that he usually keeps rigidly to the real answer. It is significant perhaps that his studies with Salieri began with fugue, but never got very far. Certainly Salieri seems never to have explored with him the effective use of the tonal answer, and this may have been one reason why, in the last months of his life, he arranged to go to Simon Sechter, the most famous contrapuntist of the time, for lessons.

In 1815 and 1816 Schubert also wrote three 'little' masses, intended for use at the normal celebration in a parish church. They seem to have been modelled on Mozart's *missae breves*, which Schubert must surely have sung as a boy in Liechtental church; and there is little doubt that they were first performed at Liechtental. The Mass in G major D167 of March 1815, the Mass in B flat D324 of November/December 1815, and the Mass in C major D452 of June/July 1816 may conveniently be considered together, for stylistically they have much in common. Following the conventions for such works, fugues are dispensed with, the Gloria and the Credo are set as unified single movements, sometimes in ternary form, and the instrumental forces are usually reduced to organ and strings, though wind parts were later added to the G major Mass. None of them is altogether free from the baroque clichés characteristic of the liturgical style, 'walking' basses, upward rushing scales in the Gloria, and ostinato accompaniment figures to define the mood. But there is much genuine Schubert to admire in them also. The Incarnatus and the Crucifixus of the B flat Mass are deeply felt, for instance, though the outer sections of the Credo strike a more perfunctory note. Much the most popular of the three is the first, the G major Mass. It too is uneven, but at its best, in the Benedictus and the Agnus Dei, it conveys a sense of lyrical sweetness and profound simplicity which Schubert learned from his beloved Mozart (Ex. 13).

Ex. 13

Only one of the three masses was published in the composer's lifetime, the Mass in C. However, this is not to be taken as an indication of neglect, as the curious history of the G major Mass illustrates. In 1847 Ferdinand Schubert handed the manuscript over to Diabelli for publication, only to discover that it had already appeared in print, in a pirated edition in Prague, as the work of a certain Kapellmeister called Robert Führer! It is an interesting comment on the ethical standards then obtaining among publishers that Ferdinand's indignant protest did not even elicit an acknowledgment.[5]

Fourteen other liturgical works belong to these years, including two settings of the *Stabat Mater*, four of the *Salve Regina*, three of the *Tantum ergo*, and several other anthems intended as graduals or offertories. They reflect very varied moods and styles, from the purely secular (*Auguste jam coelestium* D488 of October 1816, for example) to the expressive devotion of the *Stabat Mater* (D175) of April 1815, a fine setting for mixed chorus and orchestra. The figure of the Mother of God never failed to kindle Schubert's imagination. The second version, based on Klopstock's metrical German paraphrase of the hymn (D383) is on an altogether more ambitious scale. Scored for soloists, chorus, and full orchestra, it is in twelve sections, and reflects at several points Schubert's admiration for Pergolesi's famous work. It builds to a fine climax with a chorus, vocal trio and ensemble, and it is unfortunate that the 'Amen' fugue which follows rather lowers the temperature. None the less, the *Stabat Mater* deserves to be better known. It is a major work, and full of fine music.

Salve Regina was also a favourite text. The two choral settings, D379 and D386, both dating from early 1816, are attractively written in a deeply felt, homophonic style. The solo settings are more operatic in style, with a high tessitura for the voice. The version for solo soprano, orchestra and organ of July 1815 (D223), written for Therese Grob, is perhaps the most expressive of them, rivalled only by the setting for solo soprano and strings of 1819.

Schubert's only setting of the Magnificat (D486) probably dates from September 1815, though Deutsch attributed it to 1816 on the strength of a dated copy. It is in three sections, the outer ones lively and brilliant, with busy string parts and upward rushing scales, and a quiet and reflective middle section for the words 'He hath put down the mighty . . .'. The piece has some stylistic affinity with the B flat Mass, but as a whole its brilliance fails to carry conviction. The most interesting of the minor anthems are the two settings of the *Tantum ergo* of August 1816, written for similar forces and both in C major. D461, scored for four soloists, chorus and orchestra, is a solemn march, a kind of Schubertian chorus of priests, which recalls the Mozart of *The Magic Flute*. The

---

[5] Memoirs, pp. 415–16.

other version, which dispenses with three of the soloists, is more lyrical, but it also pays its tribute to Mozart.

Schubert's return to the schoolhouse in the autumn of 1813 no doubt meant a renewal of family music-making, and he welcomed the event in November by writing a new string quartet, the longest and most impressive to date, No. 8 in E flat (D87). It has two peculiarities: all the movements are in the tonic, and the order of the inner movements is reversed, the Beethovenish Scherzo coming second. The autograph has disappeared, and it has been conjectured that the unusual order was the publisher's idea rather than Schubert's.[6] It is much more likely, however, that the reflective character of the first movement suggested to the composer that the lively Scherzo should come between it and the slow movement. The arrangement is not unknown in Schubert, for it appears in the original score of the C major quartet of 1813 (D46), and again in the A major Violin Sonata of 1817. The work was published as Op. 125 No. 1 in 1830, and attributed throughout the nineteenth century to the composer's mature years. In spite of its tonal uniformity, the E flat Quartet does have variety of mood, and the contrapuntal texture of true chamber music.

The String Quartet in B flat D112, however, represents a much bigger advance on what had gone before. The autograph is precisely dated, 5 September 1814 at the beginning and 13 September at the end; at the close of the first movement Schubert added the words, 'Finished in 4½ hours'. These dates may well refer, however, to the final version, especially since the work seems to have been based on an earlier version for string trio. So at least August Reissmann asserted in his biography of the composer (1873), and the light texture and firm flowing part-writing seem to support the statement.

In this fine quartet Schubert seems to find his own individual voice for the first time, and one can even point to the exact moment in the score when this happens. The Andante sostenuto sets the pattern for some of his greatest slow movements with its alternating dark-toned and more lyrical sections. It is at the end of the first link passage that the music suddenly blossoms into a lyrical theme of Schubertian serenity (see Ex. 14).

At the end of the movement Schubert has another surprise in store for us. The placid flow of the music is arrested by a repeated unison A flat, fortissimo, which reluctantly subsides into G minor. The passage sounds like a ghostly premonition of the accented neapolitan D flat in the last bar of the C major String Quintet. The winged Finale is also predictive, the theme closely resembling that of the Scherzo of the 'Great' C major Symphony. The lyrical impetus and technical mastery of this quartet were not to be surpassed until 1820, in the C minor Quartet Movement.

[6] Maurice J. E. Brown, *Schubert: A Critical Biography* (London, 1958), p. 24.

Ex. 14

The thematic content of the G minor Quartet of March 1815 is less original. The Andantino has a Haydnesque cut, while the Menuetto has obvious echoes of Mozart's G minor Symphony. The Andantino begins like a variation movement, but develops a structure not unlike that of the corresponding movement of the B flat Quartet, straightforward treatments of the theme alternating with quieter sections in A major and D major, in which the first violin and the cello hold a kind of conversation to an accompaniment of sighing triplets. There are similar moments of stillness and relaxation in the impetuous monorhythmic Finale.

The E major Quartet of 1816 was published as Op. 125 No. 2 in the belief that it belonged to 1824. It is in fact the last of what might be called the schoolhouse quartets, though it calls for virtuosity in the players, which few amateurs would be able to offer. The influence of Mozart is again very much in evidence, both in the themes and in the non-metaphorical style of the writing. But there is a certain anonymity about the work, which is perhaps why it is the least often heard of all Schubert's quartets. The best movement is the Finale, which bubbles along happily in Haydn's best 'Gipsy Rondo' manner.

In the spring of 1816 Schubert wrote three sonatas for violin and piano which are among his best-known chamber works, popular with both amateur players and professionals. Written within a few weeks in March and April, they are intended to belong together as a group, and presumably to be published as a single opus. But if Schubert hoped for early publication, he was disappointed. They did not appear till 1836, when Diabelli brought them out under the spurious title of 'Three Sonatinas'. Technically easy, concise in form and conservative in style, they display the complete identity of form and content which Schubert, under the influence of Mozart, achieved in 1816. The music, so to speak, is all in the notes; but though they are not difficult to play, this is not to say that they do not call for precise judgment of tempo and phrasing. The first, D384 in D major, is in three movements only. The second, in A minor, with its wide leaps in the opening Allegro moderato and dynamic D minor Menuetto, carries a more restless and disturbed emotional charge, and the F major Andante explores remote tonal country in its middle section. The third sonata, D408 in G minor, has an equally fine Andante movement, and an even better Finale. Schubert's mastery of the classical language he inherited is nowhere more evident than in these delightful works.

Strictly speaking there are no Schubert concertos, not because he had no interest in the form, but because it lay outside the field of domestic music-making which was his natural element, and because he had neither the skill nor the temperament to present himself as a solo performer in his own compositions, as Mozart and Beethoven had done. In 1816, however, he seems to have had at least good amateur players on hand, for in that year he wrote three pieces which are all in effect one-movement concertos. They are the Concerto in D for violin and orchestra D345, the Adagio and Rondo in A for violin and string orchestra D438, and the Adagio and Rondo concertante in F for piano quartet D487. All three works have a slow introduction leading to an allegro in rondo form which gives ample opportunities for the soloist to show his paces. There are good melodic ideas in all of them, but a certain repetitiveness also which comes in part from the conventional form. In the Piano Quartet, in particular, the thematic material seems to be spread rather thinly. The solo parts tend to dominate throughout these works, and are not by any means easy.

Schubert wrote four operettas in 1815. The term seems preferable to the German word *Singspiel* because it covers both the form of these works—all of them have spoken dialogue—and the spirit of comic make-believe. They represent an important phase in the development of Schubert's operatic ambitions, and come closer to being viable on the stage than his first two attempts. The details are as follows:

May 1815	*Der vierjährige Posten* (The Four-Year Sentry-go) One-act operetta to a libretto by Theodor Körner.
June–July 1815	*Fernando* One-act operetta to a libretto by Albert Stadler.
July–Sept. 1815	*Claudine von Villa Bella* Three-act operetta. The libretto is by Goethe (1775), and it had already been set several times. The autograph of the first act is dated 26 July–5 August, but the other two acts have not survived. The manuscript was given to Josef Hüttenbrenner, and according to Kreissle was used to light the fire by Hüttenbrenner's servant during his master's absence in Vienna.
Nov.–Dec. 1815	*Die Freunde von Salamanka* (The Friends from Salamanka). Operetta in two acts by Johann Mayrhofer. The libretto has been lost, but the outlines of the story can be reconstructed from the score.

The Four-Year Sentry-go is based on a Gilbertian situation with obvious dramatic possibilities. Duval, with his regiment, has arrived at a village on the German frontier, and has mounted guard on a neighbouring hill. The regiment marches away, forgetting to relieve the sentries. Weary of his long watch, he descends one evening to the village, and learns that his comrades have already gone. He determines to stay in the village, makes the acquaintance of Kätchen, the daughter of Walther, the village magistrate, and marries her. As luck will have it, his old regiment marches through the village once more after an interval of four years. (Here the action of the piece begins.) Duval, fearing he will be court-martialled as a deserter, puts on his uniform and mounts guard on the very spot where he had waited in vain to be relieved. When he is recognized, the captain orders him to be arrested; but Duval, relying on his rightful duty as a sentry, threatens to shoot the first man who approaches him.[7] All ends happily when Duval is pardoned and given an honourable certificate of discharge.

The overture bubbles along briskly in the manner of Schubert's symphonic finales, but the piece is slow to get off the mark. Only after three tuneful but comparatively static scenes does the action really begin. Kätchen's aria opens with a slow and solemn prayer (Ex. 15)

---

[7] See Kreissle von Hellborn, *Franz Schubert* (Vienna, 1865). English translation by A. D. Coleridge, 1869, chap. 3, pp. 64–5.

Schubert

Ex. 15

accompanied by wind sextet, almost in Mozart's *Magic Flute* manner. Then the soldiers enter to a vigorous march leading to Schubert's first really effective operatic ensemble.

Fernando has a more extravagantly romantic plot depending, like Beethoven's *Fidelio*, on the loyalty of a wife (called Eleanora) to her husband, and her power to forgive. It ends with a chorus in praise of wedded love, but the music trails some way behind Beethoven. The surviving act of *Claudine* is more promising, and of its eight numbers two soprano solos are sometimes heard with piano accompaniment in recitals, but the piece as a whole is beyond recovery. Perhaps the most interesting of these youthful operas, however, is *Die Freunde von Salamanka*. Mayrhofer's libretto owes a good deal to *Twelfth Night*. It concerns the efforts of three young bloods to save a lady called Olivia from the attention of a conceited fop who is really interested only in her money, and who gets his come-uppance in the end by a trick of impersonation. The music is varied in mood, and the ensembles have dramatic pace. The autograph carries an inscription: 'The music is by Franz Schubert, pupil of Herr Salieri, 1815'; and one may guess that the Kapellmeister himself would not have been ashamed of his pupil's work.

Any balanced judgement of these operettas must take account of the state of public taste in Vienna. They follow the conventions of Romantic opera as Schubert had learnt them from Weigl and Gyrowetz, then highly esteemed. The libretti are probably more interesting and less trivial than most contemporary examples, and two of them (Körner's and Goethe's) had already reached the stage. But Schubert was unknown, and Salieri was no longer a force in the theatre. There is no record of any performance of any of them in the composer's lifetime.

5

New perspectives (1817–March 1821)

Schubert's decision to move to the inner city in the autumn of 1816 amounted to a declaration of faith in his own destiny as a composer. For the second time (the renunciation of the Meerfeld Endowment being the first), he had declined to take the prudent course, preferring to trust his own instinct and his own genius. Whatever we may think about Schober's morals, or his lack of them, it is to his credit that in Schubert's hour of need he opened up a way of escape from the schoolroom. But the risks involved were considerable. Schubert was proposing to support himself as a freelance composer in a world which knew nothing of such a species. The normal road to fame then lay through success in the concert hall as a virtuoso artist, or as the servant of a wealthy patron, or by serving a long apprenticeship in the opera house or the church. The first two solutions were ruled out for Schubert, the first by his own temperament and abilities, the second by the economic and social revolution which was proceeding apace. As for the third, though Vienna remained one of the great operatic centres of the world, Schubert had yet to show whether he had the flair, the influence, and the luck, to succeed.

On the other hand, the same social changes which had destroyed the sources of aristocratic patronage had created a vast new source of patronage among the professional and mercantile classes. In particular, they had created a rapidly growing demand for domestic music, for songs and piano music, both of which Schubert was well able to provide. It should not surprise us, therefore, that his main instrumental concern in 1817 seems to have been the piano sonata. What he was aiming at, to judge from the somewhat confused attempts at numbering his various finished and unfinished sonatas, was a saleable opus of three works comparable, say, with Beethoven's Op. 10 set. But that was not to be achieved until the last year of his life. In the meantime his task was to find his own voice, to adapt the conventional form of the sonata to his own mode of expression.

The story begins in 1815, when he composed a sonata in E major, D157, and one in C, D279, but failed to write a finale for either. Several fragmentary sketches survive from 1816, including five which were earlier supposed to belong together as a 'sonata in mixed keys' D459.

Recent research on the paper-types, however, has established that they relate to two distinct sonata projects, neither completed. None of the movements, in fact, sounds at all like a finale. The fragmentary and disorderly state of these early manuscripts seems to suggest that Schubert was feeling his way carefully into the keyboard sonata, over-conscious, perhaps, of the intimidating shade of Beethoven.

The A minor Sonata of March 1817, D537, is the earliest surviving complete sonata; though it lacks a Scherzo, it has a dynamic Finale in triple time, and an attractive middle movement marked 'Allegretto quasi Andantino', the song-like main theme of which was to be used later in the Rondo finale of the A major Sonata of 1828. Over the next six months he was to sketch at least five more piano sonatas, only one of which, however, can certainly be regarded as complete, the Sonata in B major of August D575. This concise, four-movement work is perhaps the first in which Schubert discovered that characteristic vein of lyricism which he was later to exploit in the D major Sonata of 1825. The work presents a certain organic unity, with a strongly rhythmical finale. Of the others, the Sonata in E minor D566, written in June, is headed 'Sonata I', as though Schubert here intended a new beginning. It pays its tribute to Beethoven's Op. 90 Sonata in the same key, and the first three movements are assured and expressive. But there is no Finale, though the Rondo in E major D506 is sometimes made to do duty as one. The Sonata in A flat D557 has three complete movements, but the status of the last one is dubious. It is in E flat, and it seems unlikely that Schubert envisaged a final movement in a key other than the tonic. The Sonata in D flat D567 is a special case, too. It has marked affinities with Beethoven. The autograph is headed 'Sonata II', and dated June 1817. The Finale is incomplete, and there is no Scherzo. A radically revised version of this sonata (D568) was published in 1829 as 'Troisième grande Sonate', with a fine Menuetto and Trio, and an extended and much improved Finale. The autograph of this final version has not survived, and it has been assumed that it, too, belongs to the summer of 1817. But Martin Chusid has argued, on stylistic grounds, for a much later date; this, coupled with the curious circumstances of its publication (see p. 136), suggest that it may belong to the spring or summer of 1826.[1]

These early sonatas are full of fine music, and most of the fragmentary ones are sometimes heard in edited and completed versions. They stand, as it were, halfway between the classical Schubert and the poet of the keyboard, showing Schubert struggling to adapt the traditional form to his own idiom. The long series of sketches and fragments seems symptomatic also of the creative hang-up which overtakes Schubert in his

---

[1] 'A Suggested Redating for Schubert's Piano Sonata in E Flat Op. 122', *Schubert-Kongress Wien*, 1978, pp. 37–44. Michael C. Tusa, 'When did Schubert revise his opus 122?', *MR*, vol. xlv, nos 3–4, Aug.–Nov. 1984, pp. 208–19. See also Reed, 'Schubert's E flat Piano Sonata: A new Date', *MT*, Sept. 1987, pp. 483–7.

middle years in regard to the sonata and the symphony. The purely structural problem relates mainly to the new status which Beethoven had given to the finale in the great works of his second period, and its relationship with the scherzo; though Schubert's lifelong interest in the fantasia seems also to indicate a temperamental preference for a looser form of organization than the sonata proper allowed. At all events, it must be significant that for six years, from 1818 to 1824, he did not complete a single work in conventional four-movement form.

Two other important instrumental works date from the late summer of 1817, the Sonata in A major for violin and piano D574, and the String Trio in B flat D581. The former exhibits a rhythmical elasticity, and an equality between the players, which marks a big advance on the three violin sonatas of 1816. Schubert reverses the usual order of the inner movements, perhaps because the theme of the final Allegro vivace closely resembles that of the Scherzo. The String Trio of September is more retrospective in style, but the part-writing is thoroughly accomplished. To September also belongs a vivacious Polonaise for solo violin and orchestra D580, entirely Schubertian both in its melodic charm and its repetitiveness.

Having made the break with the schoolroom, Schubert soon decided to end the long association with Salieri. In December 1816 he wrote a fine setting of a Metastasio recitative and aria from *Didone Abbandonata* D510. It is an accomplished exercise in the traditional Italian style, and the manuscript shows signs of Salieri's corrections. It is, however, the last to do so. Spaun tells us that Salieri was entirely out of sympathy with Schubert's growing attachment to the literature of the German Romantics, and that he 'repeatedly took Schubert to task for occupying himself with poems in the barbarous German language'.[2] As he approached his twentieth birthday, Schubert decided that it was time to stand on his own feet.

No doubt the correctness of this decision was fully endorsed by the opera singer Johann Michael Vogl, whom Schubert met in the spring of 1817. Vogl, now in his fiftieth year, had been principal baritone at the Kärntnertor Theatre for many years. His great prestige as a star of the opera was unusually combined with wide reading and a taste for the classics. He had studied law before taking to the stage, and his idea of a holiday pastime was to translate Epictetus. Rather against his own inclinations, Vogl was persuaded to meet Schubert by Schober, who also had connections with the stage. The atmosphere at the beginning of the interview was stiff with embarrassment. Schubert was never at his best when on show. But gradually Vogl thawed, impressed in spite of himself. 'You squander your thoughts without making the most of them', he said as he took his departure.[3] But soon he was singing Schubert's

<hr>

[2] Memoirs, p. 130.   [3] Memoirs, p. 132.

songs in the salons of Vienna, and was to be instrumental in establishing his fame.

Important as Vogl was to Schubert, he did not exert such a profound influence on his work as the poet, Johann Mayrhofer, whose songs dominate the year 1817. Mayrhofer (1787–1836) was a lonely and difficult man, an intellectual with a genuine poetic gift, but ugly, hypochondriac, and prickly. He had no small talk, and held himself aloof from the more frivolous activities of the Schober set, showing no interest either in women or in light reading. Only music, so Bauernfeld tells us in his witty metrical sketch of Mayrhofer's character, could make any impression on his rugged intellectualism. 'In Schubert's songs his whole being was transfigured.'[4]

What Mayrhofer's poetry did for Schubert was to reinforce his natural propensity for transcendental modes of thought, to enable him to find characteristic musical expressions for *Sehnsucht*, the Romantic yearning for the world beyond the world. The theme which recurs constantly in Mayrhofer's poetry is the longing for *das mildre Land*, the happier land. Only in the creative tension between the unsatisfactory world of the here and now, and the world of the imagination, could the Romantic find meaning in life. The universal image for this state of mind was the Wanderer, and we have seen how Schmidt's poem with that name had given birth to one of Schubert's most powerful musical images. 'There, where you are not, only there is happiness.'[5] The constant preoccupation of the Romantics with death was not morbid, though it may seem so to us, any more than the Christian belief in an afterlife is morbid. It was that which gave meaning to life, and point and poignancy to the existential moment.

The other strand in Mayrhofer's philosophy, which profoundly affected Schubert, was his belief in the special mission of the artist as the guardian of values in a world which had forsaken them. From this came the belief that there was an unbridgeable gulf between the artist and the world. These ideas gave significance to Mayrhofer's neoclassicism, and philosophical depth to the great song cycles of Müller and Schubert. Only the artist has power to transcend the evils of the world; his creative power is his only resource; so long as he still has that he can be happy. As Schubert's friend Schlechta put it in a poem called 'Des Sängers Habe' (The Minstrel's Treasure) D832: 'Shatter all my happiness, take all I have; only leave me my lyre and I shall still be glad and rich.'

The eighteen songs which Schubert wrote to Mayrhofer texts in 1817 have metaphorical strength and intellectual energy. They range from strophic songs like 'Schlaflied' (Slumber Song) to the sublimity of 'Memnon', and there is hardly a negligible song among them.

---

[4] For Bauernfeld's verse portrait of Mayrhofer see Kreissle, I, p. 50.
[5] *Der Wanderer* D489.

Sometimes, as in 'Am Strome' (By the River), the song is tinged with sweet melancholy, as Mayrhofer compares life's journey to that of the stream. 'Flow onward to the distant sea; not for you to feel at home here. I too long for kinder shores, finding no joy on earth.' Sometimes, however, the sense of doom seems to threaten the formal unity of the song. In 'Auf der Donau' (On the Danube) the thought of death is the occasion for an extended coda based on a descending chromatic bass line (Ex. 16). This motif was to recur again and again both in the songs and in the instrumental works.

Ex. 16

The note of contemplative gravity finds expression again in the famous setting of Claudius's 'Der Tod und das Mädchen' (Death and the Maiden), which established the andante rhythm of a minim followed by two crotchets as an instantly recognizable tonal image of death. This must have been a conscious association of ideas in the composer's mind, for a few weeks later he used the same rhythmic image pointedly in his setting of Spaun's 'Der Jüngling und der Tod' (The Youth and Death). The year is remarkable also for its great epic songs on classical themes: Goethe's 'Ganymed' for instance, and Schiller's 'Gruppe aus dem Tartarus' (Scene from Hades). But not all the songs of 1817 are preoccupied with the afterlife. It also produced 'Die Forelle' (The Trout), and 'Liebhaber in allen Gestalten' (The Lover in many Guises), 'Hänflings Liebeswerbung' (The Linnet's Wooing) and many more. It is arguable, indeed, that an anthology of great songs from 1817 would better represent Schubert's versatile lyrical genius than any other year of his life. Several of the greatest of them are specially written for bass voice, which must owe something to the influence of Vogl.

Schubert's new-found freedom was short-lived. In August Schober's brother, an officer in the Austrian army, was invalided home from Paris. Schober went to help him, and family business seemed to require his continued absence from Vienna till the end of the year. On 24 August Schubert wrote out a few lines called 'Farewell to a Friend', and set them to music in the key of B minor (D578). Soon afterwards he vacated his rooms in the Schober household, and returned to the schoolhouse, where he remained until the following summer.

Important instrumental works belong to the autumn of 1817. In October he began another symphony, No. 6 in C, heading the manuscript for the first time *Grosse Sinfonie*, an indication that this time he intended the work for public performance. It reflects the influence of Beethoven (especially the Beethoven of the First and Second Symphonies) and also of Rossini, whose Italian company had paid its first visit to Vienna in the autumn of 1816. In its scale and dynamic drive the work justifies its title, and there are many anticipations in it of the 'Great' C major Symphony. But Schubert is not altogether successful in assimilating these diverse influences. The effect is sometimes curiously ambivalent, as though his highly developed musical empathy left him poised between two very different styles. However, the work's scale and conception are clearly Beethoven-inspired, and it is more successful in that regard than the C minor Symphony of 1816. The Sixth Symphony was finished in February 1818.

The Overture in D major of November 1817 betrays its allegiance from the opening bars, and it became known as the 'Overture in the Italian Style' in Schubert's lifetime, though he is not responsible for the name. It is a seminal work. The sudden dynamic contrasts and apocalyptic modulations foreshadow the 'Unfinished' Symphony, while the rhythmic drive of the finale looks further ahead to the 'Great' C major. Like the Sixth Symphony, the Overture seems to be aiming at a compromise between Italian lucidity and German sublimity, but here the former is definitely in charge. The opening sections of the overture were later adapted for the overture to Schubert's music for *The Magic Harp*, a work better known to us as the *Rosamunde* overture. Schubert also wrote an overture in C major D591 which is also said to be 'in the Italian style', though with less justification.

These overtures were the first Schubert instrumental works to be played in public. On 1 March 1818 the Overture in D major[6] was played at a concert organized by the violinist Edward Jaëll. A few weeks earlier, on 6 February, the first Schubert song to appear in print was advertised in the *Wiener Zeitung*. Appropriately, it was a setting of a poem by Mayrhofer called 'Erlafsee' (Lake Erlaf), which was published as a supplement to an annual anthology of prose and verse for lovers of the countryside. It is a fine example of Schubert's power to evoke the ambivalent mood of stillness, happiness and sadness in the presence of nature, which the Romantics called *Wehmut*. These first steps along the road to fame were soon to involve him in the internal affairs of the Philharmonic Society.

About this time the Society announced its intention to promote a series of evening entertainments, social occasions which would provide an opportunity for the performance of *Hausmusik*—songs, partsongs and chamber music—as opposed to large-scale choral and orchestral works. The announcement included Schubert's name among other more famous ones, such as Haydn, Mozart, and Beethoven. This is strange enough, but soon events took a more bizarre turn. In March 1818 he made formal application for membership of the Society, making clear his wish to play an active part as an accompanist in the new series of entertainments. The application, however, was turned down by the committee, ostensibly on the ground that Schubert was not a true amateur. This was clearly a pretext, however, for many professional artists were already members, and there was nothing in the rules to debar them. The explanation can only be that some members of the committee regarded Schubert as socially or politically unacceptable.

This curious episode, the full details of which have only recently come to light,[7] is not the only evidence we have that Schubert's confidence in his own genius could inspire jealousy and misunderstanding as well as enthusiasm. In October 1818 Ferdinand Schubert, writing to his brother in Zseliz, reported that the overture to *Claudine von Villa Bella*, which had been included in the programme of a public concert, had been replaced at the last moment by Mozart's overture to *Così fan tutte*. 'Your overture comes in for much criticism. . . . The wind parts are said to be so difficult as to be unplayable . . . and a certain Scheidel . . . wanted to make out that the effect was not properly calculated, and that there were some cribs in it.'[8] It is not surprising perhaps that Schubert's

---

[6] See Hilmar: 'Das Autograph der Ouvertüre "Im Italienischen Stil", D590', *Brille* 3, pp. 11–13.

[7] Otto Biba, *Franz Schubert und die Gesellschaft der Musikfreunde in Wien, Schubert-Kongress Wien, 1978*, pp. 23–4.

[8] Docs, p. 106.

rapid rise to fame should look to some more like arrogance than genius, and his radical political and religious views must also have made enemies for him. In 1817 Mayrhofer had got together with a group of friends, including various members of Spaun's family, to publish a literary journal under the innocuous title of *Contributions to the Education of Young People*. It consisted largely of poems by Mayrhofer himself, and of extracts from Romantic authors like Jean Paul. In the eyes of the state bureaucracy, however, any expression of progressive views, even artistic ones, was subversive. After two numbers had appeared Mayrhofer's journal quietly died.

Schubert's return to the schoolroom towards the end of 1817 coincided with an improvement in the family fortunes. In December his father was appointed head of a school in the Rossau suburb, nearer to the city centre, and early in the new year the family moved to the rather more commodious accommodation there. But the change brought little consolation to Schubert; the taste of liberty and independence made the life of a schoolmaster even more claustrophobic and unbearable than before. In the first half of 1818 his spirits, and his creative genius, were at a low ebb. Apart from the completion of his Sixth Symphony, hardly anything of importance survives from this period. There are three songs, of which the most interesting is 'An den Mond in einer Herbstnacht' (To the Harvest Moon); a first draft of an attractive piano duet, the Rondo in D ('Notre amitié est invariable'); and more fragmentary sketches for piano sonatas. In May he drafted in short score two movements of a Symphony in D, D615, which do not promise any advance on what had gone before.

In the summer, however, the means of escape came from an unexpected quarter. Count Johann Karl Esterházy of Galánta, head of the Slovakian branch of the family which Haydn had served so faithfully, was in the habit of spending the summer on his estate at Zseliz, in Hungary, and the winter in Vienna. The family was musical, and the count was on the lookout for a tutor for the two young countesses Marie and Karoline, then aged fifteen and twelve. His friend Karl Unger, a professor of history and a prominent member of the Philharmonic Society, suggested that Schubert might be the man to fill the post; an introduction was arranged, and in mid-July, having secured a travel permit from the police, Schubert set off by stage coach to join the family at Zseliz.

There he found himself part of a feudal society as different from the sophistication of Vienna as can be imagined, but with a degree of financial security he had never before enjoyed. He was expected to live and board with the servants, to supervise the musical activities of the young countesses, and to put his gifts at the service of the family. In return he received about seventy-six florins a month, a modest salary indeed by aristocratic standards, but a great deal better than the best he could do as a schoolmaster. The letters of his friends and his brothers are tinged with envy at his good fortune, and his own unusually detailed letters home leave no doubt of his own relief and elation. 'Best and dearest friends', he writes to Schober shortly after his arrival, 'how are you? Are you well? I am very well. I live and compose like a god, as though that is how it had to be. Mayrhofer's 'Einsamkeit' is finished, and it is the best thing I have done, so I believe, for I was without a care . . . Thank God, now I live at last; it was time too, otherwise I should have become just another musician gone bad [*verdorbener Musikant*].'[9] The tone of his letters to the schoolhouse in the Rossau is similarly frank and high-spirited. He remembers to thank his stepmother for attending to his laundry, insists that Ferdinand should have his fortepiano, and entertains Ignaz with stories of the boorishness and ignorance of the local priests. In an often quoted letter, he paints a lively picture of the family establishment for the benefit of his friends. 'Our castle is not one of the largest, but very nicely built. It is surrounded by a very fine garden. I live in the steward's quarters. It is fairly quiet, except for about forty geese, which cackle so loudly sometimes that one cannot hear oneself speak.' He goes on to describe the steward, the doctor, the local magistrate, and the family servants, and concludes: 'The count is a bit rough, the countess proud but sensitive, and the young countesses good children. So far I have been spared a roasting.'[10]

The Mayrhofer song to which Schubert referred is a setting of a long and allegorical poem depicting the progress of man from the solitude of youth to that of old age ('Einsamkeit' D620). It is in six sections, covering the 'ages of man' in a quasi-Shakespearean manner, and the importance which the composer obviously attached to it suggests that it was specially written to provide the basis for a linked song cycle, possibly inspired by Beethoven's recently published *An die ferne Geliebte*. It is rarely performed because of is length, but it is remarkable for the pictorial richness and fluency of the piano writing; there is a lyrical assurance about the work which marks the beginning of a new phase in the development of the Romantic Lied. Something of the same pianistic expansiveness is observable in 'Das Abendrot' (The Sunset), a bass song presumably written for Karl Esterházy. The best known of the songs written at Zseliz, however, is 'Der Blumenbrief' (The Message of Flowers), a lovely strophic setting of a poem by Alois Schreiber, whose verses had recently been published.

Shortly after arriving in Zseliz, Schubert began a light-hearted love affair with the countess's chambermaid. Her name was 'Pepi' Pöckelhofer, and he refers to her in his account of the household quoted above as 'very pretty and often my companion'. What part she played in Schubert's sexual education is not known. Certainly his deeper feelings were not involved, though the two remained friends, for years later

[9] Docs, p. 93.   [10] Docs, p. 100.

she was willing to deliver Schubert's letters home on her visits to Vienna. Our information about her comes from Karl von Schönstein, a friend of the Esterházy family and an amateur singer of some distinction, whom Schubert met at Zseliz. He became one of Schubert's most enthusiastic supporters, and a fine interpreter of his songs.[11]

Schubert's ability to turn from the sublime to the merely serviceable with bewildering ease is nicely illustrated during this summer. In August, at the request of his brother Ferdinand, he hastily sketched out the so-called *Trauermesse*, or German Requiem, a setting of a versified form of the mass intended for performance at the Imperial Orphanage. With its block harmonies and simple progressions it doubtless served its purpose well, but the tradition of popular church music to which it belongs easily degenerates into sentimentality. Ferdinand later appropriated the work, and even presented it as his own in his examinations. The sketches for a Piano Sonata in F minor D625, written a few weeks later, inhabit a quite different world. The work has been compared with the 'Appassionata' Sonata in its rhythmic drive. The opening Allegro lacks the reprise, and the finale is also incomplete, though complete performing editions have been made by Erwin Ratz, Paul Badura-Skoda, and Martino Tirimo. The Adagio in D flat D505 was probably intended as the slow movement.

The most important legacy, however, of the four months spent in Zseliz was a series of fine piano duets, written as a contribution to the musical education of the young countesses. Since the duet fantasias of his schooldays Schubert had found no occasion to use the form. Now his natural genius for keyboard textures resulted in a spate of masterpieces. He began with marches and dances, three *Marches Militaires* D733, four *Polonaisen* D599, a *Deutscher* and two *Ländler*. Three full-length pieces soon followed, the eight Variations on a French Song in E minor D624, which were to be dedicated to Beethoven on their publication in 1822, a Sonata in B flat D617, and the Introduction and Variations on an Original Theme D968 A. Not all these works, admittedly, can be precisely dated, and the authenticity of the last has been questioned. The thematic material and the treatment, however, are recognizably Schubert's.

As summer gave way to autumn, the unfamiliar pleasures of life at Zseliz began to lose their attraction, and he longed for Vienna. 'If I did not get to know these people round me better every day', he writes to Ferdinand, 'things would be just as good with me as at the beginning. But now I see that I am really lonely among them, except for a couple of truly nice girls.'[12] In November he returned to the capital with the Esterházy family, and installed himself in Mayrhofer's rooms in the Wipplingerstrasse, close to the old town hall. There, on the third floor

---

[11] Memoirs, p. 100.   [12] Docs, p. 109.

of a house belonging to Frau Sanssouci, who kept the tobacconist's shop below, the two friends were to live for the next two years, devoting their lives to the service of the muses in an atmosphere of hard living, high thinking, and rough horseplay. There is little doubt that Mayrhofer's sexual orientations were abnormal; Bauernfeld implies as much in his verse portrait of the man (see Kreissle von Hellborn vol. 1, p. 50). 'He was averse to all trifling, to women as well as light literature.' The two years Schubert spent sharing rooms with Mayrhofer, and the unexplained rift between them in 1821, must be regarded as consistent with, if not as confirmation of, Maynard Solomon's thesis that homosexual practices went on in the Schubert circle. (See also page 53.)

According to Schönstein, Schubert continued to act as tutor to the young countesses through the winter months in Vienna. Certainly his association with the family can hardly have ended abruptly, since he was to return to Zseliz in 1824, and he later dedicated works both to Karl Esterházy and to the Countess Karoline. He was no longer dependent on teaching, however, for in his absence events had taken an irreversible turn for the better. Vogl had used his influence with the Imperial opera house to good effect. Before the end of the year Schubert was commissioned by the management of the Kärntnertor theatre to write the music for a projected one-act farce called *Die Zwillingsbrüder* (The Twin Brothers). Well aware that this was the opening he had been waiting for, Schubert began work at once, and on 19 January 1819 finished the score.

Die Zwillingsbrüder, by Georg von Hofmann, was a conventional farce based, like most Viennese operettas of the time, on a French original. The plot is a variant of one of the oldest ideas in the business. Franz and Friedrich Spiess are identical twins, though very different in disposition. (Both parts were played by Michael Vogl.) Lieschen, the mayor's daughter, is to be betrothed to her lover Anton on her eighteenth birthday. However, when she was born Franz Spiess deposited 1000 thalers with her father as a wedding present for her, on condition that he should have her himself if he returned before her eighteenth birthday. After many years' absence in the foreign legion, Franz returns to his native village on the fateful day to claim Lieschen for his bride. But unbeknown to him, or anybody else, his twin brother Friedrich has also appeared in the village after a long sojourn abroad. After a tangle of confusion and misunderstanding, all is happily resolved in the last scene, when the long-lost brothers are reunited, and Lieschen and Anton fall into each other's arms.

Schubert's score consists of a spirited overture and ten numbers. The most impressive writing is in the solo arias, and particularly Lieschen's, which touchingly catches the young girl's mood on the threshold of womanhood. But the tone is that of sentimental comedy rather than farce. Schubert's hopes of an early production were doomed to disappointment. Preference had to be given to Italian opera in 1819, and it was not till 14 June 1840 that *Die Zwillingsbrüder* reached the stage on a rowdy first night. The performance threatened to become a battle between contending claques. An eye witness reported: 'Schubert's friends made a lot of noise, while the opposition hissed. At the close there was a fuss until Vogl appeared and said: "Schubert is not present: I thank you in his name".'[13] In fact Schubert *was* present, with Anselm Hütten-brenner, in the gallery, having refused to put on a dress suit and appear in public. After the performance they celebrated at Lenkay's wineshop.

The critics were respectful rather than enthusiastic, and there was general agreement that Schubert's genius was not best suited to farce ('The sentiments of simple country people are interpreted much too seriously . . .' 'The composition has quite pretty things, but is kept a little too serious'),[14] and that his love of modulation left the audience uneasy. None the less, the piece made an impression, and ran for six performances with improving box-office returns. Many new works achieved only two or three performances at that time.

Meanwhile, Schubert had received another commission, this time through the good offices of Leopold von Sonnleithner, who reports on the circumstances thus: 'At the Theater an der Wien, in the summer of 1820, the designer Hermann Neefe, the technician Anton Roller and the costumier Lucca Piazza were to share a benefit. As I was related by marriage to Neefe, . . . they turned to me for advice about a composer for a projected magic opera for this benefit. They had already thought of Schubert, and I encouraged this idea by putting them in touch with Schubert himself. He at once decided to provide the composition, and it was ready in a few weeks.'[15] Hofmann was again the librettist. Schubert's friend Schlechta, who wrote a witty review of the piece, described the essential ingredients of this form of popular entertainment as 'two parts of sorcery, one good, one evil, a moonstruck lady in a ruined castle, an enraged father and a banished son, some foolish knights, a bucketful of tears, a handful of sighs and a stiff dose of the most nonsensical magic'.[16] The libretto has disappeared, but as far as can be gathered from the music, *Die Zauberharfe* (The Magic Harp) followed this prescription closely; there is also a wicked fire-demon in the cast who is finally thwarted in his evil desires by the hero and his magic harp.

The score is a substantial work, consisting of two overtures (the second played before Act III) and thirteen numbers, including six melodramas, that is scenes with spoken dialogue accompanied by music. It is full of fine imaginative music; but as a whole it is beyond recovery. In the absence of a libretto the piece lacks any formal continuity, and efforts to provide it with a new story founder on the extravagant fancy.

[13] Docs, p. 135.   [14] Docs, pp. 125 and 136.   [15] Memoirs, p. 118.
[16] Otto E. Deutsch, *Franz Schubert: Die Dokumente seines Lebens* (Bärenreiter, Kassel, 1964), p. 106.

More is the pity, for besides the quality of the music, the score shows Schubert's growing awareness of recurrent themes. The seven-bar motif with which the overture begins (Ex. 17a) serves as a motto theme for the magical power of Melinde, the sorceress, while the woodwind theme in the third number (Ex. 17b) is associated with the hero, Palmerin, and his magic harp.

Ex. 17

(a)

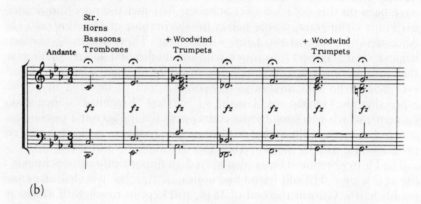

(b)

Only two numbers from this extensive score are still heard. The overture is often played, though it is now called the *Rosamunde* overture. The circumstances in which it became associated with the musical play of 1823 have never been fully explained.[17] The slow introduction, and the vivace 6/8 coda, are strongly reminiscent of the D major Overture 'in the Italian style', but it far surpasses that work in its charm and inventiveness. The Romance for the hero Palmerin (the only singing part) in the third scene was withdrawn after the first performance and replaced by an orchestral interlude, but an arrangement for solo voice and piano is sometimes heard today. The piece ran for eight perfor-

[17] For a full discussion of the history of the *Rosamunde* Overture see Maurice J. E. Brown, *Essays on Schubert* (London, 1966), pp. 250–5.

62

mances, but the receipts were disappointing. The critics praised the music; but nobody praised the play.

These operatic events, which have taken us on to the autumn of 1820, did a great deal to enhance Schubert's reputation and improve his financial position. The fee for *Die Zwillingsbrüder* was 500 florins, of which 150 florins were paid on account in July 1819, together with thirty florins for copying out the parts. A notable occasion was a second performance of the cantata *Prometheus* with pianoforte accompaniment at an evening reception at the Sonnleithners' house in January 1819. Leopold conducted, and his father Ignaz himself sang the principal part. It may well have been on this occasion that Schubert first met the poet and dramatist Franz Grillparzer, whose verses for the heroine of *Die Ahnfrau* (The Ancestress) he was to set a few weeks later. These widening contacts began to put Schubert into touch with the intellectual society of Vienna, then still a comparatively small city in which it was possible to know everybody who was anybody. His songs began to be sung in public, especially the setting of Goethe's 'Schäfers Klagelied' (Shepherd's Lament), which was sung by the court opera tenor Jäger at a public concert in February 1819, and thereafter crops up again on various concert programmes, usually sung by the same artist.

The Hüttenbrenner family also played an important part in Schubert's life at this time. His old friend and colleague Anselm, who had departed for his native Graz at the end of 1818, still kept in touch with affairs in Vienna, and Schubert's letters to him sometimes throw an interesting light on the composer's attitude to the trend of taste. Writing to Anselm in May 1819, for instance, he makes no secret of his admiration for Rossini's *Otello*. 'You cannot deny him extraordinary genius. The orchestration is often highly original, and the vocal parts also, except for the usual Italian gallopades and several reminiscences of *Tancredi*.' But he goes on to complain jokingly about the failure of the management at the Kärntnertor to produce *Die Zwillingsbrüder*. 'Even with a Vogl around, it is difficult to out-manoeuvre scoundrels like Weigl, Treitschke, etc.' Josef Weigl, whose sentimental operettas Schubert had often enjoyed, was chief conductor of the court theatres, and Georg Treitschke was staff producer and librettist at the Kärntnertor, soon to be succeeded by Georg Hofmann, Schubert's collaborator.[18]

Josef Hüttenbrenner, who arrived in Vienna just as his brother Anselm departed, was one of Schubert's most devoted admirers, and over the next few years was to become a kind of secretary and manager of the composer's affairs. On the reverse of the letter to Anselm already quoted is a note from Josef to his younger brother Heinrich, a law student with literary ambitions, urging him to try his hand at an opera libretto for Schubert. 'There is a fee to be had as well. Your names will

[18] Docs, p. 117.

be known all over Europe. Schubert will really shine like a new Orion in the musical firmament.'

It was not the opera house, however, which really set fire to Schubert's imagination in 1819, but the mountains of Upper Austria. Early in July Michael Vogl left Vienna for his annual holiday in his native Steyr, and this time Schubert went with him, his finances reinforced by the fee for *Die Zwillingsbrüder*. The experience was a kind of homecoming for both of them, for Schubert's songs were already well known at Steyr, and at Linz, some thirty miles away, through the advocacy of Vogl, Stadler, Spaun, and other members of the circle. But he, who had often celebrated the beauty of the lakes and the mountains in his songs, was now able for the first time to experience them for himself. He found himself at the centre of a circle of friends and admirers, as a guest in the house of the mining engineer, Dr Albert Schellmann. The circle was led by the local manager of the mines, Sylvester Paumgartner, a good amateur cellist, and included the iron merchant Josef von Koller and his gifted daughter Josefine. Schubert and Vogl visited Linz, Spaun's hometown, and the monastery at Kremsmünster, where Schober, Kenner, and Schlechta had all been at school. With Stadler, who was now a practising barrister in Steyr, he wrote a cantata in honour of Vogl's birthday, and a performance of the German *Stabat Mater* D383 seems to have been hastily put together. On 14 September a farewell party was held at Stadler's, and the next day the friends left for Vienna.

The long holiday was at an end, but its creative legacy survived in two great works, perhaps the first instrumental works which can be seen as wholly and characteristically Schubertian in style. The Piano Sonata in A major D664 was written for Josefine von Koller. It is the shortest of the complete sonatas. The exposition of the opening Allegro moderato occupies a mere page and a half, and the development is even shorter. Yet it conveys within its concise limits a serenity, a tempered lyricism, which reflects the happiness of those days. There is no Scherzo; the dancing 6/8 Finale brings the work to a close. But the inner stillness which lies at the heart of the work is best felt in the poetic Andante.

The stillness is characteristic also of the Quintet for piano and strings D667, called the 'Trout'. It breathes the fresh air of the mountains, but where the Sonata is concise, the Quintet is expansive, even discursive. It was commissioned by Sylvester Paumgartner, who also, so Stadler tells us, suggested using the tune of 'Die Forelle' as the theme for the variation movement. With its five movements, alternating quick and slow, and relaxed tempos, the Quintet is much closer in spirit to the eighteenth-century divertimento than to the classical four-movement quintet. Schubert includes a double bass rather than a second violin, and his purpose is plain enough. Not only does this enable him to give the cello part more melodic interest; his instinctive feeling for piano texture told him that he must avoid a competition for the middle of the keyboard, so he cleverly sets off the dotted rhythms and dancing triplets of the piano's upper octaves against a firm bass line. A kind of contest is adumbrated in the very first bars of the work between the lyrical nature of the strings and the rhythmic and decorative potential of the piano; but it is the piano which holds the upper hand throughout.

It is the piano also which defines and controls the most novel aspect of the work, its tendency to wind down to a state of musical stasis, to a slow contemplative dance. The tendency is observable in all the movements except the Scherzo; the Allegro giusto (Ex. 18) proceeds at a gentle jogtrot rather than a brisk gallop, the first Schubert finale to adopt this characteristically contemplative gait.

Ex. 18

A new generation of Romantic poets, Friedrich von Schlegel, Silbert, A.W. von Schlegel, and Novalis, dominates the songs of 1819, together with some fine new Goethe and Mayrhofer songs in October. Friedrich von Schlegel, the critic and philosopher, was the leader of the circle of established Romantic writers in Vienna; it is possible that Schubert met him through his friend Franz von Bruchmann. In February 1819 and early in 1820 Schubert set a dozen poems from the sequence called *Abendröte* (Sunsets), which express the mystical feeling for Nature as the vesture of God. 'Die Gebüsche' (The Thicket) is characteristic. 'One soul alone moves through the raging sea, and the murmured words that whisper through the leaves. . . . For him who listens inwardly, one faint sound echoes through all the sounds of this earth's motley dreams.' Schubert's questing modulations and rippling arpeggios seem to symbolize the search for God in Nature. The persistence with which he returned again and again to Schlegel's sequence in the years 1819 to 1823 suggests that he hoped to complete a publishable song cycle based upon it.

In May he discovered the mystical poet Novalis (1772–1801). But the poet's passionate love affair with death, which found expression in his

'Hymns to the Night', for once failed to fire Schubert's imagination. The best of the Novalis songs is 'Marie', a sweetly lyrical love song to the Virgin. In October he returned to Goethe with a powerfully dramatic setting of *Prometheus*, and a wonderful new setting of 'An den Mond' which fully captures the *Innigkeit* of that complex poem. To the same month belong four fine Mayrhofer songs, including two 'night poems', 'Die Sternennächte' (Starry Nights) and 'Nachtstück' (Night Piece). One other song of 1819 must be mentioned, if only because of its special significance for the composer himself. In November, he set a few lines from Schiller's ode to 'The Gods of Greece' ('Die Götter Griechenlands' D677). The poem is both a tribute to the glory that was Greece, and a lament for a lost golden age. Schubert selects only one of its sixteen verses, the one that most poignantly expresses the sense of loss. 'Beauteous world, where art thou? Return again, fair springtime of Nature; ah, your fabled dream lives only in the enchanted realm of song.' The tonal image which he finds for this poetic yearning was to become the text on which great instrumental works of 1824 were to be constructed (see Ex. 19).

Ex. 19

Writing to Mayrhofer from Linz in August in high spirits, Schubert ends enigmatically: 'Have you done anything yet? I hope so.'[19] Almost certainly the enquiry relates to a joint project for an *opera seria* based on the story of Adrastus. Eight numbers of the score of *Adrast* D137 survive together with some further sketches, all probably dating from the autumn of 1819. The story of the young prince Adrastus, banished by his father after he had accidentally killed his brother, comes from Herodotus. There are many imaginative touches in the music, but the libretto disappeared in the 1840s, and even the running order of the surviving sketches is doubtful. The score was rediscovered in the 1860s

---

[19] Docs, p. 124.

in the possession of Schubert's nephew, Eduard Schneider, and was long thought to belong to the composer's adolescent years. Recently, however, research into the manuscript paper and the script have established that it is probably a work of 1819.

Schubert's interest in serious music drama is even more strikingly illustrated by the unfinished cantata *Lazarus* of February 1820. The text, by A. H. Niemeyer, is a metrical version of the story of Lazarus (John 11) with supplementary characters borrowed or invented. Schubert's setting was planned in three acts (*Handlungen*) corresponding to the death, burial, and resurrection of Lazarus, but it breaks off in the middle of the second act. There was of course a long tradition of sacred dramatic works during Lent, when the theatres were closed. The probability is that the work was planned, possibly even commissioned, for performances at Easter, and that unforeseen circumstances intervened to prevent this. The score includes stage directions indicating the *mise en scène*, and even the movements of the singers, as though a full stage performance was envisaged. It is written for a cast of six soloists, chorus, and orchestra.

The irony is that this hybrid work, half sacred cantata, half music drama, contains the most dramatic music Schubert ever wrote, if by that we mean music which is paced, controlled, and varied entirely in accordance with the drama. There are no discrete scenes, no spoken dialogue or formal recitative. Instead there is a continuous orchestral flow, within which short motifs recur, so that each phrase seems to emerge naturally from the preceding one. Within this orchestral matrix, in quasi-Wagnerian fashion, the various solo passages, choruses, and conversational interchanges take place with a great deal of subtlety, dynamic contrast, and thematic cross-reference. A brief example of the power of the writing is given at Ex. 20, taken from the climax of the episode in which Jemina, the daughter of Jairus, tells the story of her own raising from the dead.

It seems unlikely, given Schubert's own religious views, that he could have embarked on this project on his own initiative, and it may be that his failure to finish it was the result of a lack of confidence in his own ability to do justice to the raising of Lazarus in Act III; more likely perhaps that the abandonment of *Lazarus* had something to do with a political scrape which Schubert got himself into early in March 1820.

One evening Schubert was present in the lodgings of Johann Senn, his old schoolfriend from *Konvikt* days, together with Anton Doblhoff, Johann Zechenter, Josef Streinsberg, and Franz von Bruchmann, the son of a rich merchant of liberal sympathies. Ever since the assassination of Kotzebue, the popular dramatist, who was also generally regarded as an agent of the security police, in March 1819, the political tension had been growing. Any regular association of young men of idealistic tendencies was regarded by the authorities as a cover for fanaticism and

Ex. 20

subversion. Suddenly the party in Senn's rooms was rudely interrupted by the police, and those present were, as we should say, 'taken in for questioning'. Senn, always the boldest in his resistance to injustice, made no attempt to conceal his contempt for the proceedings. But he paid dearly for his courage. After languishing in gaol for fourteen months without trial he was deported to his native Tyrol. Schubert, who is described in the official police report as 'the school assistant from the Rossau', escaped with a few bruises; but he was never to meet Senn again.[20]

It says something for the curiously schizophrenic character of Viennese society at this time, on the one hand a huge but inefficient bureaucracy, and on the other a civilized and tolerant middle class devoted to artistic pursuits, that this brush with the police does not seem to have had any adverse effect on Schubert's prospects in the opera house. The production of his operas at the court theatres in the summer was at least a *succès d'estime*; and he was soon to take up once again the search for a viable *opera seria* subject. In October 1820 he began work on a story from Indian mythology, *Sakuntala* or The Lost Ring D701. The libretto is by J. P. Neumann, a professor of physics of literary tastes and liberal views. He was later to provide the metrical version of the mass (appropriately demythologized) which Schubert set in 1827: oriental subjects had been very fashionable since the publication of Goethe's *West-östlicher Divan*. *Sakuntala* probably owes something to the influence of the orientalist Hammer-Purgstall, whom Schubert met about this time at the house of Spaun's cousin, Matthäus von Collin. However, it is the most inaccessible of all his abortive operatic projects. The libretto was never published, and is now lost. Schubert did not get beyond sketches for the first two acts, and even these were excluded from the original *Gesamtausgabe* on the advice of Brahms. They are now in the Vienna City Library. An edited version of the work was performed in Vienna in 1971 under the direction of Fritz Racek, but the score of *Sakuntala* remains virtually unknown.

The account which Spaun left of the meeting between Schubert and Hammer-Purgstall throws an interesting light on his growing fame. It was arranged at the request of Matthäus von Collin, who wanted to promote the composer's career by introducing him to influential figures in artistic circles. Present, among others, were the head of the Imperial and Royal music establishment, Count Dietrichstein, and his secretary Hofrat Mosel, Karoline Pichler, the celebrated author who presided over a famous salon in Vienna, and Ladislaus Pyrker, Patriarch of Venice, poet and liberal churchman.[21]

Yet Schubert, approaching his twenty-fourth birthday, still had no regular income. None of his compositions had yet been published in

---

[20] Docs, p. 128.   [21] Memoirs, p. 133.

permanent form, and his name was still unknown outside Vienna and a handful of provincial towns. The turning point came in the winter of 1820/21. In the autumn the private orchestra led by Otto Hatwig, which had developed into a full-size orchestra capable of mounting performances of choral masterpieces like *Messiah* and *The Creation*, had to be disbanded, depriving Schubert of the only means he had for getting his orchestral works performed. The reason was simply lack of suitable accommodation. The company had met for some time at the house of a prosperous merchant, Herr Pettenkofer, and when this gentleman unexpectedly won the first prize in a public lottery and decided to retire on the proceeds, no alternative could be found. Fortunately, Schubert's compositions were to be taken up enthusiastically in another quarter. Private concerts were held fortnightly at the house of Ignaz Sonnleithner in the Gundelhof. On 1 December 1820 an amateur tenor, August von Gymnich, made a great impression on the assembled company with a performance of 'Erlkönig', which seems to have been known up to this time only within the narrow circle of the composer's personal friends. Since no publisher had shown any interest in publishing any of Schubert's songs on the usual commercial terms, Leopold von Sonnleithner took the lead, with the support of Josef Hüttenbrenner and two others, in a scheme to publish them privately, guaranteeing the costs of production themselves.

This development led to a decisive change in the composer's circumstances. A series of private and public performances of his songs over the next few months thrust him into the limelight, and guaranteed that when the songs were offered for sale they were quickly taken up. Nearly one hundred copies of 'Erlkönig' (Op. 1) were sold in one evening when copies were put on sale at one of the Sonnleithner soirées; and before the end of the year 1821 twenty songs had been published in seven opus numbers. This sudden popularity was still narrowly based, mainly on the Goethe songs, with a sprinkling of Romantic pieces by such contemporary poets as Mayrhofer, Claudius, and Széchényi. 'Erlkönig', 'Der Wanderer' D489, and Schiller's 'Sehnsucht' (the second, recently written version, D636) crop up again and again, and so do the male-voice partsongs 'Das Dörfchen' (The Hamlet) D641 and 'Die Nachtigall' D724. At a charity concert in the Kärntnertor theatre on Ash Wednesday Vogl's performance of 'Erlkönig' drew rapturous applause. The concert, organized by Leopold Sonnleithner's uncle Josef, also included two other Schubert works, the vocal quartet 'Das Dörfchen' and a new setting of Goethe's 'Gesang der Geister über den Wassern' D714 for eight male voices and a quintet of strings. The first of these was warmly applauded, but the Goethe setting was received in puzzled silence. It is a difficult work to bring off at the best of times, and on this occasion it was not properly rehearsed.[22]

[22] Memoirs, p. 109.

The tide of fortune had turned for Schubert. About this time he applied for a post at the Court Theatre as assistant conductor, and the testimonials written on his behalf by Salieri, Mosel, and Dietrichstein have survived. Early in 1821 he was briefly employed as a coach there, working with Karoline Unger on her role as Isabella in *Così fan tutte*. The appointment, however, was short-lived; according to Leopold von Sonnleithner Schubert did not take kindly to the regular hours involved.

What his feelings were in regard to another roughly contemporary event we can only speculate. On 21 November 1820 his early love, Therese Grob, married Johann Bergmann, a master baker. Another link with the past was broken about this time, when he and Mayrhofer decided to part company. That there was an estrangement between the two is clear, though the course of events is not. Neither of these events can have disturbed his equanimity, if we are to judge from the series of remarkable compositions which flowed from his pen in December 1820.

All of them seem to be informed with imaginative flair and Promethean energy. The rhapsodic setting of Friedrich von Schlegel's 'Im Walde' (In the Forest) D708 is a paean of praise to the spirit that 'impels all thinking things, all objects of all thought, and rolls through all things'. The semiquaver figures in the pianist's right hand rush onward relentlessly for thirteen pages, foreshadowing the 'pure rhythm' of the finale of the 'Great' C major Symphony. 'Freed from all fetters, the power of thought soars aloft. Unafraid, we hear the song of the spirits borne on the wind.'

It was Schubert's destiny to rescue the partsong from its association with the glee club and the drinking party, and turn it into great art; and if the 'Song of the Spirits' does not wholly succeed, the setting of the 23rd Psalm for female voices does. The piece was written for Anna Fröhlich, the head of the singing school set up by the Philharmonic Society in 1819, who wanted a test piece for use in the school examinations. Schubert provided her with a masterpiece, which catches exactly the mood of contemplative devotion. There is no trace of *Gemütlichkeit*, and the piano part is neither optional, nor merely supportive, but equal and essential. It is perhaps the greatest of Schubert's partsongs.

To this prolific month of December 1820 belongs also a fine Mayrhofer song, 'Der zürnenden Diana' (To the Angry Diana), which foreshadows the sustained pulse and free modulation of many later songs. But the greatest work of all Schubert left unfinished, the string quartet in C minor, of which only the opening movement, the *Quartettsatz* or quartet movement, and forty-one bars of a sketch for the Andante, survive. This astonishing movement achieves formal strength and unity in its own unique way. There are two contrasted main themes, the first mysteriously chromatic, apparently derived from the incantation scene (Act I, Scene 3) in *Die Zauberharfe*, and the second, marked 'dolce', diatonic and lyrical. This second subject is heard only twice, first in E flat and the second time in B flat, a procedure which contrasts sharply with that of the other quartets. After its first entry we lose touch with the tonic C minor until the closing bars of the movement. The arrival at the dominant G major at the double barline, however, is firmly underlined, so that the movement proceeds in a great arc, from tonic to dominant and back again. The sketch for the Andante looks highly promising, and there seems nothing to explain Schubert's failure to complete the work, except perhaps his general diffidence and uncertainty in these middle years in approaching traditional four-movement forms. The simple truth may be that he did not feel able to sustain the impetus of so dynamic a work over four movements.

On 26 January 1821, Schubert gathered with fourteen members of the circle for a musical party in Schober's rooms. Schubert played and sang, a lot of punch was drunk, and the festivity went on till three in the morning. Tall and ugly but amiable Josef Huber wrote to tell his betrothed about it, leaving us the earliest surviving account of a 'Schubertiad'.[23] Such gatherings, dedicated to high art and high spirits, were to be a feature of the next few years, as Schubert's reputation spread and his circle of acquaintances was enlarged. The schoolmaster from the Rossau was to become the darling of the salons; the private man had become a public figure, albeit a somewhat reluctant one. Meanwhile the three years from 1818 to 1821 represent a significant change from song-writing to instrumental compositions and opera. Most remarkable, however, is the self-critical spirit in which he approached the piano sonata and the symphony. Much the same attitude is observable in the story of his Mass in A flat, begun in November 1819 after his return from Upper Austria. This was intended as a full-scale ceremonial mass, which Schubert planned to dedicate to the Emperor himself. There were many sketches and drafts, and the work proceeded so slowly that it was not till September 1822 that he declared himself satisfied. It is the more lyrical and idiomatic of the two mature Schubert masses, and will be considered in more detail along with the E flat Mass of 1828.

[23] Docs, p. 162.

6

The opera years (1821–3)

It is the central irony of Schubert's career that in 1820 he stood on the threshold of fame as a composer of German opera, yet he was never to fulfil his own aspirations, and the hopes of his supporters, with a major stage success. The next three years were to be dominated by various operatic projects, not one of which reached the stage. In June 1821 his additional numbers for an adaptation of Hérold's *La Clochette* were highly praised; and in December 1823 his incidental music for the romantic play *Rosamunde* won general applause. But a full-length opera of his own composition was never to be performed in his lifetime, or for a long time after his death. This reversal of fortune marks the turning point of Schubert's career, and its importance can hardly be understood without some knowledge of the political background of operatic affairs at this time.

Even in the capital cities of Germany, opera was still a primarily Italian form of entertainment, practised by Italian artists, usually in the Italian language, under the patronage of royal or aristocratic princes. It is true that Italian and French operas were frequently produced in German translations; professional singers like Vogl sang in whatever language was required of them, like their modern counterparts; and producers were similarly versatile, so that in practice there was often close co-operation between the Italian and German artists. But the German contribution to the repertory was still confined either to translations, or to *Singspiel* in the tradition of sentimental comedy. The idea of a new kind of native opera, German in language and style, and serious in intent, had taken root firmly only during the period of the revolutionary wars, along with the renaissance of German poetry and German culture. The idea was new and exciting. Gluck had never written a German opera. Mozart, encouraged by the sympathy of the Emperor Joseph II for German ideals, had written two, both comedies with spoken dialogue, though one, *The Magic Flute*, reached out beyond the commonplace to the sublime. Beethoven's only opera, *Fidelio*, had a noble theme, and nobody could deny its seriousness of purpose, but it too relied on spoken dialogue, and did not altogether escape the comic tone of the traditional *Singspiel*. The concept of through-composed, all-sung

German opera, bridging the gulf between grand opera as Cherubini and Meyerbeer understood it, and operetta, seemed as far away as ever in 1820.[1]

In Vienna, where the sympathies of the court were strongly pro-Italian, and the taste of the audience was notoriously eclectic, the battle between the two operatic schools of thought was less fierce than it had been, for instance, in Munich, or Berlin. But the enthusiasm for Rossini and his Italian company gave an edge to it. When the Italian impresario Domenico Barbaja took over the lease of the Court Theatre at the end of 1821, he gave every indication of wishing to encourage German opera, and it was that favourable situation which Schubert hoped to exploit. But Barbaja's first two seasons were dominated by the Italians. In the meantime, however, the struggle had come to a decisive climax in Berlin, where Weber's *Der Freischütz* (The Magic Marksman) was given a rapturous reception on its first production on 18 June 1821. Its success was seen as a rebuff to Gasparo Spontini, the director of the Berlin opera, whose attempts to introduce opera in the Italian language had been hissed off the stage. The enthusiasm shown for *Der Freischütz* gave a fresh impetus to the demand for German opera, and Weber was invited to come to Vienna for the first performance of it in November 1821.

These events were reflected in current journalistic gossip. In July the Vienna correspondent of the *Dresdener Abendzeitung* reported that 'the excellent songwriter Schubert is said to be busy at present composing a grand romantic opera'.[2] The reference was to *Alfonso und Estrella*, an opera in three acts, all-sung, on which Schubert and Schober planned to co-operate. In fact the report was a little premature. Serious work on the opera did not start till September; but it says something for the high hopes which were being placed upon it.

The story of *Alfonso* seems to have come out of Schober's head, with some help from Shakespeare. It is a tale of a dispossessed king, Troila, living in exile in a mountain valley, his Arden, with his son Alfonso; of the usurper Mauregato; and of their final reconciliation through the love of Alfonso and Mauregato's daughter Estrella. There is also an unscrupulous villain, called Adolfo, who plans to seize the throne for himself, and marry Estrella by force; but he too repents in the end and is forgiven. The piece dispenses with the conventional apparatus of magic; its theme (like Beethoven's in *Fidelio*) is redemption through love; and it does aim at a kind of Shakespearean universality by freeing itself from the limitations of time and space. But the weaknesses of the libretto are apparent. The stage movement is slow and clumsy, and the main action is constantly held up by the pageantry and the pastoralism. There are no minor characters of any importance, so that the action proceeds

[1] R. Engländer, 'The Struggle between German and Italian Opera at the Time of Weber', *MQ*, vol. xxxi, 1945, pp. 479–91.
[2] Docs, p. 175.

for the most part in a series of duets. The piece is full of fresh lyrical writing, especially in the love scenes of Act II. But even here it is too static. It seems to be more a succession of musical tableaux than a music drama.

In September 1821 Schubert and Schober left Vienna to spend a working holiday at St Pölten, twenty-eight miles west of Vienna. There they stayed as guests of the Bishop of St Pölten, who was distantly related to the Schober family. They divided their time between working on the opera during the day and socializing in the evening. As soon as Schober finished one act Schubert would set to work on the music, while Schober got on with the next. According to the autograph, the score of Act I was begun on 20 September and finished, at least so far as the voice-lines were concerned, on 16 October. Act II was begun two days later, but before it was finished the friends returned to Vienna, in time to attend the first performance of *Freischütz* in a savagely cut version on 3 November. Schober noted drily in a letter to Spaun that 'it did not please much'.[3] One can be sure that Schubert did not miss the new production of *Fidelio* on the following day.

Barbaja's lease of the Court Theatre officially began in the new year, but he was already in control, and was no doubt aware of the *Alfonso* project, even if he had not formally commissioned it. He had already written to Weber to ask for a new opera for the 1822 season in Vienna, and rumour had it that he was also in touch with Weigl, Poissl, and Schubert. In February 1822 Weber returned to Vienna to conduct two performances of *Freischütz*, this time without cuts, and Schubert and Schober established cordial relations with him. Schubert took him to a Concert Spirituel to hear an oratorio by Friedrich Schneider, and Schober wrote the complimentary verses which were presented to the composer, in the custom of the time, at the end of the opera.[4] The season of Italian opera which followed under Rossini's personal direction was greeted with riotous enthusiasm. Yet the Vienna correspondents of the Leipzig *Journal für die elegante Welt*, and of a Berlin periodical, could still report that the prospects for German opera looked rosy, with new operas by Weber, Weigl, Umlauff, and Schubert already in prospect.

While Schubert's operatic hopes ran high, his relations with the Philharmonic Society had entered upon a new and more promising phase. The enthusiastic public reception given to 'Erlkönig' in March 1821 had opened the doors of the musical establishment in Vienna to his songs and partsongs. In the first four months of 1821 alone, Deutsch records no fewer than thirteen public and semi-public performances, including three at the evening entertainments of the Society, and one, on 8 April, at a public concert organized by the Society. On this last occasion Schubert's contribution was once again the male-voice partsong

[3] Docs, p. 196.   [4] Docs, p. 211.

'Das Dörfchen' D598, a tuneful quartet of no great significance which was to become very popular over the next year or two. His appearance on the programme of these concerts was important, for they counted among the most important events of the season in Vienna. But his main ambition was to gain a hearing for his orchestral works. The opportunity to do so occurred in the following November, at the first concert of the new season, when his E minor Overture was included in a programme, in which Beethoven, Stadler, Romberg, and Mozart were also represented. The Overture in E minor D648 had been written in February 1819. It is seldom heard today, and its choice, in preference to one of the early symphonies, or the *Zauberharfe* Overture, seems puzzling. The longest and most elaborate of Schubert's concert overtures, it is scored for full orchestra with trombones, and is full of dynamic and harmonic contrast. But it lacks Schubertian charm. The themes are short and symphonic rather than lyrical, and the piece leaves an impression of conscious contrivance. The only critical comment to survive was guarded: 'All went well together'.[5]

For the Philharmonic Society concert of March 1822, the committee decided to ask Schubert for another male-voice quartet, and he obliged with 'Geist der Liebe' (The Spirit of Love) D747, a setting of popular verses by Friedrich von Matthisson. The piece pleased and was encored; further performances soon followed. One critic pointed to the risk of tonal monotony in the male-voice quartet, when he might perhaps more shrewdly have identified the tone of *Gemütlichkeit* which characterizes it. Schubert himself seems to have been aware of the danger of becoming too closely associated with the genre, for when the Society asked him for yet another quartet for the next season, he politely declined. 'You know yourself', he wrote to Leopold Sonnleithner, 'how the recent quartets were received; people have had enough of them. True, I might succeed in inventing some new form, but one cannot count on anything of the kind. As my future destiny lies close to my heart you who, I flatter myself, take an interest in it yourself, must admit that I should proceed cautiously, and that I cannot by any means accept the invitation, much as it flatters me.'[6]

Throughout 1821 and 1822 Schubert's work continued to be in constant demand. It was not unknown even for two different works by him to be performed on the same day. On 18 November 1821, for instance, his E minor Overture was played, as already mentioned, at the Philharmonic Society public concert at noon in the *Redoutensaal*; and on the same day at four o'clock a concert organized by the Society of Amateurs (*Dilettanten Gesellschaft*) included a performance of his setting of Schmidt's 'Der Wanderer', already a popular number on such

[5] Docs, p. 198.   [6] Docs, p. 264.

occasions. Not many composers are faced with such practical difficulties in attending performances of their work!

It seems all the more puzzling, therefore, that his association with the public concerts of the Philharmonic Society ended in March 1822, only twelve months after it began. His songs and partsongs continued to be popular at the Thursday evening entertainments of the Society, but he seems to have made no move to promote public performances of any of his symphonies or overtures until the 'Great' C major Symphony was finished in 1826. Even when he was asked for an orchestral work for a pupils' concert at the training school he once attended, he could only plead in reply that he had 'nothing for full orchestra which I could send out into the world with a clear conscience', and refer his correspondent to Beethoven's overtures. This from a man who already had six symphonies and several overtures to his credit![7] The key to this puzzling state of affairs must lie somewhere in that concern for his own destiny of which he had spoken to Sonnleithner, and especially in his anxiety to show himself worthy to assume the mantle of Beethoven.

Contemporary reports suggest that he was already regarded, in Vienna at least, as the heir apparent to the Mozart/Beethoven tradition. A diary which has recently come to light in Leningrad, for instance, throws a fascinating light on Schubert's reputation in fashionable artistic circles at this time. Peter Johann Köppen was a young man of German extraction and Russian nationality who arrived in Vienna in March 1822 in company with his friend Alexis Beresin. As a regular frequenter of the salons of Karoline Pichler, the merchant Josef Henikstein, and others, he had ample opportunity to observe Schubert as he appeared to the social and artistic establishment of Vienna. He heard Schmidt's 'Der Wanderer' sung for the first time at a reception at Henikstein's, and was moved almost to tears. On 24 April he met Schubert again at Karoline Pichler's, and recorded his impressions.

> Schubert (the composer) sang something with feeling, but little voice. The daughter of the house played Schubert's Variations on a French song with her mother. . . . The theme was especially beautiful. Schubert himself turned the pages. When he sat down at the piano Frau Pichler said: 'It reminds me of when Mozart insisted on turning the pages when I played his sonatas.' Schubert himself not very tall, rather stocky, wearing glasses.[8]

Josef Hüttenbrenner, admittedly a committed supporter, had no hesitation in comparing Schubert with Beethoven. In a letter to the publisher Peters of Leipzig, he wrote: 'Among the newer composers here Vienna again possesses a talent which has already attracted general attention, and become the darling of the public: in short, and without

---

[7] Docs, p. 265.

[8] I am indebted to Dr J. Chochlow, of Moscow, for information about this unpublished diary.

exaggeration, it is that of a second Beethoven.'[9] Yet it is doubtful whether Schubert's name was known at this time anywhere outside Germany. The first mention of his name in the London musical journal *The Harmonicon* is in 1826, though the same periodical had published the famous Trauer Waltz (Op. 9 No. 2 D365) in a corrupt form as early as October 1823, without of course mentioning the composer's name.

Schubert's own personal relations with Beethoven remain a mystery. Since they lived in the same city, and frequented the same taverns and the same music shops, it is hardly possible that they did not come face to face many times. But the evidence is conflicting, and there is no reliable record of any conversation between them. It is true, of course, that by the time Schubert arrived on the musical scene Beethoven's deafness had cut him off from any but his close friends and distinguished visitors. Moreover, the younger man's consciousness of his own genius, and his unbounded admiration for Beethoven's, would naturally tend to reinforce his shyness and embarrassment in the presence of the master. On at least two occasions, however, Schubert is reported to have visited Beethoven at his lodgings, and one of those occasions, if it took place at all, must have occurred late in 1821 or early in 1822.

In April 1822 the Variations on a French Song, for piano duet, were published by Cappi and Diabelli as Op. 10. Written at Zseliz in 1818, the work had become popular, and we have seen that Karoline Pichler and her daughter were especially fond of it. The work was dedicated to Beethoven 'by his worshipper and admirer Franz Schubert'. In later years Josef Hüttenbrenner told Luib that the composer took an engraved copy of the score to Beethoven, but did not find him at home. Albert Stadler simply said that he had been told Beethoven amiably accepted the dedication. Anton Schindler, Beethoven's friend and sometime factotum, however, left a long and circumstantial account of the interview, according to which Schubert was put off by Beethoven's comment on one point in the score, and lost his composure. But Schindler does not actually claim to have been present at the interview, and since his account was written in 1860 it can probably be regarded as a sample of his notorious capacity for historical romancing.[10]

The impression one gets of Schubert from Köppen and other contemporary witnesses is of a man at the centre of the society of his time, yet detached from it; sensitive to the trend of public taste and intellectual fashions, but jealously protective of his own destiny. Also present at the reception at Karoline Pichler's in April 1822 was a young army officer called Anton Prokesch. His friendship with the composer was not limited to such formal occasions, and his reminiscences seem to get closer to the essential Schubert. 'A young man of great hopes for music', he wrote. 'His songs have something original, deeply appealing about them,

[9] Docs, p. 232.   [10] Memoirs, p. 325.

which explains their wide circulation . . . I was much with Schubert, for though without formal education, he was agreeable because of his open-ness, his sound intelligence and his enthusiasm . . . Many an evening did we spend together in an ale-house by the Kärntnertor Theatre in the most animated conversation.' In later years Prokesch added an illumi-nating footnote to this passage. 'Great music slumbered in him, but it never came to such an awakening as he himself dreamed of and heard in his soul.'[11]

Like Shakespeare in sixteenth-century London, Schubert seems to move inconspicuously between the ale-house and the salons of the dis-tinguished. In January 1822, for instance, he was present at a party given by one Vincentius Weintridt, a professor of theology who had been dis-missed because of his rationalist views. Among the guests were a pro-fessor of classical literature, a future minister of state, and several disciples of the liberal-minded theologian, including the young painter Moritz von Schwind, and a student with literary ambitions called Eduard von Bauernfeld, both of whom were later to belong to the inner circle of Schubert's friends. For the circle was changing rapidly. Spaun departed for Linz in September 1821, not to return for five years. Old schoolfellows like Stadler and Holzapfel were busy with their own careers, conscious that Schubert had left them behind. Schubert had become ' a big noise', as Holzapfel put it in a letter to Stadler: 'I rarely see him, and we don't hit it off very well, for his world is a very differ-ent one, as it must be. His rather abrupt manner stands him in good stead, and will make a strong man and a mature artist of him.'[12]

The new circle, broadly representative of youth and talent, could be seen on parade, as it were, at the house parties held at Atzenbrugg in the summer, and at the reading parties held in the winter months. The Atzenbrugg estate was part of the property belonging to the Klosterneuburg monastery, of which Schober's uncle, Josef Derffel, was the estate manager. There Schober's numerous friends gathered by invi-tation in July for a programme of fun and games of a sophisticated kind, and expeditions into the surrounding countryside. The Atzenbrugg feasts, as they were sometimes called, took place annually from 1817 to 1822, but Schubert seems to have attended only from 1820 onwards. Here the artistic triumvirate consisting of Schober, Schubert, and the painter Leopold Kupelwieser held court. The lists of guests, which have survived, show that the company included an assortment of musicians, artists, students, and academics, all belonging to what might be called the liberal intelligentsia. Leopold Kupelwieser's atmospheric water-colours preserve the carefree mood of these golden days splendidly, and so do Schubert's own Atzenbrugg dances, later published as part of Op. 9 and Op. 18. The legacy of Atzenbrugg includes a poem by Schober and

[11] Docs, pp. 253–4.   [12] Docs, p. 211.

possibly also an enigmatic story penned by Schubert in July 1822 entitled 'My Dream'. This concerns the changing relations of a loving but severe father and a wilful son, and has been interpreted in various fanciful ways as autobiographical. But it may well be no more than a relic of some party game.[13]

The reading parties met two or three times a week in the winter months, first at Schober's, and later at the house of the painter Ludwig Mohn. They, too, were a mixture of high spirits and high thinking. We know little about the works read. All such regular meetings were regarded with suspicion by the authorities, and each member of the group had to be formally admitted under a pseudonym, chosen from German mythology or from the classics. Schober was Hagen, Schubert Volker the Minstrel, and Franz von Bruchmann Gunther. It was from a very similar group in Berlin that the texts of Schubert's two great song cycles were to emerge.

In the second half of the year 1822 events began to take a less favourable turn for Schubert. The change of fortune was signalled by the rejection of *Alfonso und Estrella*. The score was finished in February, and handed over to the new management of the Kärntnertor. By this time, however, arrangements for the summer season were far advanced. There followed a wildly enthusiastic season of Italian opera, culminating in what one critic described as 'an idolatrous orgy'. *Alfonso* was put on one side, and in the autumn Schubert, unwilling to wait indefinitely, asked for the score to be returned, so that he could try his luck elsewhere. Critical opinion, even among Schubert's friends, was divided. Court Secretary Ignaz von Mosel was said to be impressed by the work, and so was Salieri. But Vogl's sense of the theatre warned him that it would not be effective on the stage. He thought it 'altogether on the wrong lines', and doubtless his opinion carried some weight with the management.[14] He was to leave the theatre himself in November.

Josef Hüttenbrenner, acting as Schubert's agent, sent the score first to Weber in Dresden, but in spite of an encouraging initial response, nothing came of it. Nothing came either of an approach to Berlin, where the prima donna Anna Milder, whom Schubert had admired ever since her Gluck performance at the Court Theatre in 1813, expressed an interest in it. *Alfonso* had to wait till 1854 before reaching the stage at Weimar in a much edited version prepared by Liszt. Its lack of dramatic pace keeps it off the modern professional stage, though it has been heard in a concert version, and a recording exists.

During 1822 Schubert ran into financial problems in spite of the fact that the publication of his songs, which began in March 1821, had proved very lucrative. According to Sonnleithner the proceeds of the first twelve opus numbers were sufficient to clear off the composer's debts,

[13] Docs, p. 226–8.   [14] Docs, p. 230.

and provide him with some 2000 florins in addition. Such a sum, added to occasional earnings from patrons and dedicatees, must have put him in the comparatively affluent position of, say, a Kapellmeister, or a senior court official. But Schubert was a free and generous spender when money was available; he had none of Beethoven's shrewd concern for his own financial interest. Whatever the reason, he found himself temporarily in need of funds, and Diabelli chose this moment to make a cash offer for the copyright of all the works he had so far published on commission. Schubert decided, without consulting his friends, to sacrifice income for cash, and accepted 800 florins for the copyright. Having freed himself, as he doubtless saw it, from Diabelli's clutches, he then made a new agreement with Leidesdorf to provide songs on a regular basis over two years in return for 480 florins a year. These transactions offended Sonnleithner's sense of financial prudence, and Hüttenbrenner's too.

The list of compositions for 1821 and 1822 shows the extent to which Schubert's energies were concentrated on his operas. May and June 1821 are empty, apart from the two numbers for the adaptation of Hérold's *La Clochette*, which had four performances that summer under its German title, *Das Zauberglöckchen* (The Magic Bell) and a few keyboard dances. From September 1821 till the following February nothing was allowed to compete with *Alfonso*. Two other compositions only appear in January, and those specially commissioned ones: the partsong 'Geist der Liebe' for the Philharmonic Society concert, and a ceremonial work for soloists, chorus and orchestra written for performance at the Theresian Academy, a school for sons of the nobility, to mark the birthday of the Emperor. The words and the music of this laudatory piece (D748) were modelled on Haydn's anthem, 'God save Franz the Emperor'. Both these commissions were arranged by Leopold Sonnleithner. Two settings of the *Tantum ergo*, one in August 1821 (D730), and one in March 1822 (D750), were probably written for Josef Mayssen, a teacher friend of the Schubert family and organist of the parish church at Hernals, and commissioned for some special occasion. They are scored for chorus, orchestra and organ (with soloists also in the first setting).

The songs of these years, however, are of the first importance, and show a variety of mood and sureness of touch unsurpassed except in 1817 and in the composer's final years. 1821 begins with an elaborate setting of Karoline Pichler's 'Der Unglückliche' (The Hapless Man), and one of the finest of the Schiller songs, 'Sehnsucht' D636. In February Schubert fell under the spell of Goethe's collection of poems in the oriental manner, the *West-östlicher Divan*, and a series of masterpieces followed. 'Versunken' (Enthralled), 'Geheimes' (A Secret) and 'Suleika I' celebrate, each in its own way, the intimate mysteries of love. To this same period belong 'Grenzen der Menschheit' (Human Limitations), a bass song which seems to transcend the limitations of the Lied itself in a tremendous declamation of cumulative power, and further settings of two of Mignon's songs from *Wilhelm Meister*. In the autumn Mayrhofer wrote a sequence of twelve poems, allegorical and philosophic in tone, under the title *Heliopolis*. The cycle was dedicated to Schober, but it is not unlikely that they were intended as the text of a projected song cycle for Schubert, who set two of the poems in April 1822. Neither, however, is so well known as the exquisite setting of the same author's 'Nachtviolen' (Dame's Violets) in the same month.

The second half of 1822 produced a succession of wonderful songs on Romantic themes representative of the younger generation of poets, Count von Platen, Friedrich Rückert, Matthäus von Collin, Johann Senn, and Franz von Bruchmann. The last-named, whom we have already met in connection with the police raid on Senn's lodgings, was a young intellectual who had abandoned his early Catholicism for a kind of Wordsworthian deism under the influence of Schelling. He was an important influence in Schubert's social and intellectual life in these years, and introduced the composer to contemporary poetry, including that of Platen. His poems were never published, but he provided Schubert with texts for five fine songs, of which the best known is 'Am See' (By the Lake) D746, and the most remarkable in terms of depth of feeling and motivic richness 'Schwestergruss' (Sister's Greeting) D762, an elegiac song in memory of Bruchmann's sister. But all five Bruchmann settings are of uncommon interest.

Even more remarkable are three Romantic masterpieces from the pen of Matthäus von Collin, the tutor of the young Duke of Reichstadt and exponent of the new aesthetics. 'Wehmut' (Melancholy) D772 is the most perfect expression in Schubert of the mingled joy and sadness which the Romantics felt in the presence of nature. As an example of Schubert's ability to convey the whole complexity of a poem in a short, through-composed song it ranks with Goethe's 'Wandrers Nachtlied' and the Claudius 'An die Nachtigall'. Quotation is powerless to illustrate the diversity in unity of such a song. The ballad 'Der Zwerg' (The Dwarf) D771 is at the opposite extreme in scale and structure. It is a bizarre tale of beauty and the beast, with overtones of sexual domination and obsession. Throughout its five pages the left-hand octaves beat out the insistent rhythm of three quavers followed by a minim (see Ex. 21). It can hardly be an accident that its motivic cell is identical, except for a change from 3/4 to common time, with the main theme of the first movement of the 'Unfinished' Symphony. 'Nacht und Träume' (Night and Dreams) D827 contains within its twenty-nine bars the whole mystery and magic of 'holy Night'. Not all these songs, it is true, can be certainly attributed to the autumn of 1822, but it is probably safe to assume that they were written then or during the following winter. That was the time Bruchmann later spoke of as 'enchanted by music and poetry', confessing himself 'bewitched'; and it was at that time that Schubert was most under the spell of the Romantic vision.

Ex. 21

In January 1821, and again in August 1823, Bruchmann made clandestine visits to Erlangen to hear Schelling lecture on aesthetics and German mythology. There he made friends with Count August von Platen, the Romantic poet and dramatist whose homosexual disposition reinforced his sense of tragic isolation. Bruchmann introduced Platen to Schubert's songs, and in return Platen sent verses to Bruchmann for Schubert to set. 'Die Liebe hat gelogen' (Love Has Lied) D751 was written in March, and 'Du liebst mich nicht' (You Love Me Not) D756 in July. Both these songs of broken love are tragic in tone, and exploit ostinato rhythms and keys familiar to us from the Harper songs and other songs of alienation. But they are unlike any other love songs of Schubert's. There is no hint in them of the life-enhancing zest of Goethe in love, of Rückert's tenderness or even Heine's bitter irony. The mood is inward-looking, resentful and reproachful, and must owe something to Platen's catastrophic love affair with Eduard Schmidtlein in 1821. Bruchmann sent Schubert's compositions to Platen in April 1822. The whole episode leaves many questions unanswered. Who took the initiative in the exchange of courtesies between Schubert and Platen? One assumes that Bruchmann did. There seems to be little doubt that the texts are songs of homosexual love, and that both Schubert and Bruchmann must have been aware of the fact.

We can probably thank Bruchmann also for the two settings of poems by Johann Senn, who since his banishment had been eking out a precarious living in his native Tyrol. In September 1822 Bruchmann visited him there, and returned with the texts of 'Selige Welt' (Blessed World) D743 and 'Schwanengesang' (Swan Song) D744. The first is a vigorous plea for accepting gratefully whatever life offers, the second an epigrammatic greeting to death, again in the familiar 'death rhythm', in which Schubert's sense of tonal ambivalence becomes the expressive core of the song. Finally, something must be said of two groups of songs which seem to sum up Schubert's mastery of lyrical movement at the climax of his middle years. The Goethe songs of December 1822 include 'Der Musensohn' (Son of the Muses) and probably also 'Über allen Gipfeln ist Ruh' (Peace descends on every peak), the second of the Wanderer's Nightsongs; this last might stand as a vindication of the Lied in itself, for it is a perfect marriage of great poetry and great music. But in their different ways 'An die Entfernte' (To the Distant Lover), 'Am Flusse' (By the Stream), and 'Willkommen und Abschied' (Hail and Farewell) are all fine songs. The Rückert songs are equally varied in mood, and unerringly precise in their rhythmic and motivic invention, and though only one of them can be exactly dated, they belong almost certainly to the second half of 1822, or the very beginning of 1823. The five songs are all masterpieces. The best known are 'Du bist die Ruh' (You are Rest and Peace) and 'Lachen und Weinen' (Laughter and Tears); but the most astonishingly original is 'Dass sie hier gewesen' (The Aura of her Presence), a song which juxtaposes two contrasted musical worlds, the chromatic idiom of Wagner and the diatonic language of the classical masters, as symbols of the intangible presence and the tangible fact. The effect, as the song switches from the former to the latter, resembles that of a soft-focus shot being suddenly brought into close-up (see Ex. 22). There is a curious anticipation of this expressive device in the fragmentary C major Fantasie for Piano D605, which Ernst Hilmar tentatively ascribes to the summer of 1822.

Two partsongs should be mentioned because they illustrate Schubert's developing concept of the genre. 'Gott in der Natur' (God in Nature) D757 was written for Anna Fröhlich. Originally scored as a quartet for women's voices, with piano accompaniment, it is now often heard in choral versions, sometimes with orchestral accompaniment. The piece is in three main sections of which the second, characterized by bold modulations, is perhaps the best. The final section builds a climax by more conventional methods. 'Des Tages Weihe' (The Consecration of the Day) D763 is a song of thanksgiving for recovery from illness, and one of the most attractive of all Schubert's partsongs. It was written for

Ex. 22

Sehr langsam

Dass der Ost - wind Düf - te

pp >   >   sim.   pp

hau - chet in die Lüf - te   da - durch

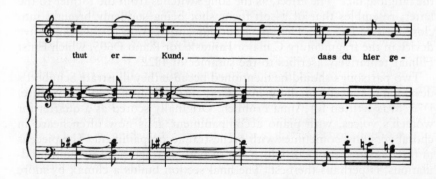

thut er ___ Kund, _____ dass du hier ge-

Ex. 22 *cont.*

we - sen, — dass du hier ge - we - sen.

Baroness Geymüller, a member of a famous banking family, who presented Schubert with fifty florins as a reward.

A revealing letter to Spaun in December 1822[15] gives us a glimpse of affairs as Schubert saw them. He begins by announcing the imminent publication of three books of songs, including two books of Goethe settings (Op. 12 and Op. 14) and another set of three dedicated to Spaun himself. Then he goes on:

> Besides these I have composed a Fantasy for piano, two hands, which is also to appear in print, dedicated to a certain wealthy person . . . With the opera there is nothing doing in Vienna. I asked to have it back and got it . . . With me things have gone quite well, apart from feeling so aggrieved by the wretched business of the opera. Do write to me soon and at length. Make out the address to the schoolhouse in the Rossau, as I live there now.

The change of address comes as a surprise, in view of Schubert's distaste for the enclosed atmosphere of the schoolroom, and the sophisticated circles he now moved in. But whether it was simply an economy measure or a symptom of ill-health, perhaps the first indication of the disease which was to strike him down in the following year, we do not know. The most interesting aspect of the letter, however, is the light it throws, and in the case of the 'Unfinished' Symphony the light it does not throw, on the two great masterpieces of the year. The Fantasie in C major, called the 'Wanderer', and the Symphony in B minor, called the 'Unfinished', both date from October/November 1822. The 'wealthy person' referred to in Schubert's letter was a certain Emanuel Karl Liebenberg, a landowner and amateur pianist, who commissioned the Fantasie. Schubert's lifelong preoccupation with monothematic structures suddenly comes to full maturity in this astonishing work. The tentative experiments in thematic transformation in the keyboard fantasias of his boyhood are here superseded in a full-length, four-movement work which was to provide the model for Liszt, César Franck, and other exponents of this structural method. The dactylic rhythm which domi-

[15] Docs, pp. 247–9.

nates three of the four linked movements is a basic unifying element, linking the outer movements with the self-quotation from 'Der Wanderer' which serves as the theme of the lovely Adagio, and gives the work its poetic depth and meaning. Over and above this there is a kind of second subject, in the E flat major theme marked 'dolce (*pp*)', which reappears refashioned in waltz time in the Scherzo (see Ex. 23). Within this unifying conception Schubert achieves an astonishing variety of pace, mood and colour, while the bravura style and unfailing invention give the work its youthful energy and charm.

Ex. 23

If the final section does not quite sustain the quality of the earlier movements, this is not because there is anything wrong with the idea of a fugal finale, but because it quickly develops into strepitoso passage work. It can fairly be said, however, that the final pages are fully in keeping with the virtuoso element in the work. It was not the composer who attached the nickname to the Fantasie, which was published in February 1823 as Op. 15. It was well spoken of on its first appearance, but made no special mark during the composer's lifetime, perhaps because of its technical difficulty. Its later popularity owes much to Liszt, whose arrangement for piano and orchestra dates from the early 1850s.

If Schubert's letter to Spaun refers to the Fantasie with a certain pride, his failure to mention the 'Unfinished' Symphony seems inexplicable. So much has been written about this problematic work that it may be well to begin by clearing up a few misunderstandings. It is not true, as is sometimes asserted, that it was written for presentation to the Styrian Music Society at Graz, which in April 1823 awarded Schubert its Diploma of Honour. Towards the end of 1823, Schubert gave the manuscript to Josef Hüttenbrenner 'out of gratitude', as Josef later put it, 'for the Diploma of Honour'. But the full score of the surviving movements dates from November 1822, long before the award of the Diploma was mooted. Moreover, it seems clear that Josef regarded the work as a personal gift to himself and his brother Anselm, and not as the property of the Styrian Music Society. It remained for many years in Josef's hands. In 1853 Anselm Hüttenbrenner made an arrangement of the two complete movements for piano duet. It was Johann Herbeck who finally wrested the score from Anselm and conducted the first performance of the work in 1865.

The intuitive mastery of the symphony, its apocalyptic and enchanted air, mark it off from Schubert's other symphonic works, making it seem almost an isolated sport, unrelated to what went before and what came after. But as we have seen, both the emotional world of the 'Unfinished', and its eruptive explosions of feeling, are foreshadowed in earlier works such as the D major Overture 'in the Italian style', *Die Zauberharfe* (particularly the incantation music), and in songs like 'Suleika I', 'Der Zwerg', 'Grablied für die Mutter' (A Mother's Funeral Song) D616 and 'Der Leidende' D432, all of them concerned with suffering, death or passion. A full discussion of the emotional terms of reference of the 'Unfinished' would involve an examination of B minor/major as the key inseparably associated in Schubert's mind with the ineluctable sadness and loneliness of the human condition. From 'Der Leidende' in 1816 to 'Der Doppelgänger' in 1828 it is Schubert's key of alienation and despair.

During the operatic years complete symphonic works are conspicuous by their absence. Recent research, however, has shown that the symphony was never very far from Schubert's thoughts. The sketches of May 1818 for two symphonic movements in short score have already been mentioned. In the spring of 1821 he drafted similarly four movements of a symphony in D, D708A, including a fine Scherzo, virtually complete in outline, and a striking forerunner of the corresponding movement of the 'Great' C major. A few months later, in August 1821, Schubert sketched a complete symphony in E, D729. This work, the autograph of which is in the library of the Royal College of Music, is a continuous outline, fully scored for the first 110 bars, and thereafter with all the leading voices inserted, so that only the detailed scoring remained to be done. The adoption of this method, which he had used for the early symphonies and was also to use for the 'Great', suggests that Schubert this time began with every intention of completing the work. Yet he did not complete it; and though the Symphonic Sketch in E is interesting, with an attractive Andante, it does not aspire either to the emotional intensity of the 'Unfinished', or to the sublimity of the 'Great'. The work has been played in various full symphonic versions, including a recent very sympathetic one by Brian Newbould, and has been recorded.

It is clear also that the 'Unfinished' was planned as a four-movement symphony, for a sketch for the Scherzo survives, almost complete except for the second half of the Trio. There are those who believe also that the Finale survives, as the B minor Entr'acte of the *Rosamunde* music, and there is something to be said for this theory; but the textual evidence, and that of the paper experts, is against it. Nor does the thematic material suggest a symphonic finale: it fits more readily into the regular sectional pattern of ballet music, for which it is effectively used in *Rosamunde* itself.

The mystery of the B minor Symphony lies not so much in the fact that it was left unfinished, for the same applies to many of Schubert's finest works, but in his attitude to his own masterpiece. As we have seen, he failed even to mention it in his letter to Spaun, and so far as we know, he never mentioned it to anyone else either, except to the Hütten-brenners. Nothing is more striking than the contrast between his indifference to the fate of the 'Unfinished', and his active concern to promote a performance of the 'Great' C major Symphony. The solution to this mystery can only derive from his anxiety to establish himself as a worthy successor to Beethoven. A public symphony in B minor was a novel concept in itself, almost a contradiction in terms. There is no such work among Haydn's or Mozart's mature symphonies, nor did Beethoven ever attempt such a thing. Moreover, Beethoven had turned the symphony into a public statement, a kind of manifesto, with social and political implications. But the world of the 'Unfinished' was a private world, and it did not seem possible that a great symphony could at such a time be made out of private grief. To look at the matter in more formal terms, any symphony to rival Beethoven's had to find a solution to what might be called the 'finale problem'; it must somehow bring to the finale a sense of consummation and catharsis, the release of tensions which had been built up throughout the earlier movements. It is difficult to imagine how such an effect could be achieved with the B minor Symphony, except indeed by such revolutionary means as were later to be used by Tchaikovsky and Mahler.

Whether there is any connection between the tragic tone of the B minor Symphony (and also of many songs of the period) and Schubert's personal circumstances is an open question, on which the truth lies beyond reach. Genius is not the slave of circumstance, and the element of emotional turbulence is not unknown in Schubert's earlier work. On the other hand, nothing in the 'Tragic' Symphony of 1816, or in the later overtures, really prepares us for the dark and demonic intensity of the 'Unfinished'. It sounds like a work born rather than made, bar succeeding bar with inevitable logic. Even the sketches in short score, though they bear witness to interesting changes in the final version, seem complete in all essentials. Yet the final score of the 'Unfinished' was contemporary with the 'Wanderer' Fantasie, a brilliant 'public' work, extrovert in style and youthful in spirit; and if many songs of the period are sombre and pessimistic, they also include 'Der Musensohn', 'Im Haine' (In the Grove), and 'Lachen und Weinen'. All one can say is that the only known event which could conceivably have occasioned the cosmic despair which invades the best of Schubert's work at this time is the onset of his serious illness. About this Kreissle, Grove, and other nine-teenth-century biographers are tactfully reticent. There is little doubt, however, that it was syphilitic. The diagnosis was first openly broached by O. E. Deutsch early in this century, and it has since been supported by various medical studies. In spite of the fact that the disease was endemic at that time in Vienna, the scientific study of it was in its infancy. The various forms of venereal disease had not then been clearly identified. The standard treatment was the application of mercury, itself a poison. Terms like 'nervous fever' and 'typhus' are widely used in the relevant documents, though not with any scientific precision. Even the chronology is in doubt. The earliest documentary evidence comes in a letter of 28 February 1823, in which Schubert apologizes to the court sec-retary Mosel for troubling him with correspondence, and explains that his state of health 'still does not permit me to leave the house'. The adverb implies that he had been ill for some time before this, and some writers assume that the symptoms first showed themselves towards the end of 1822. But there are no signs that his social life was affected before the new year. On 18 January he put in an appearance at a Schubertiad held at Mosel's house. Thereafter he disappeared from public view until the end of July, when he turned up on holiday with Michael Vogl at Linz. Some verses which survive from May sound like a bitter cry of anguish: 'Behold, as nothing in dust I lie/ A prey to grief unknown to all/ My life a pilgrimage of pain/ Now nears its everlasting end/ Destroy my life and all I am/ Cast me into Lethe's depths/ And then, O Lord, allow new life/ To thrive in purity and strength.'[16] Clearly at this time he despaired of his life. Yet in that same month he wrote a fine set of keyboard dances (D790), several songs, some sketches for a new opera (*Rüdiger* D791), and completed the vocal lines for the first act of another full-length opera, *Fierabras*.

In the letter to Mosel already referred to Schubert asks for the help of the court secretary in promoting a performance of *Alfonso* at Dresden, and concludes by making an urgent plea for the libretto which Mosel had promised to send him. Meanwhile, however, he had completed another one-act operetta. In February he came across a piece called *Die Verschworenen* (The Conspirators) by the Viennese dramatist and jour-nalist I. F. Castelli. Castelli already had successful opera books to his credit, including that of Weigl's *Die Schweizerfamilie*, and he now printed *Die Verschworenen* as an answer to composers who complained that there were no good German libretti. 'Here is one, gentlemen!' he declared in his preface. This was a challenge Schubert could not resist. He set to work and finished the score in April.

Castelli was right. *Die Verschworenen* is a good strong story, well told, and it became the basis for Schubert's most workmanlike, melodi-

---

[16] Eric Sams, 'Schubert's Illness Re-examined', *MT*, Jan., 1980, pp. 15–22.

ous, and successful opera. The story is based on the *Lysistrata* of Aristophanes, translated to the mediaeval world of the Crusades. It concerns a revolt of neglected wives against their husbands' intolerable and interminable devotion to war, and develops into a kind of battle between feminine wit and masculine machismo. There is some uncertainty as to whether Schubert wrote the part of the page Udolin as a mezzo-soprano breeches role, or for tenor; but as a whole, and in spite of some repetitive march music, the score justifies itself as the most viable Schubert operetta. The autograph, now in the British Library, consists of eleven numbers and an overture.

The subsequent history of the piece is curious. First it ran into trouble with the censors, who objected to the subversive tone of the title! Thereafter it became *Der häusliche Krieg* (Domestic Warfare). It was not heard in public until 1 March 1861, when Johann Herbeck conducted a concert performance in the Vienna Philharmonic Society's hall. The Vienna critic Hanslick recalled in later years how he sat at this first performance beside Castelli, an old man of eighty, who was astonished and moved to hear for the first time this opera of his own, written nearly forty years earlier, the existence of which he had never even suspected. The piece was enthusiastically received, and it still occasionally reappears in the repertory.

What is most attractive about *Der häusliche Krieg* is the tone of comic irony; unlike some of Schubert's earlier operettas, it does not take itself too seriously. *Fierabras*, on the other hand, Schubert's next operatic venture is a serious undertaking. It is a full-length heroic-romantic opera set in the period of Charlemagne's wars against the Moors. Like Weber's *Euryanthe*, with which it is exactly contemporary, it aims at the elusive target of a fully German grand opera though, unlike *Alfonso und Estrella*, it does include spoken dialogue. The libretto was by Josef Kupelwieser, then secretary of the Court Opera, and brother of Schubert's friend, the painter Leopold Kupelwieser. There is little doubt, therefore, that the project, even if not formally commissioned, carried the approval of Barbaja's management as part of his plan for the encouragement of German opera. On 11 October the *Theaterzeitung* reported: 'In addition to Weber's *Euryanthe* and Kreutzer's *Der Taucher* (The Diver), the theatre next to the Kärntnertor is shortly to present the first grand opera by the highly promising Schubert, the brilliant composer of 'Erlkönig': *Fierabras*, after Calderón, by the Court Secretary, Herr Kupelwieser.'[17] On 19 August the piece was passed by the censor with minor alterations. By then, as we shall see, the three-act opera was half-finished.

On 29 November, however, the *Theaterzeitung* unexpectedly reported that *Fierabras* 'is not to be performed for the present'.[18] The reason for

[17] Docs, p. 291.   [18] Docs, p. 300.

this sudden about-turn has never been fully explained. Josef Kupelwieser resigned from the theatre on 9 October, exasperated—so it is said—by the self-indulgence and arrogance of the Italian members of the company. But there is no reason why this should have led to the cancellation of the opera. Schubert himself probably gave the true explanation in a letter to Schober, who had decided in August to try his luck as an actor in Breslau. On 30 November he wrote: 'With my two operas things go very badly, too, Kupelwieser has suddenly left the theatre. Weber's *Euryanthe* turned out badly; its poor reception was in my opinion quite justified. These circumstances . . . leave me scarcely any hope for my opera.'[19] *Euryanthe*, which received its first performance on 25 October, was withdrawn after twenty performances. Where the famous Weber had failed, so the management must have argued, it would hardly be wise to risk an equally ambitious opera by the little-known Schubert.

In 1897 a revised version of *Fierabras* was produced at Karlsruhe under Felix Mottl, but until recently the conventional view that Schubert's operas do not have the dramatic edge to make them viable on the stage was not seriously challenged. In May 1988, however, a fully professional production of *Fierabras* under Claudio Abbado was much more favourably received in Vienna. As in *Alfonso* there is no lack of fine music, and after a leisurely start the first act does achieve a certain dramatic pace. Many pages of accompanied recitative bear witness to Schubert's ability to handle a scene with dramatic force and lyrical fluency. No doubt, with more experience he would have used his blue pencil to better effect. The revival of interest in recordings of the operas, however, and the success of the Vienna production suggest that at long last we may see a belated recognition of their merits.

The chronology of *Fierabras* leaves no doubt about the importance Schubert attached to his opera. The full score was begun on 25 May and the voice lines of the first two acts completed in twelve days. Several earlier sketches have survived, but even if the dates on the autograph refer only to the vocal outline, they demonstrate Schubert's phenomenal capacity for sustained creativity. On 7 June he set to work on the final act. But thereafter there is a long gap in the records until the end of July, when we find him on holiday at Steyr with Vogl, and, as he wrote to Schober, working at his opera and reading Walter Scott. For a period of some six weeks there is no note of any public appearance; no dated autograph, no record of any meetings or parties. In August Beethoven's nephew Karl wrote in the master's conversation book: 'They greatly praise Schubert, but it is said that he hides himself.'[20] There is a well-documented tradition, recorded by Kreissle and confirmed by Schubert's friends, that in the summer of 1823 he spent several weeks under treat-

[19] Docs, p. 301. On the composition history of *Fierabras* see Denny, 'Zur Chronologie im Composition-prozess des *Fierabras*', *Brille*, 9, pp. 91–103.

[20] Docs, p. 288.

ment at the Vienna General Hospital. Some authorities have suggested that this took place in May, but this seems inconsistent with the volume of creative work in that month. The commonsense solution is that Schubert's stay in hospital took place sometime after 7 June, when work was suspended on *Fierabras*, and before the last week of July, when he sought peace of mind and health once again in his beloved mountains.

Meanwhile his illness had taken its deadly course. By August the worst seemed to be over. To Schober he described himself as 'fairly well'. But 'whether I shall ever quite recover I am inclined to doubt'.[21] By mid-September he was back in Vienna. The third act of *Fierabras* was finished on 26 September, and the overture on 2 October. Meanwhile Weber had arrived for the production of *Euryanthe*. Kupelwieser's resignation was a setback, but it was not thought that this would involve more than perhaps a postponement of the opening of *Fierabras*. On 12 November Schubert was reported to be making real progress at last towards recovery, and at the end of the month was able to assure Schober that his health was firmly restored at last. The statement was true, up to a point. His creative powers were unimpaired, and his greatest compositions still lay ahead. But his health was permanently affected; he was to suffer from the secondary symptoms of the disease— headaches, sickness, aching bones, nausea, and giddiness—for the rest of his life.

Schubert formed a poor opinion of *Euryanthe*, which lacked, he thought, the tenderness and intimacy of *Freischütz*, and also its tunefulness. Significantly, it was Weber's conscious attempt to adapt his style to the needs of grand opera which he criticized. He did not see the point of the large masses of sound and the huge climaxes. Unfortunately, he made the mistake of expressing his views too frankly, and this did not do his own cause any good when the 'Romantic Play with music', *Rosamunde, Fürstin von Zypern*, reached the stage of the Theater an der Wien in December. The author was the Dresden poetess Helmina von Chézy, whom Weber had chosen to write the libretto of *Euryanthe*. In her reminiscences she described the circumstances thus:

> A young friend of mine named Kupelwieser, brother of the celebrated painter, asked me for a dramatic piece for which Schubert intended to write the music. A beautiful girl whom Kupelwieser loved, Fräulein Neumann, an actress at the Theater an der Wien, was to have the play for her benefit . . . Schubert's magnificent music was appreciated and was crowned with thunderous applause. But the story was simply not suitable. . . . Moreover, Carl Maria von Weber had fallen out with Schubert . . . who had done nothing worse than express his opinion of *Euryanthe* in his frank Viennese way.[22]

Rosamunde opened on 20 December 1823, was ridiculed by the critics as a farrago of nonsense, and was taken off after a single repeat

---

[21] Docs, p. 286.   [22] Memoirs, p. 259.

performance. The play has disappeared. Schubert's music, however, won praise from the first, and ironically it has achieved a sort of immortality denied to all the composer's more serious operatic scores. The piece served its purpose. It was hastily cobbled together to provide a first-night benefit for Emilie Neumann, who sang the title role, and she was lucky to have a genius like Schubert to give the occasion a place in the history books.

Helmina von Chézy later claimed to have written the book in five days, and signs are not wanting that Schubert was also in a hurry. Instead of writing a new overture, he took over the one he had written for *Alfonso und Estrella*. He made the same musical idea serve both for the first Entr'acte and the ballet music which followed, and borrowed some themes from earlier works for the B flat Entr'acte in Act III. The final ballet obviously derives from the same ideas as the 'Air Russe' (better known as No. 3 of the *Moments Musicaux*) which had already been published. These orchestral pieces reveal Schubert's melodic gift and feeling for instrumental colour at their best, and are often heard. But it is the vocal pieces which made the biggest impression at the original performances, and it is a pity that they are not heard more often nowadays. The Shepherds' Chorus and the Huntsmen's Chorus were enthusiastically received, and prompted Schwind to observe that they would put Weber in the shade. The Chorus of Spirits (No. 5), for male voices accompanied by horns and trombones, is a splendidly atmospheric piece. These vocal numbers were the first to be published, by Leidesdorf in the 1820s; the orchestral pieces had to wait till the 1860s. It was owing to the enthusiasm and tenacity of George Grove that the band parts, which had been stowed away after the 1823 performances, were eventually discovered. The piece we know today as the 'Rosamunde Overture' has no connection either with von Chézy's play, or with Schubert's incidental music, but is the overture to Schubert's earlier opera *Die Zauberharfe* under an assumed name.

Rosamunde marked the end of Schubert's practical involvement with the opera house. Disillusioned at last, he was to turn his attention to chamber music and to 'grand symphony'. But before we leave the climacteric year 1823, we must take note of the greatest and most original work of these middle years, the song cycle *Die schöne Müllerin* (The Fair Maid of the Mill), on which he worked intermittently during the summer and autumn.

The chronology is not altogether clear. There is a well-documented tradition that Schubert worked on his miller songs while in hospital in Vienna. If so, he must, if our assumptions are correct, have made a start in May or June. There is an autograph draft of 'Eifersucht und Stolz' (Jealousy and Pride), No. 15 in the cycle, dated October 1823; and at the end of November, in a letter to Schober, Schubert declared that he had written nothing since finishing *Fierabras* 'except a few miller songs'.[23] The inference is that the cycle was still not quite complete but if so, it must have been finished before the end of the year, or very soon after, for the publication of the work was announced by Sauer and Leidesdorf in February 1824.

The idea of a song cycle had been in Schubert's mind for years, possibly ever since the publication of Beethoven's *An die ferne Geliebte* (To the Distant Beloved) in 1816. In 1818 he had experimented with an extended song in discrete sections (on the Beethoven model) in his setting of Mayrhofer's *Einsamkeit*, and in the intervening years he had been attracted by Friedrich von Schlegel's *Abendröte* (Sunsets) sequence, and by Mayrhofer's *Heliopolis*. But when, sometime in the spring of 1823, he came across the poems of Wilhelm Müller (1794–1827) in a collection called the 'Posthumous Papers of a Travelling Hornplayer', he knew that he had found what he had been searching for. The poems are written for the voice, and combine the lyrical power of folksong with the sophisticated appeal of *Sehnsucht*.

The cycle called 'The Fair Maid of the Mill' was published at Dessau in 1821, but it had its origins in a party game played by a group of young intellectuals in Berlin some years earlier. This took the form of an elaborate charade, in which each player was given his own permanent part in the drama, and was expected to write his own part. As we have seen, the reading parties organized by the Schubertians were run on much the same lines. It is fashionable to dismiss the story of 'The Fair Maid of the Mill' as a trivial tale of a feckless youth and a fickle maid, which Schubert immortalized by his genius. But to do this is to undervalue both Müller's talent for memorable verse, and the significance of the story, which had a long and respectable ancestry stretching back into the eighteenth century. Paisiello's *La Molinara* and Goethe's mill romances were only the best-known examples of that long tradition.

Schubert adapted the poems to suit his own purpose, which was more serious, and less consciously detached and ironic, than Müller's. He omitted the verse prelude and epilogue, left out three of the poems, and emphasized with his music the allegorical elements in the story so as to make of it what I have elsewhere called 'a parable of the doom that waits on innocence in an evil world'.[24] The love of the young miller has two moments of triumph, one in 'Mein', where he mistakenly believes that his love can find fulfilment on this earth, and one in 'Trockne Blumen', where he realizes that it can only be fulfilled in death (Ex. 24).

Because there are eight strophic songs in the cycle, and several others which are modified strophic in form, it has sometimes been claimed that it represents a reversion to 'primitive models'. But there is nothing primitive about 'Ungeduld' (Impatience) or 'Die liebe Farbe' (The Favourite Colour); and as for 'Wohin?' (Whither?), 'Tränenregen' (Shower of

[23] Docs, p. 301.
[24] John Reed, '*Die schöne Müllerin* Reconsidered', ML, vol. lix, Oct., 1978, pp. 411–19.

Ex. 24

dann Blüm - lein al - le her - aus, her - aus! der

Mai ist kom - men, der Win - ter ist aus.

Tears), 'Pause' (Interlude), and 'Trockne Blumen' (Withered Flowers),
they show Schubert's mastery of lyrical movement in all its expressive
power. The sense of impassioned utterance, of subjective feeling, for
which he had striven since his early years, informs the whole cycle.

Die schöne Müllerin was published by Sauer and Leidesdorf in five
books—not four, as Schubert had intended—in 1824. The first two
books appeared in February and March, but Leidesdorf took his time
over the remainder, which were not published till August. By that time
Schubert was at Zseliz with the Esterházy family, and unable to attend
to the proofs, which were left for his brother Ferdinand to deal with. As
a result, the first edition is full of mistakes and ambiguities, not all of
which are easily resolved. The cycle was dedicated to Karl, Freiherr von
Schönstein, whom Schubert had met at Zseliz in 1818, and who became
an enthusiastic advocate of the songs.

The song cycle is the crowning achievement of four years, from the
beginning of 1820 to the end of 1823, which had been devoted almost
entirely to dramatic works and to vocal music. During these prosperous
and dynamic years, when his inventive powers were most attracted to
original forms, he wrote many small keyboard pieces, mostly dances and

characteristic miniatures, some minor liturgical works, the symphonic sketches of 1821, and two magnificent works of astonishing originality in traditional forms, the *Quartettsatz* of December 1820 and the 'Unfinished' Symphony of November 1822. But there are no chamber works, no complete symphonies, concert overtures, or string quartets. The legacy of these operatic years does, however, include two keyboard works of major importance, the 'Wanderer' Fantasie, and the Sonata in A minor D784 of February 1823. This last work marks a big advance. The dramatic and lyrical elements are nicely balanced; the slow movement shows in wonderfully original form that outer serenity with an undercurrent of disruptive emotion which was to recur so often in Schubert's mature work; and the Finale, with its scherzo-like main theme and lyrical episodes, makes an effective conclusion. The work has a dark Romantic tone and a dynamic thrust which is new in Schubert's piano sonatas. But it is in three movements only. He was not to return to conventional four-movement form till 1824, after a gap of seven years.

7

Poetry and disillusion (1824)

By the turn of the year the Schubert circle was in a sad state of disarray. The triumvirate of the arts which had disported itself at Atzenbrugg, and at the reading parties in Vienna, was now widely dispersed. Schober was in Breslau, where his plan to devote his talents to the drama had not, it seems, been received with universal acclamation. Leopold Kupelwieser was on his way to Rome in company with a Russian aristocrat, Alex von Beresin, whom we met in the last chapter as the friend and patron of Peter Köppen. Kupelwieser had entered upon this expedition with some reluctance, since it meant parting with his fiancée as well as with his friends, but the prospect of an extended tour of Italy, with all expenses paid, was not to be spurned. Spaun was still attending to his official duties in Linz. Of the inner circle of Schubert's friends, only Schwind and Bruchmann remained in Vienna; and as for Schubert himself, he was soon to commit himself to a further period of service with the Esterházy family, which would keep him in Zseliz throughout the summer months.

Moreover, the circle was torn by conflicting loyalties and intrigues. Schubert's illness, and Schober's absence, seem to have taken the heart out of it. The twice-weekly reading parties had been revived at Mohn's in November, but the membership had been infiltrated by the hearties, whom Schwind referred to as 'our billiard-playing fraternity'.[1] In December Schwind was on the point of resigning, because the meetings were wholly taken up with money matters and practical jokes. Even Bruchmann had to admit that things were no longer what they were; at the Schubertiads it was tacitly felt that 'we are no longer as sound at the core as we used to be'. The reading parties struggled on through the winter in spite of internal tensions, only to be finally wound up in March 1824.[2] Schubertiads were few and far between. On 11 November Schubert was well enough to attend a musical party at Bruchmann's, at which Vogl sang gloriously, so Bruchmann reported to Kupelwieser, and toasts were drunk to absent friends. But only one other such gathering is reported that winter, and though Schubert's indisposition must have

---

[1] Docs, p. 305. [2] Docs, pp. 302, 303, 304, 305.

played a part in this, personal feelings were also involved. Relations between Schubert and Bruchmann were cool. Bruchmann, having got himself engaged to the daughter of a highly placed master-of-the-horse, and being urged by his father to settle down to the serious business of life, had returned to his law studies. Schubert complained, in a letter to Schober, that 'he seems to conform to the ways of the world, and thereby already he loses his halo, which in my judgment consisted in his steadfast disregard for all worldly considerations'.[3]

Schober also bears some responsibility for the general decline of the circle. For some time he had been conducting a secret affair with Bruchmann's sister Justina, in which Schwind acted as go-between. Though Bruchmann was aware of what was going on, the affair was kept from Justina's parents, presumably because of Schober's permissive views and self-indulgent life style. The affair caused a deep rift in the circle, in which Schubert and Schwind sided with Schober.

One consequence of the dispersal of the circle is that we are not short of information about the matter. There is a regular correspondence between Schwind and Schober, and another between Kupelwieser and his betrothed, a warm-hearted and intelligent young woman called Johanna Lutz. Schubert's own letters to his friends, and to his family, are unusually frank and serious in tone. Many of these letters have survived, giving us a much fuller picture of events and attitudes than we could otherwise expect. There are many references, for instance, to the state of Schubert's health. After his return from Upper Austria in September 1823 there had been a general disposition among his friends to believe that his complete recovery was only a matter of time. That must have been his own hope and belief too, for he was able to assure Schober in his letter of 30 November that 'my health, thank God, is firmly restored at last'. On New Year's Eve he was well enough to attend the party at Mohn's, though closely attended by his medical adviser, Dr Bernhardt. But in January the reports of friends take on a more cautious tone. Schubert is 'fairly well' (22 January) or 'almost completely well' (7 January), but in constant communication with his doctors. In February, Schwind reports that he had been put on a strict diet and confined to his room, a treatment which seems to have done him good, at least temporarily. He gave up the wig he had been wearing to conceal his shaven head, and Schwind reported (6 March) that he was much better, though still on a diet. But in April there are renewed complaints of aching bones, and of his inability to sing or play the piano. All these comments and reports are allusive and circumstantial, but their total import is not to be denied. Schubert was suffering from the secondary effects of his illness, and was to do so from time to time for the rest of his life.[4]

On the last day of March he opened his heart to Kupelwieser in a long

---

[3] Docs, p. 300.   [4] Docs, pp. 319, 324, 331, 342, 343.

and unusually serious letter, confessing that he was 'the most wretched and unhappy creature in the world'.

> Think of a man whose health will never be right again, and who in sheer despair over this always makes things worse instead of better. Think of a man, I say, whose brightest hopes have come to nothing; for whom the happiness of love and friendship have nothing to offer but, at the best, pain; whose passion for beauty (at least the sort that inspires) threatens to forsake him. I ask you, is he not a miserable, unhappy being?—'My peace is gone, my heart is sore, I shall find it never, nevermore.' I may well sing this every day now, for every night, when I go to bed, I hope I may not wake again, and every morning only recalls yesterday's grief.[5]

Yet such is the resilience of genius, that out of his despair came a whole series of instrumental masterpieces. The first four months of the year were among the most productive of his life. In the same letter to Kupelwieser, after recalling the failure of his operas, the collapse of the reading parties, and the lost happiness of the Atzenbrugg days, he went on: 'So far as songs are concerned, I have not done much that is new, but I have tried my hand at several instrumental things, for I wrote two quartets for violins, viola and cello, and an Octet, and I intend to write another quartet and generally speaking to pave my way to grand symphony in this way.'

This represented a deliberate change of direction. The break with the opera house was complete. For four years he had devoted his time and talents to the stage, and it had brought him nothing but failure and disappointment. Now he would follow in Beethoven's footsteps and concentrate on chamber music and grand symphony. He had at some time promised to write incidental music for a dramatic fairy tale by J. G. Seidl, a popular Viennese journalist and poet, and had been given the script. But the memory of *Rosamunde*'s fate was too bitter. When he left Vienna in May for Zseliz he left the script behind, taking with him instead some borrowed scores of Mozart's string quintets. Ferdinand sent the libretto on to him in July, together with an early edition of the Bach preludes and fugues, but Seidl's urgent appeals for the score were left unanswered.[6]

The year 1824 was not only a change of direction so far as composition was concerned; it represented also a turning away from the pursuit of public acclaim, a retirement into private and family life. Significantly, when disaster struck, Schubert returned from the inner city to the schoolhouse in the Rossau. The decision must have been motivated to some extent by the need for economy; the services of fashionable doctors like Schäffer and Bernhardt did not come cheap. But it was also a return to the security of home and family. It has sometimes been suggested that Schubert's illness must have widened the breach between him

[5] Docs, p. 339.   [6] Docs, pp. 357, 359.

and his father. If so, there is no evidence of it in their surviving correspondence. On the contrary, they seem to have kept in close touch during Schubert's absence in Zseliz, and though Franz's letters home have not survived, his father's letter of 14 August is written in affectionate terms. There are no reproaches, only tactful reminders about Schubert's social obligations and many expressions of natural affection. As for Schubert and his brother Ferdinand, trouble seems to have drawn them closer together.[7]

In April Count Esterházy left Vienna with his family to spend the summer as usual as Zseliz. Schubert, however, delayed his departure until 25 May, for reasons which we can only conjecture. Among them perhaps was the desire not to miss Beethoven's public concert on 7 May, at which the Choral Symphony, and movements of the Missa Solemnis, were given their first performance. Six years had elapsed since Schubert was last at Zseliz, and circumstances now dictated that he should be treated as a guest rather than a hired employee. This time he was allowed his own room in the castle, took his meals with the family, and was given a salary of 100 florins a month. The young countesses had of course grown up in the meantime. Marie, now 21, was already an accomplished pianist, and Karoline an impressionable eighteen-year-old. With the help of Karl von Schönstein's excellent baritone voice a vocal quartet could be mustered for the evening's musical entertainment. One September morning at breakfast, so Schönstein relates, the Countess Rosine showed Schubert a poem of La Motte Fouqué's which had taken her fancy, and suggested he might set it as a vocal quartet. Schubert took the verses away, pleased with the idea, and set to work. By evening the thing was finished, and tried out with Schubert himself at the piano. The following evening the individual parts were ready, and a more polished performance was possible. This piece, called 'Gebet' (Prayer) D815, is a substantial work of some fourteen pages, and one of Schubert's best partsongs (Ex. 25). The autograph remained in the possession of the Esterházy family for many years before they allowed it to be published. As Schönstein noted, Schubert revelled in this sort of challenge: he could 'shake the most glorious things out of his sleeve'.[8]

Under the influence of such day to day contact with genius, a kind of *amitié amoureuse* seems to have developed during the summer between Schubert and the young Countess Karoline. One imagines it to have been a kind of mutual attraction, no more and no less, between two unhappy people, each susceptible to the ennobling power of music. The composer's feelings for the ideal and the unattainable found a focus in the young girl, while her poetic instincts found fulfilment in his music. The relationship could never have been anything but entirely platonic, and that perhaps was its value and importance to both of them. Schubert's

---

[7] Docs, p. 367.   [8] Memoirs, p. 102.

Ex. 25

Ex. 25 cont.

reference to the 'attractions of a certain star' in a letter to Schwind sums it all up, for a star is by its nature beautiful, remote, and unattainable.[9]

Schubert's letters from Zseliz show him in chastened mood. Writing to Schober in September, he reflects that unhappiness must be the lot of every sensible person in a miserable world. 'If only we were together, you, Schwind, Kuppel and I, any misfortune would seem to me but a trivial matter; but here we are, separated, each in a different corner, and that is what makes me unhappy. I want to exclaim with Goethe: "Who will bring back one hour of that sweet time?".' But there is more in his mood than a lament for lost happiness. He encloses with this letter to Schober some verses he had written entitled 'Klage an das Volk!' (Complaint to the People), in which he inveighs against the triviality and subservience of the age. 'The idle time, which hinders the fulfilment of all greatness, destroys me too. Even golden verse is foolishly mocked by the people, no longer attentive to its powerful message. Only by the gift of sacred art can we still image forth the strength and achievements of former times, allay the pain which can never be reconciled with fate.' Schubert felt deeply, as Beethoven did, the decline in standards of taste and the failure of liberal principles which marked the 1820s in Vienna. The prosperous middle classes, finding themselves free to exploit their artistic tastes, but denied all political power, seemed prepared to settle for a cosy accommodation with Metternich's absolutism. The spirit of Biedermeier was in the ascendant, and Schubert was reflecting here on the position of the artist in a hostile and unsympathetic world.[10]

Characteristically, this sombre mood found expression in a vein of deep poetic feeling. The A minor String Quartet of February is, in emotional terms, a Romantic excursion to the land of lost content, taking as its text the line of Schiller which Schubert had set in November 1819: 'Beauteous world, where art thou? Return again, fair springtime of Nature.' (See Ex. 19.) Eight years had elapsed since Schubert's last complete quartet, the one in E major of 1816, and the contrast between that work and the A minor Quartet D884 could hardly be more striking. The former seems entirely classical in style and form, looking back to Mozart. The latter retains the traditional form, it is true, even to the title of 'Menuetto' for the third movement. But in style and idiom it belongs to a different world, the emotional world of Romantic song. So much is clear from the opening bars. Hitherto Schubert had always moulded his first subjects on short dynamic motifs, suitable for development, reserving his longer and more lyrical ideas for his second subjects. Here the Allegro ma non troppo begins (like a song) with a two-bar introduction, followed by a song-like theme eight bars long which moves (*pp*) smoothly and introspectively first from tonic minor to dominant major, and finally to tonic major (see Ex. 26a). The linking material is based on

---

[9] Docs, p. 370.   [10] Docs, pp. 374–5.

Ex. 26

(a)

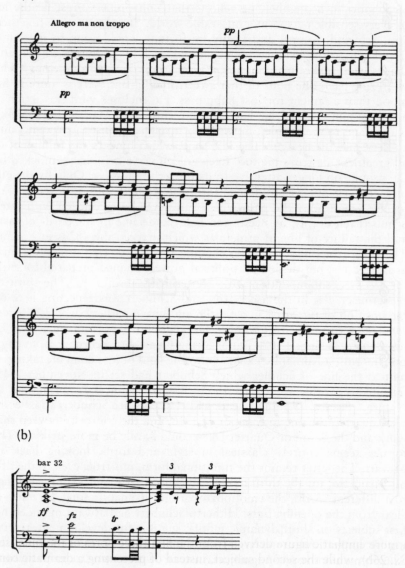

(b)

(c)

a more emphatic figure derived from the first three notes of the tune (see Ex. 26b), while the second subject, instead of presenting a dramatic contrast to the first, conforms to the same mood and movement (see Ex. 26c). In its unity of mood, the movement is quasi-monothematic; and though the first subject is heard complete five times in the course of it, and the second subject three times, neither of these tunes outstays it welcome.

For the Andante Schubert borrowed, or perhaps borrowed back, the tune he had used in the B flat Entr'acte of the *Rosamunde* music, as the basis for a set of variations in which the mood of wistful nostalgia is only briefly interrupted by a stormy excursion to E flat major. The Menuetto begins with a direct quote from his setting of Schiller's poem (see Ex. 19), while the Finale abandons the impetuous style of earlier quartets. Marked Allegro moderato, its deliberate 2/4 gait recalls the tempo giusto of the finale of the 'Trout' Quintet.

After its first performance, given by the Schuppanzigh Quartet on 14 March, Schwind accurately diagnosed its special quality. Writing to Schober in Breslau he said: 'Schubert's quartet was performed, rather slowly in his opinion, but clearly and tenderly. As a whole it is very smooth, but in such a way that the tune stays in one's head, as with songs, all feeling and thoroughly expressive.'

Schubert envisaged the A minor work as the first of a group of three quartets, and it was published as Op. 29 No. 1. Yet the Quartet in D minor ('Death and the Maiden') had to wait till 1831 for publication, and there is no clear record of any public performance in the composer's lifetime. It was written in March, immediately after the completion of the A minor Quartet. The work's familiar title is not on the autograph, but its aptness was recognized from the first, both because the whole quartet does seem to be, in a metaphorical sense, about death, and because its emotional centre is the Andante con moto, a wonderful set of variations on a harmonic sequence taken from the second half of the Claudius song written in February 1817. Here there is no trace of sentimentality or self-pity, only a clear-eyed searching for the beauty that lies beyond tears. The lyrical and the dynamic elements are held in balance, both within movements and between them. The hard-driven opening Allegro, defiant and resolute in tone, ends in a final page of pure poetry. Even in the Presto finale the *con forza* second subject provides an appropriate foil to the headlong career of the main theme. In popular estimation the D minor Quartet has always ranked as Schubert's greatest, and in this case time seems to have upheld the verdict.

To the first three months of the year belong also two other instrumental works and an important group of songs. The Variations for flute and piano D802 were almost certainly written for Ferdinand Bogner, a prominent member of the Philharmonic Society (he married into the Fröhlich family) and an expert flautist. The work consists of an Introduction, Theme, and seven variations on the tune of 'Trockne Blumen' from *Die schöne Müllerin* cycle, the last an extended finale in march form. Schubert seems to have used the commission mainly as an opportunity for technical display on the part of the soloist. But there is something incongruous about the whole idea, and much of the work seems wholly out of sympathy with the song, though its musicality is beyond question. It is sometimes played as a violin and piano duo.

The Octet in F for strings and woodwind, however, is a quite different story. It was commissioned by Ferdinand Count Troyer, the steward
of the Archduke Rudolf, and a good amateur clarinettist; and it was
modelled, at his suggestion, on Beethoven's Septet, Op. 20. It closely
resembles that work in form and instrumentation, though it surpasses its
model in a variety of mood and depth of poetic feeling. To Beethoven's
four string instruments Schubert added a second violin; the three wind
instruments (clarinet, bassoon and horn) are the same. The six movements in general alternate between quick and slow, and the two outside
movements both have slow introductions which play an important part.
The Octet is quintessential Schubert. It is written in the spirit of the classical divertimento and draws equally upon the vernacular and the classical tradition, and with equal mastery. The Trio of No. 5, for instance,
elevates the folk-dance to the level of great music (Ex. 27). The variation movement (No. 4), based on an aria from Schubert's 1815 opera *Die
Freunde von Salamanka*, is less impressive, but the Adagio is full of lyrical and contrapuntal magic, sunlight, and shadow. No work bears more
eloquent testimony to Schubert's universality, his facility within a wide
range of styles.

Ex. 27

109

The sense of the darkness within, an awareness of the abyss which seems to haunt Schubert's imagination from 1822 onwards, and which obtrudes even in the most serene of his slow movements, finds open expression in many of his songs, and not least in the four Mayrhofer songs of March 1824. Schubert had written no Mayrhofer songs since 1822, and his name is conspicuously absent from the list of subscribers to the collection of his friend's poems which appeared early in 1824. For reasons which are not clear, there had been no contact between them. Now, perhaps in an attempt to make amends, Schubert chose four texts, three of which chimed in with his disenchanted mood. 'Abendstern' (Evening Star) is an apostrophe to the star of love, remote and unattainable, which 'sows no seed, sees no fruit, and bears its grief alone'. The song's insistent pulse—three quavers followed by a dotted crotchet—symbolizes the star's enigmatic self-sufficiency. 'Auflösung' (Dissolution) is a rhapsodic address to the setting sun, as a symbol of the transitory nature of the physical universe and the immortality of art: 'dissolve, world, and never more disturb the sweet ethereal choirs'. Schubert's setting is Wagnerian in conception. The continuous sounding of the tonality of G major is orchestrated with right-hand arpeggios of a distinctive ingenuity, and with dynamic levels which range from *pp* to *fffz*. The song is a tour de force, full of mystical fire. 'Der Sieg' (Victory) D805 is comparatively unknown, but undeservedly so, for it is one of the most positive and direct statements of Mayrhofer's longing for that 'unclouded life, so pure, and deep, and clear', in which the spirit is released from the bonds of the body, and the imagination is renewed. Schubert's setting is a solemn hymn with a more resolute, apocalyptic middle section. These, with 'Gondelfahrer' (Gondolier), are the only solo songs which can with certainty be ascribed to 1824, though it is possible that others, for example Schiller's 'Dithyrambe' and Goethe's second 'Suleika' song, may belong there. There is no doubt, however, that 1824 is the least productive year of all, so far as songs are concerned, a fact which must reflect Schubert's preoccupation with instrumental music.

As in 1818, Zseliz offered a special stimulus to the composition of piano duets. The young countesses were privileged that summer to participate in a series of original masterpieces. To June belong the two works, each of which in its own way bears witness to Schubert's admiration for Beethoven. The so-called 'Grand Duo' Sonata (Schubert himself referred to it simply as a 'grand sonata for four hands') is a four-movement work, so generous in its proportions, symphonic in style, and so full of orchestral effects, that many Schubert lovers, from Schumann to Donald Tovey, have been tempted to regard it as a symphony in disguise. In a sense they were right. The 'Grand Duo' is clearly written as a 'public' work; its scale, the thematic allusions to Beethoven's second symphony, the symphonic nature of the themes and the epic impersonal tone, all suggest that Schubert was deliberately 'working his way toward grand symphony' when he wrote it. But equally clearly it was not intended as a symphony, still less as the grand symphony he had determined to write. The work has been orchestrated by Joachim and others, but the results, however interesting, fail to carry full conviction.

The Variations on an Original Theme, Op. 35, on the other hand, are idiosyncratic and fully Schubertian, a private work in spite of the traditional form, and in spite of the fact that it found an early sponsor (a certain Count Anton Berchtold) and was published in 1825. The influence of Beethoven is still felt, but only in the pulse, which is haunted by the marching rhythm of the Allegretto of Beethoven's A major Symphony. Schubert's variation movements sometimes sound unadventurous, but not this one. Here his command of tonality and power of melodic transformation, the variety of mood and *Bewegung*, constantly delight and surprise. The work is beautifully written for the medium and belongs, with the great works of 1818 and 1828, among the classics of duet literature.

Much the same can be said of two other four-hand pieces, though the chronology of one of them is doubtful. The Six Grand Marches with Trios, Op. 40, published by Sauer and Leidesdorf in 1825, were almost certainly written at Zseliz, though the autograph is lost, and an earlier date is possible. They are Schubert's finest set of marches. Again the variety of mood achieved within this familiar form is striking. The elegiac No. 5, a funeral march worthy of rank beside Chopin's, stands alongside the brisk and sprightly No. 2, and the military pomp of No. 4. *The Divertissement à l'hongroise* stands alone as Schubert's only conscious essay in the popular Hungarian style. The germ of the work was a short piece called 'Hungarian Melody', which he wrote on 2 September 1824. Based on the familiar stamping rhythm of the Hungarian dance, it was used later as the basis of an extended finale for the *Divertissement*.

The complete work is in three movements, the outer ones unified rhythmically, and by a prevailing G minor/major tonality, the middle one a short march in C minor. This ingenious scheme gives the work the scale and weight of a sonata coupled with the appeal of those 'characteristic' dances which were coming into fashion. Some critics, influenced perhaps by the popularity of the *Divertissement* during the nineteenth century, have condemned it for its 'triviality' and rhythmic monotony. It is not surprising, for instance, that Mendelssohn, with his sophisticated taste and devotion to the classical tradition, should have been repelled by it. It remains true, however, that the *Divertissement* is a splendid vindication of Schubert's respect for the vernacular tradition, and his ability to use it for his own purpose. The work was dedicated to the opera singer Katharina von Lászny, and published as Op. 54 by Artaria in April 1826.

A notebook of Schubert's attributed to 1824 consists for the most part of epigrammatic observations on life and art, and gives us an insight into the reflective and introspective side of his personality. Like the correspondence with Schober, it reveals a man at odds with the world, and scornful of its values. 'Enviable Nero!' he exclaims, 'You were strong enough to destroy a loathsome people to the strains of strings and song.' And again: 'There is no one who understands the joy and pain of others. We always believe that we are coming together, and always we move only side by side. What torture it is, for those who recognize this!' But this strange document also bears witness to his belief that the imagination is nourished by adversity, for 'pain sharpens the understanding and strengthens the mind'. The artist, he insisted, should not concentrate on his art and shut out the rest of his life. 'One kind of beauty should inspire mankind throughout life, it is true; but the glow of that inspiration should illuminate everything else.'[11]

The glow that illuminates his own work in 1824 comes from that vein of poetry he had found in the two great string quartets of February and March. It illuminates the duet masterpieces of the summer, and even the group of six linked *Deutsche* D820 which he wrote in October. Arranged in two groups, each consisting of a main dance and two trios, this minor masterpiece is among the most poetic of all his keyboard dances. So too are the four *Ländler* for piano duet (D814), written in July.

In mid-October Schubert returned to Vienna in the company of Karl von Schönstein. Schubert was suffering from one of his intermittent attacks of gastritis and begged leave to travel with him, though he was not due to return till November. How far this story should be taken at face value, or whether it should be explained, in part at least, by Schubert's longing for Vienna after several months in the country, it is difficult to say. It may be significant, however, that he did not return to the inner city, but went back to his room in the schoolhouse at the Rossau, where he lived until the following spring.[12]

The final months of the year were uneventful. The social life of the circle was at a low ebb. There are no records of Schubertiads until the new year, and the reading parties had ceased to be. *Der kurze Mantel* (The Short Cloak), Seidl's musical play, duly appeared at the Theater an der Wien on 6 October, but not with Schubert's music. The attempt to interest Weber in *Alfonso* had failed, and Schubert's other operas were forgotten. In November Schubert wrote a sonata for piano and arpeggione, or bowed guitar, an instrument newly invented by J. G. Staufer, who probably also commissioned the sonata. The instrument failed to catch on, and the sonata (D821) is now usually heard as a sonata for piano and viola or cello.

[11] Docs, pp. 336–7.
[12] Memoirs, pp. 101–2. See also Docs, pp. 380–1 for Schönstein's account of the journey home.

One publishing event calls for notice, because it points towards the future. On 11 December Leidesdorf announced the appearance of his second 'Album musical' for Christmas and the New Year. It included two contributions from Schubert, the Kosegarten song 'Die Erscheinung' (The Apparition) D229, and a piano piece called 'Les Plaintes d'un Troubadour', which is more familiar to us as No. 6 of the *Moments Musicaux*, Op. 94. The history of these characteristic keyboard pieces in ternary form is of interest and importance, for they were to father a whole literature of Romantic music. They seem to have been invented by the Bohemian composer Tomášek (1774–1850), who published the first examples in 1807. His favourite pupil, Jan Voříšek (or Worzischek), took the idea with him when he went to Vienna to complete his studies. There he met Kiesewetter and other members of the Schubert circle, and in 1818 accepted the post of conductor to the Philharmonic Society. He met Schubert at the house of Ignaz Sonnleithner, and though their relations do not seem to have been close, there is little doubt that the pieces which Schubert wrote for Leidesdorf's album (another had been included in the first edition of 1823) owed something to Voříšek's example. If so, history owes him a special debt of gratitude, for Schubert was to find in the ternary form and the ostinato rhythms of these evocative pieces a splendid medium for his own genius.

8

Grand symphony (1825–6)

The records of Schubert's social and creative life during the ensuing winter months are curiously thin. There are no major works between October 1824 and April 1825. Until February, when he moved to new quarters in a house next door to Schwind's lodgings, he remained quietly at home in the Rossau, firmly refusing social engagements and taking afternoon walks with his brothers. There Schwind visited him regularly, and by dint of much persuasion got him to come out and meet Anna Hönig, the daughter of a formidable academic lawyer, with whom Schwind had fallen in love. But Schubert was in an obstinately unsociable mood, and his indifference to the social conventions on one such occasion upset the volatile Schwind, who was naturally anxious to impress the Hönig family.[1] On 29 January the first of a weekly series of Schubertiads was held at the house of Josef Witteczek, the son-in-law of that Professor Watteroth in whose honour Schubert's *Prometheus* cantata had been performed, but we do not find Schubert's name among the list of guests. Nor is there any mention of the usual New Year celebrations.

This is not the only circumstantial evidence we have that Schubert's health had again taken a turn for the worse during these winter months. In his biography of the composer Kreissle refers to the 'well-authenticated fact' that the song 'Der Einsame' (The Recluse) was written, appropriately in a way, while Schubert was a patient in hospital.[2] The song appeared as a supplement to the Vienna *Zeitschrift für Kunst* in March 1825, and it is generally supposed that it was written not later than January. If so, the inference is inescapable that Schubert spent some part of that month in hospital. 'Der Einsame' is one of two fine songs written to texts by Karl Lappe. How Schubert came upon the poems is not known, for they were not published till 1836, but whatever the source, he made of 'Der Einsame' and the companion piece, 'Im Abendrot' (Sunset Glow), masterpieces of subjective feeling in contrasted moods.

Our main source of information on these matters is Schwind. On 14 February he wrote to Schober:

[1] Docs. p. 424–5.   [2] Kreissle, I, p. 317.

Schubert is well, and busy again after a certain inertia . . . We meet daily, and so far as I can I share his whole life with him. . . . There is a Schubertiad at Enderes's every week; that is to say, Vogl sings. Apart from him the company consists of Witteczek, Esch, Schlechta, Gross, Riepl—a mixture of familiar faces only. The new Variations for four hands are something quite extraordinary. The theme is as grand as it is languid, as 'scientifically' correct—don't laugh—as it is free and noble. In eight variations these features are quite independently and vigorously treated, yet each one seems to be the theme over again. You would be astonished by the characterisation of the marches, and the unprecedented depth [*Innigkeit*] and loveliness of the trios. He is now doing songs.[3]

Schwind's description of the Schubertiads plainly implies that Schubert himself was unable to be present. Karl Enderes was a legal colleague of Witteczek's, and shared rooms with him. The variations, and the marches for four hands, are the ones written at Zseliz in the previous summer and autumn, while the songs referred to in the last sentence quoted may be the earliest Sir Walter Scott songs, possibly those from *The Legend of Montrose* (D830) and *The Pirate* (D831). But three important partsongs were also written about the turn of the year. 'Wehmut' (Melancholy), 'Ewige Liebe' (Eternal Love), and 'Flucht' (Flight) are for male voices, and they all aim to escape from the naïve *Gemütlichkeit* of the sociable partsong. It is significant that after the first public performance of 'Flucht' in March, one critic remarked that it was 'extremely difficult to perform'. The three works were published in October 1828 by Pennauer. Only one solo song can with certainty be ascribed to February, but it is an important one. 'Des Sängers Habe' (The Minstrel's Treasure) D832 is a setting of verses by Schubert's old schoolfriend, Franz von Schlechta. 'I can bear every loss, every misfortune', says the minstrel, 'so long as I can keep my zither, the symbol of my art and my genius.' Schubert translated the last verses from the third person to the first, as though to emphasize their application to himself, and wrote a strangely moving song, despairing, defiant, and triumphant by turns.

In February 1825, also, Schwind took Schubert to visit Eduard Bauernfeld, a promising young dramatist. The two men had met briefly at the house of Professor Weintridt in 1822. Bauernfeld was a keen musician, who had long admired Schubert's music, but had not previously been a member of the circle. On this occasion, however, they played duets together, and within a few weeks they were toasting each other in brotherhood. For the remaining years of the composer's life Bauernfeld's diary and reminiscences provide a valuable source of information about the life of the circle. Schubert, Schwind and Bauernfeld became regular companions in nightly visits to the inn and the coffee-house, though the association never had quite the intimacy and cohesion of that earlier

[3] Docs, p. 401.

triumvirate of the arts, Schubert, Schober and Kupelwieser, in Atzenbrugg days. But then the circle itself had changed character under the stress of personal quarrels and the demands of a career. In March the Schober–Justina affair came to a crisis, when Bruchmann decided to force the secret engagement between the two into the open. The air resounded with charges, counter-charges and recriminations, and the circle split down the middle. Schubert and Schwind cut themselves off from Bruchmann and refused to meet him. That level-headed, good-natured girl, Johanna Lutz, thought they had behaved like children. 'After all, it is none of their business', she wrote to her betrothed in Rome. 'If they don't like him, that is their affair. But their behaviour is childish. However, their affection and loyalty to Schober is nice.' She was very glad to report also to Kupelwieser that Schubert 'is now very busy and regular in his habits'.[4]

In the spring, while the circle disintegrated under the stress of these quarrels, Schubert devoted his time and energy to the composition of piano sonatas. The unfinished sonata in C major D840 and the sonata in A minor D845 are the first four-movement sonatas he had attempted since 1817. The autograph of the C major work, now sadly split up, is a first draft dated April 1825. The first two movements are pure Schubert both in style and in content, and the third is superb. The Trio is complete, and the Menuetto breaks off after 80 bars, when in sight of a return to the opening theme. So far, the work is undeniably both great and characteristic. But once again Schubert ran into trouble with the finale, a light-hearted rondo which lacks the weight to clinch the matter. He abandoned it after 272 not very inspired bars. The autograph was given by Ferdinand Schubert to Schumann in 1839, and was published by Whistling, of Leipzig, in 1861 with the misleading subtitle of *Reliquie* (Relic).

The autograph of the A minor sonata is lost, and it is not clear whether it preceded or followed the C major work, but it is safe to assume that it was finished before Schubert's departure for Steyr in mid-May, for he took it with him when he left. The opening Moderato (see Ex. 28(a)), like the similarly marked movement of the companion piece, exploits the composer's gift for melodic extension and elaboration. It begins with an arpeggio-based figure, which proceeds in familiar fashion from tonic minor to dominant major. A variant of the opening bars (see Ex. 28(b)) plays a leading role in the development and the coda. Its insistent tread has sinister implications, which are strikingly confirmed by its appearance in a song which is exactly contemporary, 'Totengräbers Heimweh' (Gravedigger's Longing). The unison theme is used as an accompaniment to the words 'Abandoned by all, cousin only to death, I wait at the brink, staring longingly into the grave'. Schubert can hardly

[4] Docs, p. 406.

Ex. 28

(a)

(b)

have been unaware of the significance of this self-quotation, which throws a fascinating light on his state of mind.

The Andante con moto is a splendid set of variations on a noble theme carrying the tune in the inner voices; it blossoms into lyrical triplets at the end very much in Beethoven's manner. The level is fully maintained in the third movement, this time very properly called Scherzo, with its Trio in F major. The Finale is another rondo, but here the movement is sustained by a powerful rhythmical impetus which culminates in repeated accented chords, hinting prophetically at the closing pages of the 'Great' C major Symphony.

The A minor Sonata was published by Pennauer early in 1826 as 'Première grande Sonate' and received a warm welcome from the discerning few. A review of the Leipzig *Allgemeine musikalische Zeitung* of 1 March 1826, the first extended public notice of a Schubert instrumental work, gave a detailed account of the piece, and linked it with 'the greatest and freest of Beethoven's sonatas'. It characterized the tone acutely as that of 'suppressed but sometimes violently erupting sombre passion, alternating with melancholy seriousness'.

The lyrical themes, expansive treatment, and poetic tone of these two great sonatas may be said to adapt the traditional form to the emotional world of Romantic song, and to point the way to the last three sonatas of 1828. Like the two string quartets of 1824, they mark the inception of what may be called, without misleading implications, Schubert's third period.

The summer months saw a re-enactment of the long holiday in Upper Austria which Schubert and Vogl had enjoyed in 1819. In mid-May Schubert left Vienna to join Vogl at Steyr, taking with him the manuscript of the A minor piano sonata, the songs from Scott's *The Lady of the Lake*, which he had just completed, and four-hand works for piano. He had always turned to the mountains for recuperation and peace of mind. Now he found also health, and the assurance that his genius was understood and greatly valued.

His letters home during this period are noteworthy for their zest and self-confidence, as he described the warm welcome he and Vogl received wherever they went. 'I find my compositions everywhere,' he wrote, 'especially at the monasteries of Florian and Kremsmünster, where with the aid of a gallant pianist I produced my four-handed Variations and marches with encouraging success.' Others remarked on his outgoing mood and self-assurance. At Linz he was just too late to meet his old friend Josef von Spaun, who had been sent off to a new post at Lemberg; but he stayed with Spaun's brother-in-law, Anton Ottenwalt, who reported: 'Schubert looks so well and strong, is so bright and relaxed, so genial and communicative, that one cannot but be sincerely delighted. By the way', he added, 'he had been working on a symphony in Gmunden, which is to be performed in Vienna this winter.' This was the

long-projected grand symphony. But before we come to that problematic work, it may be helpful to set out the course of events during this
memorable summer.[5]

Schubert arrived in Steyr on about 20 May, and stayed there with Vogl
for two weeks, renewing acquaintance with old friends, and visiting the
monastery at Kremsmünster nearby. Between 24 and 27 May there was
also an expedition to Linz, about 30 miles away, where he stayed with
Ottenwalt. Here there was a regular Schubert supporters' club, formally
constituted as the Linz Philharmonic Society in 1821. During Schubert's
convalescence in 1823 both he and Vogl had been enrolled as honorary
members; his songs, dances, and duet pieces were already widely known.
There was an especial welcome for the two artists at Steyregg Castle,
some five miles to the east, the home of Count Weissenwolf and his
musical wife Sophie, where regular Schubertiads were held; and at the
monastery of St Florian nearby.

On 4 June they left Steyr for the little town of Gmunden on Lake
Traun, where they stayed in the house of Ferdinand Traweger. There
the evenings were spent making music, while Schubert, enchanted by the
lakeside scenery, worked during the day on the first draft of his symphony. There were also musical parties at Ebenzweier Castle, three miles
away along the lakeside, where Therese Clodi, the eldest of four children, managed the house and estate on behalf of her blind father.
Schubert called her the 'lady of the lake', a graceful allusion to her
enthusiasm for Ellen's songs from Scott's poem. He wrote home:

> It was like being at home at Traweger's, very free and easy. With the arrival of
> Privy Councillor von Schiller, who is king of the whole Salzkammergut, we
> dined, Vogl and I, every day at his house, and made music there too. So we did
> at Traweger's. My new songs from Walter Scott's 'Lady of the Lake' especially
> were a great success. Much surprise was felt about my devoutness, which I have
> expressed in a hymn to the Holy Virgin; it seems to touch all hearts, and inspires
> a feeling of devotion. I believe the reason is that I never force myself to be
> devout, and never compose hymns or prayers or anything of the sort except
> when the mood takes me; but then it is usually the right and true devotion.

This is put a little strongly, perhaps, for his father's benefit, though it
is certainly true of Ellen's third song, the famous 'Ave Maria'. Later in
the same letter there is a striking passage which reflects the inner peace
he had found since leaving Vienna. He comments, jocularly but a little
unsympathetically perhaps, on Ferdinand's hypochondriac tendencies,
and exclaims: 'As though death were the worst thing that can happen to
us creatures! If he could only see these divine mountains and lakes, the
sight of which threatens to overwhelm and engulf us, he would not love
this petty human life so much, nor think it anything but great good fortune to be consigned to the earth's mysterious power to create new life.'[6]

[5] Docs, pp. 430, 435.   [6] Docs, pp. 434–7.

From Gmunden the friends returned to spend a week at Linz and visit Steyregg again. From 25 July to 15 August they were back at Steyr, providing an opportunity for Schubert to catch up with his correspondence. Then they set off on a spectacular three-day journey up to Bad Gastein via Kremsmünster, Neumarkt, and Salzburg. Schubert was so moved by this excursion into the heart of the Salzkammergut that he later began a detailed account of the journey for his brother Ferdinand. His travelogue is often vivid and revealing but, unfortunately, he left it unfinished. The visit to Gastein, which lasted almost three weeks, was the high point of the summer. There he continued to work on the symphony, finding in the sublimity of the mountains and the Salzbach Falls the inspiration he sought. There too he renewed acquaintance with Ladislaus Pyrker, the Patriarch of Venice, to whom his Op. 4 songs had been dedicated in 1821, and set two of his poems, 'Das Heimweh' (Homesickness) and 'Die Allmacht' (Omnipotence), the latter an apostrophe to the God revealed in Nature. He also wrote another piano sonata at Gastein, that in D major D850, more extrovert and dynamic than the two he had written in the spring, but equally Romantic in tone.

On 4 September Schubert and Vogl proceeded by easy stages back to Gmunden, where they arrived about 10 September. The second half of the month they spent at Steyr, and the first few days of October once more at Linz. After farewell parties at Steyregg and at Ottenwalt's the two friends went their different ways, Vogl to Italy, where he planned to spend the winter, and Schubert back to Vienna. He travelled in company with the pianist, Josef von Gahy, his favourite duet partner, and arrived home on or about 6 October.

The autograph score of the 'Great' C major Symphony, in the archive of the Philharmonic Society in Vienna, is a marvellously revealing document, from which it is obvious that the work was originally sketched in the form of a continuous outline score, the leading voices filled in in the appropriate places, leaving the detailed scoring to be completed later. Schubert was very careful and systematic about the preparation of his major scores, using different coloured inks for different phases of the work, and making extensive use of margins for corrections and additions. Moreover, a cursory examination of the autograph is enough to establish that the outer movements, and the Trio, must have undergone radical reconstruction, in the course of which some of the original folios have been discarded and others, of a different type, inserted in their place. Modern techniques for identifying and classifying different music papers make it possible to give tentative dates to these alterations, so that we can now see that the gestation period of the work stretched over many months, beginning in the summer of 1825 and probably extending into the spring or summer of 1826.

All this makes it difficult to understand why Grove's hypothesis of a missing 'Gastein' symphony was not seriously challenged for nearly one hundred years. But an aura of sanctity surrounds a dated autograph, and the date on the first page of the score (there is no title page) is—or seems to be—March 1828. Since this is so, Grove argued, the 'Great' C major must belong to the last year of the composer's life, and must be quite distinct from the symphony drafted in the summer of 1825, common-sense objections and stylistic evidence notwithstanding.

It is only in recent years that scholars have come to accept that there may be other explanations for the date; either that Schubert, for his own purposes, removed the original title page with its dedication to the Philharmonic Society and redated the work; or, that '1828' is a mis-reading of '1825' or even '1826'. Whatever the truth of this may be, the hypothesis of a missing 1825 symphony has now been discredited. The 'Great' C major Symphony is now seen as the culmination, in 1825 and 1826, of Schubert's long self-preparation for grand symphony, and as the realization of his lifelong ambition to write a great 'public' work com-parable with Beethoven's.

And what of the symphony itself? One way to characterize it is to say that it and the 'Unfinished' Symphony represent the two contrasted faces of his genius; the latter, in a minor key, intensely personal and dramatic, concise, emotionally and thematically homogeneous, its tone that of sombre passion constantly interrupted by violent explosions of feeling; the former in a major key, lyrical and discursive, externally rather than internally structured, proceeding in a series of extended paragraphs, some of which take on the scale almost of separate movements; and, except for the climax of the Andante con moto, markedly extrovert, aiming at celebration and sublimity. In short, the two works seem to sum up the contrast between the private and the public composer.

There are significant parallels between the 'Great' and the Choral Symphony of Beethoven, the first performance of which Schubert had heard in May 1824. Both works are retrospective in form, looking back to the classical four-movement symphony, but carrying the cumulative tension through to the end, so as to achieve the effect of catharsis. Both have the character of a summing-up. Just as the Ninth Symphony embodies in their final form ideas and ideals which had occupied Beethoven's mind for thirty years, so the themes and formal devices used in the 'Great' can almost all be traced back to Schubert's early years; to the symphonies, particularly the first three and the sixth, to the overtures 'in the Italian style' and to *Rosamunde*, and to the piano sonatas of 1825. What is different is the scale, and the sense of sublimity which per-vades the whole.

Both Beethoven's Ninth Symphony and Schubert's 'Great' C major seem to embody a philosophical message, but here the differences begin. Beethoven's message is quite explicit in the affirmation of his Finale; his commitment is to the ideals of peace, freedom, and the brotherhood of man, as expressed in Schiller's ode. Schubert's commitment is to the

Romantic doctrine of Nature as the vesture of God. It is implicit in the symphony, but explicit in the exactly contemporary song, 'Die Allmacht' to a text by Johann Ladislaus Pyrker, D852: 'Great is Jehovah the Lord, for heaven and earth proclaim his might'. It is a curious fact that in January 1826, when, it may be surmised, Schubert was still wrestling with the finale of his symphony, he wrote an elaborate choral setting of Pyrker's verses D875, the thematic material of which is closely related to that of the solo song. The autograph, which disappeared during the nineteenth century and was only rediscovered in 1952, is seventeen pages long, and consists of an extended Allegro maestoso and concluding fugue. The piece was abandoned unfinished, and if the quality of the fugue does not suggest that Schubert deprived us of a masterpiece, the scale of the work, and its close links with the symphony, are interesting in the light of Beethoven's choral finale, which must still have been fresh in Schubert's mind. It may not be altogether coincidental, either, that the development section of his finale begins with a woodwind theme which instantly recalls Beethoven's Ninth.

That instinctive feeling for wind tone which had been evident in Schubert's orchestration since his earliest years comes to full maturity in the 'Great' C major Symphony. The evocative writing for horns and trombones is justly famous, surpassing Beethoven, while the woodwind parts, especially in the inner movements, are a joy. Significantly, some of the happiest examples were the result of afterthoughts, as the autograph plainly shows.

Yet Schubert's musical personality is entirely his own. The C major Symphony is his greatest public work. It belongs to the conscious, esemplastic side of his genius, and does not, like the 'Unfinished', seem to emerge unbidden from subconscious levels of the imagination. None the less, it is *the* essential Schubert symphony, uniquely expressive of that belief in the unity of man and Nature for which he stood, and the first of the great Romantic symphonies.

The Piano Sonata in D major, also written at Gastein, is the second of the three sonatas to be published in the composer's lifetime. Instead of the withdrawn, contemplative lyricism of the C major and A minor sonatas it shows dynamic and extrovert brilliance, aptly embodied in the upward surge of the opening bars (Ex. 29). However, the sonata has a kind of dual personality. Florestan sets the tone for the work, and retains the upper hand in the opening Allegro and the Scherzo; but Eusebius keeps interrupting, and has the last word. For the sonata ends, like Beethoven's last sonata, with a whisper. This conjunction of poet and virtuoso is perhaps least successful in the Andante con moto, where it is not always easy to reconcile the legato line of the song-like theme with the elaborate rhythmic variations imposed upon it. The final Rondo is based on a dance tune in dotted rhythm, sometimes thought to be beneath the dignity of a piano sonata, but in fact just one more proof

Ex. 29

of Schubert's ability to enlist the vernacular style to serve his own purposes. The D major Sonata was published as Op. 53 in April 1826, and
dedicated to Karl Maria von Bocklet.

One must suppose that Schubert's main concern after his return to
Vienna was to revise and complete his symphony, for little else of importance seems to have been written during the last three months of the
year, except songs and compositions for piano duet. Of the songs of
1825, the most important are the settings of poems from the 'Verse
Journal' (*Poetisches Tagebuch*) of Ernst Schulze (1789–1817), whose
short and tragic life follows a familiar Romantic pattern, and the Walter
Scott songs. Schulze died of tuberculosis, like Keats, but his life had been
blighted earlier by the death of his beloved Cäcilie. His poems depict a
man overwhelmed by a sense of loss. Schubert found in them something
to match his own mood, and set them with a rhythmic and imaginative
power which anticipates *Winterreise*. 'Im Walde' (In the Forest) foreshadows 'Erstarrung' (Benumbed) in the later cycle; 'Lebensmut'
(Courage) anticipates 'Mut', and 'Tiefes Leid' (Deep Sorrow)
'Wasserflut' (Flood). The greatest of the Schulze songs, however, is full
of a wistful sense of lost happiness. 'Im Frühling' (In Springtime) is a
kind of theme and variations for piano and voice. 'The happiness of love

passes away, leaving only love itself, and, alas, sorrow.' Schubert's setting, written in March 1826, catches the mood of joy remembered, sadness regained, with wonderful assurance. It is one of his very greatest
songs.

The settings of songs from Sir Walter Scott's narrative poem, *The
Lady of the Lake*, which had been so much admired at Steyregg and
Ebenzweier, date from the spring of 1825. In an attempt to exploit
Scott's enormous European vogue, Schubert planned to publish them
both with the original English words and in a German translation, and
(with one exception) they were so published in 1826. Schubert underestimated the difficulties, however; the translation he used, by Adam
Storck, does not always conform to the metrical scheme of the original.
Schubert knew no English, and wrote the songs to match the German
text, so that adjustments have to be made when the songs are sung in
English. Like the Schulze songs, the Scott songs are unified by their ostinato rhythms, but tinged with a kind of epic nostalgia. At their best, as
in Ellen's three songs, they seem to breathe the very air of Romantic his-
toricism, with their harp-like figuration and horn calls.

Apart from songs, piano duets had become one of Schubert's most
reliable sources of income. 1825 and 1826 saw a whole series of such
works, many of which can be dated only approximately by reference to
the subsequent publication. His ability to give poetic depth to familiar
popular forms such as the march, waltz, and polonaise is constantly
exploited. The six *Polonaisen* D824 published in the summer of 1826,
for instance, were written in the preceding spring; so, probably, was the
Sonata in E minor D823, of which the middle movement is a splendid
example of variation form. The B minor theme, marked Andantino, is
spare and hieratic (Ex. 30a); but it blossoms in Variation 4 into pure
poetry (Ex. 30b) in the transcendental key of B major. Since the word
'sonata' had by this time become something of a liability in commercial
terms, the publisher, Thaddäus Weigl, decided to publish the three
movements separately under French titles. The opening march appeared
as a 'Divertissement en forme d'une Marche brillante et raisonnée' in
June 1826, and the other two movements a year later.

The Grande Marche funèbre in C minor D859 was certainly written
in December 1825, for it is an occasional piece prompted by the death
of the Russian Emperor, Alexander I, on 1 December. Similarly, the
Grande Marche héroïque in A minor D885 must belong to the following spring, for it was published in September to catch the public interest in the coronation of his successor Nikolaus I. Both works were
published by Pennauer. But of much more interest musically are the two
Characteristic Marches in C, D886, published by Diabelli in 1829, the
origin of which remains a mystery. These lively 6/8 pieces have delighted
generations of duet players.

The steady flow of four-hand piano works, and the attempt to exploit

Ex. 30

(a)

Ex. 30 *cont.*

the fashionable appeal of Walter Scott, are not the only evidence we have of Schubert's willingness to meet the demands of publishers, and the expectations of the public, so far as he could do so without compromising his concern for his art. Early in 1825 he met Jakob Craigher, a prosperous businessman and amateur poet whose travels had given him a formidable reputation as a linguist. Craigher gave Schubert manuscript copies of his poems, including 'Die junge Nonne' (The Young Nun), a dramatic monologue with which the composer brought the Romantic ballad to a new expressive peak. In April Schubert set Colley Cibber's poem, 'The Blind Boy', in a German translation made by Craigher, which matches the metrical scheme of the English original. After his return from Upper Austria in October, Schubert met Craigher again and asked for his help in preparing bilingual editions of songs by well-known authors, in the hope of interesting foreign publishers. This resulted, for instance, in the publication of three songs by Goethe and Bruchmann in July 1826 with both German and Italian texts and, in May 1827, of 'Der Wachtelschlag' (The Quail's Cry) similarly. It is also possible that Craigher provided the German texts for the three Italian songs for bass voice D902, published in September 1827. But it cannot be said that this stratagem did much to enhance Schubert's reputation outside Austria. As we have seen, the A minor Piano Sonata received a warm and on the whole discerning notice in the Leipzig *Allgemeine musikalische Zeitung* (March 1826), and about the same time the Vienna correspondent of the London *Harmonicon* made a brief reference to the 'young composer Schubert', who 'continues to labour indefatigably in the composition of songs'. But these and similar laconic references to Schubert's activities in various German periodicals mean little. The significant fact is that no publisher outside Austria could be persuaded to publish anything of Schubert's before 1828, when Probst of Leipzig at last agreed to bring out the E flat Piano Trio. As for Paris and London, Schubert's name was still virtually unknown there.

Yet the steadily rising tally of publications and performances points quite clearly to his growing reputation in Vienna. The yearly total of new song-publications, for instance, increases from twelve in 1825 to twenty-three in 1826, twenty-five in 1827 and forty-nine in 1828. In these same years his compositions appear with increasing frequency in the programmes of private concerts, and especially those of the fortnightly musical entertainments (*Abendunterhaltungen*) of the Philharmonic Society. According to statistics prepared by Otto Biba, the archivist of the Society, from 1825 Schubert was second only to Rossini in the list of most frequently featured composers at these concerts.[7] The indirect evidence points in the same direction also. In December 1825 the *Wiener Zeitung* carried an advertisement for an 'extremely good likeness of the composer Franz Schubert'. It was an engraving by Johann Passini, based on the portrait water-colour by W. A. Rieder. The accompanying blurb spoke of 'the composer of genius, sufficiently well known for his fame in the musical world, who has delighted his hearers so often, especially with his vocal compositions'.

It seems that Schubert had also begun to play an official part in the life of the Philharmonic Society. In September 1825, during his absence in Upper Austria, he had been elected a deputy member of the Council of Representatives, the official governing body of the Society. This led in 1827 to his election as a full member of the representative body, a position of some influence. To be sure, it is difficult to think of Schubert as a conscientious committee man. But at least these facts establish that he was no completely unknown genius, working in isolation from the society in which he lived.

Meanwhile, the Schubert circle slowly re-established itself during the autumn and winter of 1825/6. But it was a different circle, with a different nucleus. At the beginning of July Schober had returned from Breslau, having decided to switch his allegiance from the drama to poetry, and prepare his poems for publication. Leopold Kupelwieser also had returned from Italy during Schubert's absence. He and his faithful Johanna planned to be married in September 1826, and what with the claims of matrimony and those of his career, we do not hear much more of Kupelwieser in the annals of the Schubertians. The new triumvirate of the arts, Schubert, Schwind and Bauernfeld, could not quite recapture the glory of the old, and Schubert and Schwind continued to complain about the decline of the circle. It is the diary of the satirical and articulate Bauernfeld that best conveys the slightly raffish tone that now seems to characterize the circle. 'Schubert is back', he wrote in October, 'life in the pub and the coffee-house with friends, often till two or three in the morning . . . Schober is the worst. Admittedly he has nothing to do, and actually does nothing, for which Moritz [von Schwind] often reproaches him.'[8] For the customary grand party held at Schober's on New Year's Eve Bauernfeld wrote an elaborate pantomime, poking fun

[7] Otto Biba, 'Schubert's Position in Viennese Musical Life', *NCM*, vol. iii, no. 2, Nov., 1979, pp. 106–13.
[8] Docs, p. 469.

at the individual excesses and weaknesses of the Schubertians (especially Schober). Ominously, Schubert was absent, not feeling well enough to attend. Ill-health was by no means his only worry at this time. Financial embarrassment, the increasingly senseless behaviour of the censor and the security police, the short-sightedness of publishers and the decline in standards of taste all combined to make 1826 a year of bleak prospects. After the euphoria of the summer, and the triumphs of Gmunden and Gastein, the following autumn and winter seemed more like a slough of despond.

It was not that Schubert was without recognition, or without appropriate fees for his work. In October, Artaria had paid him 200 florins for the seven songs from *The Lady of the Lake*, and in January he accepted 120 florins from Thaddäus Weigl for the D major piano sonata and the *Divertissement à l'hongroise*. Such fees were fair, even favourable, in comparison with, say, Beethoven's, or Weber's. The mere fact that Schubert's songs and piano works were much in demand for publication in almanacs and periodicals, and that at least nine Viennese publishers were willing to acquire his compositions is proof that he was not gravely exploited. But income is one thing, living expenses are another, especially in Vienna, where accommodation was extremely costly, and doubtless doctors' fees also. Josef von Spaun, who was posted back to Vienna in April 1826 to take charge of the Public Lottery Office, put it fairly and succinctly in his reminiscences. 'Back in Vienna again from Lemberg', he wrote, 'I found Schubert in the full flowering of his talent. At last he was getting more recognition and receiving payment for his works, even though this was miserable in comparison with their worth. His position had improved, though it still continued to be unsatisfactory.'[9]

His friends recognized that what Schubert needed was an official post with a regular income, if possible without official duties which would encroach on his freedom to compose. Such an ideal solution seemed in the spring of 1826 to be almost within reach. The death of the first Kapellmeister, Salieri, and of the court organist, Voříšek, in 1825 had opened up new opportunities at the top of the musical establishment of the Court. The post of first Kapellmeister had already been filled by the promotion of Salieri's deputy, Josef Eybler, but the position of second Kapellmeister, carrying with it the duties of court organist, remained vacant. In April Schubert submitted his formal application for this post to the Emperor, setting out brief details of his long association with the Imperial Chapel, his record as a composer, and, in suitably tactful language, his need of the money. In such matters, however, administrative wheels ground almost as slowly as the mills of God. It was not till December that the problem was resolved, and then only by

[9] Memoirs, p. 136.

a technical ploy designed to save money. Josef Weigl, the conductor of the Court Theatre, was invited to take over the duties of court organist as well as his own, in return for a modest increase in his annual lodging allowance! It was a disappointment, though Schubert is reported to have said that he was glad so good a man had got the job.

Meanwhile, a change of management at the Kärntnertor theatre had revived Schubert's interest in the opera. The possibility of a collaboration with Bauernfeld had suggested itself in 1825, when the friendship between the two men began. Bauernfeld's first play to reach the stage was not be produced until 1828, shortly before Schubert's death, but his enthusiasm for the drama augured well for the plan. At that time, however, Schubert favoured an opera based on the story of Ernst Schulze's *Die bezauberte Rose* (The Enchanted Rose), a Romantic poem with all the ingredients of fairies, spells, princes and shepherd boys, and a princess who has been turned into a rosebud, all too familiar in the genre. Bauernfeld, however, had a better idea, an opera based on the mediaeval tale of the Count of Gleichen, who fell in love with a Saracen princess, named Suleika, while away on a crusade, married her, and brought her home to settle down in a happy *ménage à trois* with his wife, the Countess Ottilie. The story had obvious dramatic possibilities, and would appeal to the fashionable interest in oriental romance which Goethe had successfully exploited. On the other hand, a plot based on a bigamous marriage seemed certain to fall foul of the censors. In 1825, moreover, Barbaja's lease on the Court theatres was due to come up for renewal, and the prospects for a new German opera were anything but rosy. Gossip suggested that future audiences would be in for a diet of ballet and Italian opera.

In the event, things did not turn out so badly. After a long delay, it was announced that Barbaja would take over a new lease of the Kärntnertor in April 1826. In June Ignaz von Mosel, a firm admirer of Schubert's music and a champion of German opera, became Director of the Court theatres, and though this was an administrative post with no direct responsibility for artistic policy, it was no doubt intended to help in keeping the Italians under control. Barbaja, through his deputy Duport, made it known that he would be interested in new operas from German composers, including Schubert. In these circumstances it was agreed that Bauernfeld should go ahead and prepare a libretto based on the 'Count of Gleichen' story as soon as possible. As it happened, Bauernfeld had decided in April to go on a tour of Carinthia and Upper Austria with his friend, Ferdinand von Mayerhofer, a young army officer. This meant a long absence from Vienna, but Bauernfeld welcomed this as an opportunity to get to work on the libretto. 'Hail to thee, Boredom, mother of the Muses!' he confided to his diary, with a neat quote from Goethe's 'Venetian Epigrams', 'thus I thought of the libretto for Schubert, and set to work on *Der Graf von Gleichen*.' By the end of May the thing was finished.[10]

Bauernfeld's letters from the provinces are full of fun and high spirits. Meanwhile, however, the circle in Vienna was in the doldrums. Schober was ill, and Schwind's affair with Netti Hönig was going badly. The weather was appalling; Schubert complained of lack of money and his inability to work. He had planned to join up with Bauernfeld and Mayerhofer in the summer at Linz, but the plan had to be abandoned. 'I cannot get to Gmunden, or anywhere else', he wrote on 10 July 1826, 'for I have no money at all, and altogether things go very badly for me.'[11] The travellers finally arrived back at the end of July. In October *Der Graf von Gleichen* was banned by the censor, but Schubert proposed to set the text none the less. Some eighty-eight pages of sketches, mostly in outline score on two or more staves, do in fact survive in the Vienna City Library. They belong to the summer of 1827. But the hopes of a new deal for German opera soon evaporated, and it is clear that Schubert, discouraged by his failure to get a hearing for *Alfonso*, for the time being put the project out of mind.

Michael Vogl, who had surprised his friends on his return from Italy by announcing his forthcoming marriage to Kunigunde Rosa, now tried to promote Schubert's interest by encouraging him to apply for a post as a coach to the new management of the opera house. According to Anton Schindler, who left a long circumstantial account of the affair in his memoirs, Schubert submitted a trial score which was rehearsed at an audition under his own direction. The soprano, a young actress called Nanette Schechner, complained that the orchestra was too heavy in the climaxes, but Schubert refused to make any concessions, and finally stormed out with the score under his arm. Schindler is a notoriously unreliable witness, and his story certainly loses nothing in sensational detail in the telling. However, there is nothing inherently improbable about it, nor is it inconsistent with what we know of Schubert's temperament, and of his attitude to his own work. In his insistence on the subordinate function of the interpreter, and the primacy of the composer, he was just as uncompromising and inflexible as Beethoven.[12]

It is a relief to turn from this catalogue of disappointments to the one solid achievement of the summer, the composition of his last, some would say his greatest, string quartet, D887 in G major. It has always had a special appeal for Schubert-lovers, though it has been comparatively slow to establish itself in the affections of the general public, perhaps because it lacks those metaphorical associations which contribute to the popularity of its two great predecessors. The A minor Quartet is 'about' disenchantment, and the loss of innocence. The D minor Quartet is 'about' death. But what is the G major Quartet about? The first move-

---

[10] Docs, pp. 523, 530.   [11] Docs, p. 538.
[12] For Schindler's account see Memoirs, pp. 309–11.

ment is an extended discussion of the tonality of G major, and in particular of the complementarity of light and dark in its make-up. The motto theme which occurs three times alternates between major and minor so as to emphasize the instability of the third (Ex. 31). Not only is the tune of the Andante un poco mosso poised similarly between E minor and E major; its middle section is a tonal battle which threatens to destroy the tonic itself. Only in the third movement does Schubert explore the implications of the third as a stable tonic. The Scherzo, in B minor, is based on the Neapolitan relationship between G and F sharp, while the Trio (the emotional centre of the work) links G major and B major with a wonderfully heart-easing tune. The Finale is a moto perpetuo 6/8 movement in Schubert's tarantella-like manner, but not so fierce and hard-driven as the finale of the D minor Quartet.

Ex. 31

Looked at in the context of Schubert's complete *œuvre*, this searching examination of the tonality of G is significant. In view of the popularity of G major as a lyrical key, it seems surprising, to say the least, that Schubert had not used this key before in a major instrumental work. But he had used it frequently in his songs, and not only for 'simple' songs like 'Heidenröslein' and Matthisson's 'Stimme der Liebe' (The Voice of Love) D418, but always with his own unique awareness of the emotional potential of the major/minor shift, and often with an explicitly transcendental implication in the text. Outstanding examples are the setting of Claudius's 'An die Nachtigall', 'Die Gebüsche', and 'Todesmusik' (Death Music), and the magnificent setting of Mayrhofer's 'Auflösung' D807. If the G major String Quartet does not have the obvious extra-musical associations of the A minor and the D minor quartets, it would be quite wrong to regard it as something apart from the main stream of Schubert's work, a kind of digression into absolute music. On the contrary, it offers perhaps the best demonstration of the essentially metaphorical nature of his musical language; the affective links with the songs are crucial. There are unmistakable pre-echoes of *Winterreise*, especially in the Andante, and it shares with the Schulze settings the tone of melancholy nostalgia, and the driving rhythms.

The autograph of the G major Quartet is dated 20 June 1826 at the beginning, and 30 June at the end. But the work probably began to take shape in the composer's mind much earlier in the year. He had intended to complete a group of three quartets since the beginning of 1824, and was no doubt reminded of the fact in February, when the D minor Quartet was successfully rehearsed at the house of his friend Franz Lachner, the Bavarian musician and composer who had recently been appointed assistant conductor at the Kärntnertor theatre. His ambition would have received a further nudge on 21 March, when Beethoven's Quartet in B flat Op. 130 had been given its first performance at the last public concert of the Philharmonic Society's season. Schubert spent much of June at Währing, then a pleasantly rural suburb some miles from the city, and it may well have been there that he worked at the fair copy of the G major Quartet during the last ten days of the month. It is almost certain that the quartet was privately performed during the following winter, probably again at Lachner's, and the first movement may well have been the one included in Schubert's public concert in March 1828. But the first fully authenticated complete public performance was given by the Hellmesberger Quartet on 8 December 1850 at the Philharmonic Society, and the work was published by Diabelli in the following year.

In June 1826 Schubert received a flattering invitation from the Swiss publisher H. G. Nägeli to contribute to a new collection of piano sonatas. This was to appear under the grand title of 'The Portal of Honour', and contributions were invited from Weber, Mendelssohn, Ries, and Moscheles among others. Schubert replied promptly, accepting the proposal, and asking for a fee of 120 florins in advance. Nägeli seems to have demurred at this, for the negotiations got no further; and when the G major sonata came to be finished, in October, it was sold to the Viennese publisher Tobias Haslinger. The incident, however, may have prompted Schubert to make another attempt to get his work published outside Austria.

In August 1826 he made an approach to the most reputable music publishers in Germany. He wrote in almost identical terms to Probst, and to Breitkopf & Härtel, both of Leipzig, offering the Octet for wind and strings, string quartets, piano sonatas, and four-hand piano pieces.[13] Härtel sent a pompously worded letter in reply, declaring his wish to 'establish a pleasant mutual relationship', and offering to publish one work on a trial basis without any fee, in exchange for some free copies. To this Schubert did not bother to reply. Probst, however, was more forthcoming, though cautious. He asked to see some songs and piano pieces ('not too difficult'). Schubert sent three compositions (we do not know which) through Artaria, asking eighty florins each for them, rather

---

[13] Docs, pp. 546, 547.

more than Artaria had paid for the D major Sonata. At this point Probst
let the matter drop, excusing himself on the ground that he was too busy
for the moment with the complete works of Kalkbrenner. So much for
Schubert's hopes of making a name for himself in Germany.

In the autumn the tangled story of the 'Great' C major Symphony
reached its climax. Schubert completed the score in the spring or summer of 1826. Fortunately, modern techniques for dating the various
kinds of manuscript paper used in its make-up enable us to clarify the
evolution of the final form with reasonable confidence. When Schubert
returned to Vienna in October 1825 he brought with him an outline
sketch in open score of the first three movements and a large part of the
Finale. His task over the next few months was to complete the orchestration and expression marks, and at the same time to make a thorough
revision of what he had done. This involved not only countless minor
changes, additions and deletions, but alteration of some of the main
themes, and major reconstructions of the coda of the first movement and
of the Trio. The history of the main theme of the Allegro ma non
troppo, for instance, shows the care with which this process was under-
taken, and illustrates the retrospective character of the work. It began
life as the opening theme of the Allegro con brio of the Symphony No.
3 in D major of 1815. In the outline sketch this took a more nakedly
rhythmic form, at some cost to the thematic interest. The final form,
which had to be inserted as a correction wherever the theme occurs, is
clearly an improvement. (See Ex. 32.) Schubert's original plan for the
movement envisaged a return of the theme of the andante Introduction
at the climax of the main movement. But he must have decided that the
build-up to this climax needed strength, for he later inserted three extra
sheets at this point (bars 591–646). The operation involved the cancellation of one whole page of the original sketch, which can still be seen in
the autograph.

Ex. 32   (a)

Symphony no. 3 in D

Allegro con brio

(b)

'Great' C major : first draft

Allegro ma non troppo

Ex. 32 *cont.*   (c)

'Great' C major : final version

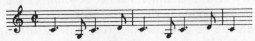

A similar radical reconstruction took place at bars 43–122 in the Trio. The effect of these and similar changes was to make an already long work even longer, and to intensify the climaxes. The Finale was the last movement to be completed. The last 155 bars are written on similar paper to that used in the G major String Quartet, and probably date from the spring or summer of 1826.[14]

Schubert's hopes for a public performance of his symphonic masterpiece rested on the Philharmonic Society, for he was in no position at this time to face the financial risk involved in sponsoring his own concert. (Even Beethoven had found the concert of 7 May 1824, at which the Ninth Symphony was first performed, a source of trouble, anxiety, and financial loss.) Accordingly, he wrote to the Committee early in October to notify the Society of his intention to dedicate to them 'as a native artist, this, my Symphony, and to commend it most courteously to their protection'. In reply the Committee decided to give Schubert an honorarium of 100 florins, 'not as a fee, but as a token of the Society's sense of obligation towards you'.[15] The intention seems to have been to recognize Schubert's claim to the consideration of the Committee as a much respected member and representative, without giving any firm undertaking in advance to perform the work. By the end of the year the score had been handed over to the Society, and the Committee agreed to have the parts copied as a necessary step towards a performance. The parts were ready in the summer (the copyists' receipts have survived in the archive of the Society) and at some time in the ensuing autumn or winter the work was played through at one of the regular practices of the Society's orchestra. The outcome, as Leopold Sonnleithner described it in later years, was that the symphony was 'provisionally put on one side, because of its length and difficulty'. So it had to wait until March 1839, when Schumann's enthusiasm brought about its first performance under Felix Mendelssohn's direction at the Leipzig Gewandhaus.

Schubert biographers have conducted a contentious post-mortem on these events, in which less than justice has been done to the role of the Philharmonic Society. It is not true, as is sometimes claimed, that the Society rejected the symphony, or that it was filed away and forgotten. Certainly it was not till 1839, after the Leipzig première, that the Society

---

[14] Robert Winter, 'Paper Studies and the Future of Schubert Research', *Schubert Studies*, ed. Eva Badura-Skoda and Peter Branscombe (Cambridge, 1982), pp. 209–311.

[15] *Docs*, pp. 559, 560.

got round to planning a complete performance, and on that occasion the plan was frustrated by the refusal of some of the professional players to give the necessary rehearsal time. Taking account of the undemanding standards of taste in Vienna in the 1820s, however, and the general reaction against the sublime and the intellectual, it is difficult to see what else the Society could have done. In fact, it was not till the last forty years of the century that the symphony began to find a place in the repertory, largely through the advocacy of Grove and Manns in London, and Hallé in Manchester.

The combination of traditional form with an enlargement and enrichment of content, which underlies the concept of the 'Great' C major Symphony, is characteristic also of two instrumental works of October 1826, the Piano Sonata in G major and the Rondo in B minor D895 for piano and violin. The Sonata presents an interesting contrast with the String Quartet written in the same key a few months earlier. Where the Quartet is concentrated, highly charged, and in places at any rate rigorously intellectual in tone, the Sonata is lyrical and serene. Instead of the fragmentary motifs which serve in the Quartet as the basis for discussion, the Sonata begins with a long cantabile paragraph firmly rooted in G major, reminiscent, in mood at least, of the opening of Beethoven's Fourth Piano Concerto; and it ends with a leisurely rondo, as innocent as a child's game, and only faintly tinged with nostalgia even in the C minor episode. The third movement, which reverts to the title of Menuetto, is in B minor, with an enchanting Trio in B major. The autograph of this thoroughly Schubertian work, now in the library of the Royal College of Music, confirms what the relaxed style of the Sonata suggests, that it came easily off the pen. Yet at the same time it reveals everywhere the care with which Schubert revised his work. The nineteenth-century notion that he never made sketches or revised will not survive a study of any of his major scores. It is clear, for instance, that the Andante of this sonata was recast not once but twice, and the composer's second, and sometimes his third, thoughts are evident throughout the score.

One rather mysterious fact about the G major Sonata is that the autograph is headed 'IV. Sonate fürs Pianoforte allein October 1826'. The numeral IV is puzzling. The two complete sonatas of 1825 had already been published as 'Première grande Sonate' and 'Seconde grande Sonate'; but where, then, is no. 3? It is generally assumed that Schubert had taken the unusually far-sighted course of reserving No. 3 for the unfinished C major ('Reliquie') Sonata of spring 1825, intending to complete that work later. But it seems to have been overlooked that a 'Troisième grande Sonate' does in fact exist. It is the Sonata in E flat D568, published by Pennauer a few months after Schubert's death as Op. 122. Because this E flat sonata is a revised version of the D flat sonata of June 1817 it has hitherto been assumed that it must belong to the same period. However, the internal evidence, and particularly the masterly reshaping of the two outer movements and extension of the recapitulations, suggest otherwise. The more likely explanation is that, some time between the publication of the D major sonata, in April, and October 1826, Schubert took up the three-movement sonata in D flat and thoroughly revised it for publication, before handing it over to Pennauer.[16]

The Rondo in B minor exhibits the same generous proportions as the G major sonata, but is a much less poetic work. It was written as a vehicle for the young Bohemian violinist Josef Slawjk (Slavík), who had arrived in Vienna earlier in the year and struck up a friendship with Schubert. There is an extended Introduction, marked Andante. The main episode is in G major, and the outer sections are based on two contrasted themes, the first scherzo-like, and the second a brisk march in D major. The piece ends with a brilliant Più mosso version of the march in B major. It is a virtuoso work which inspires respect rather than affection. Early in 1827 it was given a first performance at a soirée arranged by Artaria, who published it in April, appropriately Frenchified as 'Rondeau brillant'.

1826 is a thin year for songs, though they make up in quality what they lack in quantity. In March he set several poems by J. G. Seidl, a government official and fashionable journalist whose poems had recently been published. The Seidl songs are characteristic of Schubert's mature song style, which finds its own way to combine the formal perfection of the strophic song with the expressive fluency and pliancy of the through-composed *Gesang*. All the Seidl songs show his instinctive flair for discovering the precise unifying gait (*Bewegung*) for the verses, within which his command of modulation and melodic variation can do its work unhindered. The best known of them is 'Der Wanderer an den Mond' (The Wayfarer to the Moon), but 'Im Freien' (In the Open) and 'Wiegenlied' (Cradle Song) are just as magical in their different ways. All of them display a subtle and sophisticated sensitivity to the unique mood of the poem, and some (especially 'Sehnsucht' D879) have the undertow of gloom which was to sound so eloquently in *Winterreise*.

Two fine settings of poems by Schubert's old schoolfriend Franz von Schlechta belong also to March. 'Totengräber-Weise' (Gravedigger's Ditty) is an extraordinary song built on a four-bar tolling phrase treated with continuous modulation, in such a way as to encompass sadness, resolution and wonder in turn. 'Fischerweise' (Fisherman's Ditty) can hardly be bettered as an example of Schubert's mature mastery of the modified strophic song.

In January 1826 he paid his last tribute to Goethe, with four settings of Mignon's songs from *Wilhelm Meister*. Two of these look back to the earlier settings of 1821, and one, the final solo version of 'Nur wer die Sehnsucht kennt', even further back to 'Ins stille Land' of 1816. The duet

---

[16] See note 1 on page 51.

version of the same lyric is effective in its somewhat operatic manner, but it cannot be said that either of the new settings reaches the elusive goal of a definitive version of the famous lines. The Goethe songs were published by Diabelli as Op. 62 in March 1827.

Schubert was more successful with Shakespeare, three of whose lyrics he set in July while staying at Währing with Schober. He used the translations in the new Vienna Shakespeare, which relied for the most part on the work of A. W. Schlegel and also on some new translations by Bauernfeld and Ferdinand Mayerhofer. 'Ständchen' (Hark, hark, the lark . . .) and 'An Silvia' (Who is Sylvia) show the world's two greatest song-writers in triumphant collaboration. The words inevitably summon up the music, and vice-versa. Schubert is never greater than when, as in these songs, he appears to be at his simplest.

It remains to mention two partsongs, both written in September, which provide further evidence of Schubert's intention to rescue the form from triviality. 'Nachthelle' (Night's Brightness) is an atmospheric piece for male-voice quartet and a 'damnably high tenor' solo, as Ferdinand Walcher put it in a note to the composer. It captures admirably a mood of luminous serenity. 'Grab und Mond' (Moonlit Grave) is more sombre, and less successful. The texts are both by Seidl.

The G major Sonata and B minor Rondo are the last compositions which can be certainly ascribed to the year 1826. November and December are blank. Instead, the year dwindled away in a succession of parties at 'The Green Anchor', which happened this autumn to be in favour as a nightly rendezvous for the circle, and at Bogner's coffee house. Thanks to the diaries of Franz and Fritz von Hartmann, two young law students from Linz who attached themselves to the circle, we have a pretty clear picture of events, as they appeared to normally intelligent but not particularly sensitive outsiders. In December, for instance, references to the 'Anchor' and to Bogner's recur with monotonous regularity, and the party seems rarely to have broken up before 11.30. On 15 December there was a 'big, big Schubertiad' at Spaun's, supposedly the one featured in Schwind's famous drawing, 'A Schubert Evening at Josef von Spaun's'. Franz von Hartmann tells us there was 'a huge gathering'. Vogl sang 'almost 30 songs', and Schubert and Gahy played duets gloriously. Hartmann was particularly moved by the six Grand Marches for duet. 'When the music was over, there was a glorious feed, and then dancing. . . . At 12.30, after a warmhearted parting with the Spauns and Enderes, we saw Betty home and went to the "Anchor", where we found Schober, Schubert, Schwind, Derffel and Bauernfeld still there. Merry. Home. To bed at 1 o'clock.'[17]

This was one of the few bright interludes in a dull and overcast autumn and winter. There was another on 17 September, when the

[17] Docs, pp. 571–2.

circle assembled to celebrate the marriage of Leopold Kupelwieser and Johanna Lutz. Schubert insisted on playing dances, and Schwind made a speech. But the sad truth was that the old circle had disintegrated, and the new circle seemed to have degenerated into a set of quarrelsome Bohemians. Vogl too had retired into matrimony. Bauernfeld, who could never resist the temptation to exercise his satiric gift at the expense of his friends, offended Schober, and complained that he was bored by the antics of the circle. Schwind gloomed over his ill-starred love affair. Schober relapsed into his customary idleness. Underlying these personal frustrations there were more serious worries about the political situation and the public mood. The secret police seemed to be acting in a spirit of mindless repression. In April the authorities suddenly decided to take action against a harmless club of artists, writers and intellectuals called 'Ludlam's Cave', devoted to the arts, and in particular to the art of witty and spontaneous entertainment. Having raided the club in the middle of the night, the police proceeded to put most of the distinguished writers and artists in Vienna into prison. The dramatist Grillparzer, who gives an account of the matter in his memoirs, describes how the following morning the police took statements and cross-examined their victims 'as though the safety of the state were at risk'. In the face of such stupidity, it seemed that art could only take refuge in escapism, and the public in light entertainment. The great hit of the autumn was 'The Girl from Fairyland, or The Peasant as Millionaire', a magic play by the gifted dramatist Ferdinand Raimund with music by Josef Drechsler. By a curious chance, when Bauernfeld took up his official post as a secretary on probation in September, among the first papers to appear on his desk were those relating to the 'Ludlam's Cave' affair. When the raid occurred, both Schubert and Bauernfeld were applicants for membership of the club; so, as Bauernfeld remarked, if they had been a little earlier, or the police raid a little later, he might have had to assist at the inquiry into his own behaviour![18]

As always in bad times, Schubert's thoughts often turned towards the mountains, but circumstances ruled out a holiday. Towards the end of the year, however, a pianist friend of his called Johann Baptist Jenger took the matter in hand. Jenger came from Graz, and had played the decisive role in the award of a Diploma of Honour to Schubert in April 1823 by the Styrian Music Society. On 29 December he wrote to Marie Pachler in Graz: 'Friend Schubert has firmly resolved to travel to Graz next year, but if he does not get there with me it will again come to nothing, like this year. I kiss your hand, dear lady, for the kind offer to let me have a room in your grand new house, and shall accept it with the greatest pleasure when the time comes.' In January the arrangements were settled.[19]

---

[18] Memoirs, p. 241.   [19] Docs, p. 583.

As a postscript to a mainly depressing year, attention may be drawn to a little-known miniature work of a strikingly original and idiosyncratic kind. In February 1826 a young friend of Schubert's, Adolf von Pratobevera, wrote a verse play for private performance on his father's birthday. At the end of the play a kind of valediction was to be recited against a background of music, which Schubert with his usual generosity agreed to provide. 'Fare you well, fair earth! Only now, as joy and sorrow pass away, do I understand you . . . Joy I take with me, you I leave behind.' To these words Schubert wrote music (Ex. 33) which in its inner stillness and serenity anticipates the mood of the last piano sonatas and the String Quintet. He had often used melodrama in his operas, but usually at moments of drama and tension. Its use here, to heighten the sense of peace and reconciliation, is perfectly conceived.

Ex. 33

9

The winter journey (1827)

1827 is the climacteric year. The contrast between man and artist reaches baffling proportions; the task of reconciling Schubert's private life with the inner world of his imagination becomes so difficult as to seem irrelevant. The Schubertians transferred their allegiance from the 'Green Anchor' to the 'Castle of Eisenstadt', and the diaries of the brothers Hartmann record a relentless succession of parties, interspersed with an occasional reception or Schubertiad. Schober in later life hinted at even wilder excesses. In June 1868, when he was in his seventies, Schober entertained a party of journalists with a story about a forgotten love affair of Schubert's. Ludwig Frankl, who wrote the story down, says it concerns a young woman called Gusti Grünwedel. According to Schober, Schubert was in love with her, and she was well-disposed towards him, but Schubert was too modest. When Schober suggested that he ought to marry her, Schubert protested that no woman could possibly love him. He jumped up, rushed out of the room without his hat, flushed with anger . . . telling himself again and again that no happiness was granted to him on earth. Schubert then let himself go to pieces, according to Schober. 'He frequented the city outskirts and roamed around in taverns, at the same time composing his most beautiful songs in them, just as he did in the hospital too . . . where he found himself as the result of excessively indulgent sensual living and its consequences.'[1] Yet 1827 is the year of *Winterreise*, of the two great piano trios and two sets of Impromptus for piano; a year especially characteristic of his mature genius. His friends were well aware that there were two contradictory sides to his nature. Mayrhofer spoke of it as 'a mixture of tenderness and coarseness, sensuality and candour, sociability and melancholy'.[2] Bauernfeld, with his dramatist's detachment, analysed it more closely: 'If there were times, both in his social relationships and in his art, when the Austrian character appeared all too violently in the vigorous and pleasure-loving Schubert, there were also times when a black-winged demon of sorrow and melancholy forced its way into his vicinity; not altogether an evil spirit, it is true, since, in the dark con-

---

[1] Memoirs, pp. 265–6.   [2] Memoirs, p. 14.

centrated hours, it often brought out songs of the most agonising beauty.' Bauernfeld goes on to speak of an idealized love at work in his friend, mediating, reconciling, and compensating, a love with which the Countess Karoline was associated as a kind of benevolent muse.[3]

Even his closest friends were shocked by the sustained pessimism of *Winterreise*. Spaun recalls: 'For a time Schubert's mood became more gloomy and he seemed upset. When I asked him what was the matter he merely said: "Well, you will soon hear and understand." One day he said to me, "Come to Schober's today. I will sing you a cycle of awe-inspiring songs." We were quite dumbfounded by the gloomy mood of these songs, and Schober said he only liked one song, 'Der Lindenbaum' [The Linden Tree]. To which Schubert replied: "I like these songs more than all the others, and you will get to like them too." '[4] It is probable that this informal recital took place in the spring of 1827, and that what Schubert sang was not the whole cycle as we know it, but the twelve songs of Part I, which were written in February and March 1827 and published by Haslinger in January 1828. For it is clear from the autograph that the two parts were written separately and at different times. Part I is dated at the beginning 'February 1827'. The twelfth song, 'Einsamkeit' (Loneliness), is written in D minor, the key of the opening song, and at the end of it Schubert wrote 'Finis', a clear indication that he regarded the cycle as complete. Part II, dated 'October 1827', is headed 'continuation of *Winterreise*', and is for the most part a fair copy of earlier drafts.

The explanation for this curious procedure is that Wilhelm Müller's cycle of poems was itself written and assembled in stages. Schubert's source for Part I was the 1823 almanac *Urania*, in which the twelve poems appeared in the same order as in Schubert's setting. Subsequently Müller added twelve more poems, and rearranged the whole cycle in the second volume of the 'Posthumous Papers of a Travelling Horn Player', which appeared in November 1824. Schubert seems to have come across this revised version of the cycle at some time in the summer of 1827, when the manuscript of Part I was already probably on its way to the printer. What he did then was to set the extra poems in the order in which he came to them, numbering the additional songs from one to twelve, as though they formed a separate work. The final order of Schubert's cycle is thus in part due to chance, which may account for the fact that the continuity of *Winterreise* is less convincing than that of *Die schöne Müllerin*. The proofs of Part II of *Winterreise* were, it is said, corrected by the composer on his deathbed. It appeared at the end of 1828.

The two great song cycles share the same landscape and the same mythology, and should be seen as complementary, in spite of differences

---

[3] Memoirs, p. 234.   [4] Memoirs, pp. 137–8.

in tone and structure. Looked at in isolation, the earlier work is sometimes underrated as folkish and whimsical, while *Winterreise* is often regarded simply as an expression of suicidal despair, regardless of the stoicism of its conclusion. Together they constitute Schubert's greatest achievement. But whereas *Die schöne Müllerin* has a real, though shadowy, plot involving three principal characters, *Winterreise* is a wholly interior drama. The only human figure to emerge, other than the protagonist, is the pitiable hurdy-gurdy man of the final song. His complaint is not against individual wrongs, but against fate itself. He belongs to the same tribe as the Harper in *Wilhelm Meister*, and, like Byron's Manfred, he is denied even the consolation of death.

This gives to *Winterreise* a tragic stature beyond that of the earlier cycle, a depth and universality which it is not fanciful to call Shakespearean. Its last scene can move to tears, as Shakespeare does, with the totally unexpected yet inevitably right: 'Strange old fellow, shall I go with you? Wilt grind out your music to my songs?' Arnold Feil has compared the scene to Feste's song at the end of *Twelfth Night*, an ironic comment on the drama which reconciles us to the human condition. But an equally apt parallel would be Lear and his Fool, bravely contemplating the death of faith and compassion with a smile and a song.

> Come, let's away to prison:
> We two alone will sing like birds i' the cage.
> When thou dost ask me blessing I'll kneel down,
> And ask of thee forgiveness.

The footsteps of the Wanderer echo through the work, usually in 2/4 time and in a minor key; while the songs of delusion and derangement, like 'Frühlingstraum' (Dream of Spring), 'Täuschung' (Illusion), 'Die Nebensonnen' (The Mock Suns), and 'Der Leiermann' (The Hurdy-Gurdy Man) are in triple time and take A minor/major as their tonal centre. These tonal associations, however, cannot be reduced to a rational scheme. Schubert's attitude to such matters was not schematic but pragmatic and instinctive, as he showed by lowering the keys of five of the songs in the course of publication. The order of the songs is a more controversial question. There are grounds for believing that Müller's final order puts the songs in a more narrative context than Schubert's. 'Die Post' (The Post), for instance, works better at No. 6 than at No. 13, and 'Frühlingstraum' at No. 21 than at No. 11. But on the propriety of altering Schubert's order, as has been done by several artists in this century, opinions differ. Müller's title, by the way, is *Die Winterreise*, but Schubert omitted the article both on his autograph and in the first edition.

While Schubert was absorbed in the composition of Part I of *Winterreise*, all Vienna talked of Beethoven's approaching end. As concern mounted, the news spread far beyond the city. The Philharmonic

Society of London sent him a present of £100 to relieve him of financial worries, while the publisher Schott sent a dozen bottles of wine. J. N. Hummel, the famous pianist and composer, made a special journey from Weimar to pay his last respects, and among the many visitors was Schubert's old friend Anselm Hüttenbrenner, from Graz. A crowd of many thousands assembled on 29 March to watch the funeral procession as it moved slowly through the city to the burial ground at Währing, at its head a collection of pall bearers and torch carriers, Schubert among them, representing the art of music from all parts of the empire. Fritz von Hartmann tell us in his diary that at the end of the long day he returned to the 'Castle of Eisenstadt', where he found Schubert, Schober, and Schwind, and stayed talking with them of Beethoven and his work late into the night.

For Schubert, Beethoven's work was both an ideal to aim at, and a standard by which to be judged. 'Who can do anything after Beethoven?' he is said to have remarked once to Spaun. Now the master was dead, he was not alone in regarding himself in a sense as the legitimate heir. Anton Schindler evidently thought so too, for he handed over to Schubert the Rellstab poems Beethoven had not found an opportunity to set. According to Schindler, Beethoven himself ratified the notion. 'Truly there is a divine spark in this Schubert,' he is reported to have said, when Schindler took him some of Schubert's songs on his deathbed. But whether Schubert actually visited Beethoven before his death is not clear. Anselm Hüttenbrenner asserted 'as an absolute fact' that Schubert accompanied him on a visit to the dying man shortly before his death. But corroborative evidence is lacking.[5]

The international concern over Beethoven's illness and death throws into sharp relief Schubert's failure to make his mark outside Vienna and the neighbouring cities. When Hummel and his pupil Ferdinand Hiller met Schubert during this eventful month of March 1827, neither had heard of him before. Hiller described the circumstances in his reminiscences.

A childhood friend of Hummel's, the former singer Buchwieser . . . was most enthusiastic about Schubert, and at her house he was presented to the famous Kapellmeister. We dined there several times in the company of the quiet young man and his favourite singer, the tenor [*recte* baritone] Vogl. The latter already elderly, but full of fire and life, had very little voice left, and Schubert's piano playing, in spite of not inconsiderable fluency, was very far from being that of a master. And yet I have never heard the Schubert songs sung as they were then! . . . I can still see my portly master, with his simple sincerity, as he sat in a comfortable armchair in the big drawing-room, to one side of the piano. He said little, but big tears were running down his cheeks. It was a revelation.

[5] Memoirs, p. 66.

Next morning Hiller called on Schubert, to find him busily composing. When he remarked on the young man's industry, the reply was: 'I write for several hours every morning. When one piece is finished, I begin another.'[6]

This encounter would never have taken place, presumably, but for Hummel's accidental association with Buchwieser, who was known to Schubert as Katharina von Lászny, to whom he dedicated his *Divertissement à l'hongroise*. The young English musician and critic Edward Holmes was less fortunate. He arrived in Vienna in July intent on making a thorough survey of the musical life of the city, for his object was to follow in Burney's footsteps and make an appraisal of the state of music in Germany. But it is clear that he never even heard Schubert's name mentioned, or if he did, he did not think it important enough to record; for though his book has a good deal to say about Viennese music in general (he found it very disappointing), and the Abbé Stadler in particular, there is no mention of Schubert. When Heinrich Hoffmann von Fallersleben, the folklorist from Breslau, visited the city in June he spent several days trying to track Schubert down, without success. Finally he found the composer at an inn in the suburb of Grinzing, but he was thoroughly disillusioned by his unprepossessing appearance, and found him in no mood to have his social activities interrupted. The entry in Hoffmann's diary reads: 'Grinzing. The old fiddler was playing something by Mozart . . . We spotted Schubert with a girl from where we were sitting; he came over to us and we never caught sight of him again.'[7]

Schubert was temperamentally averse to the social limelight, and his reclusive tendency must have been reinforced by his radical views on politics and religion, and by the complaisant and comfort-loving conventions of the age. (Had not Beethoven himself been well content with his reputation as an eccentric recluse?) But there are, of course, simpler and more objective explanations for his seeming invisibility to foreign observers. In 1827 he was thirty, an age at which Haydn was unknown outside Austria, and Beethoven only on the threshold of fame. Even in Vienna, he was known only as a composer of songs and keyboard pieces, for none of his orchestral works, and only a handful of his liturgical and chamber works, had so far been published. (The 478 numbers published in his lifetime included only one string quartet, one piano trio and one of his early Masses, that in C major.) Moreover, public interest, and that of the growing critical press, was focussed upon the opera, and particularly on the immensely fashionable Italian opera. It was the age of Rossini, and of the virtuoso performer, who could draw huge audiences and vast sums of money wherever he went. Schubert had neither the inclination nor the ability to compete in this market. He never per-

---

[6] Memoirs, pp. 282–3.   [7] Memoirs, pp. 285–6.

1 Franz Theodor Schubert.
Oil painting by Carl Schubert

2 Ferdinand Schubert. Oil painting
(unfinished) by his nephew Ferdinand

3 Therese Grob.
Oil painting by Heinrich Hollpein

4 Joseph von Spaun.
Pencil drawing by Moritz von Schwind

5 Franz von Schober.
Oil painting by Leopold Kupelwieser

6 Johann Mayrhofer.
Crayon sketch by Ludwig Michalek
after Moritz von Schwind

7 Moritz von Schwind.
Self-portrait

8 Franz von Bruchmann.
Etching from the original drawing
by Leopold Kupelwieser

9 The Kärntnertor Theatre

10 Schubert's room
at Zseliz

11 Schubert.
Pencil drawing by Leopold Kupelwieser (1821)

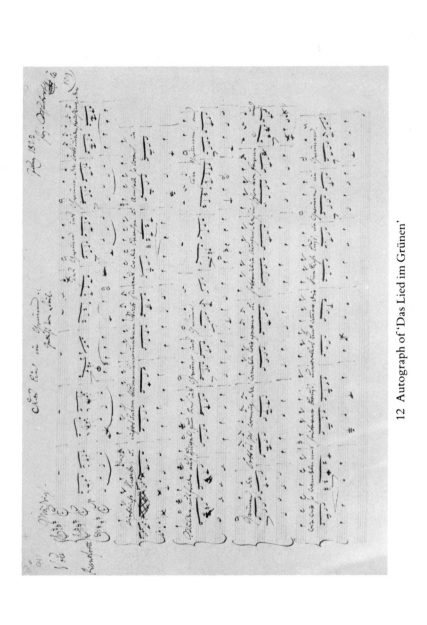

12 Autograph of 'Das Lied im Grünen'

13 Wilhelm Müller, author of
Die schöne Müllerin and of *Winterreise*.
From an unsigned original

14 Johann Michael Vogl. Original
drawing by Franz von Schober

15 Karl Freiherr von Schönstein.
Lithograph by Josef Kriehuber

16 Anna Fröhlich.
Crayon sketch by Heinrich Thugut

17 View of Gmunden.
Pen-and-ink drawing by Carl Schubert

18 View of Gastein

19 Excursion of the Schubertians from Atzenbrugg to Aumühl.
From the water-colour by Leopold Kupelwieser

formed in public as a solo pianist, though he did occasionally appear as accompanist for his own songs at the evening entertainments of the Philharmonic Society. In a sense, he was the victim of his own success as a songwriter, and of his own retiring disposition. Even his closest friends thought of him primarily as a songwriter, and doubted that he would ever rival Mozart or Beethoven as an instrumental composer.

Yet it seems to have been his cherished ambition to establish himself as Beethoven's successor. So much is clear from the great works of 1827 and 1828, many of which were either directly 'inherited' from the master, or strongly influenced by him. In the former class are the cantata *Mirjams Siegesgesang*, the Rellstab songs, and the C major String Quintet; in the latter the three great Piano Sonatas of 1828, the E flat Mass, the two Piano Trios, and the A minor Sonata movement for piano duet called *Lebensstürme* (Storms of Life). The chronology of these works is often difficult to determine, because dated autographs in the last two years of Schubert's life are less common than in his early years; and even where they are available, they may conceal a long period of gestation. The history of the three last Piano Sonatas, for instance, is much more complicated than the dated autograph suggests. The death of Beethoven and the meeting with Hummel seem to have strengthened Schubert's resolve to succeed as a composer in classical instrumental forms, and it may well be that the great chamber works of his last year began to take shape in his mind from that time.

In the early months of the year, his creative energy was concentrated on the first part of *Winterreise*. Apart from that, only a few other songs and partsongs survive. But publications continued to issue from the press in a steady stream. Tobias Haslinger, who had taken over the influential Steiner establishment in May 1826, lost no time in coming to an understanding with Schubert. He began in January with a set of twelve keyboard dances of the sort which Schubert could rattle off by the dozen, the so-called *Valses Nobles* D969, followed by the G major Piano Sonata D894 of October 1826. This appeared in April as a set of separate movements, individually titled, in order to avoid, presumably, the old-fashioned world 'sonata' and appeal to the new generation of keyboard players. Haslinger played an important part in promoting Schubert's name. Before the composer's death ten opus numbers appeared under his imprint, including important works such as *Winterreise* and the Impromptus, Op. 90, for piano. He seems also to have encouraged Schubert to set songs by well-known contemporary poets like Rochlitz and Seidl. Two sets of songs by these authors came out in May, including such favourites as 'Der Wanderer an den Mond' (The Wayfarer to the Moon) and 'An die Laute' (To the Lute). The Rochlitz songs had been composed in January.

After Part I of *Winterreise* came a group of partsongs, and one solo song of the first rank, a setting of verses by another contemporary poet,

Friedrich Reil. 'Das Lied im Grünen' (The Song of the Greenwood) D917 is a tribute to spring, and to its infallible power to heal and renew. The hint of mortality in the last verse casts a momentary shadow, soon dispelled. The mood is more carefree, less contemplative, than that of 'Im Frühling', the Schulze song written a year earlier, but the two masterpieces seem complementary. They represent Schubert's mature mastery of the through-composed song at its best.

Of the many fine partsongs of the year, two at least claim attention for their high quality and the circumstances surrounding their composition. 'Nachtgesang im Walde' (Night Song in the Forest) D913 was commissioned by the horn-player Josef Lewy, and first performed at his private concert on 22 April. Scored for male-voice quartet with an accompaniment of four horns, it is an extended work which begins in pastoral mood and culminates in a lively allegro. The setting of Franz Grillparzer's 'Ständchen' (Serenade) D920 for alto solo and female choir was written for Anna Fröhlich, the head of the Philharmonic Society's singing school, as a birthday present for one of her pupils, Louise Gosmar, Leopold Sonnleithner's fiancée. The piece was given its first performance outside Louise's window one evening in August. Schubert's infallible instinct for a precise *Bewegung*, and his mastery of piano figuration, enabled him to catch the mood of happy conspiracy exactly. It is perhaps the best of the partsongs of the year.

Before we come to the great instrumental works of 1827, something must be said of two enterprises with a less happy outcome. The *Deutsche Messe* or German Mass D872 was commissioned by J. P. Neumann, the author of the text. Neumann was a liberal churchman (he had written the libretto for Schubert's oriental opera *Sakuntala* in 1820) whose aim was to provide simple hymns for the congregation to sing during the celebration of the Mass. There are eight hymns and an epilogue. The work evidently met a need, for both text and music were quickly published and many arrangements of the music were made, though they were not published under Schubert's name until 1870. Since the intention was to bring the music within the compass of a congregation with no musical training, it is hardly fair to criticize the work for its unrelieved block harmonies, simple tunes and elementary progressions. The truth is, however, that it does not escape from the sentimentality which clings to so much popular nineteenth-century liturgical music, and its emollient piety soon begins to cloy.

The sketches for Bauernfeld's opera, *Der Graf von Gleichen* (The Count of Gleichen), were begun on 19 June, and must have kept the composer busy for some weeks. Sketches for twenty-one scenes of the two-act opera survive, with a few other fragmentary sketches. Schubert had of course long worked out his own routine for such work. Generally the voice line is written out in full, usually (but not always) with the text, and leading voices in the accompaniment inserted here and there in short score. The manuscript of the libretto and the sketches themselves are in the Vienna City Library, but they remain unpublished and unknown. Johann Herbeck arranged three numbers for a concert performance in October 1868, but the arrangement has never been published. No. 14, the Crusaders' Chorus, was arranged and published by Fritz Racek in 1962. Schubert seems to have been content to rely sometimes upon his own earlier ideas. No. 13, for instance, is a reworking of the Goethe song 'Wonne der Wehmut' (Joy in Sadness) of August 1815, while No. 20c, a soprano aria, borrows its main idea from the 1814 Matthisson song 'Die Betende' (The Girl at Prayer). But so far as can be judged, there is little in these sketches to remind us of the flair and originality which characterize earlier dramatic works like *Lazarus* and *Die Zauberharfe*. Schubert evidently put the work on one side until such time as a stage performance seemed possible; he is said, however, to have discussed it with Bauernfeld on his deathbed.

Schubert may have put the opera sketches aside to return to *Winterreise*, for first drafts of two of the songs from Part II have survived, probably from July or August. The most significant achievement of these summer months, however, was undoubtedly the composition of the first set of four Impromptus, later published by Haslinger as Op. 90. Schubert cannot be credited with having invented the form; the word came into use in Vienna in the early 1820s as a name for a short keyboard piece, usually in ternary form, written in the manner of an extemporization. The real father of the short characteristic keyboard piece was Tomášek, whose influence on Schubert, through his pupil Voříšek (1791–1825) has already been noticed (see page 113). But Schubert's command of tonality and movement, and his natural flair for dance rhythms and ternary form, found their most assured and characteristic expression in such pieces, so that his Impromptus and *Moments Musicaux* have set a standard for a whole literature of nineteenth-century music. The title, in any case, was not Schubert's but Haslinger's. The first page of the autograph has a note in the publisher's hand, 'Impromptu No. 1 in C minor'. The first two of the set appeared in December 1827, the other two, for some unexplained reason, not till 1857.

The spontaneity, combined with economy of means and clarity of form, in these pieces marks them off from the sonatas, making them specially representative of the essential Schubert, freed from the constraints of sonata form. Yet the distinction is a fine one. Schumann concluded, on the evidence of the key sequence and thematic cross-references, that the second set of Impromptus, Op. 142, written later in the year, is really a sonata in disguise; and since Schubert suggested to Schott of Mainz that they might be published either as a set or separately,[8] presumably

8 Docs, p. 739.

he did not regard the matter as very important. Admittedly, the earlier set is more varied in mood, style and tonality, more idiosyncratic in fact. The first Impromptu, in C minor, is quintessential Schubert both in its theme (is it not a sort of extemporary treatment of the tune of 'Der Wegweiser'?) and in its monothematic structure. No. 2 in E flat is a brilliant keyboard study with a contrasted middle section, and No. 3 an atmospheric nocturne, full of Romantic feeling, in G flat. No. 4 again assumes the character of an extemporization. It begins with a rippling arpeggio figure and an ambiguous pulse; but after exploring various tonalities, a kind of yearning cello tune wells up in the left hand. The Trio section in C sharp minor brings an interval of tonal stability and poetic sadness.

The autograph fair copy of the second set of Impromptus, Op. 142, is dated December 1827, but the existence of a sketch for the first in the set suggests that composition began some months earlier. The four pieces are numbered five to eight, leaving no doubt that they were intended as a sequel to the first set. The first and the last have a strong Hungarian flavour, with wide leaps and stamping rhythms, and both exploit Schubert's tendency to take off on a tonal digression, spinning a web of pure sound from an arpeggio figure or just a scale passage. No. 2 is a wistful Allegretto, and No. 3 a set of variations on the familiar tune from the *Rosamunde* Entr'acte in B flat.

Like the Impromptus, the six *Moments Musicaux* belong to the family of short characteristic keyboard pieces of Bohemian origin, though the provenance of Schubert's pieces is more obscure. Two of them had already been published in Sauer and Leidesdorf's annual 'Musical Album', No. 3 in December 1823 and No. 6 a year later. When the other four were composed is an open question, for the autograph has not survived. But we do know that Schubert was much occupied with small-scale piano pieces in the summer of 1827. Sketches for two such pieces have survived (D916B and 916C) which the paper experts confidently ascribe to the summer or early autumn. Some months earlier he had written a short piano work in ternary form, which is a 'Moment Musical' in all but name, quite perfect in its expressive economy. But with characteristic generosity he presented it to his young friend Ferdinand Walcher, who was due to leave Vienna to join his ship at Venice. It is known as the Allegretto in C minor D915 (Ex. 34).

In spite of their diversity of mood, there is an impressive consistency of style in the *Moments*. All reveal the composer's liking for monothematic procedures, and, except for the first number, in C major, they all inhabit the same tonal territory, lying between F minor, A flat, and D flat/C sharp. They rely for the most part on Schubert's preference for sectional structure and ternary form, and on his infinite capacity for inventing a precise movement or gait. The quasi-balletic quality in these hauntingly beautiful pieces might be adduced in support of the proposi-

Ex. 34

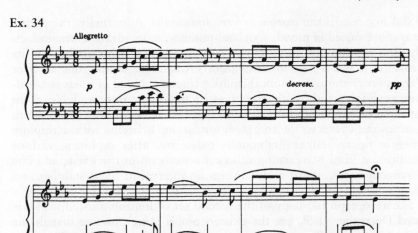

tion that Schubert was primarily a dance composer. The third, in F minor, is a near relation of the G major ballet music from *Rosamunde*. The sixth, in A flat, is a contemplative Menuet and Trio, coloured by the composer's tonal magic. The fifth is a study in Schubert's favourite dactylic rhythm. The second and the fourth are perhaps the most poetic, the latter a Romantic excursion on a baroque theme. Einstein was wrong perhaps to suggest that the *Moments* represent Schubert's last word as a keyboard composer, for the last three piano sonatas were still to come; but nothing is more idiosyncratic, more typical of the essential Schubert, than these eloquent miniatures. Their appeal is universal. They were published in July 1828 by Leidesdorf as *Momens musicals* (*sic*) in two books, Op. 94.

In September the long-projected visit to Graz took place at last. Schubert's friend Johann Jenger, a native of Graz, had made all the arrangements with Marie Pachler, the talented wife of the advocate Karl Pachler, who acted as host to the visitors. Marie was a fine pianist, who had even made an impression, as a young woman in 1817, on Beethoven's musical and emotional susceptibilities. Graz was a provincial capital with a lively musical life, and the Pachlers were at the centre of it. Schubert was well known there through his links with the Hüttenbrenners and with Jenger, so he was welcomed very much as a celebrity. In the first week a party was made up to hear Meyerbeer's opera *Il Crociato in Egitto* (The Crusader in Egypt), the German text of which had been prepared by Schubert's old collaborator Josef Kupelwieser, now secretary at the opera house in Graz. There was also a grand charity concert at which Schubert accompanied his own songs, and various excursions into the countryside took place.

Schubert took the opportunity to broach the possibility of a production of *Alfonso und Estrella*, and promised to recover the score from the Kärntnertor theatre and sent it to Karl Pachler. But nothing came of it. Ultimately the score did reach Graz, where it languished unperformed for many years before Ferdinand Schubert claimed it back. For three weeks Schubert blossomed in the warmth of his welcome. He was always at his best on these provincial excursions, and there is no hint of illness or indisposition. Back in Vienna, however, he was conscious of the very different social and cultural climate. Writing his thank-you letter to Marie Pachler, he adds: 'Already I find that I was too happy in Graz, and that I cannot yet get accustomed to Vienna. Admittedly, it is quite big, but then it is devoid of cordiality, openness, genuine thought, meaningful words, and especially of sensible behaviour. There is so much confused chatter that one hardly knows whether one is being clever or stupid, and inward calm is seldom or never achieved.'[9] The creative legacy of this bright interval in a sombre year seems to have been slight. In Graz Schubert wrote two songs to texts suggested by Marie Pachler, one of them an unremarkable setting of the Scottish ballad 'Edward' in Herder's translation (D923). The other is something of a curiosity, for it was for many years attributed to Karl von Leitner, the Graz poet. The real author of 'Heimliches Lieben' (Secret Love) D922, however, was Louise von Klenke, mother of Helmina von Chézy. The poem is a Sapphic ode full of passion. Schubert's vocal line floats serenely above a running accompaniment in triplets. The set of twelve 'Grazer Walzer' D924 and the 'Grazer Galopp' D925 must have been written down either during the holiday or very soon after Schubert's return, for they were published in January 1828 by Haslinger. The mood of the dances is bright and unclouded (the key centres are E major and A major) and though they lack the emotional depth of some of Schubert's dances, they illustrate once again his flawless command of tonality and form (Ex. 35).

The Leitner songs of the autumn represent a more substantial legacy of the Graz visit. Schubert had set Leitner's 'Drang in die Ferne' (The Urge to Roam) D770 in 1822, but it was Marie Pachler who persuaded him to return to this poet. A wonderful sequence of songs followed in

Ex. 35

[9] Docs, p. 670.

the period October to January, as typical of Schubert's mature song style as anything outside the great song cycles. The ability to capture and define a mood with a precise gait and an appropriate keyboard figure is splendidly illustrated in 'Die Sterne' (The Stars) D939, 'Der Winterabend' (The Winter Evening) D938 and 'Des Fischers Liebesglück' (Fisherman's Bliss); and even the sentimental verses entitled 'Vor meiner Wiege' (By my Cradle) D927 provide Schubert with an opportunity to explore once again the B minor tonality he had always associated with the thought of death.

Schubert's ability to compose the slight and unpretentious alongside the sublime has often been noticed, and there is a curious example of it in November, when he seems to have worked almost simultaneously on the E flat Piano Trio and the comic vocal trio *Der Hochzeitsbraten* (The Wedding Roast) D930. The provenance of this latter work, a sort of miniature operetta, is a puzzle. The text is by Schober, a sketch about two lovers caught redhanded in the act of poaching on the eve of their wedding day. An amorous huntsman succumbs to the blandishments of the bride-to-be and all ends happily with an irresistible yodelling finale. It is hardly a work which Schubert would have embarked upon, one feels, without some hope of performance or other inducement; in fact it was produced at the Josefstadt theatre shortly after the composer's death. One possible clue to the mystery is that Schubert's friend, Franz Lachner, had shortly before been enlisted as assistant conductor at the Kärntnertor theatre. Maurice Brown suggested that it was Lachner who was responsible for the publication of the youthful jeu d'esprit *Die Advokaten* (The Lawyers) D37 in May 1827, a work of similar scale and appeal. It may well be that Lachner, anxious to promote Schubert's operatic interests, planned to use 'The Wedding Roast' as a curtain-raiser.[10]

We turn now to the chamber works of the last three months of 1827, which, like those of the first three months of 1824, represent a creative peak in Schubert's life. Already we are on controversial ground, for although the surviving autograph of the Piano Trio in E flat D929 leaves no room for doubt that it was begun in November 1827, the provenance of the B flat Piano Trio D898 is shrouded in mystery. The autograph is missing, and no direct documentary evidence as to its date survives. Left to do the best they can with guesses based on stylistic traits, commentators have opted for various dates ranging from 1825 to 1828. In recent years, however, circumstantial evidence of a factual kind has come to light which makes it possible to conclude with some confidence that it was composed, as Kreissle said in the 1860s, 'a little earlier' than the E flat Trio.

The main considerations are these. The Adagio movement in E flat D897, sometimes called 'Notturno', is generally thought to have been intended originally as the slow movement of the B flat Piano Trio. It has tonal and stylistic affinities with the familiar Andante un poco mosso, but is clearly inferior to that fine movement. The autograph of this movement, which Schubert presumably rejected, has survived, and the paper experts tell us that the paper is identical with that which Schubert was using in the autumn of 1827 for the E flat Piano Trio and the fair copy of *Winterreise*. Moreover, in the first edition of the B flat work, which appeared in 1836, and in earlier publishers' catalogues and indexed lists of Schubert's works, it is always referred to as 'premier Grand Trio', an indication that this designation probably derives from the autograph. More significantly perhaps, there is clear documentary evidence that at the beginning of 1828 Schubert had two 'new Trios' in the market. One was played at his private concert on 26 March, and Leopold Sonnleithner put on record his clear recollection that this was the Piano Trio in E flat D929.[11] However, on 18 January, in a letter to Anselm Hüttenbrenner, Schubert had reported that 'a new Trio of mine' had been played at Schuppanzigh's, and that 'it pleased very much'.[12] This must be a reference to the public concert given by the Schuppanzigh Quartet on 26 December in the hall of the Philharmonic

[10] See Brown, *Essays on Schubert* (London, 1966), pp. 244–7.
[11] Memoirs, p. 115.　　　　　　　　　　　　　[12] Docs, p. 714.

Society. There is independent confirmation, in fact, that this concert included a Schubert trio. Now it was an established convention of the age that 'new' in this context meant that the work had not been played in public before. If therefore the work played in March was the E flat Trio, it is a reasonable conclusion that the work played in December was the 'premier Grand Trio' in B flat.[13]

We come back then to Kreissle's statement that the B flat Trio was written just before the companion work, in September/October 1827. If a more speculative gloss may be added, is it not likely that the lyrical energy of the work owed something to the Styrian countryside which had given him a new lease of life in September? The mountains had always acted as a catalyst for Schubert, and there is something of the vernal freshness of the 'Trout' Quintet about the B flat Trio. Schubert's friend Feuchtersleben remarked that he returned from Graz 'full of enthusiasm, but richer by only two songs'. But he may well have been speaking out of ignorance. The 'boundless longing' of the B flat Trio (the phrase is Schumann's) may at least have taken shape in his mind during the happy days in Graz.

If this enables us to assign a probable date to the work, it does not altogether dispose of the mystery, for the B flat Trio is never mentioned specifically in Schubert's correspondence with publishers in the course of 1828; and though it was known to exist, it was not published until June 1836. The most plausible explanation of this long gap between the first performance and publication is that it was sold, and presumably paid for, after its successful public debut, and then, for reasons which remain obscure, put aside. Such delays were not unusual (the Octet for wind and strings, the String Quintet, and the G major Quartet all had to wait till the 1850s for publication), but it remains mysterious.

Comparison between the two great piano trios has been a favourite occupation of critics ever since Schumann, in his review of the B flat Trio in 1836, characterized it, somewhat dubiously perhaps, as 'passive, lyrical and feminine' in contrast to the 'more spirited, masculine and dramatic tone' of the later work. The composer's lyrical and architectonic powers are at their best in the opening Allegro moderato, based on two happily contrasted but equally delightful subjects. The Scherzo looks back to that of the 'Trout' Quintet, turning its theme upside down, and in the final Rondo Schubert plunders the music of the village band to enliven the sobriety of classical form. The 'pipe and drum' episodes are a joy to Schubert-lovers, and the movement is kept going with a witty little theme which sounds like an about-turn in music (see Ex. 36). Is it only coincidence that this theme reproduces the notes from the Andante of the 'Trout' Quintet?

[13] See Eva Badura-Skoda, 'The Chronology of Schubert's Piano Trios', *Schubert Studies*, pp. 277–95.

Ex. 36

The tune is used for the brisk Presto coda, bringing this unfailingly inventive work to a lively conclusion.

The Piano Trio in E flat is more discursive, but even richer in incidental detail. Like the companion piece, it makes very effective use of terraced sequences in the development sections, a characteristic of Schubert's mature chamber music style. The incorporation of the theme of the Andante within the fabric of the finale is a masterly and original touch. Both the Trio and the concluding 6/8 Allegro moderato pay their tribute to vernacular folk rhythms, while the Scherzando makes deft use of canonic imitation. But it is the Andante con moto which at once commands attention by its attractive theme and pacing rhythm of four steady quavers to the bar. There is a well-authenticated tradition, recorded by Leopold Sonnleithner in 1858[14] and documented by Alois Fuchs in 1844, that Schubert borrowed this theme from a Swedish song which he heard the tenor Isak Albert Berg sing at the Fröhlichs' house. Berg was a young Swedish singer who stayed in Vienna for about a fortnight early in November 1827, and appeared at receptions which Schubert also attended. The song has recently been rediscovered and identified by Manfred Willfort, and the opening bars are given in Ex. 37a.

Ex. 37

(a)   Se solen sjunker (Original key D minor)

Se   so-len sjunker ner ____ back hö-ga ber-gens topp   för ____

[14] Memoirs, p. 115.

154

(b) Schubert: E flat Piano Trio

It is apparent that the *gehende Bewegung*—the walking gait—of the song and of Schubert's theme are the same, but the resemblance in fact goes further. For the characteristic turns of the trio theme, in the cello's third bar, for instance, and the drop of a fifth in its tenth bar, are revealed by a full comparison to be inspired adaptations of features in the song.[15] The song is called 'Se solen sjunker' (The sun has set).

[15] M. Willfort, 'Das Urbild des Andante aus Schuberts Klaviertrio D929', *Österreichische Musikzeitschrift*, vol. xxxiii, 1978, pp. 277–83.

Sketches for the E flat Piano Trio survive from November 1827. After the first performance at Schubert's concert on 26 March the composer shortened the finale by some ninety-nine bars, and instructed the publisher that the cuts were to be strictly observed in the first edition. The parts appeared in October 1828 from Probst of Leipzig, but it is doubtful whether Schubert received them before his death.

The two piano trios brought to this favourite classical form a new sense of tonal balance between strings and keyboard, and a new tonal inventiveness. Having made his own unique contribution to one form, he turned to another, the fantasia, which had attracted him since boyhood. There are two ways, broadly speaking, of reconciling the freedom and spontaneity which belong to the form by its nature with the sense of organic unity which it must achieve if it is to succeed as a work of art. The first may be called the method of thematic transformation; this treats the fantasia as basically a monothematic form, in which one seminal idea is adapted to sit the changing moods of the piece. This method had inspired Schubert's adolescent experiments with the form (especially the Fantasie in C minor for four hands D48) and the great 'Wanderer' Fantasie of November 1822. The other method may be called the method of cyclical organization, and has more affinity with the rondo. Here various contrasting musical ideas are used, the piece is conceived as a sequence of discrete sections rather than as an organic whole, and a sense of unity is achieved through repetition and recurrence. This method lends itself readily to extension and elaboration. Schubert had experimented with it in the Rondo in B minor for violin and piano of October 1826 D895, and he now turned to it again. Like the Rondo in B minor, the Fantasie in C for violin and piano was written for the Czech virtuoso Josef Slawjk, and the first performance was given at his concert on 26 January 1828. Like most of Schubert's mature chamber works, it has a formal link with the songs, for its centre piece is a set of florid variations on the Rückert song, 'Sei mir gegrüsst' (I greet you) D741. Grouped round this central section are six others based on three main ideas. The tempos move from the Andante molto introduction to Allegro vivace at the end, with intervening sections marked Allegretto and Andaninto, while the key system is based on C major and its circle of thirds, A minor/major, A flat, and E flat. The elaborate organization seems to have mystified the audience at the first performance, as well as the critics, and it must be admitted that it seems to concede too much to brilliance and virtuosity. Only the Vienna correspondent of the London *Harmonicon* found a good word to say for it.[16] Once again, however, the tonal effects are striking, so much so that—in the introduction for instance—Schubert seems to make orchestral demands on his two players.

[16] 'A new Fantasia for pianoforte and violin, possesses merit far over the common order.'

The Fantasie in C, written in December 1827, can be regarded as the forerunner of a much greater work. For in January he drafted the Fantasie in F minor for piano duet, his greatest work for four hands, which brings to the cyclical form of organization a diversity in unity and emotional depth unique in the literature of four-handed works. The piece is in four linked movements, which follow a conventional sonata pattern. But the long-legged theme in F minor which has the first and the last word, and holds the structure together, anchors the whole work to a mood of contemplative sadness and resolution. The tonal scheme, moreover, exhibits a perfect Schubertian symmetry, the predominant F minor/major of the outer sections set off by the Neapolitan key of F sharp in the inner movements. The Largo makes a wistful gesture in the direction of Rossini, while the Scherzo (Allegro vivace) rivals Beethoven in its drive and assurance. The final section acknowledges its status by reverting to a contrapuntal treatment of earlier material, but at the end Schubert looks back to the F minor tune after a long pause which sounds like the musical equivalent of a cardiac arrest, and the mood of reconciliation and regret is restored. The work draws eclectically on a variety of musical sources, yet its unity, and its authentic Schubertian quality, remain unassailable.

This discussion of the F minor Fantasie has taken us beyond the close of 1827, in order to draw attention to the link between it and the Fantasie in C. Meanwhile the good health and euphoria of the Graz visit had quickly evaporated. Schubert had promised Frau Pachler that he would write a short easy duet for her and her small son, Faust, to play on Karl Pachler's nameday. So on 12 October he duly sent off a little March in G (D928), adding his best wishes to Karl, and an ominous postscript: 'I hope that your grace is in better health than I, for my usual headaches are already plaguing me again.'[17] A few days later he had to excuse himself from a party at Netti Hönig's, and in November he was unable to keep a luncheon engagement. There was nothing in these social non-events to alarm Schubert's friends, but it is clear that the various gastric and other ailments which had bothered him since his illness were by no means cured.

---

[17] Docs, p. 679.

10

The final phase (1828)

On New Year's Eve the Schubertians gathered as usual in Schober's rooms. According to Franz von Hartmann's diary, it turned out to be a lively evening. In addition to the Hartmann brothers there were present Schober, Spaun, and Schubert (who had been once again a tenant of Schober's since March), the pianist Josef von Gahy, Schwind, and Bauernfeld, the scholar and teacher Karl Enk, and Eduard Rössler, a young doctor from Pest. 'On the stroke of twelve we toasted each other in Malaga and drank to a happy new year. Bauernfeld then read a poem on this point of time.'[1] At two o'clock the visitors left to go on to Bogner's coffee house. Bauernfeld's poem, which was to appear a few days later in the Vienna *Zeitschrift für Kunst*, is a meditation on time's revenges. Towards the end it seems to take a prophetic turn: 'The magic of speech, the source of all song, it too, though divine, will cease to flow. The voice will no longer ring out in the throng, for the singer too has a time to go. As the stream hastens toward the sea, so the singer—to the source of all poetry.'[2] The Schubertians had reason to be conscious that their days of irresponsible youth were over. Bauernfeld himself was now a civil servant, trying hard to establish himself as a dramatist. Spaun was to be married in April. Schwind was soon to move to Munich to further his career as a painter, while the Hartmann brothers were due to end their studies and return to Linz in August. Bauernfeld's words are therefore more likely to refer to the ineluctable passage of time than to the possibility of Schubert's death before the end of the year, which came as a surprise to his friends.

The carnival season began with a relentless round of parties, and with the revival of the reading parties at Schober's after an interval of nearly four years. Thanks to Franz von Hartmann, who was a regular attender, we can compile a fairly complete list of the literary fare provided. The meetings were held weekly on Saturday evenings, and continued through to August with occasional breaks. The favourite authors were Heinrich von Kleist, the enemy of the political and cultural establishment, seven of whose *Novellen* were read early in the year; Tieck in

[1] Docs, p. 703.   [2] Docs, p. 703.

March and April; Goethe; and Schober himself, whose only published book of verse, *Palingeneses* (a collection of sonnets on biblical themes), was read in February and March. Also mentioned are Heine (*Reiseideen*), Friedrich von Schlegel and Karl Immermann. Clearly the Schubert circle was determined to keep abreast of current literary trends.

On 28 January Spaun organized a special Schubertiad to celebrate his engagement to Franziska Roner. At Schubert's own suggestion Bocklet, Schuppanzigh, and Linke were invited, and a performance was given of the Piano Trio in E flat and of the Variations on an Original Theme in A flat for piano duet D813. These details we owe to Spaun, though he does not identify by name the individual works played.[3] He adds that this splendid occasion was the last of its kind. Schubert's new Fantasie in C for violin and piano D934 was given its first performance at Josef Slawjk's concert on 20 January, and met with a cool reception. The real achievement of the month, however, was the drafting of the F minor Fantasie for piano duet, already discussed. The very full sketches which survive are mainly on two staves, dated 'January 1828'. A comparison with the fair copy of April throws a revealing light upon Schubert's compositional methods at this time. In January he came to a halt during the Scherzo, doubtless dissatisfied with the march tune he first thought of. In the final version this tune is discarded in favour of the familiar fleet-footed theme. Elsewhere the general tendency is towards extension of climaxes and clarification of ideas.[4] The fourth movement, for instance, is strengthened and lengthened by the repetition of the double forte climax and by an inspired insertion of five extra bars in the coda. As is the case with the 'Great' C major Symphony, some of the most effective and characteristic moments in the work are shown to be the result of the composer's second thoughts. Both works seem to be sustained by the Romantic search for sublimity. The F minor Fantasie was dedicated to Karoline, Countess Esterházy, and published by Diabelli in March 1829.

Early in February two letters arrived unexpectedly from publishers soliciting works for publication, a further indication of Schubert's rapidly growing reputation. In 1826 his approach to Probst of Leipzig had proved fruitless. Now Probst wrote to ask him to send whatever compositions he had available. The letter from Schott of Mainz was equally accommodating, and rather more business-like. It is noticeable also that the many reviews of Schubert's published works in this last year of his life are markedly more respectful and discriminating; indeed, a series of discerning reviews by G. W. Fink, the editor of the Leipzig *Allgemeine musikalische Zeitung*, may well have alerted Probst and Schott to the importance of Schubert's work, not to mention its commercial potential. In reply to Schott, Schubert wrote on 21 February to offer the E flat Piano Trio, two string quartets (those in D minor and G

---

[3] Memoirs, p. 138.
[4] John Reed, *Schubert: The Final Years* (London, 1972), pp. 180–4.

major presumably), the Impromptus for piano (second set), the two recent fantasias, and the comic trio *Der Hochzeitsbraten*. As an afterthought he added a string of unpublished works, operas, a symphony and a mass, 'only in order to acquaint you with my striving after the highest in art'.[5] Schott's reply asked for eight works to be sent for inspection, but said little about fees, except to request the composer to fix 'the lowest fee possible'.[6] There the matter rested for some weeks, while Schubert busied himself with the preparations for his public concert.

This was the realization of a long-cherished ambition. Ever since the collapse of his operatic hopes, it had been recognized in the circle that the only way to promote Schubert's interests would be to mount a concert entirely devoted to his own works. Beethoven's public concert of 7 May 1824 had sparked off a serious discussion of the project, but the financial risk involved, and the lack of enthusiasm shown for Beethoven's concert, had persuaded Schubert against the idea. But now he seemed to have good reason to hope for a successful outcome. At Jenger's instigation, the hall of the Philharmonic Society was put at his disposal free of charge. He had always been generous with his help for other people's concerts; now they rallied to his support. Vogl promised to take part. So did the tenor Ludwig Tietze and the hornist Josef Lewy. Schuppanzigh was ill and unable to attend, but his colleagues in the famous quartet agreed to perform a movement from 'a new quartet'—probably the one in G major—and (with Bocklet at the piano) a piano trio. Josefine Fröhlich brought her choir of young ladies from the Conservatoire to sing the partsong *Ständchen* D920, and the male-voice choir of the Philharmonic Society contributed a rousing chorus, *Schlachtlied* (Battle Song) D912. The hall was full, the programme was received with enthusiasm, and Schubert was left with a profit of more than 300 gulden, in those days a substantial sum.

Perhaps the most interesting of the vocal items in this programme, the only work specially written for the concert, was the setting of Rellstab's verses entitled 'Auf dem Strom' (On the River) D943, for tenor solo with accompaniment of piano and horn obbligato. The unusual forces are no doubt to be explained by the availability of Tietze and Lewy, but Schubert's facility turns them into a minor masterpiece of exceptional interest. Rellstab's poem is a song of farewell, at first glance a man's valediction to his lover as his boat slowly recedes from the shore. But it soon becomes clear that the words have a deeper, more symbolic, meaning. The speaker is taking leave, not only of his love, but also of his life. 'Oh, how I shudder with horror before that dark wilderness, far from every friendly shore, where no island is to be seen; no song can reach me from the shore, to bring sad tears. Only the storm blows cold across

---

[5] Docs, p. 740.   [6] Docs, p. 745.

the grey and angry sea.' Schubert's setting uses a pair of related stro-
phes, the odd-numbered verses in E major and the even ones in the rel-
ative minor, so that the song, like the poem, seems to work on two
emotional levels, and the seemingly conventional means—the arpeggio-
based figures, the echo phrases on the horn, and the gentle rise and fall
of the voice—take on deeper and more tragic overtones. It has been
pointed out by Rufus Hallmark[7] that the song has significant emotional
and thematic links with Beethoven, and that the minor tune of the even-
numbered verses is an obvious allusion to the funeral march in the
Eroica Symphony (see Ex. 38).

Ex. 38

What makes this all the more curious is that Schubert originally
planned his concert for 21 March, but postponed it for a week, so that
it actually took place on 26 March, the anniversary of Beethoven's
death. Moreover, it is generally accepted that the Rellstab poems had
come to Schubert from Beethoven's *Nachlass* through the agency of
Schindler. What it comes to, then, is that Schubert chose a text handed

---

[7] 'Schubert's *Auf dem Strom*', *Schubert Studies*, pp. 25–46.

on to him from Beethoven, as tragic in tone as his own *Winterreise*, had it performed on the anniversary of the master's death, and based his setting partly on an allusion to Beethoven's best-known and most characteristic symphony. It is not necessary to assume that he was here engaged in a process of Elgarian mystification; more likely he was simply paying a deeply felt compliment to his great predecessor, and at the same time staking out his own claim to be a representative of 'the highest in art'.

The short cantata *Mirjams Siegesgesang* (Miriam's Song of Victory) D942 seems also to have been intended originally for performance at Schubert's concert. It is written for soprano solo, SATB chorus, with piano accompaniment, though according to Leopold Sonnleithner Schubert intended to provide full orchestration,[8] so presumably time did not allow for the piece to be properly prepared and the two choral items were put in to replace it. It was well known that Beethoven had at one time promised to write an oratorio for the Philharmonic Society, for which Franz Grillparzer was to have provided the text, and that he spent much time in his last months studying the scores of Handel oratorios, some of which are said to have been handed on, after his death, to Schubert. It must be of some significance therefore that *Mirjams Siegesgesang* is recognizably Handelian in style and that its text is by Grillparzer. The soprano solo part was written for Anna Fröhlich's sister Josefine, and it was Anna Fröhlich who arranged for the first performance to be given at the Memorial Concert of 30 January 1829. The work is in six linked sections. Franz Lachner was responsible for the orchestrated version used at the Memorial Concert. The consciously archaic tone of Miriam's Song probably militates against it, for it is neither *echt* Handel nor idiosyncratic Schubert. But the composer's infallible musicality ensures that it is effective in performance.

Elated by the success of his concert, Schubert resumed the correspondence with Schott, offering to send the Piano Trio, the second set of Impromptus, and the male-voice quintet *Mondenschein* (Moonlight) D875 for 160 gulden. On the same day he sent a belated reply to Probst's letter of 9 February, offering him the Piano Trio and various other unspecified works, and asking for a fee of 60 gulden 'per sizable book'. This phrase was intended to apply to books of songs or minor piano pieces, but Probst chose to interpret it in his own way, and promptly sent off 60 gulden, asking for the Trio in return. In the meanwhile Schott had decided to reject the Trio, which left Schubert with no alternative but to send it off to Probst. This he did on 10 May, protesting that he never intended to let it go for so small a fee, and adding precise instructions for its performance.

The cuts indicated in the last movement are to be strictly observed. Be sure to have it performed for the first time by capable people, and most particularly

[8] Memoirs, p. 12.

see to a continual uniformity of tempo at the changes of the time-signature in the last movement. The minuet at a moderate pace and *piano* throughout, the trio, on the other hand, vigorous except where *p* and *pp* are marked.[9]

The correspondence dragged on through the summer months, while Schubert's impatience to see his work in print increased as his health deteriorated. His anxiety, coupled with the curiously meticulous instructions to Probst, suggest that he was fully aware of the possibility that he had little time left.

On 9 May Bauernfeld noted in his dairy: 'Today Schubert (with Lachner) played his new wonderful four-hand Fantasie to me.'[10] Earlier in the day the two friends had been present at Paganini's fourth recital, and Schubert, always generous when in funds, paid for both tickets. The Viennese had taken to Paganini with their usual immoderate enthusiasm, ,and their insatiable appetite for news of the Italian virtuoso was responsible for the fact that Schubert's concert was comprehensively ignored by the musical press. Not that the Schubertians themselves were immune to the general infection. This was Bauernfeld's second, and probably Schubert's third, visit. Jenger had written to Marie Pachler in extravagant terms about the new star in the musical firmament, while Schubert himself, enraptured by Paganini's cantabile, had written to Anselm Hüttenbrenner 'I heard an angel sing in the Adagio'.[11]

In April, as usual, he wrote songs. At least, he drafted several Rellstab songs, including 'Herbst' (Autumn) and possibly also 'Lebensmut' (Courage), 'Liebesbotschaft' (Message of Love) and 'Frühlingssehnsucht' (Longing for Spring). But the chronology of the Rellstab songs is unclear. The fair copy is dated August 1828, and attached to the autograph of the Heine songs, but Schubert's intention was to publish them as a separate group. The only other composition which can certainly be ascribed to April is the fair copy of the F minor duet Fantasie, and the mature lyricism and mastery of the Rellstab songs fits in with April well enough.

His main concern in the summer months, however, was with liturgical works and piano pieces. The three *Klavierstücke* D946 belong to May, and seem to fall in the same category as the Impromptus, though the autograph has neither title nor numbering. The first and third are in ternary form, with stormy and impetuous outer sections and more lyrical and tranquil middle sections; the keyboard writing is often strikingly improvisatory. The most interesting of the three pieces is the second in E flat, a poetic sonata rondo with interludes in C minor/major, A flat minor and B minor. It is built upon a haunting 6/8 tune of great beauty (Ex. 39), adapted from the chorus which opens Act III of Schubert's 1823 opera *Fierabras*.

[9] Docs, p. 774.   [10] Docs, p. 773.   [11] Memoirs, p. 67.

Ex. 39

The three *Klavierstücke* were not written as an integrated work, and the third may well be earlier than May 1828. They were not published till 1868, when they were assembled and edited by Brahms.

Two fine works for piano duet, written about the same time, represent Schubert's last contribution to the four-hand medium he had so richly endowed. The first, a sonata movement marked Allegro ma non troppo, was published by Diabelli in 1840 under the title *Lebensstürme* (Storms of Life), a sobriquet which is at least in keeping with the work's restless questing spirit. Well-contrasted subject groups are accommodated within a powerful forward drive, the tonality is wide ranging, and the development section is one of the best Schubert ever wrote. Like the 'Grand Duo' sonata, the work seems to invite orchestration, so strong are the instrumental overtones in the writing. Both formally and in its Promethean spirit the work seems to represent a return to earlier models, and its effectiveness in performance makes one wonder whether Schubert was once again 'working his way towards grand symphony'. Yet the piece could hardly present a bigger contrast with the symphonic sketches (D936A) which he also began to draft during the summer months. The *Lebensstürme* movement surprises by its organic unity and strength; the symphonic sketches by their lack of definition and a certain amorphous quality.

The Grand Rondo in A, D951, has always been thought of as a companion piece to the *Lebensstürme* movement D947, and it may well have been intended as the finale of a sonata which Schubert failed to complete. It was finished in June, and published in December by Artaria. Marked Allegretto quasi Andantino, it is based on one of the composer's loveliest and sunniest tunes, handled with all his mastery of tone and texture. The single contrasted interlude, in C major, does not perhaps quite sustain the magic of the rest, but who will complain, when Schubert is able to delight and surprise us for more than 300 bars without moving far from the key of A major?

The indications we have of Schubert's state of mind during his last summer are not reassuring. Meeting one day by chance with the actor Heinrich Anschütz, he began to talk about the ending of Barbaja's lease of the Kärntnertor, which had expired in June. 'Thank goodness,' said Schubert, 'we are rid of this barbarous music!' And when Anschütz protested that the Italians had given people a great deal of pleasure, 'All very well,' came the reply, 'but don't talk to me about music. It often seems to me as though I no longer belonged to this world.'[12] It may have been said as an ironic jest, but the fact was that the headaches, attacks of giddiness, and gastritis which had returned after his holiday at Graz were still troubling him. This may well be the real explanation of the constant complaints of lack of money, which in themselves seem surprising. There is no sign that his income from publications, commissions and fees had been drying up. Rather the reverse; and the proceeds from his concert had been a useful windfall. Yet the return visit to Graz which he and Jenger had promised to make foundered miserably in the end through lack of funds. In April the only doubt appeared to be not whether, but when, the visit would take place. But soon doubts begin to arise. On 6 September Jenger reported that Schubert was expecting an early improvement in his financial circumstances (from the fee for the E flat Piano Trio?), and planned to arrive in Graz 'with a new operetta'—*Der Hochzeitsbraten* perhaps? Three weeks later, however, the whole project had to be abandoned. 'Nothing will come of the trip to Graz this year,' Schubert wrote to Jenger, 'for money and weather are wholly unfavourable.'[13]

There was not much reassurance to be gained from the circle either. The reading parties went on into August, but Schubert was an irregular attender, and seems to have spent several weeks in June and July at Währing with Schober. Schwind, after agonies of indecision, had at last got himself engaged to Netti Hönig, and though their plans were by no means secure, felt obliged to further his career by attending the academy at Munich. Bauernfeld's first play, due to be produced in September,

---

[12] Memoirs, pp. 223–4.   [13] Docs, p. 807.

proved to be a flop, and was taken off after four performances. Vogl and Spaun had taken up matrimony, while Mayrhofer had come to terms with life as the paid servant of a regime he detested. Only Schubert, and of course Schober, seemed unable to look forward to some settled station in life, and even Schubert in these last months of his life appeared to be preparing himself for a position as Kapellmeister.

The evidence for this lies in the series of liturgical and sacred works which occupied him from May to October, and in the decision to seek lessons in fugue and counterpoint from Simon Sechter, the court organist and acknowledged master in such matters. The Mass in E flat D950, which was begun in June, is certainly the greatest of the liturgical works of 1828; its greatness, however, can only be fully appreciated in the context of the age. It is necessary first to consider the story of Schubert's ambitions as a church composer, and of his Mass in A flat D678, over which he spent more time, and took more trouble, than over any other single work.

Church music was in Schubert's blood. He was trained in the art and craft of music as a choirboy, first in the parish church of Liechtental and then in the Imperial and Royal Chapel. It was his first mass, written at the age of seventeen, which drew public attention to his genius, and he produced liturgical works throughout his working life. From the first the Mass in A flat was planned on the most ambitious lines. It was begun in November 1819 and Schubert worked at it off and on for three years, with numerous sketches and amendments. Writing to Spaun on 7 December 1822 he said: 'My Mass is finished, and is to be produced before long. I still have the old idea of dedicating it to the Emperor or the Empress, as I think it a success.'[14]

In one sense it certainly was. The A flat Mass is a bold and original attempt to combine the new expressionist language Schubert had developed in his songs with the conventional form of the rite. But he underestimated the difficulties involved in getting its innovatory style accepted. The fact that his own religious beliefs had much more in common with the deism of the Enlightenment than with the strict orthodoxy of the court may not have mattered much, for this rationalist faith still had many adherents both inside and outside the church, and many of those who professed it—men such as Pyrker, Spendou, and Neumann—were his friends and patrons. More importantly, he was not best equipped to deal with those sections of the Mass which were traditionally reserved for fugal treatment, and the Viennese court seems to have been strongly conservative in such matters. He had an instinctive grasp of canonic devices, and could use them with force and facility; but the set-piece fugues in the Gloria and the Credo are a different matter. His lack of assurance in the use of counter-themes and tonal answers too often suggests that he is imprisoned in the form, rather than liberated by it.

[14] Docs, p. 248.

In the A flat Mass Schubert wisely omitted all set fugues except the 'Cum sancto Spiritu' at the end of the Gloria, and his first attempt at that failed to satisfy him. The Mass was finished in September 1822. In January 1826 it was carefully revised, and he wrote a second version of the 'Cum sancto Spiritu' based on a shorter and more interesting subject. But when he took this revised version of the Mass to Josef Eybler, Kapellmeister at the Royal Chapel, he was told that, good as the work was, it was not in the style the Emperor approved.[15] Not surprisingly, the E flat Mass of 1828 reverts to much more traditional models. There are fully-worked fugues in all the usual places, and much contrapuntal treatment elsewhere. The main key scheme is confined to E flat and its near relations. Thus the two great Masses of Schubert's maturity are contrasted in much the same way as the two great symphonies of 1822 and 1825–6; while the first is lyrical, organic, innovative, and idiosyncratic, the later work reflects those tendencies which influenced both Schubert and Beethoven in their final phase: a reversion to traditional forms, a revival of interest in contrapuntal techniques, and above all, a Romantic concern for sublimity.

Both masses exploit Schubert's genius for orchestral tone fully, and both employ trumpets as well as trombones. The great moments in the E flat Mass, the threefold cry of wonder at the opening of the Sanctus, the 'Domine Deus', the opening of the Gloria, and the Agnus Dei, all reveal a mastery of antiphonal effects in the use of brass, woodwind, strings, and voices which Schubert had not achieved before (see Ex. 40).

Ex. 40(a)

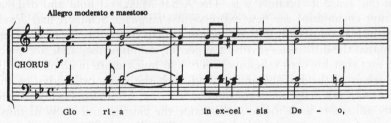

---

[15] Memoirs, p. 177.

Ex. 40(b)

The hushed pleading of the chorus ('Miserere, miserere nobis') against the inexorable chant of the brass in the 'Domine Deus' is perhaps the most moving moment in all Schubert's six Masses. The Mass in E flat was probably written for the church of the Holy Trinity at Alsergrund, where Schubert's boyhood friend, Michael Leitermayer, was organist. Beethoven's funeral service had taken place there, and it was at Schubert's own request, so it is said, that the first performance was given there on 4 October 1829, eleven months after the composer's death.

Whether the Mass was commissioned by the church of the Holy Trinity is not clear, but the setting of *Glaube, Hoffnung und Liebe* (Faith, Hope and Love) D954 certainly was. It was written for the dedication service for the recast bell on 2 September 1828. The text, by Friedrich Reil, is linked to the theme of St Paul's famous chapter, though it is not a paraphrase. Schubert's setting, for male-voice quartet and SATB chorus with wind-band accompaniment, is serenely diatonic and homophonic in Haydn's manner. Indeed, his ability to disguise himself as other composers is especially striking in the last years of his life; he could write like Beethoven, Rossini, or Haydn at will, not to mention composers yet unborn like Brahms, Wolf, and Richard Strauss. By a curious coincidence, a rather Brahmsian song with the same title ('Glaube, Hoffnung und Liebe' D955) was written at about the same time, but the author is Christoff Kuffner and it has no connection with the choral work.

Also commissioned was the setting of Psalm 92 ('It is a good thing to give thanks unto the Lord') for baritone solo and SATB quartet and chorus. It was written for Salomon Sulzer, the cantor of the new Vienna synagogue which had been inaugurated in 1826. The Jews were only now recovering from a long period of oppression in Vienna, and something like a renaissance of Jewish culture was taking place. As a compliment to Sulzer, and perhaps as a gesture of sympathy for the Jewish cause, Schubert set the Jewish text of the psalm, and did his best to accommodate the non-metrical structure of Jewish poetry.[16] This work (Psalm 92 D953) was written in July.

The circumstances in which the *Hymnus an den heiligen Geist* ('Hymn to the Holy Ghost') D948 was written are not known, but it is a substantial work for male-voice quartet and chorus with a middle section, marked 'Un poco più mosso', for chorus only. The a cappella version was written in May, and in October Schubert added parts for a wind band of 13 players, including trombones. The piece makes some concession to the demand for sweet undemanding piety, especially in its main theme, and indeed these choral works belong to the category of serviceable occasional works rather than great masterpieces. But the extensive series of such liturgical works in his last year argues not only that his services were in demand, but that he was looking to them as a permanent source of income. Significantly, in October he wrote a new four-part version of the Benedictus for his Mass in C, which had been published in 1825. The original version was written for Therese Grob, and its high tessitura had evidently proved a stumbling block in performance. Diabelli issued the new version separately in 1829.

Throughout the summer Schubert's health continued to give cause for concern. He was now under the care of Dr Ernst Rinna, a court physician whose fees must have added to the strain on Schubert's resources. Rinna was a believer in fresh air and exercise. On his advice Schubert moved out to the Wieden suburb at the beginning of September, to live with his brother Ferdinand. The area was then being opened up as a residential suburb, and it is said that the sanitary arrangements were still incomplete. Whatever the reason, the expected improvement in his condition did not take place. But his friends were inclined to regard his indispositions as just one of the facts of life, and nobody was seriously alarmed. As for his creative power, in August and September it reached a peak which set the seal on his life's work. In those two months he completed the Rellstab and the Heine songs, the String Quintet, and the three great Piano Sonatas in C minor, A major and B flat.

The autograph of the songs is dated August 1828. Unless we are prepared to reject categorically the testimony of Schindler, and of Rellstab himself, however, we must suppose that the texts of the Rellstab songs came to Schubert's possession from Beethoven's *Nachlass* in 1827, and some of them were certainly set in the spring of 1828. As for the Heine

[16] Elaine Brody, 'Schubert and Sulzer Revisited', *Schubert Studies*, pp. 47–60.

songs, Schönstein was consistently firm in his contention that they were written long before Schubert's last illness, though his dates have been proved faulty. The Schubertians were reading Heine in January 1828, and Deutsch's conjecture that they were sketched in January and February 1828 seems reasonable. It is probable, therefore, that the autograph represents the last stage in the selection and revision of songs which had been sketched earlier. In any case, the association of the two groups of songs in one publication was entirely the publisher's idea. Early in October Schubert offered the Heine songs to Probst, a clear indication that he was still at that time thinking in terms of two separate publications. Haslinger saw the commercial advantage of linking all Schubert's 'last songs' together, and it was he who invented the title *Schwanengesang* (Swan Song). For good measure he added the Seidl song, 'Die Taubenpost' (The Carrier Pigeon) D965A, a lovely song which serves as a kind of epitaph to Schubert's lyrical genius, but one which has no connection whatever with either Rellstab or Heine. In the end Haslinger published the fourteen songs in two books, the second of which included the last of the Rellstab songs, the Heine group, and 'Die Taubenpost'. In this way Schubert's intentions were finally frustrated, and even the integrity of the two groups was ignored.

It is the mark of Schubert's genius that he developed a different style for every poet he set, and the Rellstab and Heine songs can be clearly differentiated, though they touch the same deep pessimism—and the same key of B minor—in 'In der Ferne' (Far from Home) and 'Der Doppelgänger' (The Ghostly Double). The Rellstab group have more variety of emotional colour, and their lyrical mastery reminds us often of *Die schöne Müllerin* rather than *Winterreise*, especially in 'Liebesbotschaft' (Message of Love) and 'Frühlingssehnsucht' (Longing for Spring). The formal perfection of 'Ständchen' has made it perhaps the best known serenade in music. 'Kriegers Ahnung' (Warrior's Foreboding) looks like a reversion to the earlier form of the sectional ballad; yet its tone is set by the double-dotted theme of the opening, which returns like a muffled drum-beat as the singer, in the closing bars, bids his sweetheart goodnight. 'Aufenthalt' (Resting Place) is another Wanderer song, reminding us of the Schulze songs in its ostinato rhythm, but less headlong, more resolute, as though passionate protest had mellowed to stoic strength. 'Abschied' (Parting) is a more good-humoured leave-taking, for the young man who rides out of the town has life before him, as well as a journey. Its jogtrot rhythm can be almost hypnotic; it brings this wonderful cycle to a smiling close.

Heine is a greater poet than Rellstab, as well as a more acerbic and epigrammatic one. To match this mood of bitter irony, Schubert's settings, with the sole exception of 'Das Fischermädchen' (The Fisher Girl), exhibit a spare but intense expressiveness which represents the final achievement of his lyrical genius. 'Ihr Bild' (Her Likeness) is a magical

distillation of the torment of lost happiness. 'Am Meer' (By the Sea) and
'Die Stadt' (The Town) bring the expressive language of the classical age
within reach of Debussy and Strauss. 'Der Doppelgänger' is perhaps the
greatest of the Heine songs. It is neither pure song nor pure recitative,
but a kind of impassioned declamation based on a harmonic sequence
in B minor which has close thematic links with the E flat Mass.
Schubert's traffic with the Lied had begun in 1811 with imitations of
Zumsteeg's eighteenth-century ballads; here, seventeen years later, he
brings it into the emotional world of Hugo Wolf.

The unity of the Heine songs is reinforced by a vague continuity of
theme, and by close musical associations between them; for they inhabit
the same tonal territory as the first group of piano Impromptus Op. 90
and the *Moments* Op. 94, based on the 'circle of thirds', C, E flat, G, B
flat, A flat, C flat (= B minor/major), D flat. This strongly implied unity,
however, is to some extent obscured by the fact that Schubert's order is
different from Heine's. If the songs are rearranged in Heine's order—
'Das Fischermädchen', 'Am Meer', 'Die Stadt', 'Der Doppelgänger', 'Ihr
Bild', 'Der Atlas'—the narrative thread and the tonal relationships present themselves more forcefully. This has led some authorities to assume
that Schubert's original order must have been the same as Heine's, an
attractive hypothesis, but one which remains in the present state of
knowledge unproven.[17]

The correspondence with Schott and Probst dragged on inconclusively
through the summer months. Schott, having begun as though he wanted
to publish everything of Schubert's he could lay hands on, finally asked
for only two works, the second set of Impromptus and the vocal quintet *Mondenschein*. Then, having consulted his Paris advisers, he changed
his mind about the Impromptus, on the ground that they were 'too difficult for trifles', and haggled over the fee for *Mondenschein*. This dis-
mal news was conveyed to Schubert at the end of October, as the effects
of his final illness began to make themselves felt. Meanwhile Probst, who
had received the E flat Piano Trio in May, seemed to have done very little about it. At the beginning of October Schubert lost patience, and
wrote to the publisher in terms which are all too revealing about his
state of mind:

> Sir, I beg to enquire when at last the Trio will appear. Can it be that you have
> not yet got the opus number? It is Op. 100. I await the appearance of it with
> longing. I have composed among other things three sonatas for piano solo,
> which I would like to dedicate to Hummel. Also I have set several songs by
> Heine of Hamburg which were extraordinarily well liked here, and lastly com-
> posed a Quintet for 2 violins, viola and 2 cellos. I have played the sonatas in
> several places with great success, but the Quintet is still to be tried out in the

---

[17] Harry Goldschmidt, 'Welches war die ursprüngliche Reihonfolge in Schuberts Heine-
Liedern?', *Deutsches Jahrbuch der Musikwissenschaft für 1972* (Leipzig, 1974), pp. 52–62.
Richard Kramer, 'Schubert's Heine', *NCM*, Spring 1985, pp. 213–25.

coming days. Let me know if any of these compositions would perhaps suit you. Respectfully I remain, Frz. Schubert.[18]

Probst replied by return of post, apologizing for the delay in the publication of the Trio. But on the possibility of accepting further works he was guarded, asking only to see the Heine songs, which Schubert did not send. Significantly, he ends with a request for more easy works for piano duet, for which there was a rapidly growing market.[19] The correspondence is a striking confirmation of the fact that even at the end of his life Schubert was still regarded as a composer of songs and popular piano music, and not taken seriously as a chamber music composer.

The last three piano sonatas show the same tendency to revert to classical models that we have noticed in the case of the 'Great' C major Symphony and the E flat Mass. Attempts to reshape the sonata in a concise, organically unified form which are observable in the A minor Sonata of 1823 D784, and in some earlier fragmentary sonatas of his middle years, are abandoned, and Schubert returns to the four-movement model, but on a scale expansive enough to accommodate the emotional world of the songs. It is not simply that the Andantino of the A major Sonata D959 is a near relation of the Schober song 'Pilgerweise' (Pilgrim's Song) D789, and that the main theme of the opening movement of the B flat Sonata D960 recalls Mignon's song 'So lasst mich scheinen', especially in its second setting of April 1821, D727. The emotional tone of the sonatas, and to a large extent their musical idiom, is taken over from the songs. Their emotional antecedents derive in particular from the Mignon songs, from the melodrama 'Abschied von der Erde' D829, and from the Heine songs.

The influence of Beethoven, which has often been noticed in these sonatas, is strongest in the C minor Sonata D958. The resemblance between the opening theme and the subject of Beethoven's C minor Variations is obvious enough, while the Adagio is unmistakably Beethovenish. Even the impetuous 6/8 Finale may well owe something to the Presto finale of Beethoven's Op. 31 No. 3. But this is nothing new; much the same comment could be made about the Tragic Symphony of 1816 or the 'Grand Duo' Sonata of 1824. Less often noticed is the fact that the Menuetto is based on a familiar Schubert theme, which appears as early as his very first string quartet (D18) of 1810 or 1811. Where the C minor Sonata is dynamic and dramatic, the A major work is lyrical and *feierlich*. The opening Allegro is pure Schubert in its discursive inventiveness. A tiny phrase lifted from the end of the exposition becomes in the development the basis of a delightful passage characteristic of the composer's command of figuration and tonality. There is a sense of serenity, of controlled feeling about the sonata, rudely shattered, however, in the middle of the Andantino. The 3/8 theme has much

---

[18] Docs, pp. 810–11.   [19] Docs, pp. 813–14.

the same pulse and shape as the corresponding movement of the B flat Sonata, but here a storm of rushing scales and trills suddenly irrupts into the stillness, only to subside just as suddenly three pages later. This procedure may be compared with that in the corresponding movements of the G major String Quartet and the C major String Quintet. Schubert's tendency to make these sudden changes of mood can be traced as far back as the Andante of the String Quartet in B flat of November 1812 (see pp. 12–13) and seems to be a mark of that emotional ambiguity which is a feature of his art.[20] The serene Finale borrows a theme from the A minor Sonata of March 1817 D537 and finds its own pre-echo in the lovely Schulze song of 1826, 'Im Frühling' (In Springtime).

The Sonata in B flat D960 is the most personal and poetic of them all. The veiled melancholy of the opening Molto Moderato is punctuated by ominous bass trills and pregnant pauses. Perhaps the most magical episode in the whole movement is the bridge passage which leads back to the recapitulation. The Andante sostenuto is a slow contemplative dance, a ternary movement in C sharp minor which moves at the end to the major in a passage of rhapsodic stillness and poetry. The tone of reconciliation and valediction in this wonderful work is unmistakable, and gives it a special place in the affections of Schubert lovers. It is only in this century, however, that Schubert's achievement in these three great sonatas has been fully recognized by the critics and a wider audience. For many years their length and expansiveness hindered their acceptance as worthy to be set beside Beethoven. It was that great Schubertian Sir Charles Hallé who first brought them to public notice in England in the 1860s in his annual series of piano recitals in London. After the First World War Schnabel, and later Brendel, were largely responsible for reawakening public awareness of Schubert's keyboard masterpieces.

The autographs of these last three sonatas are dated September 1828 and headed 'Sonate I', 'Sonate II' and 'Sonate III', thus realizing at long last Schubert's ambition to publish a set of sonatas to rival Beethoven's Op. 2 and Op. 10 sets. Schubert's declared intention to dedicate the three works to Hummel provides some circumstantial support for the notion that their conception in his mind went back to the events of March 1827. By the time Diabelli got round to publishing them, however, Hummel was dead; instead, Diabelli dedicated them to a younger champion of Schubert's genius, Robert Schumann.

We know even less about the origins of the String Quintet in C D956 than we do about the last piano sonatas, because neither sketches nor fair copy have survived. It is fair to assume, from the letter to Probst already quoted, that Schubert turned to the Quintet after finishing the sonatas towards the end of September, but it seems unlikely, to say the least, that he would embark on such a profound and ambitious work

---

[20] Hugh Macdonald, 'Schubert's Volcanic Temper', *MT*, Nov., 1978, pp. 949–52.

without his usual preliminary sketches. It was well known that Beethoven had promised Diabelli a string quintet as early as 1824; a twenty-four-bar sketch for the work had been found among his papers and published as 'Ludwig van Beethoven's last Musical Thought'. The projected quintet was to have been in C major. What more appropriate than that Schubert should accept responsibility for Beethoven's unfinished business?

The String Quintet has its deliberate textural roughnesses, its 'hard sayings', and its total impact would be diminished if they were not there. For part of its greatness at least is its universality. It aims to include everything, the confident vigour of the Scherzo and the lingering valediction of the Trio, the poetic vision of the Adagio and the pragmatic good humour of the Finale. Surely no tune could more clearly express the belief that life is good and happiness is manageable than this:

Ex. 41

Yet the whole work sounds like a reluctant leave-taking. It is the final and definitive expression of Schubert's poetic vision, of that Romantic longing for the world beyond the world which he learnt from Mayrhofer and Goethe and a hundred others. For many listeners that conscious longing is best summed up in the dark lyricism of the second subject of the opening Allegro ma non troppo, but it is present, too, in the quizzical little syncopated march tune which emerges just before the end of the exposition and proceeds to dominate the development. (It sounds like a Schubertian comment on Beethoven's famous inscription over the finale of his F major String Quartet: 'Must it be?—It must be.') And the poetic vision is reflected and symbolized by the Neapolitan relationship, the emphatic accenting of the tonic by the note a semitone higher, which permeates the work. In the Adagio this relationship is presented in schematic form, the middle section in F minor, turbulent and rhythmically angular, set off against the outer sections in the stillness of E major. Even after the return of the poetic vision, echoes of the emotional storm still rumble on in the second cello part, and it returns momentarily but ominously, in the last bars of the movement. As though to endorse the finality of this tonal symbolism, Schubert brings the whole work to a close with an emphatic reassertion of C major against the disruptive pull of D flat (Ex. 42). As Browning's Abt Vogler put it, 'Hark, I have dared and done, for my resting place is found, The C major of this life: so, now I will try to sleep.'

Ex. 42

It was Thomas Mann who said of the String Quintet that it is the music one would like to hear on one's deathbed, and indeed it is difficult to listen to it without feeling that Schubert must have had some premonition of the approaching end. Yet his life in October went on quite in accordance with normal routines. At the beginning of the month, probably at Rinna's suggestion, he went on foot to Eisenstadt in Hungary to visit Haydn's grave. The expedition involved a walk of about fifty miles, covered in three days; nothing exceptional for those

175

days, though it hardly suggests a man close to death. His companions on this holiday were Ferdinand, and probably also two of Ferdinand's close friends, Josef Mayssen, a teacher and choirmaster in the suburb of Hernals, and Johann Rieder, who occupied a similar position at the church of the Holy Trinity at Alsergrund. It may not be a coincidence, therefore, that Schubert returned to liturgical works in October, first making a fair copy of the orchestral version of the 'Hymn to the Holy Ghost', written in May, and then turning to two new works, the Offertorium *Intende voci* D963 and the *Tantum ergo* D962. The former is a substantial work for tenor solo, mixed chorus, and full orchestra with trombones, with a good deal of contrapuntal part-writing. The *Tantum ergo*, for similar forces, is equally effective in its more homophonic style. It is a fair assumption that both these pieces were intended for performance at Alsergrund, where Rieder seems to have had appropriate forces at his disposal.

Some time in October also Schubert arranged to take a course of lessons in counterpoint with Simon Sechter, the court organist, then the leading authority on fugue, but today remembered only as the tutor of Schubert, Liszt, and Bruckner. If it seems astonishing to us that a man who had just completed the three great piano sonatas and the String Quintet should seek instruction from an academic expert in an outmoded style, it must be remembered that the eighteenth-century view of composition as a 'scientific' discipline which could be acquired by patient study was still widely accepted, and that modern ideas of genius as a mysterious God-given faculty beyond the need for systematic training would have seemed very strange to Schubert, or to Beethoven, who had himself in his early thirties sought instruction in the art of word-setting from Salieri, the recognized expert in such matters. To Schubert's friends there would have been nothing outrageous in the proposal, particularly in the context of his apparent wish to find a post as a Kapellmeister. Indeed, it had been canvassed often before 1828, and it is said that the only member of the circle to speak against it was Karl Pinterics, the gifted amateur and collector of Schubert's songs. On or about 4 November Schubert actually attended at Sechter's rooms for his first lesson. The manuscript record of this fascinating event has survived; it was discovered by Christa Landon in 1968 in the archive of the Vienna *Männergesangverein*, and it throws a remarkable light on Schubert's motives for embarking on a course of study with Sechter so late in his short life. For it was concerned with what was for him the nub of the problem, methods of varying the real answer, the successive statements of the fugal subject, so as to give life and flexibility to the composition. At the end of the lesson Sechter wrote out a fugue subject based on the musical equivalent of Schubert's own name, presumably intending that this should be worked out before the next lesson. But Schubert was already a sick man. The second lesson never took place, and it was

Sechter himself who wrote the fugue on the composer's name as a memorial to him after his death.[21]

Schubert's last two songs, written in October, turn away from the pessimism of *Winterreise* and the Heine songs to the enchanted world of pure melody. 'Die Taubenpost' (The Carrier Pigeon) has already been mentioned. The poet sends messages to his love by pigeon post, and the name of the secret messenger is—Longing (*Sehnsucht*). The tune dances along as if captivated by its own delight, only to pause momentarily at the final revealing couplet. 'Der Hirt auf dem Felsen' (The Shepherd on the Rock) D965 is a recital piece specially written for Anna Milder-Hauptmann, the prima donna of the Berlin opera, whom Schubert had first heard and admired as a schoolboy, when she appeared with Vogl at the Kärntnertor. It is scored for soprano and clarinet (the piano accompaniment is purely supportive) and it calls for two virtuoso performers. In the right hands it is irresistible. Yet the text is a contrived affair in three discrete sections, two of them abstracted from Müller, and one, so it is said, from Helmina von Chézy. 'The Shepherd on the Rock' is not perhaps the greatest Schubert, but only he could have written it. After the first performance, which Milder gave in March 1830, the piece disappeared for the rest of the century, to be rediscovered in 1902 at a concert of the Vienna Schubert Society.

A problematic set of sketches for a symphony in D remains to remind us that Schubert's symphonic ambitions had not been satisfied with the completion of the 'Great' C major. Until recently the seven leaves containing these sketches were assumed to belong to May 1818, along with other sketches (D615). Recent research into the script characteristics, however, and the paper-types has established that they must be much later, and are among the composer's last works. According to the experts two types of paper are represented, one of which points to an origin in the summer of 1828, while the other suggests a later date still, probably October. The sketches are all on two staves, and include alternative drafts without any clear indication of sequence, number of movements, or of the composer's ultimate intentions. Evidently Schubert's ideas had not yet advanced to the stage at which a continuous outline score, such as he had adopted for the 'Great' C major and for the symphonic sketch in E of August 1821, could be attempted. Nor do these 1828 sketches have anything like the coherence and continuity of the surviving sketches for the 'Unfinished' Symphony. Yet there is internal evidence that this is indeed a late work. The beginning of what is assumed to be the first movement (Schubert marks it '*Anfang*') has a repetitive figure reminiscent of the opening of the B flat Piano Trio, and of the *Klavierstück* in C, D916B, of 1827 (see Ex. 43).

[21] Alfred Mann, 'Zu Schuberts Studien im strengen Satz', *Schubert-Kongress Wien, 1978*, pp. 127–39.

Ex. 43

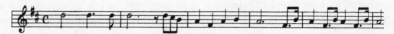

A Scherzo, also in D major, is based on two themes which are developed contrapuntally, a reminder of Schubert's growing interest in contrapuntal techniques. Without any question, however, the most interesting sketch is for an Andante in B minor, a spare and sombre movement in 3/4 time with a quasi-Mahlerian tone of elegiac self-absorption (see Ex. 44).

Ex. 44

It is difficult to conceive that such world-weary music as this originated in the same month as 'Der Hirt auf dem Felsen' and 'Die Taubenpost', though such contrasts are by no means unknown in Schubert. The sketches have been sympathetically realized as a three-movement symphony by Brian Newbould, and a version is now available on record.[22] New light has been thrown on this problematic work by a recent article by Daniel Jacobson and Andrew Glendening, who make a convincing case for the view that the sketches were intended as the first stage of a symphony designed as a public tribute to Beethoven.[23]

On the last day of October he went out with Ferdinand and friends for an evening meal at 'The Red Cross' in the Himmelpfortgrund, near the old schoolhouse where he had grown up. No sooner had he tasted the fish, however, than he began to feel ill. This time the attack marked

[22] Brian Newbould, 'Schubert's Last Symphony', *MT*, May, 1985, pp. 272–5.
[23] See *Brille*, 15 (June 1995), pp. 113–26.

the onset of his final illness, though nobody realized as much at the time. For the next two weeks, however, life went on much as usual. On the following day he attended a performance of his brother Ferdinand's Requiem Mass at Hernals church, and afterwards went for a three-hour walk. His first lesson with Sechter took place on 4 November. About the same time he dined with the Fröhlich family, and spent a convivial evening with Schönstein. Spaun called to see him, and found him well enough to check the fair copy Spaun had made of the setting of Psalm 23 (D706) for a ladies' choir at Lemberg. 'There is nothing really the matter with me,' he declared on this occasion, 'except that I am so exhausted I feel as if I were going to fall through the bed.'[24] A few days later he wrote his last letter to Schober. 'Dear Schober, I am ill. I have eaten nothing for eleven days, and drunk nothing, and I totter feebly and shakily from my chair to bed and back again. Rinna is treating me. If I take anything I bring it up at once.' And he went on to ask for reading matter, and in particular for novels by the fashionable Fenimore Cooper.[25]

On or about 14 November he took to his bed permanently. But he was still completely *compos mentis* and able to converse normally with his friends. He expressed a wish to hear Beethoven's recently published string quartet in C sharp minor, Op. 131, and according to the violinist Karl Gross a performance was specially arranged in his bedroom. Schubert was full of enthusiasm, and so moved that it was feared the excitement might aggravate his condition. When Rinna fell ill himself, he handed over the case to a colleague, Josef von Vering, a specialist in venereal diseases. On 16 November a conference between Vering and another doctor, Johann Wisgrill, took place at the bedside. Vering's diagnosis was gloomy. He later told his nephew, Gerhard von Breuning, that he had regarded the case as hopeless from the beginning because of the 'advanced decomposition of the blood'. Vering thought that the origins of the disease were to be looked for much earlier. But he may have foreseen the possibility of a lapse into coma, for a male nurse was called in to help Ferdinand's wife Anna, and Schubert's stepsister Josefa, who had been giving devoted attention to the patient.

On Monday 17 November he was still fully conscious. Bauernfeld and Lachner came to see him, and the talk was about opera, in particular *Der Graf von Gleichen*. Later in the day, however, he became delirious, and the next day his condition rapidly worsened. The end came at 3 o'clock on Wednesday afternoon, 19 November.

The cause of death was entered on the death certificate as *Nervenfieber*. This imprecise term was the one generally used to describe a collapse of the central nervous system resulting in coma. It tells us nothing about the reason for the final collapse which set in only forty-eight

[24] Memoirs, p. 139.   [25] Docs, pp. 819–20.

hours before death, though there have been many conjectures. According to Deutsch, Schubert was suffering from typhoid fever brought on by insanitary conditions in the Wieden suburb. But his symptoms are not those normally associated with typhoid fever. Schubert remained rational and articulate until the last stage of his illness. Many members of the circle, including Mayerhofer, Bauernfeld, Lachner, and the doctor Vering saw his death as only the last phase of a process which had begun in 1823 with his serious illness. Without doubt the secondary effects of that infection must have taken their toll in later years, and maybe the treatment for it also, for the only known remedy in those days was the application of mercury, itself toxic. It has even been suggested that the immediate cause of death was the onset of the tertiary stage of syphilis. It may be so, though there are serious objections. The truth is that the cause of death was not clear even to Schubert's own doctors. They left no detailed data on which a more accurate diagnosis could be based, and the hospital records of the time, if they ever existed, have disappeared. His final collapse and death came as a shock and a surprise to his friends, and its immediate cause remains a mystery.[26]

In one sense, however, it is an irrelevant mystery. For the evidence accumulates that whatever his friends thought, Schubert himself recognized the irreversible nature of his disorder, and felt himself to be living, so to speak, in the presence of death. 'Sometimes it seems to me as though I no longer belonged to this world,' he had said to Anschütz, and Ferdinand's account of his last recorded utterance has a strangely apt finality. 'All day long he wanted to get up, and he continued to imagine that he was in a strange room. A few hours later the doctor appeared . . . But Schubert looked fixedly into the doctor's eyes, grasped at the wall with a feeble hand, and said slowly and seriously: "Here, here is my end!" '[27] The evidence of his own work, however, is the really significant thing. Nobody can study his songs and his chamber compositions, particularly those of the last three years, without realizing the constant companionship he found in the idea of death. He inherited the belief of the early Romantics in death as friend to life, and he re-enacted that belief in his own life.

The funeral service was held in the parish church of St Joseph, Margereten, on Friday 21 November. The burial was planned to take place there also, but the arrangements were changed at the last minute. Early on the Friday morning Ferdinand wrote to his father, to propose that the body should be interred in the Währing cemetery, which he knew to be his brother's own wish. 'For on the evening before his death, though only half-conscious, he said to me: "I implore you to transfer me to my room, not to leave me here in this corner under the earth; do I

---

[26] For a full discussion of the evidence, and a more positive summary of it, see Sams, loc. cit., p. 106. See also H. D. Kiemle, 'Woran starb Schubert eigentlich?', *Brille* 16, pp. 41–51.

[27] Memoirs, p. 38.

then deserve no place above the earth?" I answered him, "Dear Franz, rest assured, believe your brother Ferdinand, whom you have always trusted, and who loves you so much. You are in the room where you have always been, and lie in your own bed." And Franz said: "No, it is not true: Beethoven does not lie here".'[28] A memorial service was held at the Augustiner church in the inner city on 23 December, followed by an informal gathering of friends at Spaun's house.

In 1829 a fund was launched to pay for a permanent memorial to the dead composer, which was erected in the summer of 1830. The project was organized by a small group led by Grillparzer and the Fröhlichs. Grillparzer himself drafted a number of possible inscriptions. The one finally chosen read: 'The art of music here entombed a rich possession, but even fairer hopes.' Much facile and unfair criticism has been levelled at Grillparzer for this, on the ground that he failed to appreciate the greatness of Schubert's actual achievement. Since that achievement was not to be fully acknowledged till a century had passed, Grillparzer can perhaps be excused for not being gifted with second sight. The truth was that none of the composer's friends was fully aware of the range and depth of his genius; much of his greatest work was to remain unpublished, unknown, and undiscovered for many decades yet.

Grillparzer also wrote some doggerel verses about Schubert, which Kreissle later declared 'sum up his friend's influence and individuality as an artist'. Freely translated, they at least give an indication of the composer's single-minded dedication to his art.

> I am Schubert, and I claim
> To answer to no other name.
> I can only play my part
> By honouring the highest art.
> I can't command your presence here.
> It's not my way to interfere.
> If you praise, or if you blame,
> That's all one, I shan't complain.
> Do you like the path I tread?
> Then fine, just follow where I led.[29]

The worst feature of the conspiracy of silence about Schubert's life during the nineteenth century has been that it opened the way to a whole series of critical misconceptions and mythical interpretations. We have had Schubert the 'natural' composer, the impoverished Bohemian of popular anecdote, the eternal youth of Capell's brilliant sketch,[30] and the slightly epicene youth of operetta. Grillparzer's ironic little sketch at

---

[28] Docs, p. 825.

[29] See Kreissle von Hellborn, vol. 2, p. 170.

[30] See Capell, *Schubert's Songs* (London, 1928). New edition, ed. Martin Cooper, 1973, chap. 1.

least brings us nearer to the truth than these extravagant fancies. For behind that bland manner and unprepossessing appearance he cherished a fierce pride in his own genius, an invincible tenacity of purpose. He believed absolutely in the truth of his own vision, and knew that it was his right, in the end, that he should rest beside Beethoven.

Appendix A

Calendar

Year	Age	Life	Contemporary musicians and events
1797		Franz Peter Schubert born, 31 Jan, in the Himmelpfortgrund, Vienna, son of Franz Theodor Schubert, schoolmaster, and Elisabeth, née Vietz.	Napoleon's north Italian campaign. Peace of Campo Formio, Oct. Donizetti born, 25 Nov. Beethoven aged 27, Cherubini 37, Haydn 65, Hummel 19, Meyerbeer 6, Rossini 5, Salieri 47, Ignaz Schubert 12, Ferdinand Schubert 3, Karl Schubert 2, Weber 11.
1798	1		First (private) performance of Haydn's *The Creation*, 30 Apr.
1799	2		Napoleon becomes First Consul.
1800	3		Beethoven gives his first public concert, 2 Apr. Battle of Marengo, 4 June; Austrians driven out of Italy.
1801	4	Schubert family moves to the house in the Säulengasse called 'The Black Horse'.	Peace of Lunéville, 2 Feb. Bellini born, 1 Nov.
1802	5	Schubert introduced to the keyboard by his brother Ignaz.	Peace of Amiens, Mar.
1803	6		Zumsteeg dies, 27 Jan. Berlioz born, 11 Dec.
1804	7	Schubert's uncle Karl Schubert dies, 29 Dec.	First (private) performance of the *Eroica* Symphony, Feb. Franz II gives up the title of Holy Roman Emperor and becomes Franz I, Emperor of Austria.

Year	Age	Life	Contemporary musicians and events
1805	8	Schubert sings in the choir of Liechtental church, and is introduced to the violin by his father.	First public performance of *Eroica* Symphony, Apr. Vienna occupied by the French army under Napoleon, Nov. Battle of Austerlitz, 2 Dec.
1806–1807	9–10	Schubert studies singing, keyboard, and counterpoint under Michael Holzer, choir master of Liechtental church.	
1808	11	Vacancies in the choir of the Imperial Chapel advertised, May. Auditions for choirboys held under the direction of Kapellmeister Salieri, 30 Sept–1 Oct. Schubert enters the *Konvikt* as a choral scholar, Oct. Meets Josef von Spaun.	Part I of Goethe's *Faust* published.
1809	12	Schubert plays violin in the student orchestra at the Seminary.	Mendelssohn born, 3 Feb. Austria declares war on France, 9 Apr. The Seminary is hit by a French shell, 11 May. Vienna occupied by the French army, 12 May–20 Oct. Haydn dies, 31 May. Austrian army defeated at Wagram, July. Metternich becomes Foreign Minister. Peace of Vienna, Oct. Period of rapid inflation in Vienna.
1810	13	Earliest surviving compositions, including song sketches, a Fantasie for piano duet (D1), and possibly a string quartet (D18).	Chopin born, 22 Feb; Schumann born, 8 June.
1811	14	Earliest surviving complete songs, including 'Hagars Klage' (D5), 'Der Vatermörder' (D10), and probably 'Leichenfantasie' (D7). Other compositions include an Overture for strings (D8), a Fantasie for piano duet (D9), and a symphonic sketch (D2B). Schubert's first opera, *Der Spiegelritter*, begun, Dec. Studies keyboard under the	Devaluation of the currency, and introduction of the *Wiener Währung*, or local currency, 15 Mar. Liszt born, 22 Oct.

Year	Age	Life	Contemporary musicians and events
		court organist, Wenzel Ruzicka.	
1812	15	Schubert's mother, Elisabeth, dies, 28 May. Begins lessons in counterpoint with Salieri, 18 June. Schubert's last appearance as a chorister, 26 July, his voice having broken. Many exercises in voice-setting for Salieri. Other compositions include an Overture in D (D26), church compositions, a sonata movement for piano trio (D28), string quartets, and songs.	
1813	16	Probable date of Schubert's visit to the Court Theatre, Jan, with Spaun and Theodor Körner to see Vogl and Milder in Gluck's *Iphigénie en Tauride*. Schubert's father marries Anna Kleyenböck, aged 29, daughter of a silk merchant, 25 Apr. Schubert recommended for an endowment to enable him to continue his studies, 13 Sept. Imperial decree, 22 Oct, approving the award of the Meerfeld Endowment to Schubert on condition that he reaches the required standard in the new term. Schubert renounces the Meerfeld Endowment, Nov. Symphony No. 1 in D finished, 28 Oct. *Des Teufels Lustschloss* begun, 30 Oct. Other compositions include several string quartets, an Octet for wind instruments (D72) and Minuets for piano and for string quartet.	Wager born, 22 May. Theodor Körner dies of wounds received in action, 26 Aug. Verdi born, 10 Oct. Battle of the nations at Leipzig, 16–19 Oct.
1814	17	Schubert enters the Normal School of St Anna, Jan, to train as a primary school-	Paris surrenders to allied armies, 30 Mar; Napoleon leaves France for Elba, 20

Year	Age	Life	Contemporary musicians and events
		teacher, and passes the qualifying examination in Aug. Present at the first performance of *Fidelio* (final version), 23 May. Composition of String Quartet in B flat (D112), 5–13 Sept. Parish church at Liechtental celebrates its centenary, 25 Sept. F.p. of Schubert's first Mass in F at Liechtental church, 16 Oct. Revised version of *Des Teufels Lustschloss* completed, Oct. Composes his first Goethe song, 'Gretchen am Spinnrade', Oct. Symphony No. 2 in B flat begun, 10 Dec. Love affair with Therese Grob begins. Autumn: Music practices in the Schubert home become a regular weekly event, with dances and orchestral music arranged for strings. Compositions of 1814 include the Mass No. 1 in F, the String Quartet in B flat Op. 168, Sept, and thirteen Matthisson songs.	Apr; Congress of Vienna assembles, Sept. Grand Beethoven concerts held in the Redoutensaal, at which the A major Symphony, the 'Battle Symphony', and *Der glorreiche Augenblick* are played, 29 Nov. and 2 Dec. Formal establishment of the *Gesellschaft der Musikfreunde*, the Vienna Philharmonic Society.
1815	18	Schubert teaches in his father's school but continues his association with Salieri and with his friends at the Seminary. The flood of compositions in this year includes two symphonies (Nos. 2 and 3), four operas, two Masses and other liturgical works, dances and sonata movements for piano, a string quartet in G minor and about 150 songs. Autumn: The orchestral practices held at the Schubert home outgrow the school-	Napoleon escapes from Elba, 26 Feb; The Hundred Days; Battle of Waterloo, 18 June. Student unrest in Vienna, autumn.

Year	Age	Life	Contemporary musicians and events
		room, and move to the house of Franz Frischling in the Dorotheagasse. First meeting with Schober, and with Anselm Hüttenbrenner.	
1816	19	Applies (unsuccessfully) for a post as music teacher at the Normal School at Laibach, Feb. Spaun's request for permission to dedicate the first volumes of the projected edition of Schubert's songs to Goethe is ignored, Apr. Schubert contributes to the fiftieth anniversary celebrations of Salieri's arrival in Vienna, 16 June. F.p. of the cantata *Prometheus*, Schubert's first paid commission. First meeting with Leopold Sonnleithner, 24 July. Schubert moves to Schober's rooms in the inner city, and gives up teaching. End of the Therese Grob affair. The orchestral practices resume under the leadership of Otto Hatwig. Regular association with Salieri ends, Dec. Compositions of the year include two symphonies (Nos. 4 and 5), a Mass, a string quartet in E, and over 100 songs; also the first *opera seria, Die Bürgschaft* (incomplete).	Beethoven piano sonata played in public at Linke's farewell concert, 18 Feb. First visit of the Italian opera company to Vienna offers opportunity to hear *Tancredi* in Italian, 17 Dec, and *L'inganno felice*, 26 Nov.
1817	20	First meeting with Michael Vogl in Schober's rooms, ?Mar. Friendship with Mayrhofer deepens Schubert's understanding of Romantic thought and of neo-classical themes. Schober leaves Vienna, Aug, to assist his brother Axel. Soon after Schubert vacates his rooms	First issue of *Beiträge zur Bildung für Jünglinge*, edited by Mayrhofer.

Year	Age	Life	Contemporary musicians and events

at Schober's and returns to the schoolhouse. Josef Hüttenbrenner arrives in Vienna, late summer, and becomes an enthusiastic propagandist for Schubert's work. Schubert's father is promoted to the headship of the school in the Rossau suburb, Dec. The most important compositions of 1817 are the song settings of Mayrhofer, Goethe, and Claudius; a series of six pianoforte sonatas, Mar– Aug, the Symphony No. 6 in C, begun Oct, and the two Overtures 'in the Italian style', Nov.

1818 21 Schubert family moves to the schoolhouse in the Rossau suburb, Jan. There Schubert may have resumed teaching temporarily. The Mayrhofer song 'Erlafsee' is published as a supplement to the 'Pictorial Pocket Book'— the first Schubert song to appear in print, 6 Feb. The Overture 'in the Italian style', D590, played at a public concert in the Theater an der Wien, 1 Mar. (First Schubert orchestral work to be played in public.) Schubert's application to join the Phil. Soc. as a practising member is blocked by the Committee. Overture 'in the Italian style' again played at a public concert, 17 May. From July, employed as music tutor to the Esterházy family at Zseliz in Hungary. There he met the baritone singer Karl von Schönstein and wrote a series of works for piano duet

Vienna Phil. Soc. advertises its intention to promote a series of 'evening entertainments', including Schubert's name among the list of attractions, Jan. First of the Phil. Soc.'s 'evening entertainments' held, 12 Mar. The Chief of Police, Sedlnitzky, reports growing concerning about student unrest, May. Anselm Hüttenbrenner returns to Graz, Oct. His brother Josef takes up a post in Vienna, Dec.

Year	Age	Life	Contemporary musicians and events
		for the young countesses. Returns to Vienna, Nov. 19, sharing Mayrhofer's lodgings in the Wipplingerstrasse. Commissioned, on Vogl's recommendation, to write the music for a one-act farce, *Die Zwillingsbrüder*, for the Kärntnertor theatre. Important works of 1818: the Symphony No 6 in C (completed Feb), the Sonata in B flat for piano duet (D617), the unfinished F minor piano sonata of Sept (D625), and the Rondo in D for piano duet, Jan.	
1819	22	Schubert is introduced into the Sonnleithner circle, Jan. Leopold Sonnleithner organizes a repeat perform-ance of the *Prometheus* cantata, 8 Jan. Score of *Die Zwillingsbrüder* completed, 19 Jan. 'Schäfers Klagelied' (Goethe) sung by the tenor Jäger at a public concert at the 'Roman Emperor' inn, 28 Feb. (First Schubert song to be sung in public.) He receives 180 florins on account from the Court Theatre for *Die Zwillingsbrüder*, and for copying the parts, June. Early July–mid Sept: Schubert and Vogl on holiday at Steyr and Linz. Main works of 1819: *Die Zwillingsbrüder*, Overture in E minor, Feb, *Adrast* (unfinished sketches for an *opera seria*), Piano Sonata in A major (D664), Quintet for Piano and Strings (the 'Trout'), and the Mass in A flat, begun Nov.	Murder of Kotzebue by a young student in Mannheim, 23 Mar. Conference of German states at Carlsbad under Metternich's leadership agrees new repressive measures to combat student radicalism. Carlsbad Decrees promulgated, Sept. Count Collorado, a leader of liberal opinion, visits Vienna and makes contact with Johann Senn and other members of the Schubert circle. Lanner and J. Strauss join forces to form the popular quintet.
1820	23	Composes the dramatic oratorio *Lazarus*, Feb.	Therese Grob marries Josef Bergmann, Nov.

Year	Age	Life	Contemporary musicians and events
		Schubert, with Senn, Bruchmann and others, arrested during a police raid on Senn's rooms, Mar. Directs a performance of Haydn's 'Nelson' Mass at Alt-Lerchenfeld church, 4 Apr. Overture in E minor (D648) played at the Assembly Hall in Graz, 7 Apr. First public performance outside Vienna. Haydn's *The Creation* performed, 13 Apr, under Hatwig's leadership at the music practices. *Die Zwillingsbrüder* produced at the Kärntnertor theatre, 14 June. It runs for six performances. Schubert at Atzenbrugg, July. *Die Zauberharfe* produced at the Theater an der Wien, 19 Aug. It runs for eight performances. The orchestral practices come to an end, Sept, finding no suitable accommodation. 'Erlkönig', sung by August von Gymnich at a soirée at Sonnleithner's, 1 Dec, makes a big impression, and leads to a plan to publish Schubert's songs privately. Schubert and Mayrhofer part company at end of the year. Schubert lives alone in rooms nearby for the next few months. Compositions of the year include *Lazarus*, Feb, *Die Zauberharfe*, May–Aug, *Sakuntala*, sketched, Oct. 23rd Psalm, Dec, *Quartettsatz*, Dec, 'Gesang der Geister über den Wassern', Dec. Songs by Mayrhofer and Friedrich von Schlegel.	
1821	24	Schubert applies, Jan, for an appointment at the	Bruchmann goes to Erlangen to hear Schelling lecture,

Year	Age	Life	Contemporary musicians and events

Kärntnertor as composer or conductor, submitting testimonials from Dietrichstein, Salieri, Weigl, and Mosel. He is employed temporarily as a coach during Feb, but the experiment is not a success. Gymnich sings 'Erlkönig' at an 'Evening Entertainment' of the Phil. Soc., 25 Jan, a first appearance in these programmes. A grand party at Schober's at which Schubert's songs are sung, 30 Jan. The first Schubertiad? Schiller's 'Sehnsucht' (D636) performed at the Phil. Soc. soirée, 8 Feb. At a charity concert held at the Kärntnertor, 7 Mar, three Schubert works are performed, including 'Erlkönig', sung by Vogl and accompanied by Anselm Hüttenbrenner. The event established Schubert's fame in Vienna. Publication of Schubert's Op. 1 ('Erlkönig') on commission from Cappi and Diabelli is announced, 4 Apr. Schubert's vocal quartet 'Das Dörfchen' performed at a public concert organized by the Phil. Soc, 8 Apr. Receives a fee of 50 florins for his coaching work at the opera. Hérold's *Das Zauberglöckchen* produced at the Kärntnertor, 20 June, with two extra numbers by Schubert, for which he is paid 100 florins. Schubert at Atzenbrugg, July. Symphonic sketch in E (D729) written, Aug. Schubert and Schober at St Pölten work together on *Alfonso und Estrella*, Sept–

and there meets Platen, whom he introduces to Schubert's songs, Jan. Dietrichstein becomes Director of the Court theatres. Death of Napoleon, 5 May. Metternich becomes State Chancellor, 25 May. Weber's *Freischütz* gets a rapturous reception on its first production in Berlin, 18 June. Spaun takes up a new post at Linz, 23 Sept. Barbaja commissions a new opera from Weber for Vienna, Nov. First performance of *Der Freischütz* at the Kärntnertor, in a savagely cut version, 3 Nov.

Year	Age	Life	Contemporary musicians and events
		Oct. Schubert's E minor Overture included in the final public concert of the year organized by the Phil. Soc., 18 Nov. The chief compositions of the year are songs (especially Goethe songs in the spring), *Alfonso und Estrella* (completed Feb 1822), and two incomplete symphonic sketches.	
1822	25	First meeting of Schubert and Bauernfeld at Professor Weintridt's, 21 Jan. Schubert a frequent visitor at sought-after salons such as Karoline Pichler's, Henikstein's, and Geymüller's, Feb–Apr. Score of *Alfonso und Estrella* finished, 27 Feb. Schubert's vocal quartet 'Geist der Liebe' performed at the Phil. Soc.'s public concert, Mar. Schubert becomes a full member of the Phil. Soc. Extended article by Hentl in the Vienna *ZfK* on Schubert's songs, 23 Mar. Early autumn: Schubert breaks with Diabelli, and sells the copyright on his published songs. Enters into an agreement with Leidesdorf. Management of the Court opera turns down *Alfonso und Estrella*. Schubert returns to the schoolhouse in the Rossau, Oct. Attends New Year's Eve celebrations at Schober's. Major works of 1822: A flat Mass No. 5, completed Sept, Symphony in B minor (the 'Unfinished'), the 'Wanderer' Fantasy for piano, Oct–Nov, and many fine songs to Romantic texts by Platen, Mayrhofer, Rückert, Bruchmann, Schober, Senn, and Goethe.	Barbaja takes over the lease of the Kärntnertor theatre. Appreciative article on Schubert's songs in the Vienna *AmZ*, 19 Jan. Weber arrives in Vienna for opening of opera season, Feb. Weber conducts *Der Freischütz* at the Kärntnertor without cuts, 7 and 9 Mar. Rossini arrives for Italian opera season, 23 Mar, which ends in a riot of enthusiasm, 14 July. Rochlitz visits Vienna and meets Schubert. Vogl leaves the Court opera, Nov. According to Schlösser, Schubert present at the new production of *Fidelio*, final version, 4 Nov. Liszt, living with his father in Vienna from 1821 to 1823, gives his first public concert, 1 Dec.

Year	Age	Life	Contemporary musicians and events
1823	26	Schubert turns down a request, Jan, for another male-voice quartet for the forthcoming Phil. Soc. concert. First indication of Schubert's serious illness, which obliges him to keep to his room, 28 Feb. Schubert is proposed as an honorary member of the Styrian Philharmonic Society at Graz, 10 Apr. Schubert's condition worsens. His poem, 'My Prayer', suggests that he fears for his life, May. Begins work on the opera *Fierabras* and completes the score of Act I on 30 May. Completes Act II of *Fierabras*, 5 June. About this time, probably early June to mid-July, Schubert spent several weeks in hospital. During this period he is believed to have worked on *Die schöne Müllerin*. Schubert left Vienna for a convalescent holiday at Steyr and Linz, end July to mid-Sept. Here he read Walter Scott and continued work on *Fierabras*. Act III of *Fierabras* finished, 26 Sept. Schubert returns to Vienna to lodge with 'tall Huber' in the inner city. Work on *Die schöne Müllerin* continued, Oct, Schubert and Weber meet at Steiner's, 28 Oct, and disagree about the merits of *Euryanthe*. Schubert's music for the 'Romantic Play' *Rosamunde* is highly praised, but the piece fails, 20/21 Dec. The circle in decline. Major works of 1823: Piano sonata in A minor (D784), Feb. *Die Verschworenen*, Mar, *Fierabras*, May–Oct, *Die schöne Müllerin*, finished Nov. *Rosamunde*, Nov–Dec.	Vienna correspondent of a Leipzig periodical reports the presence of 'the musical director Schubert' at Mosel's musical evening, 18 Jan. Schober moves to Breslau to try his hand at acting, and does not return till 1825, Aug. Bruchmann goes to Erlangen to attend Schelling's lectures on mythology, Aug. Weber arrives in Vienna to direct production of *Euryanthe*, 21 Sept. Première of *Euryanthe* at the Kärntnertor, 25 Oct. The piece is withdrawn after two performances. Leopold Kupelwieser leaves Vienna for Italy as companion to Beresin, 7 Nov.

Year	Age	Life	Contemporary musicians and events
1824	27	Schubert's health, though improved, continues to give cause for concern. He concentrates on writing chamber music and songs. F.p. of the A minor String Quartet at Schuppanzigh's subscription concert at the Musik-Verein, 14 Mar. In a frank and revealing letter, 31 Mar, to Leopold Kupelwieser in Rome, Schubert announces his intention to work towards grand symphony through chamber music. Schubert present at Beethoven's concert, hears the first performance of the Choral Symphony and parts of the Missa Solemnis, 7 May. Leaves Vienna for Zseliz, where he again acts as tutor to the Esterházy family. There he writes a magnificent series of works for piano duet, and falls in love in Platonic fashion with the young countess Karoline. He returns, with Schönstein, mid-Oct. Feels ill again, Oct, and returns to live in the school-house in the Rossau till February 1825. Major works of 1824: String Quartets in A minor and D minor ('Death and the Maiden'); Octet for strings and wind; 'Grand Duo' sonata; Variations on an original theme in A flat Op. 35; Six Grand Marches Op. 40; *Divertissement à l'hongroise*; Arpeggione Sonata; Mayrhofer songs, Mar.	Smetana born, 2 Mar. Reading parties suspended, 2 Apr. Bruckner born, 4 Sept.
1825	28	Schubert, in poor spirits, leads a quiet life at home. He	Barbaja's lease of the Kärntnertor theatre runs

Year	Age	Life	Contemporary musicians and events

may have spent a further short period in hospital during Jan. Schwind takes Schubert to see Bauernfeld, Feb, and the acquaintance ripens into friendship. Schubert moves, Feb, into rooms in Frühwirth's house in the suburb of Wieden, next door to the Schwind family residence. Disclosure of Schober's secret engagement to Justina Bruchmann results in an open breach in the circle, Mar. Wilhelm Rieder paints Schubert's portrait, May. Schubert leaves Vienna to join Vogl at Steyr, *c.* 20 May. Excursion to Linz, St Florian, and Steyregg Castle, 24–7 May. They move on to Gmunden on Lake Traun, 4 June, where they stay for six weeks. There Schubert works on the first draft of his 'Great' C major Symphony. The travellers move to Linz, 15 July, and on 25 July return to Steyr. About 10 Aug they leave Steyr to travel via Salzburg to Gastein, 18 Aug, where they stay till 4 Sept. There Schubert meets the Patriarch of Venice, Ladislaus Pyrker, and continues to work on his symphony. They reach Gmunden, 10 Sept, and on 17 Sept are back at Steyr. After a further excursion to Linz and Steyregg they return to Vienna on 6 Oct. Schubert receives a fee of 220 florins from Artaria for his 'Lady of the Lake' songs, Oct. An engraving of Schubert, 'the composer of genius', after Rieder's

out. In July the theatre closes until Apr 1826, 31 Mar. Salieri dies, 7 May. Op. 19 (Goethe songs) published with dedication to the author, but without Goethe's permission, 6 June. Schober returns to Vienna, 2 July. Leopold Kupelwieser returns to Vienna from Rome, 7 Aug. Schubert is elected to the representative body of the Phil. Soc., Sept. J. P. F. Richter (Jean Paul) dies, 14 Nov.

Year	Age	Life	Contemporary musicians and events
1825	28	portrait, is advertised for sale, 9 Dec. Bauernfeld's satirical play on the circle is read at the New Year's Eve party at Schober's. Schubert was too ill to attend. Main works of 1825: Piano Sonata in C (the 'Reliquie'); Piano Sonata in A minor (D845); Scott songs; C major Symphony (finished 1826); Piano Sonata in D major; Pyrker songs, Aug, and Schulze songs, Dec.	
1826	29	Rehearsal of D minor Quartet (at Lachner's?), 30 Jan. Schubert makes cuts and other changes. Schubert formally petitions the Emperor for the post of Vice-Kapellmeister in the Court Chapel, 7 Apr. (He is shortlisted but not selected.) Schubert and Bauernfeld agree to do an opera together, Apr, and decide on 'The Count of Gleichen' as the subject. Farewell party, 15 Apr, for Bauernfeld and Mayerhofer, who depart on a tour of Carinthia. There Bauernfeld writes the libretto of the opera, returning with it at the end of July. The Swiss publisher Nägeli approaches Schubert through Karl Czerny and asks him for a piano sonata, June. Schubert spends a few weeks as Währing, July, with Schober and his mother. There he writes the Shakespeare songs and finishes the G major String Quartet. Abortive approach to the publishers Probst, and Breitkopf & Härtel, of Leipzig, Aug. Schubert ill,	Schubert's father, Franz Theodor Schubert, made a freeman of the city, 23 Feb. Schuppanzigh quartet plays Beethoven's Op. 130 quartet and Op. 97 piano trio at the Musik-Verein, 21 Mar. The London *Harmonicon*, in its Vienna report, Mar, mentions Schubert patronizingly as continuing 'to labour indefatigably in the composition of songs'. Barbaja takes over a new lease of the Kärntnertor, and makes known his interest in new German operas, Apr. Spaun returns to Vienna to take up an official post, Apr. Police raid on the 'Ludlams Höhle' club excites derision of Vienna's artistic community, Apr. Death of Weber in London, 5 June. Michael Vogl marries Kunigunde Rosa, 26 June. According to Schindler, Schubert was seriously considered for a post as assistant conductor at the Kärntnertor, but the audition ended in open disagreement, *c.* Aug. Leopold Kupelwieser

Year	Age	Life	Contemporary musicians and events
		and short of money. Dedicates his C major Symphony to the Phil. Soc., and hands over the completed score, Oct. In return he receives an honorarium of 100 florins. The libretto of *The Count of Gleichen* is banned by the censor. Schubert none the less declares that he will compose the opera. A 'big, big Schubertiad', held at Spaun's, 15 Dec, the original inspiration of Schwind's famous drawing of 1868, 'A Musical Evening at Josef von Spaun's'. Chief compositions of 1826: String Quartet in G major, June; Piano Sonata in G major, Oct; Rondo in B minor for violin and piano, Dec; Goethe, Shakespeare, Seidl and Schulze songs.	marries Johanna Lutz, 17 Sept. The 'Ludlams Höhle' society suppressed by the police, Oct. Bauernfeld takes up an official position in the lottery office, Oct. Première of Raimund's 'The Girl from Fairyland', with music by Drechsler, scores immediate success, 10 Nov.
1827	30	Karl Maria von Bocklet and Josef Slawjk play Schubert's Rondo in B minor for violin and piano at Artaria's, Jan. Schubert moves into rooms in Schober's house in the Tuchlauben, Mar. Meeting with Hummel and Hiller at Frau von Lázny's, Mar. Schubert visits Beethoven on his deathbed, with Schindler, Teltscher and the brothers Hüttenbrenner, Mar. First public performance of the Octet at Schuppanzigh's last subscription concert of the season, 16 Apr. 'Nachtgesang im Walde' performed at Josef Lewy's concert, 22 Apr. Schubert and Schober stay at the 'Empress of Austria' in Dornbach, May. Schubert is elected a full representative	Beethoven seriously ill. Weigl appointed Vice-Kapellmeister in the Court Chapel, Jan. Schubert's songs again mentioned in the London *Harmonicon*, Feb. Schindler takes 'about sixty' Schubert songs to show to Beethoven on his deathbed, Feb. Death of Beethoven, 26 Mar. His funeral, 29 Mar. Edward Holmes and Marie Novello stay in Vienna, 8–18 July, during their musical tour of Germany, but make no mention of Schubert. Fallersleben and Panofka, in search of Schubert, track him down at Dornbach, 8 Aug, but the experience proves disenchanting. 'Erlkönig' is played at a

Year	Age	Life	Contemporary musicians and events
		member of the Phil. Soc., 12 June. Schubert and Jenger stay in Graz as guests of Karl and Marie Pachler, 3–20 Sept. Return to Vienna 24 Sept. Schubert, unwell, apologizes for his absence from Anna Hönig's party, 15 Oct. The Schuppanzigh ensemble plays 'a new piano trio' by Schubert (probably the Trio in B flat Op. 99) at the Musik-Verein, 26 Dec. New Year's Eve party at Schober's. Compositions of 1827: *Winterreise* (Part I Feb/ Mar, Part II finished Oct); *Der Graf von Gleichen* sketches, begun June; Four Impromptus Op. 90, summer?; Four Impromptus Op. 142, Dec; *Moments Musicaux* nos. 1, 2, 4, and 5, summer?; Piano Trio Op. 99 in B flat, Sept– Oct?; Piano Trip Op. 100 in E flat, Nov; Fantasie in C for violin and piano, Dec; Leitner songs, autumn.	musical evening in Berlin, with Mendelssohn accompanying, 13 Nov. Marriage of Countess Marie Esterházy to Count Breunner-Enkevoerth.
1828	31	Weekly reading parties resumed at Schober's. At Slawjk's concert, the Fantasie in C for violin and piano fails to impress, 20 Jan. Special Schubertiad in honour of Spaun and his new fiancée, 28 Jan. Two German publishers, Probst of Leipzig and Schott of Mainz, approach Schubert independently, inviting MSS. for consideration, 9 Feb. Schubert's public concert, in the Phil. Soc. hall, is a great success, and makes a substantial profit, 26 Mar. Schubert treats Bauernfeld to a ticket for Paganini's concert,	Appreciative essay on Schubert's songs (Opp. 79, 80, and 81) by G. W. Fink in the Leipzig *AmZ*, 23 Jan. Paganini arrives in Vienna, 16 Mar. Schwind's engagement to Netti Hönig is at last announced. Paganini concert, 13 Apr. Spaun's marriage to Fanny Roner, 14 Apr. Leopold Sonnleithner marries Louise Gosmar, 6 May. Barbaja's lease of the Kärntnertor runs out, June. Death of Katharina von Lászny, 3 July. Bauernfeld's first play, 'The Suitors', fails on its first production, 5 Sept.

Year	Age	Life	Contemporary musicians and events
		4 May. Schubert and Lachner play the F minor duet Fantasie for the first time in Bauernfeld's rooms, 10 May. Schubert sends Probst the E flat Trio. On 23 May he sends Schott the four Impromptus Op. 142 and the vocal quartet *Mondenschein*, which are later returned. Schubert makes an expedition to Heiligenkreuz and Baden with Lachner and Schickh, 3–4 June. The publisher Brüggemann of Halberstadt invites MSS. from Schubert, 21 June. Schubert spends much time this summer out of town, probably with Schober again at Währing, July. He writes to Probst confirming the opus number of the E flat Trio, 1 Aug. On his doctor's advice he moves, 1 Sept, to the new Wieden suburb, where he stays with his brother Ferdinand. His health, however, does not improve. He writes urgently to Probst, begging for news of the E flat Trio, and offering the publisher the three final Piano Sonatas, the String Quintet, and the Heine songs, 2 Oct. He joins Ferdinand, Josef Mayssen and Johann Rieder on a walking expedition to Eisenstadt to see Haydn's grave, 6–8 Oct. A letter from Schindler, 11 Oct, urging him to go to Pest and arrange a concert of his own works, remains unanswered. Schubert is taken ill while dining at the 'Red Cross', 31 Oct. He goes for a three-hour walk with Ferdinand and Josef Mayssen,	Schwindt goes to Munich to attend the Academy there, 22 Oct.

199

Year	Age	Life	Contemporary musicians and events

3 Nov. Goes with Josef Lanz for a lesson with Sechter on counterpoint, 4 Nov, but fails to appear for the next lesson. He dines with Schönstein and others, and spends a convivial evening, 9 or 10 Nov. In his last letter, 12 Nov, to Schober, he asks for reading matter. Karl Holz arranges a performance of Beethoven's Quartet in C sharp minor Op. 131 at Schubert's request, *c.* 14 Nov. His doctors, Josef Vering and Johann Wisgrill, are pessimistic about Schubert's chances of recovery. Bauernfeld and Lachner visit Schubert and discuss opera prospects. Later he becomes delirious, 17 Nov. He suffers hallucinations and falls into a coma, 18 Nov. Schubert dies, 3 pm, 19 Nov. Compositions of 1828: Fantasie for piano duet in F minor, Jan–Apr; Heine songs; Rellstab songs; Sonata movement in A minor for piano duet (*Lebensstürme*); Grand Rondo in A for piano duet; Mass No. 6 in E flat, June–July; piano sonatas in C minor, A major and B flat, finished Sept; String Quintet in C major, finished ?Oct; 'Der Hirt auf dem Felsen' (The Shepherd on the Rock).

Berlioz 25, Bruckner 4, Chopin 18, Liszt 17, Mendelssohn 19, Rossini 36, Schumann 18, Verdi 15, Wagner 15

Appendix B

List of works

I STAGE WORKS

D no.	Title	Text	Date	Remarks
11	Der Spiegelritter	Kotzebue	Dec. 1811–1812	Singspiel, incomplete
84	Des Teufels Lustschloss	Kotzebue	Oct. 1813–Oct. 1814	2 versions
190	Der vierjährige Posten	Körner	May 1815	Singspiel
220	Fernando	Stadler	June/July 1815	Singspiel
239	Claudine von Villa Bella	Goethe	Begun 26 July 1815	Singspiel. Acts 2 and 3 lost (see p. 56)
326	Die Freunde von Salamanka	Mayrhofer	Nov./Dec. 1815	Singspiel
435	Die Bürgschaft	(?)	Begun 2 May 1816	Act 3 incomplete
647	Die Zwillingsbrüder	Hofmann	Finished Jan. 1819	Singspiel
137	Adrast	Mayrhofer	(?) Autumn 1819	Incomplete
644	Die Zauberharfe	Hofmann	Summer 1820	Zauberspiel
701	Sakuntala	Neumann	Oct. 1820	Incomplete
723	Das Zauberglöckchen	Treitschke	Spring 1821	2 additional nos. only
732	Alfonso und Estrella	Schober	Sept. 1821–Feb. 1822	Grand opera
787	Die Verschworenen (alias Der häusliche Krieg)	Castelli	March/April 1823	Singspiel
791	Rüdiger	Mosel	May 1823	2 nos. only sketched
796	Fierabras	J. Kupelwieser	May–Oct. 1823	Grand opera
797	Rosamunde	Helmina v. Chézy	Nov./Dec. 1823	Incidental music
918	Der Graf von Gleichen	Bauernfeld	June/July 1827	Sketches only
981	Der Minnesänger			Lost

Schubert

II ORCHESTRAL MUSIC

Symphonies

D no.	Title	Date	Remarks
2B	Sketch for symphony in D (formerly D997)	(?) 1811	30 bars only.
82	No. 1 in D	Oct. 1813	
125	No. 2 in B flat	10 Dec. 1814–24 March 1815	
200	No. 3 in D	24 May–19 July 1815	
417	No. 4 in C minor ('Tragic')	Finished 27 April 1816	
485	No. 5 in B flat	Sept.–3 Oct. 1816	
589	No. 6 in C	Oct. 1817–Feb. 1818	
615	Piano sketches for a symphony in D	May 1818	2 mvmts only
708A	Piano sketches for a symphony in D	(?) Spring 1821	
729	No. 7 in E	Aug. 1821	Outline sketch in open score
759	No. 8 in B minor ('Unfinished')	Oct.–Nov. 1822	
944	No. 9 in C ('Great')	1825–1826	
936A	Piano sketches for a symphony in D	Summer and autumn 1828	3 movmts

Overtures

D no.	Title	Date	Remarks
2A	Sketch for an overture in D (formerly 996)	(?) 1811	62 bars only
4	In D, for the comedy *Der Teufel als Hydraulicus*	(?) 1812	
12	In D	(?) 1812	
26	In D	Finished 26 June 1812	
470	In B flat	Sept. 1816	
556	In D	May 1817	
590	In D	Early 1818	'In the Italian style'
591	In C	Nov. 1817	'In the Italian style'
648	In E minor	Feb. 1819	

The following operatic overtures are also sometimes heard in the concert-hall:

11	*Der Spiegelritter*	B flat
84	*Des Teufels Lustschloss*	F

190	*Der vierjährige Posten*	D	
239	*Claudine von Villa Bella*	E	
326	*Die Freunde von Salamanka*	C	
647	*Die Zwillingsbrüder*	D	
644	*Die Zauberharfe*	C minor/major	Now known as the *Rosamunde* Overture
732	*Alfonso und Estrella*	D minor/major	
796	*Fierabras*	F minor/major	

Concertante music

345	Concerto in D	1816	Solo violin and orchestra
438	Rondo in A	June 1816	Solo violin and string orchestra
580	Polonaise in B flat	Sept. 1817	Solo violin and orchestra

III CHAMBER MUSIC

For wind instruments and wind with strings

2D	(Formerly 995) Six Minuets for Wind Instruments	1811	(2 ob, 2 cl, 2 bn, 2 hn, trbn)
2F	Trio for Wind Instruments	1811	Fragment
72	Wind Octet in F (2 ob, 2 cl, 2 bn, 2 hn)	Finished 18 Aug. 1813	2 mvmts survive complete
79	Wind Nonet in E flat minor (*Eine kleine Trauermusik*)	Sept. 1813	(2 cl, 2 bn, dbn, 2 hn, 2 trbn)
96	Arrangement of W. Matiegka's Notturno	26 Feb. 1814	(fl, vla, vcl, guitar)
803	Octet for Wind and Strings	Feb.–1 March 1824	(cl, hn, bn, 2 vln, vla, vcl, db)

Strings with piano

28	Piano Trio in B flat	27 July–28 Aug. 1812	Sonata in 1 mvmt
487	Adagio and Rondo concertante in F	Oct. 1816	For piano quartet
667	Piano Quintet in A (the 'Trout')	Autumn 1819	(pf, vln, vla, vcl, db)
897	Piano Trio movement in E flat ('Notturno')	(?) Oct. 1827	
898	Piano Trio in B flat	(?) Sept.–Oct. 1827	
929	Piano Trio in E flat	Nov. 1827	

Piano and one other instrument

| 384 | Sonata in D for violin and piano | March 1816 | |

385	Sonata in A minor for violin and piano	March 1816	
408	Sonata in G minor for violin and piano	April 1816	
574	Sonata in A for violin and piano	Aug. 1817	
802	Introduction and Variations on 'Trockne Blumen' for flute and piano	Jan. 1824	
821	Sonata in A minor ('Arpeggione')	Nov. 1824	Now usually played as sonata for piano and cello (or viola)
895	Rondo brillant in B minor for violin and piano	Oct. 1826	
934	Fantasie in C for violin and piano	Dec. 1827	

Music for strings

N.B. Nos. given for early string quartets do not correspond with those given in most published editions.

2C	(Formerly 998) Fragment of a string quartet movement	(?) 1811	
3	Fragment of a string quartet movement in C	(?) Summer 1812	
8	Overture in C minor for string quintet	29 June 1811	
18	String Quartet No. 1 in mixed keys	1810 or 1811	
94	String Quartet No. 2 in D	1811 or 1812	
32	String Quartet No. 3 in C	Sept.–Oct. 1812	
36	String Quartet No. 4 in B flat	19 Nov. 1812–21 Feb. 1813	
46	String Quartet No. 5 in C	3–7 March 1813	
68	String Quartet No. 6 in B flat	8 June–18 Aug. 1813	2 mvmts only
74	String Quartet No. 7 in D	22 Aug.–Sept. 1813	
86	Minuet in D for string quartet	(?) 1813	
87	String Quartet No. 8 in E flat	Nov. 1813	
87A	Andante in C	Nov. 1813	Fragment
89 and 90	Five minuets and six trios: five Deutsche and seven trios, for string quartet	Nov. 1813	
103	String quartet mvmt in C minor	23 April 1814	Incomplete
112	String Quartet No. 9 in B flat	Sept. 1814	

173	String Quartet No. 10 in G minor	25 March–1 April 1815	
353	String Quartet No. 11 in E	1816	
354	Four comic Ländler for two violins in D	Jan. 1816	
355	Eight Ländler for solo violin	Jan. 1816	(?) First parts
370	Nine Ländler in D for (?) violin	Jan. 1816	of proposed violin duets
374	Eleven Ländler for solo violin	Feb. 1816	
471	String Trio in B flat	Sept. 1816	Incomplete
581	String Trio in B flat	Sept. 1817	
703	String Quartet movement No. 12 in C minor (*Quartettsatz*)	Dec. 1820	41 bars of incomplete Andante
804	String Quartet No. 13 in A minor	Feb.–March 1824	
810	String Quartet No. 14 in D minor ('Death and the Maiden')	March 1824	
887	String Quartet No. 15 in G	Finished 20–30 June 1826	
956	String Quintet in C	Sept.–Oct. 1828	

IV PIANO MUSIC

For four hands

1	Fantasie in G	8 April–1 May 1810	
1C	Fragment of a sonata movement in F	(?) 1810	
9	Fantasie in G minor	Sept. 1811	
48	Fantasie in C minor ('Grande sonate')	April–June 1813	
592	Arrangement of the Overture in D major (590)	Dec. 1817	
597	Arrangement of the Overture in C (591)	End of 1817	
599	Four Polonaises	July 1818	
602	*Trois Marches héroiques*	(?) Summer/ autumn 1818	
968A	Introduction and four variations on an original theme, with finale (formerly 603)	(?) 1818 or 1824	
968	Allegro moderato in C and Andante in A minor ('Sonatine')	(?) 1818	

608	Rondo in D ('Notre amitié est invariable')	Jan. 1818	2 versions
617	Sonata in B flat	Summer/autumn 1818	
618	Deutsche in G with 2 Trios and 2 Ländler in E	Summer/autumn 1818	
618A	Polonaise in B flat	July 1818	
624	Eight Variations on a French Song in E minor	Sept. 1818	
733	Three *Marches Militaires*	(?) Summer/autumn 1818	
668	Overture in G minor	Oct. 1819	
675	Overture in F minor/major	(?) Nov. 1819	
773	Overture to *Alfonso und Estrella* (arrangement)	1823	
798	Overture to *Fierabras* (arrangement)	End 1823	
812	Sonata in C ('Grand Duo')	June 1824	
813	Eight Variations on an Original Theme in A flat	June/July 1824	
814	Four Ländler	Summer 1824	
818	*Divertissement à l'hongroise* in G minor	(?) Autumn 1824	
819	Six Grandes Marches	Summer/autumn 1824	
823	*Divertissement sur des motifs originaux* in E minor (Sonata published as three separate movements: Marche brillante et raisonnée, Andantino varié, Rondeau brillant)	(?) Autumn 1825	
824	Six Polonaises	Early 1826	
859	*Grande Marche funèbre* in C minor	Dec. 1825	
885	*Grand Marche héroique* (for Coronation of Nicholas I of Russia)	Sept. 1826	
886	(See 968B) Two Characteristic Marches in C	(?) 1825–26	
908	Eight Variations on a theme from Hérold's 'Marie'	Feb. 1827	
928	*Kindermarsch* in G (for Faust Pachler)	12 Oct. 1827	
940	Fantasie in F minor	Jan.–April 1828	
947	Sonata movement in A minor (*Lebensstürme*)	May 1828	
951	Rondo in A	June 1828	
952	Fugue in E minor (for organ or piano)	3 June 1828	

Sonatas, Fantasies, Variations, and related pieces for piano solo

2E	(Formerly 993) Fantasie in C minor	(?) 1811	
347	Allegro moderato in C	(?) 1813	
156	Ten Variations in F	Feb. 1815	
157	Sonata in E	Feb. 1815	No finale
178	Adagio in G	8 April 1815	2 versions
279	Sonata in C	Sept. 1815	No finale
346	Allegretto in C	(?) 1815	Incomplete
348/ 349	Andantino and Adagio in C	(?) Summer 1817	Incomplete
459	Sonata in E	Aug. 1816	2 mvmts only
459A	Three pieces, Adagio, Scherzo, and Allegro patetico	(?) 1816	Earlier associated with 459
537	Sonata in A minor	March 1817	3 movements
557	Sonata in A flat	May 1817	3 movements
566	Sonata in E minor	June 1817	3 movements. Incomplete
567	Sonata in D flat	June 1817	3 movements
570/ 571	Sketches for three movements of a sonata in F sharp minor	July 1817	
604	Andante in A	(?) Summer 1817	Possibly slow mvmt for 570/1
575	Sonata in B	Aug. 1817	
576	13 Variations on a theme by Anselm Hüttenbrenner	Aug. 1817	
593	2 Scherzos in B flat and D flat	Nov. 1817	
605A	Fantasie in C ('Grazer Fantasie')	(?) 1818	
612	Adagio in E	April 1818	
613	Sonata in C	April 1818	2 mvmts, both incomplete
625	Sonata in F minor	Sept. 1818	3 mvmts, 2 incomplete
505	Adagio in D flat	(?) Sept. 1818	Possibly slow mvmt for 625
655	Incomplete sketch for sonata mvmt in C sharp minor	April 1819	
664	Sonata in A	(?) Summer 1819	3 mvmts
605	Fantasie in C	(?) Summer 1822	Incomplete
760	Fantasie in C (the 'Wanderer')	Nov. 1822	
769A	Incomplete sonata mvmt in E minor	(?) 1823	

784	Sonata in A minor	Feb. 1823	3 mvmts
900	Allegretto in C minor	(?) 1823	Incomplete
840	Sonata in C ('Reliquie')	Spring 1825	Incomplete
845	Sonata in A minor	Spring 1825	
850	Sonata in D	Aug. 1825	
568	Sonata in E flat	(?) Summer 1826	Revised version of 567
894	Sonata in G	Oct. 1826	
916B	Piano piece in C	(?) Summer 1827	Sketch
916C	Piano piece in C minor	(?) Summer 1827	
958	Sonata in C minor	Finished Sept. 1828	
959	Sonata in A	Finished Sept. 1828	
960	Sonata in B flat	Finished Sept. 1828	

Shorter Characteristic Pieces

606	March in E with Trio	(?) 1818	
718	Variation on a waltz by Diabelli	March 1821	
780	6 *Momens musicals* (*sic*)		
	No. 3	1823	('Air Russe')
	No. 6	1824	('Plaintes d'un Troubadour')
	Nos. 1, 2, 4, and 5	(?) Summer 1827	
817	'Hungarian Melody' in B minor	2 Sept. 1824	See also D818
844	'Albumblatt': Waltz in G	16 April 1825	For Anna Hönig
899	Four Impromptus Op. 90	(?) Summer 1827	
915	Allegretto in C minor	26 April 1827	For Ferdinand Walcher
935	Four Impromptus Op. 142	Dec. 1827	
946	3 Piano Pieces, in E flat minor, E flat, and C	May 1828	

Dances for Piano

Of the 400 or so keyboard dances which survive, not many can be precisely dated. The main collections are these:

128	12 Wiener Deutsche	(?) 1812	
41	20 Minuets with Trios	1813	10 others have been lost
299	12 Ecossaises	Autumn 1815	
145	12 Waltzes, 17 Ländler, and 9 Ecossaises	1815–July 1821	
681	8 Ländler	*c.* 1815	4 others lost
146	20 Waltzes	1815	(nos. 1, 3–11)
		Feb. 1823	(nos. 2, 12–20)

365	36 Original Dances	1816–July 1821	
378	8 Ländler in B Flat	13 Feb. 1816	
380	3 Minuets each with 2 Trios	22 Feb. 1816	
420	12 Deutsche	1816	
421	6 Ecossaises	May 1816	
529	8 Ecossaises	Feb. 1817	
697	6 Ecossaises in A flat	May 1820	
734	16 Ländler and 3 Ecossaises	*c.* 1822	('Hommage aux belles Viennoises')
735	Galopp and 8 Ecossaises	*c.* 1822	
781	12 Ecossaises	Jan. 1823	
779	34 Valses Sentimentales	*c.* 1823	
783	16 Deutsche and 2 Ecossaises	Jan. 1823–July 1824	
790	12 Deutsche	May 1823	
820	6 Deutsche Tänze	Oct. 1824	Composed at Zseliz
977	8 Ecossaises	(?) 1825	
969	12 Walzer ('Valses Nobles')	(?) 1826	
924	12 Grazer Walzer	(?) Oct. 1827	

V LITURGICAL AND SACRED WORKS

24E	Fragmentary sketches for a Mass in F	(?) Summer 1812	
27	Salve Regina in F	28 June 1812	Sop., orch., organ
31	Kyrie in D minor	25 Sept. 1812	Soloists, SATB, orch.
45	Kyrie in B flat	1 March 1813	SATB
49	Kyrie in D minor	Finished 15 April 1813	Soloists, SATB, orch.
56	Sanctus	21 April 1813	Canon for 3 voices
66	Kyrie in F	May 1813	SATB, orch., organ
71A	Alleluja in F	(?) July 1813	Canon for 3 voices
105	Mass No. 1 in F	May–July 1814	See also 185
106	Salve Regina in B flat	28 June–1 July 1814	Tenor and orch.
739	Tantum ergo in C	1814	SATB, orch.
136	Offertory: Totus in corde	(?) 1815	Tenor (or sop.) and orch., organ
167	Mass No. 2 in G	March 1815	Missa brevis
175	Stabat mater in G minor	April 1815	SATB and orch., organ
181	Offertory: Tres sunt (A minor)	April 1815	SATB, orch., organ

184	Gradual: Benedictus es, Domine	April 1815	SATB, orch., organ
185	Dona nobis pacem	April 1815	Alternative version for 105
223	Salve Regina in F (revised 1823, with wind parts added)	5 July 1815	Sop., orch., organ
324	Mass No. 3 in B flat	Begun Nov. 1815	Missa brevis
379	Salve Regina (German text)	21 Feb. 1816	SATB, organ
383	Stabat mater in F minor/ major	Begun 28 Feb. 1816	German text by Klopstock
386	Salve Regina in B flat	Early 1816	SATB
452	Mass No. 4 in C	June–July 1816	Missa brevis. See also 961
453	Requiem in C minor	July 1816	Fragment
460	Tantum ergo in C	Aug. 1816	Sop., SATB, orch.
461	Tantum ergo in C	Aug. 1816	Soloists, SATB, orch.
486	Magnificat	(?) Sept. 1815 or 1816	Soloists, SATB, orch.
488	Auguste jam coelestium	Oct. 1816	Sop., ten., and orch.
621	German Requiem (Trauermesse)	Aug. 1818	Soloists, SATB, orch.
676	Salve Regina in A	Nov. 1819	Sop. and str. orch.
678	Mass No. 5 in A flat	Nov. 1819– Sept. 1822	Revised Jan. 1826? Two versions of Cum sancto Spiritu
689	*Lazarus* (the Easter Cantata)	Feb. 1820	Soloists, SATB, orch.
696	6 Antiphons for Palm Sunday	March 1820	SATB
730	Tantum ergo in B flat	16 Aug. 1821	Soloists, SATB, orch., organ
750	Tantum ergo in D	20 March 1822	SATB, orch., organ
755	Kyrie in A minor	May 1822	Fragment
811	Salve Regina in C	April 1824	TTBB
872	*Deutsche Messe*	Early autumn 1827	SATB, organ. Second version with orch.
948	*Hymnus an den heiligen Geist*	May 1828	Quartet TTBB and choir TTBB. Orchestrated Oct. 1828
950	Mass No. 6 in E flat	June–July 1828	

953	Der 92. Psalm	July 1828	Soloists, SATB. Text in Hebrew
954	*Glaube, Hoffnung und Liebe*	Aug. 1828	Soloists, SATB, piano or wind instruments
961	Benedictus in A minor	Oct. 1828	Soloists, SATB, orch. Alternative setting for 452
962	Tantum ergo in E flat	Oct. 1828	Soloists, SATB, orch.
963	Intende voci (Offertory)	Oct. 1828	Tenor, SATB, orch.

VI CHORUSES, PARTSONGS, AND CANTATAS FOR SEVERAL VOICES

D no.	Title	Author	Date	Notes
For mixed voices				
642	Viel tausend Sterne prangen	Eberhard	(?) 1812	Quartet, SATB, pf
47	Dithyrambe	Schiller	29 March 1813	Fragment
168	Begräbnislied	Klopstock	9 March 1815	Chorus SATB, pf
168A	Osterlied	Klopstock	9 March 1815	Chorus SATB, pf
232	Hymne an den Unendlichen	Schiller	11 July 1815	Quartet SATB, pf
294	Namensfeier	Anon.	27 Sept. 1815	Soloists and chorus STB, orch.
330	Das Grab	Salis-Seewis	28 Dec. 1815	Chorus SATB, pf
439	An die Sonne	Uz	June 1816	Quartet SATB, pf
440	Chor der Engel	Goethe	June 1816	Chorus SATB
451	Prometheus	Dräxler	June 1816	Lost
472	Kantate zu Ehren von Josef Spendou	Hoheisel	Sept. 1816	Soloists and chorus
609	Die Geselligheit	Unger	Jan. 1818	Quartet SATB, pf
643A	Das Grab	Salis-Seewis	1819	Quartet SATB
666	Kantate zum Geburtstag Michael Vogls	Stadler	10 Aug. 1819	Trio STB, pf
748	Am Geburtstag des Kaisers	Deinhard-stein	Jan. 1822	Chorus SATB, soloists, orch.

D no.	Title	Author	Date	Notes
763	Des Tages Weihe	Anon.	22 Nov. 1822	Quartet SATB, pf
815	Gebet	Fouqué	Sept. 1824	Quartet SATB, pf
875A	Die Allmacht	Pyrker	Jan. 1826	Chorus SATB, pf. Incomplete
985	Gott im Ungewitter	Uz	(?) 1827	Quartet SATB, pf
986	Gott der Weltschöpfer	Uz	(?) 1827	Quartet SATB, pf
930	Der Hochzeitsbraten	Schober	Nov. 1827	Trio STB, pf
936	Kantate für Irene Kiesewetter	Anon.	26 Dec. 1827	Chorus SATB, soloists, pf 4 hands
826	Der Tanz	Anon.	Early 1828	Quartet SATB, pf
942	Mirjams Siegesgesang	Grillparzer	March 1828	Chorus SATB, sop. solo, pf

Various early exercises in partwriting for mixed voices with Italian texts not included above.

For men's voices

D no.	Title	Author	Date	Notes
37	Die Advokaten	Engelhart	25–27 Dec. 1812	Trio TTB, pf
38	Totengräberlied	Hölty	(?) 1813	Trio TTB
51	Unendliche Freude (1)	Schiller	15 April 1813	Trio TTB
53	Vorüber die stöhnende Klage	Schiller	18 April 1813	Trio TTB
54	Unendliche Freude (2)	Schiller	19 April 1813	Trio TTB or BBB. 2 versions
55	Selig durch die Liebe	Schiller	21 April 1813	Trio TTB
57	Hier strecket der wallende Pilger	Schiller	29 April 1813	Trio TTB
58	Dessen Fahne Donnerstürme wallte	Schiller	May 1813	Trio TTB
62	Thronend auf erhabnem Sitz	Schiller	9 May 1813	Trio TTB
63	Wer die steile Sternenbahn	Schiller	10 May 1813	Trio TTB
64	Majestätsche Sonnenrosse	Schiller	10 May 1813	Trio TTB

D no.	Title	Author	Date	Notes
65	Schmerz verzerret ihr Gesicht	Schiller	11 May 1813	Trio TTB sketch
67	Frisch atmet des Morgens lebendiger Hauch	Schiller	15 May 1813	Trio TTB
43	Dreifach ist der Schritt (1)	Schiller	8 July 1813	Trio TTB
69	Dreifach ist der Schritt (2)	Schiller	8 July 1813	Canon for 3 voices
70	Dreifach ist der Schritt der Zeit (3)	Schiller	8 July 1813	Trio TTB
71	Die zwei Tugendwege	Schiller	15 July 1813	Trio TTB
75	Trinklied	Schäffer	29 Aug. 1813	Bass, chorus TTBB, pf
80	Zur Namensfeier meines Vaters	Schubert	27 Sept. 1813	Trio TTB, guitar
60	Hier umarmen sich getreue Gatten	Schiller	3 Oct. 1813	Trio TTB
88	Verschwunden sind die Schmerzen	Schubert	15 Nov. 1813	Trio TTB
110	Wer ist gross?	Anon.	24–25 July 1814	Bass, chorus TTBB, orch.
129	Mailied	Hölty	*c.* 1815	Trio TTB
140	Klage um Ali Bey	Claudius	1815	Trio TTB
148	Trinklied	Castelli	Feb. 1815	Tenor, chorus TTB, pf
236	Das Abendrot	Kosegarten	20 July 1815	Trio, SSB, pf
242	Trinklied im Winter	Hölty	(?) Aug. 1815	Trio TTB
243	Frühlingslied	Hölty	(?) Aug. 1815	Trio TTB
267	Trinklied	Anon.	25 Aug. 1815	Quartet TTBB, pf
268	Bergknappenlied	Anon.	25 Aug. 1815	Quartet TTBB, pf
269	Das Leben ist ein Traum	Wannovius	Aug. 1815	Trio TBB, pf
277	Punschlied	Schiller	29 Aug. 1815	Trio TTB, pf
147	Bardengesang	Ossian	20 Jan. 1816	Trio TTB
331	Der Entfernten (1)	Salis-Seewis	*c.* 1816	Quartet TTBB
337	Die Einsiedelei (1)	Salis-Seewis	*c.* 1816	Quartet TTBB
338	An den Frühling (2)	Schiller	*c.* 1816	Quartet TTBB

D no.	Title	Author	Date	Notes
356	Trinklied	Anon.	1816	Solo voice and chorus TTBB, pf acc. lost
364	Fischerlied (2)	Salis-Seewis	1816–17	Quartet TTBB
377	Das Grab (3)	Salis-Seewis	11 Feb. 1816	Quartet TTBB, pf
387	Die Schlacht	Schiller	March 1816	Solo voice, chorus TTBB, pf. Sketch
407	For Salieri's 50th anniversary celebration	Schubert	Early June 1816	Tenor, quartet TTBB, pf
423	Andenken	Matthisson	May 1816	Trio TTB
424	Erinnerung	Matthisson	May 1816	Trio TTB
427	Trinklied im Mai	Hölty	May 1816	Trio TTB
428	Widerhall	Matthisson	May 1816	Trio TTB
494	Der Geistertanz (4)	Matthisson	Nov. 1816	Quintet TTBBB
513	La Pastorella al Prato	Goldoni	(?) 1817	Quartet TTBB, pf
538	Gesang der Geister über den Wassern (2)	Goethe	March 1817	Quartet TTBB
569	Das Grab (4)	Salis-Seewis	June 1817	Unison chorus
572	Lied im Freien	Salis-Seewis	July 1817	Quartet TTBB
598	Das Dörfchen	Bürger	Dec. 1817	Quartet TTBB, pf
635	Leise, leise, lasst uns singen	Anon.	*c.* 1819	Quartet TTBB
656	Sehnsucht (Nur wer die Sehnsucht kennt) (4)	Goethe	April 1819	Quintet TTBBB
657	Ruhe, schönstes Glück der Erde	Anon.	April 1819	Quartet TTBB
705	Gesang der Geister über den Wassern (3)	Goethe	Dec. 1820	TTBB, pf. Sketch.
714	Gesang der Geister über den Wassern (4)	Goethe	Dec. 1820– Feb. 1821	Octet (4T, 4B) and strings.
724	Die Nachtigall	Unger	Spring 1821	Quartet TTBB, pf
422	Naturgenuss	Matthisson	(?) Summer 1822	Quartet TTBB, pf

D no.	Title	Author	Date	Notes
709	Frühlingsgesang (1)	Schober	Early 1822	TTBB
740	Frühlingsgesang (2)	Schober	Early 1822	Quartet TTBB, pf. Earlier version 709
710	Im Gegenwärtigen Vergangenes	Goethe	(?) March 1821	Quartet TTBB, pf
747	Geist der Liebe (2)	Matthisson	Jan. 1822	Quartet TTBB, pf
983	Jünglingswonne	Matthisson	(?) 1822	Quartet TTBB
983A	Liebe	Schiller	(?) 1822	Quartet TTBB
983B	Zum Rundetanz	Salis-Seewis	(?) 1822	Quartet TTBB
983C	Die Nacht	(?) Krummacher	(?) 1822	Quartet TTBB
809	Gondelfahrer (2)	Mayrhofer	March 1824	Quartet TTBB, pf
822	Lied eines Kriegers	Anon.	31 Dec. 1824	Bass, unison chorus, pf
825B	Flucht	Lappe	Early 1825	Quartet TTBB
835	Bootgesang	Scott/Storck	1825	Quartet TTBB, pf
847	Trinklied aus dem 16. Jahrhundert	Gräffer	July 1825	Quartet TTBB
848	Nachtmusik	Seckendorf	July 1825	Quartet TTBB
825	Wehmut	H. Hüttenbrenner	(?) 1825	Quartet TTBB
825A	Ewige Liebe	Schulze	(?) 1825	Quartet TTBB
865	Widerspruch	Seidl	(?) 1826	Quartet TTBB. Also as solo song
875	Mondenschein	Schober	Jan. 1826	Quintet TTBBB, pf
892	Nachthelle	Seidl	Sept. 1826	Tenor, quartet TTBB, pf
893	Grab und Mond	Seidl	Sept. 1826	Quartet TTBB
901	Wein und Liebe	Haug	Spring 1827	Quartet TTBB
903	Zur guten Nacht	Rochlitz	Jan. 1827	Bar. solo, chorus TTBB, pf

D no.	Title	Author	Date	Notes
912	Schlachtlied (2)	Klopstock	28 Feb. 1827	Double chorus TTBB
913	Nachtgesang im Walde	Seidl	April 1827	Quartet TTBB, 4 hns
914	Frühlingslied	Pollak	April 1827	Quartet TTBB. Also as solo song (919)
916	Das stille Lied	Seegemund	May 1827	Quartet TTBB. Incomplete
984	Der Wintertag	Anon.	(?) After 1820	Quartet fragment TTBB, pf (Pf. part is lost)
920	Ständchen	Grillparzer	July 1827	Alto, chorus TTBB, pf

For women's voices

D no.	Title	Author	Date	Notes
269	Das Leben ist ein Traum	Wannovius	25 Aug. 1815	Trio SSA
706	Der 23. Psalm	M. Mendelssohn	Dec. 1820	Quartet SSAA, pf
757	Gott in der Natur	Kleist	Aug. 1822	Quartet SSAA, pf
836	Coronach	Scott/Storck	1825	Chorus SSA, pf
920	Ständchen	Grillparzer	July 1827	Alto, chorus SSAA, pf

For unspecified voices

Various voice-setting exercises for Salieri, mostly of texts by Metastasio and Schiller, 1812 and 1813.

D no.	Title	Author	Date	Notes
169	Trinklied vor der Schlacht	Körner	12 March 1815	Double unison chorus, pf
170	Schwertlied	Körner	12 March 1815	Solo voice and unison chorus, pf
183	Trinklied	Zettler	12 April 1815	Solo voice, unison chorus, pf
189	An die Freude	Schiller	May 1815	Solo voice, unison chorus, pf
199	Mailied	Hölty	24 May 1815	Duet for voices or hns

D no.	Title	Author	Date	Notes
202	Mailied (Der Schnee zerrinnt)	Hölty	26 May 1815	Duet for voices or hns
203	Der Morgenstern	Körner	26 May 1815	Duet for voices or hns
204	Jägerlied	Körner	26 May 1815	Duet for voices or hns
205	Lützows wilde Jagd	Körner	26 May 1815	Duet for voices or hns
244	Willkommen, lieber schöner Mai	Hölty	(?) Aug 1815	Canon for 3 voices
253	Punschlied: im Norden zu singen	Schiller	18 Aug. 1815	Duet
357	Gold'ner Schein	Matthisson	May 1816	Canon for 3 voices
442	Das grosse Halleluja	Klopstock	June 1816	Trio or 3 part chorus
443	Schlachtlied	Klopstock	June 1816	Chorus, pf. See also 912
521	Jagdlied	Werner	Jan. 1817	Unison chorus, pf

VII SOLO SONGS

For ease of reference, the songs are listed in alphabetical order under titles.
Where necessary, the first line is also given. See under *Die schöne Müllerin*,
Winterreise, and *Schwanengesang* for individual songs contained therein.

D no.	Title	Author	Date
645	Abend	Tieck	Jan. 1819. Sketch
650	Abendbilder	Silbert	Feb. 1819
382	Abendlied ('Sanft glänzt die Abendsonne')	Anon.	24 Feb. 1816
499	Abendlied ('Der Mond ist aufgegangen')	Claudius	Nov. 1816
276	Abendlied ('Gross und rotentflammet')	Stolberg	28 Aug. 1815
495	Abendlied der Fürstin	Mayrhofer	(?) Nov. 1816
856	Abendlied für die Entfernte	A. W. v. Schlegel	Sept. 1825
690	Abendröte	F. v. Schlegel	(?) 1820–March 1823
235	Abends unter der Linde (1)	Kosegarten	24 July 1815
237	Abends unter der Linde (2)	Kosegarten	25 July 1815
265	Abendständchen: an Lina	Baumberg	23 Aug. 1815
806	Abendstern	Mayrhofer	March 1824
475	Abschied: nach einer Wallfahrtsarie	Mayrhofer	Sept. 1816
829	Abschied von der Erde	Pratobevera	Feb. 1826 (Melodrama)
406	Abschied von der Harfe	Salis-Seewis	March 1816

D no.	Title	Author	Date
578	Abschied von einem Freunde	F. Schubert	24 Aug. 1817
95	Adelaide	Matthisson	1814
211	Adelwold und Emma	Bertrand	June 1815
904	Alinde	Rochlitz	Jan. 1827
241	Alles um Liebe	Kosegarten	27 July 1815
153	Als ich sie erröten sah	Ehrlich	10 Feb. 1815
477	Alte Liebe rostet nie	Mayrhofer	Sept. 1816
361	Am Bach im Frühling	Schober	(?) 1816
344	Am ersten Maimorgen	Claudius	(?) 1816
878	Am Fenster	Seidl	March 1826
160	Am Flusse (1)	Goethe	27 Feb. 1815
766	Am Flusse (2)	Goethe	Dec. 1822
504	Am Grabe Anselmos	Claudius	4 Nov. 1816
746	Am See ('In des Sees Wogenspiele')	Bruchmann	(?) 1822
124	Am See ('Sitz ich im Gras')	Mayrhofer	7 Dec. 1814
539	Am Strome	Mayrhofer	March 1817
195	Amalia	Schiller	19 May 1815
122	Ammenlied	Lubi	Dec. 1814
166	Amphiaraos	Körner	1 March 1815
462	An Chloen ('Bei der Liebe reinsten Flammen')	Jacobi	Aug. 1816
363	An Chloen ('Die Munterkeit ist meinen Wangen')	Uz	1816. Incomplete
283	An den Frühling (1)	Schiller	6 Sept. 1815
587	An den Frühling (2)	Schiller	Oct. 1817
259	An den Mond (1) ('Füllest wieder Busch und Tal')	Goethe	19 Aug. 1815
296	An den Mond (2)	Goethe	(?) Autumn 1819
193	An den Mond ('Geuss lieber Mond')	Hölty	17 May 1815
468	An den Mond ('Was schauest du so hell')	Hölty	7 Aug. 1816
614	An den Mond in einer Herbstnacht	Schreiber	April 1818
447	An den Schlaf	Anon.	June 1816
518	An den Tod	Schubart	1817
197	An die Apfelbäume wo ich Julien erblickte	Hölty	22 May 1815
765	An die Entfernte	Goethe	Dec. 1822
189	An die Freude	Schiller	1815
654	An die Freunde	Mayrhofer	March 1819
303	An die Geliebte	Stoll	15 Oct. 1815
394	An die Harmonie	Salis-Seewis	March 1816
905	An die Laute	Rochlitz	Jan. 1827
737	An die Leyer	Bruchmann	(?) 1822–23
547	An die Musik	Schober	March 1817

D no.	Title	Author	Date
497	An die Nachtigall ('Er liegt und schläft')	Claudius	Nov. 1816
196	An die Nachtigall ('Geuss nicht so laut')	Hölty	22 May 1815
372	An die Natur	Stolberg	15 Jan. 1816
270	An die Sonne ('Sinke, liebe Sonne')	Baumberg	(?) Aug. 1815
272	An die Sonne ('Königliche Morgensonne')	Tiedge	25 Aug. 1815
478(3)	An die Türen will ich schleichen (formerly 479)	Goethe	Sept. 1816
457	An die untergehende Sonne	Kosegarten	July 1816–May 1817
530	An eine Quelle	Claudius	Feb. 1817
113	An Emma	Schiller	17 Sept. 1814
115	An Laura	Matthisson	2–7 Oct. 1814
860	An mein Herz	Schulze	Dec. 1825
342	An mein Klavier	Schubart	c. 1816
161	An Mignon	Goethe	27 Feb. 1815
315	An Rosa ('Warum bist du nicht hier')	Kosegarten	19 Oct. 1815
316	An Rosa ('Rosa, denkst du an mich?')	Kosegarten	19 Oct. 1815
369	An Schwager Kronos	Goethe	(?) 1816
288	An sie	Klopstock	14 Sept. 1815
891	An Silvia	Shakespeare	July 1826
99	Andenken	Matthisson	April 1814
542	Antigone und Oedip	Mayrhofer	March 1817
585	Atys	Mayrhofer	Sept. 1817
543	Auf dem See	Goethe	(?) March 1817
943	Auf dem Strom	Rellstab	March 1818; pf and hn acc.
774	Auf dem Wasser zu singen	Stolberg	1823
81	Auf den Sieg der Deutschen	(?) Schubert	Autumn 1813
201	Auf den Tod einer Nachtigall (1)	Hölty	25 May 1815
399	Auf den Tod einer Nachtigall (2)	Hölty	13 May 1816
853	Auf der Bruck	Schulze	(?) March 1825
553	Auf der Donau	Mayrhofer	April 1817
611	Auf der Riesenkoppe	Körner	March 1818
151	Auf einen Kirchhof	Schlechta	2 Feb. 1815
807	Auflösung	Mayrhofer	March 1824
297	Augenlied	Mayrhofer	(?) Early 1817
458	Aus 'Diego Manazares' (Ilmerine)	Schlechta	30 July 1816
753	Aus 'Heliopolis' ('Im kalten rauhen Norden')	Mayrhofer	April 1822

D no.	Title	Author	Date
754	Aus 'Heliopolis' ('Fels auf Felsen')	Mayrhofer	April 1822
134	Ballade	Kenner	(?) Early 1815
866(2)	Bei dir allein	Seidl	(?) Summer 1828
496	Bei dem Grabe meines Vaters	Claudius	Nov. 1816
669	Beim Winde	Mayrhofer	Oct. 1819
653	Bertas Lied in der Nacht	Grillparzer	Feb. 1819
631	Blanka	F. v. Schlegel	Dec. 1818
626	Blondel zu Marien	Anon.	Sept. 1818
431	Blumenlied	Hölty	May 1816
258	Bundeslied	Goethe	Aug. 1815
263	Cora an die Sonne	Baumberg	22 Aug. 1816
282	Cronnan	Ossian	5 Sept. 1815
411	Daphne am Bach	Stolberg	April 1816
627	Das Abendrot	Schreiber	Nov. 1818
155	Das Bild	Anon.	11 Feb. 1815
868	Das Echo	Castelli	(?) 1826–27
219	Das Finden	Kosegarten	25 June 1815
250	Das Geheimnis (1)	Schiller	7 Aug. 1815
793	Das Geheimnis (2)	Schiller	May 1823
309	Das gestörte Glück	Körner	15 Oct. 1815
442	Das grosse Halleluja	Klopstock	June 1816
456	Das Heimweh	Hell	July 1816
917	Das Lied im Grünen	Reil	June 1827
532	Das Lied von Reifen	Claudius	Feb. 1817
652	Das Mädchen ('Wie so innig')	F. v. Schlegel	Feb. 1819
117	Das Mädchen aus der Fremde (1)	Schiller	16 Oct. 1814
252	Das Mädchen aus der Fremde (2)	Schiller	12 Aug. 1815
281	Das Mädchen von Inistore	Ossian	Sept. 1815
623	Das Marienbild	Schreiber	Aug. 1818
280	Das Rosenband	Klopstock	Sept. 1815
231	Das Sehnen	Kosegarten	8 July 1815
174	Das war ich (1)	Körner	26 March 1815
174	Das war ich (2)	Körner	(?) June 1816. Fragment
926	Das Weinen	Leitner	Autumn 1827
871	Das Zügenglöcklein	Seidl	(?) March 1826
775	Dass sie hier gewesen	Rückert	(?) 1822/23
857(1)	Delphine	Schütz	Sept. 1825
291	Dem Unendlichen	Klopstock	15 Sept. 1815
221	Der Abend ('Der Abend Blüht')	Kosegarten	15 July 1815
108	Der Abend ('Purpur malt')	Matthisson	July 1814
524	Der Alpenjäger ('Auf hohem Bergesrücken')	Mayrhofer	Jan. 1817

D no.	Title	Author	Date
588	Der Alpenjäger ('Willst du nicht das Lämmlein hüten')	Schiller	Oct. 1817
833	Der blinde Knabe	Cibber/Craigher	Early 1825
731	Der Blumen Schmerz	Majláth	Sept. 1821
622	Der Blumenbrief	Schreiber	Aug. 1818
800	Der Einsame	Lappe	(?) Jan. 1825
350	Der Entfernten	Salis-Seewis	(?) Spring 1816
699	Der entsühnte Orest	Mayrhofer	(?) March 1817
225	Der Fischer	Goethe	5 July 1815
402	Der Flüchtling	Schiller	18 March 1816
515	Der Flug der Zeit	Széchényi	(?) 1821
693	Der Fluss	F. v. Schlegel	March 1820
15	Der Geistertanz (1)	Matthisson	*c.* 1812. Incomplete
15A	Der Geistertanz (2)	Matthisson	*c.* 1812. Incomplete
116	Der Geistertanz (3)	Matthisson	14 Oct. 1814
560	Der Goldschmiedsgesell	Goethe	May 1817
254	Der Gott und die Bajadere	Goethe	18 Aug. 1815
990	Der Graf von Habsburg	Schiller	(?) 1818 Sketch
405	Der Herbstabend	Salis-Seewis	March 1816
490	Der Hirt	Mayrhofer	8 Oct. 1816
965	Der Hirt auf dem Felsen	Müller/v. Chézy	October 1828; pf and cl acc.
30	Der Jüngling am Bache (1)	Schiller	24 Sept. 1812
192	Der Jüngling am Bache (2)	Schiller	15 May 1815
638	Der Jüngling am Bache (3)	Schiller	April 1819
300	Der Jüngling an der Quelle	Salis-Seewis	(?) 1821
385	Der Jüngling auf dem Hügel	H. Hüttenbrenner	Nov. 1820
545	Der Jüngling und der Tod	Spaun	March 1817
594	Der Kampf	Schiller	Nov. 1817
692	Der Knabe	F. v. Schlegel	March 1820
579	Der Knabe in der Wiege	Ottenwalt	Sept. 1817
367	Der König in Thule	Goethe	Early 1816
932	Der Kreuzzug	Leitner	Nov. 1827
432	Der Leidende	Anon.	May 1816
207	Der Liebende	Hölty	29 May 1815
861	Der liebliche Stern	Schulze	Dec. 1825
209	Der Liedler	Kenner	(?) Jan. 1815
141	Der Mondabend	Kumpf	1815
264	Der Morgenkuss	Baumberg	22 Aug. 1815
172	Der Morgenstern	Körner	12 March 1815
764	Der Musensohn	Goethe	Dec. 1822
794	Der Pilgrim	Schiller	May 1823
663	Der 13. Psalm	M. Mendelssohn	June 1819
255	Der Rattenfänger	Goethe	19 Aug. 1815
149	Der Sänger	Goethe	Feb. 1815

D no.	Title	Author	Date
482	Der Sänger am Felsen	Pichler	Sept. 1816
517	Der Schäfer und der Reiter	Fouqué	April 1817
256	Der Schatzgräber	Goethe	19 Aug. 1815
536	Der Schiffer ('Im Winde, im Sturme')	Mayrhofer	(?) 1817
694	Der Schiffer ('Friedlich lieg ich')	F. v. Schlegel	March 1820
633	Der Schmetterling	F. v. Schlegel	(?) March 1820
805	Der Sieg	Mayrhofer	March 1824
565	Der Strom	Anon.	(?) Autumn 1817
77	Der Taucher	Schiller	Sept. 1813–end 1814
375	Der Tod Oscars	Ossian	Feb. 1816
531	Der Tod und das Mädchen	Claudius	Feb. 1817
213	Der Traum	Hölty	17 June 1815
713	Der Unglückliche	Pichler	Jan. 1821
906	Der Vater mit dem Kind	Bauernfeld	Jan. 1827
10	Der Vatermörder	Pfeffel	26 Dec. 1811
742	Der Wachtelschlag	Sauter	(?) 1822
931	Der Wallensteiner Lanzknecht beim Trunk	Leitner	Nov. 1827
489	Der Wanderer ('Ich komme vom Gebirge her')	Schmidt	Oct. 1816
649	Der Wanderer ('Wie deutlich das Mondes Licht')	F. v. Schlegel	(?) Feb. 1819
870	Der Wanderer an den Mond	Seidl	(?) March 1826
271	Der Weiberfreund	Cowley/Ratschky	25 Aug. 1815
938	Der Winterabend	Leitner	Jan. 1828
320	Der Zufriedene	Reissig	23 Oct. 1815
785	Der zürnende Barde	Bruchmann	Feb. 1823
707	Der zürnenden Diana	Mayrhofer	Dec. 1820
771	Der Zwerg	M. v. Collin	(?) Nov. 1822
933	Des Fischers Liebesglück	Leitner	Nov. 1827
6	Des Mädchens Klage (1)	Schiller	(?) 1811
191	Des Mädchens Klage (2)	Schiller	15 May 1815
389	Des Mädchens Klage (3)	Schiller	March 1816
832	Des Sängers Habe	Schlechta	Feb. 1825
510	Didone Abbandonata	Metastasio	Dec. 1816
514	Die abgeblühte Linde	Széchényi	(?) 1821
852	Die Allmacht	Pyrker	Aug. 1825
104	Die Befreier Europas in Paris	Mikan	16 May 1814
634	Die Berge	F. v. Schlegel	(?) March 1820
102	Die Betende	Matthisson	Autumn 1814
519	Die Blumensprache	(?) Platner	(?) Oct. 1817
246	Die Bürgschaft	Schiller	Aug. 1815
329	Die drei Sänger	Bobrik	23 Dec. 1815
393	Die Einsiedelei (1)	Salis-Seewis	(?) March 1816
563	Die Einsiedelei (2)	Salis-Seewis	May 1817

D no.	Title	Author	Date
390	Die Entzückung an Laura (1)	Schiller	March 1816
577	Die Entzückung an Laura (2)	Schiller	Aug. 1817. Incomplete
579B	Die Erde (formerly 989A)	Matthisson	Autumn 1817
229	Die Erscheinung	Kosegarten	7 July 1815
182	Die erste Liebe	Fellinger	12 April 1815
159	Die Erwartung	Schiller	May 1816
550	Die Forelle	Schubart	(?) Early 1817
262	Die Fröhlichkeit	Prandstetter	22 Aug. 1815
430	Die frühe Liebe	Hölty	May 1816
290	Die frühen Gräber	Klopstock	14 Sept. 1815
646	Die Gebüsche	F. v. Schlegel	Jan. 1819
712	Die gefangenen Sänger	A. W. v. Schlegel	Jan. 1821
444	Die Gestirne	Klopstock	June 1816
677	Die Götter Griechenlands ('Schöne Welt, wo bist du?')	Schiller	Nov. 1819
404	Die Herbstnacht	Salis-Seewis	March 1816
828	Die junge Nonne	Craigher	1824/early 1825
400	Die Knabenzeit	Hölty	13 May 1816
214	Die Laube	Hölty	17 June 1815
210	Die Liebe ('Freudvoll und leidvoll')	Goethe	3 June 1815
522	Die Liebe ('Wo weht der Liebe hoher Geist?')	Leon	Jan. 1817
751	Die Liebe hat gelogen	Platen	Spring 1822
673	Die Liebende schreibt	Goethe	Oct. 1819
446	Die Liebesgötter	Uz	June 1816
308	Die Macht der Liebe	Kalchberg	15 Oct. 1815
194	Die Mainacht	Hölty	17 May 1815
866(3)	Die Männer sind méchant	Seidl	(?) Summer 1828
238	Die Mondnacht	Kosegarten	25 July 1815
788	Die Mutter Erde ('Des Lebens Tag ist schwer')	Stolberg	April 1823
534	Die Nacht ('Die Nacht ist dumpfig')	Ossian	Feb. 1817
358	Die Nacht ('Du verstörst uns nicht')	Uz	(?) June 1816
208	Die Nonne	Hölty	29 May–16 June 1815
466	Die Perle	Jacobi	Aug. 1816
745	Die Rose	F. v. Schlegel	(?) March 1820
50	Die Schatten	Matthisson	12 April 1813
795	Die schöne Müllerin (Song Cycle) Das Wandern Wohin?	W. Müller	Summer/autumn 1823

D no.	Title	Author	Date
	Halt!		
	Danksagung an den Bach		
	Am Feierabend		
	Der Neugierige		
	Ungeduld		
	Morgengruss		
	Des Müllers Blumen		
	Tränenregen		
	Mein		
	Pause		
	Mit dem grünen Lautenbande		
	Der Jäger		
	Eifersucht und Stolz		
	Die liebe Farbe		
	Die böse Farbe		
	Trockne Blumen		
	Der Müller und der Bach		
	Des Baches Wiegenlied		
289	Die Sommernacht	Klopstock	14 Sept. 1815
247	Die Spinnerin	Goethe	Aug. 1815
186	Die Sterbende	Matthisson	(?) May 1815
176	Die Sterne ('Was funkelt ihr so mild')	Fellinger	6 April 1815
313	Die Sterne ('Wie wohl ist mir im Dunkeln')	Kosegarten	19 Oct. 1815
939	Die Sterne ('Wie blitzen die Sterne so hell')	Leitner	Jan. 1828
684	Dis Sterne ('Du staunest, o Mensch')	F. v. Schlegel	(?) 1819–20
670	Die Sternennächte	Mayrhofer	Oct. 1819
307	Die Sternenwelten	Fellinger	15 Oct. 1815
965A	Die Taubenpost	Seidl	Oct. 1828
230	Die Täuschung	Kosegarten	7 July 1815
866(1)	Die Unterscheidung	Seidl	(?) Summer 1828
409	Die verfehlte Stunde	A.W. v. Schlegel	April 1816
391	Die vier Weltalter	Schiller	(?) March 1816
691	Die Vögel	F. v. Schlegel	March 1820
778A	Die Wallfahrt	Rückert	(?) 1822/23
801	Dithyrambe	Schiller	(?) 1824
93(1)	Don Gayseros I ('Don Gayseros')	Fouqué	(?) End of 1815
93(2)	Don Gayseros II ('Nächtens klang die süsse Laute')	Fouqué	(?) End of 1815
93(3)	Don Gayseros III ('An dem jungen Morgenhimmel')	Fouqué	(?) End of 1815
770	Drang in die Ferne	Leitner	(?) End of 1822
776	Du bist die Ruh	Rückert	(?) 1823
756	Du liebst mich nicht	Platen	1822

D no.	Title	Author	Date
445	Edone	Klopstock	June 1816
923	Eine altschottische Ballade	tr. Herder	Sept. 1827
620	Einsamkeit	Mayrhofer	July 1818
837	Ellens Gesang I ('Raste, Krieger')	Scott/Storck	Spring 1825
838	Ellens Gesang II ('Jäger, ruhe von der Jagd')	Scott/Storck	Spring 1825
839	Ellens Gesang III ('Ave Maria')	Scott/Storck	April 1825
584	Elysium	Schiller	Sept. 1817
33(1)	Entra l'uomo allor che nasce	Metastasio	Autumn 1812
413	Entzückung	Matthisson	April 1816
749	Epistel: Musikalischer Schwank	M. v. Collin	Jan. 1822
98	Erinnerung	Matthisson	Sept. 1814
586	Erlafsee	Mayrhofer	Sept. 1817
328	Erlkönig	Goethe	Oct. 1815
434	Erntelied	Hölty	May 1816
226	Erster Velust	Goethe	5 July 1815
607	Evangelium Johannis	Pericope for the Mass	Spring 1818
526	Fahrt zum Hades	Mayrhofer	Jan. 1817
351	Fischerlied (1)	Salis-Seewis	(?) 1816
562	Fischerlied (2)	Salis-Seewis	May 1817
881	Fischerweise	Schlechta	(?) March 1826
857(1)	Florio	Schütz	Sept. 1825
450	Fragment aus dem Aeschylus	Mayrhofer	June 1816
700	Freiwilliges Versinken	Mayrhofer	(?) 1817
455	Freude der Kinderjahre	Köpken	July 1816
896	Fröhliches Scheiden	Leitner	Autumn 1827. Sketch
520	Frohsinn	Castelli	Jan. 1817
686	Frühlingsglaube	Uhland	Sept. 1820
398	Frühlingslied ('Die Luft ist blau')	Hölty	13 May 1816
919	Frühlingslied ('Geöffnet sind des Winters Riegel')	Pollak	(?) Spring 1827
854	Fülle der Liebe	F. v. Schlegel	Aug. 1825
285	Furcht der Geliebten	Klopstock	12 Sept. 1815
544	Ganymed	Goethe	March 1817
171	Gebet während der Schlacht	Körner	March 1815
719	Geheimes	Goethe	March 1821
491	Geheimnis	Mayrhofer	October 1816
233	Geist der Liebe ('Wer bist du, Geist der Liebe')	Kosegarten	15 July 1815
414	Geist der Liebe ('Der Abend schleiert Flur und Hain')	Matthisson	April 1816

D no.	Title	Author	Date
100	Geisternähe	Matthisson	April 1814
142	Geistesgruss	Goethe	(?) 1815
143	Genugsamkeit	Schober	(?) 1815
484	Gesang der Geister über den Wassern	Goethe	Sept. 1815. Incomplete
831	Gesang der Norna	Scott/Spiker	Early 1825
955	Glaube, Hoffnung und Liebe	Kuffner	Aug. 1828
808	Gondelfahrer	Mayrhofer	March 1824
448	Gott im Frühlinge	Uz	June 1816
218	Grablied	Kenner	24 June 1815
454	Grablied auf einen Soldaten	Schubart	July 1816
616	Grablied für die Mutter	Anon.	June 1816
778	Greisengesang	Rückert	(?) Autumn 1822
716	Grenzen der Menschheit	Goethe	March 1821
118	Gretchen am Spinnrade	Goethe	19 Oct. 1814
564	Gretchens Bitte	Goethe	May 1817. Incomplete
396	Gruppe aus dem Tartarus (1)	Schiller	March 1816. Incomplete
583	Gruppe aus dem Tartarus (2)	Schiller	Sept. 1817
5	Hagars Klage	Schücking	March 1811
552	Hänflings Liebeswerbung	Kind	April 1817
257	Heidenröslein	Goethe	19 Aug. 1815
922	Heimliches Lieben	Klenke	Sept. 1827
726	Heiss mich nicht reden (1)	Goethe	April 1821
877(2)	Heiss mich nicht reden (2)	Goethe	(?) Jan. 1826
312	Hektors Abschied	Schiller	19 Oct. 1815
945	Herbst	Rellstab	April 1828
502	Herbstlied	Salis-Seewis	Nov. 1816
322	Hermann und Thusnelda	Klopstock	27 Oct. 1815
651	Himmelsfunken	Silbert	Feb. 1819
890	Hippolits Lied	Gerstenberger	July 1826
463	Hochzeitlied	Jacobi	Aug. 1816
295	Hoffnung ('Schaff, das Tagwerk meiner Hände')	Goethe	(?) Oct. 1819
251	Hoffnung (1) ('Es reden und träumen')	Schiller	7 Aug. 1815
637	Hoffnung (2)	Schiller	(?) 1817
240	Huldigung	Kosegarten	27 July 1815
659	Hymne (1) ('Wenige wissen das Geheimnis')	Novalis	May 1819
660	Hymne II ('Wenn ich ihn nur habe')	Novalis	May 1819
661	Hymne III ('Wenn alle untreu werden')	Novalis	May 1819
662	Hymne IV ('Ich sag es jedem')	Novalis	May 1819

D no.	Title	Author	Date
227	Idens Nachtgesang	Kosegarten	7 July 1815
317	Idens Schwanenlied	Kosegarten	19 Oct. 1815
736	Ihr Grab	Engelhardt	(?) End of 1822
902(3)	Il modo di prender moglie	Anon.	1827
902(2)	Il traditor deluso	Metastasio	1827
799	Im Abendrot	Lappe	(?) Jan. 1825
880	Im Freien	Seidl	March 1826
882	Im Frühling	Schulze	March 1826
738	Im Haine	Bruchmann	(?) 1822
708	Im Walde ('Windes Rauschen')	F. v. Schlegel	Dec. 1820
834	Im Walde ('Ich wandre über Berg')	Schulze	(?) March 1825
464	In der Mitternacht	Jacobi	Aug. 1816
403	Ins stille Land	Salis-Seewis	March 1816
573	Iphigenia	Mayrhofer	July 1817
866(4)	Irdisches Glück	Seidl	(?) Summer 1828
521	Jagdlied	Werner	Jan. 1817
215	Jägers Abendlied (1)	Goethe	20 June 1815
368	Jägers Abendlied (2)	Goethe	Early 1816
909	Jägers Liebeslied	Schober	Feb. 1827
728	Johanna Sebus	Goethe	April 1821. Incomplete
419	Julius an Theone	Matthisson	30 April 1816
990A	Kaiser Maximilian	H. v. Collin	(?) 1818
321	Kennst du das Land	Goethe	23 Oct. 1815
415	Klage ('Die Sonne steigt')	Matthisson	April 1816
512	Klage ('Nimmer trag' ich länger')	Anon.	(?) 1817
371	Klage ('Trauer umfliesst mein Leben')	Anon.	(?) Jan. 1816
436	Klage an den Mond	Hölty	12 May 1826
323/ 991	Klage der Ceres	Schiller	Nov. 1815–June 1816
496A	Klage um Ali Bey	Claudius	(?) 1815 or 1816
23	Klaglied	Rochlitz	1812
217	Kolmas Klage	Ossian	22 June 1815
528	La Pastorella al Prato	Goldoni	Jan. 1817
302	Labetrank der Liebe	Stoll	15 Oct. 1815
777	Lachen und Weinen	Rückert	(?) 1822–23
301	Lambertine	Stoll	12 Oct. 1815
388	Laura am Klavier	Schiller	March 1816
508	Lebenslied	Matthisson	Dec. 1816
395	Lebensmelodien	A. W. v. Schlegel	March 1816
937	Lebensmut ('Fröhlicher Lebensmut')	Rellstab	(?) 1827
883	Lebensmut ('O wie dringt das junge Leben')	Schulze	March 1826

D no.	Title	Author	Date
39	Lebenstraum	Baumberg	(?) 1810. Sketch
7	Leichenfantasie	Schiller	1811
509	Leiden der Trennung	H. v. Collin	Dec. 1816
298	Liane	Mayrhofer	Oct. 1815
352	Licht und Liebe	M. v. Collin	(?) 1822. Duet
222	Lieb Minna	Stadler	2 July 1815
698	Liebeslauschen	Schlechta	Sept. 1820
164	Liebesrausch (1)	Körner	March 1815
179	Liebesrausch (2)	Körner	8 April 1815
206	Liebeständelei	Körner	26 May 1815
558	Liebhaber in allen Gestalten	Goethe	May 1817
535	Lied ('Brüder, schrecklich brennt die Träne')	Anon.	Feb. 1817
284	Lied ('Es ist so angenehm')	(?) Schiller	6 Sept. 1815
483	Lied ('Ferne von der grossen Stadt')	Pichler	Sept. 1816
373	Lied ('Mutter geht durch ihre Kammern')	Fouqué	15 Jan. 1816
107	Lied aus der Ferne	Matthisson	July 1814
830	Lied der Anne Lyle	Scott	(?) Early 1825
109	Lied der Liebe	Matthisson	July 1814
843	Lied des gefangenen Jägers	Scott/Storck	April 1825
474	Lied des Orpheus	Jacobi	Sept. 1816
596	Lied eines Kindes	Anon.	Nov. 1817
822	Lied eines Kriegers	Anon.	31 Dec. 1824
360	Lied eines Schiffers an die Dioskuren	Mayrhofer	(?) 1822
416	Lied in der Abwesenheit	Stolberg	April 1816
473	Liedesend	Mayrhofer	Sept. 1816
273	Lilla an die Morgenröthe	Anon.	25 Aug. 1815
902(1)	L'Incanto degli occhi	Metastasio	1827
343	Litanei auf das Fest aller Seelen	Jacobi	Aug. 1816
711	Lob der Tränen	A. W. v. Schlegel	(?) 1818
248	Lob des Tokayers	Baumberg	Aug. 1815
150	Lodas Gespenst	Ossian	17 Jan. 1816
327	Lorma (1)	Ossian	28 Nov. 1815. Incomplete
376	Lorma (2)	Ossian	10 Feb. 1816. Incomplete
319	Luisens Antwort	Kosegarten	19 Oct. 1815
549	Mahomets Gesang (1)	Goethe	March 1817. Incomplete
721	Mahomets Gesang (2)	Goethe	March 1821. Incomplete
503	Mailied	Hölty	Nov. 1816
658	Marie	Novalis	(?) May 1819
215A	Meeres Stille (1)	Goethe	20 June 1815

D no.	Title	Author	Date
216	Meeres Stille (2)	Goethe	21 June 1815
305	Mein Gruss an den Mai	Kumpf	15 Oct. 1815
541	Memnon	Mayrhofer	March 1815
429	Minnelied	Hölty	May 1816
152	Minona	Bertrand	8 Feb. 1815
42	Misero pargoletto	Metastasio	(?) 1813
381	Morgenlied ('Die frohe neubelebte Flur')	Anon.	24 Feb. 1816
266	Morgenlied ('Willkommen rotes Morgenlicht')	Stolberg	24 Aug. 1815
685	Morgenlied ('Eh die Sonne früh aufersteht')	Werner	1820
561	Nach einem Gewitter	Mayrhofer	May 1817
827	Nacht und Träume	M. v. Collin	(?) 1822
119	Nachtgesang ('O gib vom weichen Pfühle')	Goethe	30 Nov. 1814
314	Nachtgesang ('Tiefer Feier schauert')	Kosegarten	19 Oct. 1815
687	Nachthymne	Novalis	Jan. 1820
672	Nachtstück	Mayrhofer	Oct. 1819
752	Nachtviolen	Mayrhofer	April 1822
162	Nähe des Geliebten	Goethe	27 Feb. 1815
695	Namenstaglied	Stadler	March 1820
188	Naturgenuss	Matthisson	(?) May 1815
846	Normans Gesang	Scott/Storck	April 1825
513A	Nur wer die Liebe kennt	Werner	(?) 1817
310	Nur wer die Sehnsucht kennt (1)	Goethe	18 Oct. 1815
359	Nur wer die Sehnsucht kennt (2)	Goethe	1816
481	Nur wer die Sehnsucht kennt (3)	Goethe	Sept. 1816
877(4)	Nur wer die Sehnsucht kennt (4)	Goethe	Jan. 1826
877(1)	Nur wer die Sehnsucht kennt (5)	Goethe	Jan. 1826. Duet
874	O Quell, was strömst du rasch und wild	Schulze	(?) March 1826
548	Orest auf Tauris	Mayrhofer	March 1817
278	Ossians Lied nach dem Falle Nathos	Ossian	(?) Sept. 1815
551	Pax Vobiscum	Schober	April 1817
76	Pensa, che questo istante	Metastasio	Sept. 1813
467	Pflicht und Liebe	Gotter	Aug. 1816
392	Pflügerlied	Salis-Seewis	March 1816
500	Phidile	Claudius	Nov. 1816
540	Philoktet	Mayrhofer	March 1817

D no.	Title	Author	Date
789	Pilgerweise	Schober	April 1823
674	Prometheus	Goethe	Oct. 1819
253	Punschlied: im Norden zu singen	Schiller	18 Aug. 1815
17(1)	Quell' innocente figlio	Metastasio	(?) Autumn 1812
138	Rastlose Liebe	Goethe	19 May 1815
397	Ritter Toggenburg	Schiller	13 March 1816
114	Romanze ('Ein Fräulein klagt' im finstern Turm')	Matthisson	Sept. 1814
144	Romanze ('In der Väter Hallen ruhte')	Stolberg	April 1816. Incomplete
907	Romanze des Richard Löwenherz	Scott/Müller	(?) March 1826
476	Rückweg	Mayrhofer	Sept. 1816
163	Sängers Morgenlied (1)	Körner	27 Feb. 1815
165	Sängers Morgenlied (2)	Körner	1 March 1815
121	Schäfers Klagelied	Goethe	30 Nov. 1814
761	Schatzgräbers Begehr	Schober	Nov. 1822
910	Schiffers Scheidelied	Schober	Feb. 1827
443	Schlachtgesang	Klopstock	June 1816
527	Schlaflied	Mayrhofer	Jan. 1817
744	Schwanengesang ('Wie klag ich's aus')	Senn	(?) Autumn 1822
957	*Schwanengesang* (Song Cycle)		Finished Aug. 1828
	Liebesbotschaft	Rellstab	
	Kriegers Ahnung	Rellstab	
	Frühlingssehnsucht	Rellstab	
	Ständchen	Rellstab	
	Aufenthalt	Rellstab	
	In der Ferne	Rellstab	
	Abschied	Rellstab	
	Der Atlas	Heine	
	Ihr Bild	Heine	
	Das Fischermädchen	Heine	
	Die Stadt	Heine	
	Am Meer	Heine	
	Der Doppelgänger	Heine	
	(Die Taubenpost is listed separately)		
318	Schwangesang ('Endlich stehn die Pforten offen')	Kosegarten	19 Oct. 1815
559	Schweizerlied	Goethe	May 1817
170	Schwertlied	Körner	12 March 1815
762	Schwestergruss	Bruchmann	Nov. 1822
123	Sehnsucht ('Was zieht mir das Herz so')	Goethe	3 Dec. 1814
516	Sehnsucht ('Der Lerche wolkennahe Lieder')	Mayrhofer	(?) Spring 1817

D no.	Title	Author	Date
52	Sehnsucht ('Ach, aus dieses Tales Gründen') (1)	Schiller	15–17 April 1813
636	Sehnsucht (2)	Schiller	(?) Early 1821
879	Sehnsucht ('Die Scheibe friert, der Wind ist rauh')	Seidl	March 1826
180	Sehnsucht der Liebe	Körner	8 April 1815
741	Sei mir gegrüsst	Rückert	1822
743	Selige Welt	Senn	(?) Autumn 1822
433	Seligkeit	Hölty	May 1816
286	Selma und Selmar	Klopstock	14 Sept. 1815
35(1)	Serbate, O dei custodi	Metastasio	Dec. 1812
198	Seufzer	Hölty	22 May 1815
293	Shilrik und Vinvela	Ossian	20 Sept. 1815
896A	Sie in jedem Liede	Leitner	Autumn 1827
306	Skolie ('Lasst im Morgenstrahl des Mai'n')	Deinhardstein	15 Oct. 1815
507	Skolie ('Mädchen entsiegelten')	Matthisson	Dec. 1816
469	So lasst mich scheinen (1) and (2)	Goethe	Sept. 1816. Fragments
727	So lasst mich scheinen (3)	Goethe	April 1821
877(3)	So lasst mich scheinen (4)	Goethe	Jan. 1826
78	Son fra l'onde	Metastasio	13 Sept. 1813
628	Sonett I	A. W. v. Schlegel	Nov. 1818
629	Sonett II	A. W. v. Schlegel	Nov. 1818
630	Sonett III	Gries	Dec. 1818
410	Sprache der Liebe	A. W. v. Schlegel	April 1816
889	Ständchen ('Hark, hark, the lark')	Shakespeare	July 1826
187	Stimme der Liebe (1) ('Abendgewölke schweben hell')	Matthisson	(?) May 1815
418	Stimme der Liebe (2)	Matthisson	29 April 1816
412	Stimme der Liebe ('Meine Selinde!')	Stolberg	April 1816
720	Suleika I ('Was bedeutet die Bewegung')	M. v. Willemer	March 1821
717	Suleika II ('Ach um deine feuchten Schwingen')	M. v. Willemer	(?) End 1824
126	Szene aus 'Faust'	Goethe	Dec. 1814
533	Täglich zu singen	Claudius	Feb. 1817
73	Thekla: eine Geisterstimme (1)	Schiller	22–23 Aug. 1813
595	Thekla: eine Geisterstimme (2)	Schiller	Nov. 1817
876	Tiefes Leid	Schulze	Dec. 1825 or March 1826
274	Tischlerlied	Anon.	25 Aug. 1815

D no.	Title	Author	Date
234	Tischlied	Goethe	15 July 1815
758	Todesmusik	Schober	Sept. 1822
101	Todtenopfer	Matthisson	April 1814
44	Totengräberlied	Hölty	19 Jan. 1813
842	Totengräbers Heimwehe	Craigher	April 1825
869	Totengräber-Weise	Schlechta	1826
275	Totenkranz für ein Kind	Matthisson	25 Aug. 1815
465	Trauer der Liebe	Jacobi	Aug. 1816
888	Trinklied ('Bacchus, feister Fürst des Weins')	Shakespeare	July 1826
183	Trinklied ('Ihr Freunde und du goldner Wein')	Zettler	12 April 1815
523	Trost ('Nimmer lange weil ich hier')	Anon.	Jan. 1817
671	Trost ('Hörnerklänge rufen klagend')	Mayrhofer	Oct. 1819
97	Trost, an Elisa	Matthisson	1814
546	Trost im Liede	Schober	March 1817
120	Trost im Tränen	Goethe	30 Nov. 1814
682	Über allen Zauber	Mayrhofer	(?) Autumn 1819
884	Über Wildemann	Schulze	March 1826
862	Um Mitternacht	Schulze	Dec. 1825
554	Uraniens Flucht	Mayrhofer	April 1817
287	Vaterlandslied	Klopstock	14 Sept. 1815
177	Vergebliche Liebe	Bernard	6 April 1815
792	Vergissmeinnicht	Schober	May 1823
59	Verklärung	Pope/Herder	4 May 1813
715	Versunken	Goethe	Feb. 1821
688	Vier Canzonen		Jan. 1820
	(1) Non t'accostare all'urna	Vittorelli	
	(2) Guarda, che bianca luna	Vittorelli	
	(3) Da quel sembiante appresi	Metastasio	
	(4) Mio ben ricordati	Metastasio	
786	Viola	Schober	March 1823
579A	Vollendung (formerly 989)	Matthisson	Autumn 1817
632	Vom Mitleiden Mariä	F. v. Schlegel	Dec. 1818
228	Von Ida	Kosegarten	7 July 1815
927	Vor meiner Wiege	Leitner	Autumn 1827
224	Wandrers Nachtlied I ('Der du von dem Himmel bist')	Goethe	5 July 1815
768	Wandrers Nachtlied II ('Über allen Gipfeln ist Ruh')	Goethe	(?) Dec. 1822
772	Wehmut	M. v. Collin	(?) Nov. 1822
261	Wer kauft Liebesgötter?	Goethe	21 Aug. 1815
478(2)	Wer nie sein Brot mit Tränen ass (1)	Goethe	Sept. 1816
478(2)	Wer nie sein Brot (2)	Goethe	Sept. 1816

D no.	Title	Author	Date
478(2)	Wer nie sein Brot (3)	Goethe	Autumn 1822
325	Wer sich der Einsamkeit ergibt (1)	Goethe	13 Nov. 1815
478(1)	Wer sich der Einsamkeit ergibt (2)	Goethe	Sept. 1816
639	Widerschein	Schlechta	1819 or 1820
525	Wie Ulfru fischt	Mayrhofer	Jan. 1817
855	Wiedersehn	A. W. v. Schlegel	Sept. 1825
498	Wiegenlied ('Schlafe, schlafe, holder, süsse Knabe')	Anon.	Nov. 1816
304	Wiegenlied ('Schlummer sanft!')	Körner	15 Oct. 1815
867	Wiegenlied ('Wie sich der Äuglein kindlicher Himmel')	Seidl	(?) 1826
767	Willkommen und Abschied	Goethe	Dec. 1822
401	Winterlied	Hölty	13 May 1816
911	*Winterreise* (Song Cycle) Gute Nacht Die Wetterfahne Gefrorne Tränen Erstarrung Der Lindenbaum Wasserflut Auf dem Fluss Rückblick Irrlicht Rast Frühlingstraum Einsamkeit Die Post Der greise Kopf Die Krähe Letzte Hoffnung Im Dorfe Der stürmische Morgen Täuschung Der Wegweiser Das Wirtshaus Mut Die Nebensonnen Der Leiermann	Müller	Feb.–Oct. 1827
896B	Wolke und Quelle	Leitner	(?) End of 1827. Sketch
260	Wonne der Wehmut	Goethe	20 Aug. 1815
362	Zufriedenheit (1)	Claudius	(?) April 1816
501	Zufriedenheit (2)	Claudius	Nov. 1816
492	Zum Punsche	Mayrhofer	Oct. 1816
83	Zur Namensfeier des Herrn Andreas Siller	Anon.	28 Oct.–4 Nov. 1813

Appendix C

Personalia

Appendix C gives brief biographies of those people who figures most importantly in Schubert's life, those who most influenced his work or thought, and some of the scholars and performers who helped to bring Schubert's work to the attention of the public during the nineteenth century. It was decided not to include in Appendix C anyone born after Schubert's death (1828). Johannes Brahms (b. 1833) is the honourable exception to this rule.

Artaria, Matthias (1783–1835). Member of a well-known family of Austrian music publishers. He operated independently in Vienna from 1818 to 1833, and published three important Schubert works in 1826.

Assmayr, Ignaz (1790–1862). Pupil of Salieri at the same time as Schubert. He became second court organist in 1825 and Kapellmeister in 1846.

Barbaja, Domenico (?1778–1841). Italian impresario. His first lease of the court theatres in Vienna ran from the beginning of 1822 to March 1825. A second lease of the Kärntnertor theatre began in April 1826. Barbaja presided over enormously successful seasons of Italian opera, but he also commissioned Weber's *Euryanthe*, and encouraged other German opera composers.

Barth, Josef (1781–1865). Tenor in the Imperial Chapel choir. He took part in many performances of Schubert partsongs in the Philharmonic Society entertainments and other concerts.

Bauernfeld, Eduard von (1802–90). Viennese dramatist and man of letters. He first met Schubert in January 1822, but the acquaintance only ripened into a close friendship three years later. Bauernfeld played duets with Schubert and was the sole auditor of the first performance of the F minor Duet Fantasie. His satirical talent made him a somewhat critical observer of the antics of the Schubert circle; however, his diary and his reminiscences provide an important primary source of information about the last years of the composer's life.

Beresin, Alexis von. Russian aristocrat, resident in Vienna 1822–3 in the course of his grand tour. His companion on the first part of his journey was P. J. Köppen (q.v.), who later went his own way. Beresin left Vienna for Italy in November 1823 with a new companion, Schubert's friend Leopold Kupelwieser, the painter. In August 1824 Beresin died suddenly in Sicily. Kupelwieser returned to Vienna a year later.

Bernhardt, J. Medical doctor and amateur writer. He attended Schubert in the early stages of his illness, in 1823 and 1824. He wrote an opera libretto which Schubert failed to set. Possibly in recompense, the composer dedicated to him the Six Grand Marches for piano duet, Op. 40.

Bocklet, Karl Maria von (1801–81). Pianist. He began his career as a violinist in the orchestra of the Theater an der Wien, but later became a solo pianist and teacher. Schubert dedicated to him the D major Sonata of August 1825.

Bogner, Ferdinand (1786–1846). Flautist, and professor at the Vienna Conservatory. He married Barbara Fröhlich (q.v.) in 1825, and was a prominent member of the Philharmonic Society. The Variations on the 'Trockne Blumen' theme for flute and piano were probably written for him.

Brahms, Johannes (1833–97). The great German composer was a fervent admirer of Schubert's works. He said of Schubert's songs that there is none from which we cannot learn something. Brahms's significant collection of Schubert manuscripts was bequeathed to the Philharmonic Society. He orchestrated a number of songs, and his chorus for female voices, Op. 113/13, uses the melody of *Der Leiermann* as a direct tribute to Schubert. Brahms edited the symphonies for the Breitkopf & Härtel critical edition of Schubert's works.

Bruchmann, Franz von (1798–1867). Son of a rich merchant and patron of the arts in Vienna, Bruchmann was a very important link between Schubert and the circle of Romantically minded poets and philosophers in Vienna in the years 1820 to 1823. He abandoned his Catholicism for a Romantic pantheism based on the teachings of Friedrich von Schlegel and Schelling. He made special journeys to Erlangen to hear Schelling lecture, and there met the poet and dramatist von Platen, whom he introduced to Schubert's work. Bruchmann took a leading part in the reading parties, and provided Schubert with the texts of several fine songs. He withdrew from the circle in 1825, after the exposure of Schober's secret affair with his sister Justina, and later became a Redemptorist priest.

Castelli, Ignaz (1781–1862). Patriot, songwriter and dramatist. He wrote the libretto of *Die Verschworenen* (The Conspirators) as a challenge to German composers, but did not discover that Schubert had taken up the challenge until 1861. His memoirs give a lively account of the frustrations of artistic life in Vienna under the censorship.

Chézy, Wilhelmine von (1783–1856), née Klenke. German playwright and author. She came to Vienna from Dresden in 1823 for the production of *Euryanthe* (November 1823), and while there wrote the Romantic play *Rosamunde*, for which Schubert provided incidental music. In her memoirs she speaks generously of Schubert's music, and modestly of her own part in the production.

Claudius, Matthias (1740–1815). German poet, thirteen of whose poems Schubert set in 1816 and 1817. His sincere feeling for the simple pleasures of life, and fresh observation of nature, played an important part in Schubert's development as a songwriter.

Clodi, Therese (*c.*1801–after 1847). The Clodi family were friends and relations of the Spauns. They lived at Ebenzweier Castle by the side of Lake Traun, three miles from Gmunden. There they entertained Schubert and Vogl during the holiday tour of 1825. Schubert called Therese, who looked after the whole family, the 'lady of the lake', an amiable allusion to his enthusiasm for Scott's poem, and to the popularity of his Scott songs.

Collin, Matthäus von (1779–1824). Matthäus and his brother Heinrich (1772–1811) were important figures in the Romantic movement in Vienna. Matthäus was a professor of philosophy, who became tutor to the young Duke of Reichstadt, Napoleon's son, in 1815. He wrote the words of three of

Schubert's most intensely Romantic songs, 'Der Zwerg', 'Nacht und Träume', and 'Wehmut'.

Craigher, Jakob Nikolaus (1797–1855). Merchant, traveller, diplomat, and poet. His command of European languages made him a useful translator. In 1825 Craigher agreed to provide Schubert with metrical translations of songs by well-known poets, so that they could be published in alternative language versions. He also wrote the words of 'Die junge Nonne'.

Dankesreither, Johann Nepomuk von (1756–1823). Bishop of St Pölten. Schubert and Schober (a distant relation of Dankesreither) stayed as guests on the Bishop's estate in the autumn of 1821, while working on *Alfonso und Estrella*, and at other times too. The three Harper's songs, Op. 12, were dedicated to him.

Diabelli, Anton (1781–1858). Directed the firm of Diabelli & Co., successor to Cappi & Diabelli, until 1853. He published more than 40 opus numbers of Schubert's work during the composer's lifetime, bought all the surviving unpublished songs, and other works, from Ferdinand Schubert in 1829, and published the 50 books of the *Nachlass* from 1830 to 1850. Diabelli, himself a composer, was a bold and innovative editor, and did not scruple to interfere with Schubert's autographs in the process of making them more acceptable, as he thought, to the public.

Dietrichstein, Moritz, Count (1775–1864). *Hofmusikgraf* (administrative head of the court musical establishment) in Vienna, and a strong supporter of Schubert, who dedicated his Op. 1, 'Erlkönig', to him.

Doblhoff, Anton von (1800–72). A politically-minded member of the circle, he was a pupil of Senn (q.v.), and came under suspicion of the police about the time of Senn's arrest and banishment. None the less, he had a distinguished career in the Civil Service, culminating in a term as Minister of Education.

Doppler, Josef (b. 1792). In 1867 he told Grove that he had been present at Schubert's christening. He was well known to the Schubert family as a boy, and took part in the early music practices at the schoolhouse. In later years he became general manager of Spina's publishing house, successor to Diabelli & Co.

Ebner, Leopold (1791–1870). Played violin in the student orchestra at the *Konvikt*, where he met Schubert. Like his friend Stadler (q.v.) he made a collection of Schubert songs in manuscript, which is now in the library of Lund University, Sweden.

Eckel, George Franz (1797–1869). Played first flute in the student orchestra at the *Konvikt*. He became a distinguished physician and veterinary surgeon. In 1858 he wrote down his memoirs of Schubert, remarkable for their detailed and perceptive account of the composer's physical appearance and temperament.

Enderes, Karl (1787–1861). Law officer, botanist, and member of the circle. He lived with Witteczek (q.v.) *c*.1824–5 on the Kärntnertorstrasse, where Schubertiads were frequently held.

Esterházy, von Galánta, Johann Karl Count (1775–1834). He married in 1802 the Countess Rosina Festetics (1784–1854). With their three children, Marie (b.1802), Karoline (b.1805), and Albert (b.1813), they lived at Zseliz in Hungary in the summer months, and at Penzing near Vienna from November to May. Schubert tutored the young countesses at Zseliz in 1818 and 1824, and kept in touch with the family during their visits to Vienna. Karoline, the 'certain attractive star' of Schubert's mature years, married Count Karl Folliot in 1844, but the marriage was annulled.

Eybler, Josef (1765–1846). Austrian composer, friend of Mozart and Haydn. He succeeded Salieri as Hofkapellmeister in 1824. His attachment to traditional liturgical style is reflected in his refusal to accept Schubert's A flat Mass for performance at court.

Fries, Moritz von (1777–1826). Banker, patron of the arts, and connoisseur. He was the dedicatee of Schubert's Op. 2, *Gretchen am Spinnrade.*

Fröhlich, A musical family of four sisters, daughters of a nobleman turned merchant, who lived by themselves in the Spiegelgasse. Anna (1793–1880) sang soprano, and taught singing in the school opened by the Philharmonic Society in 1819. Barbara (b.1798) was a mezzo, who married the flautist Ferdinand Bogner (q.v.) in 1825. Katharina, Grillparzer's 'eternal beloved', was a soprano and Josefine a contralto. The Fröhlich sisters were closely involved in Philharmonic Society affairs, and through them with Schubert. For Anna he wrote his finest partsongs as test pieces for the student choir. Grillparzer lived for many years with the Fröhlichs, whom Bauernfeld dubbed the *Grillparzen.*

Fuchs, Alois (1799–1853). Civil servant and musicologist. He worked as an assistant to Kiesewetter (q.v.) in the War Office, and collected autographs and first editions. In the 1840s he compiled a thematic catalogue of Schubert's works, later supplemented by Ferdinand Schubert.

Gahy, Josef von (1793–1864). Civil servant and pianist. Born in Hungary, he came to Vienna *c.*1817, and worked in the same office as Spaun. He was Schubert's favourite duet partner, and a famous performer of the keyboard dances. The celebrated story about the Rondo in D for piano duet (D608 'Notre amitié est invariable') is probably apocryphal.

Gosmar, Louise (1803–1858). A pupil of Anna Fröhlich's, she married Leopold Sonnleithner in 1828. For her birthday in August 1827 Schubert wrote the partsong 'Ständchen' (Serenade) to a text specially written by Grillparzer.

Grillparzer, Franz (1791–1872). Austrian poet and dramatist. He was related to the Sonnleithner family on his mother's side. He met Schubert *c.*1820, and followed his career closely, but the two men were never intimate. Grillparzer wrote the inscription for Schubert's tombstone and took a leading part, with the Fröhlich family, in organizing the official subscription for a memorial to him.

Grob, Therese (1798–1875). Schubert's first love married a master baker, Johann Bergmann, in November 1820, but died childless. Her mementos of Schubert, including the songbook he compiled for her in 1816, were jealously guarded for many years by the family descendants of her nephew. They are now in private possession at Bottmingen bei Basel.

Grove, Sir George (1820–1900). Civil engineer, Secretary of the Crystal Palace Company 1852–73, and polymath. His *Dictionary of Music and Musicians* was first published in four volumes (1879–89). Grove's essays on Beethoven, Schubert, and Mendelssohn contained therein were models for their time, as were his programme notes, and were regarded as authoritative well into the twentieth century. Inevitably, some of his judgements, notably his theory of a missing 'Gastein Symphony', have had to be rejected, but the history of Schubert's reputation in England owes perhaps more to his enthusiasm and pragmatic wisdom than to anyone else.

Gymnich, August (1786–1821). A tenor singer and civil servant, who played a prominent part in Philharmonic Society affairs. His performance of 'Erlkönig' at Sonnleithner's on 1 December 1820 led directly to Schubert's sensational success over the following twelve months. He died unexpectedly in the autumn of 1821.

Hallé, Sir Charles (1819–1895). German born pianist and conductor, well known as the founder and conductor of the Hallé orchestra, but deserves to be better known for his missionary zeal on behalf of such composers as Berlioz and Schubert, whose work was neglected in the nineteenth century, and particularly for his enthusiastic advocacy of Schubert's piano sonatas. In his annual series of piano recitals at St James Hall in London he not only played all Beethoven's 32 sonatas in chronological order several times; in 1868 he played all the available eleven Schubert sonatas, many of them for the first time in England, and edited the first edition of them for Chapell & Co., thus challenging deliberately the common nineteenth-century view that Schubert's sonatas were not worthy to be set beside Beethoven's because of their length and diffuseness.

Hartmann, Franz von (1808–75) and Fritz (1805–50). They were members of a musical family in Linz, close friends of the Spauns; their diaries record their enthusiasm for Schubert's music. They studied law at the university, Fritz from 1823 and Franz from 1824. But it is not till 1827, when they were both in Vienna and active members of the circle, that they tell us a good deal about its composition and somewhat Bohemian attitude to life and art.

Haslinger, Tobias (1787–1842). Haslinger took over the much respected Steiner publishing house in May 1826 and steadily expanded the business. In 1827 an 1828 he published important Schubert works, including the G major piano sonata, *Winterreise*, and two Impromptus.

Hatwig, Otto (1766–1834). Violinist, and leader of the orchestra at the Burg Theatre. In the autumn of 1815 he took over the leadership of the semi-professional orchestra which had originated in the practices in the Liechtental schoolhouse. Under his guidance the orchestra grew in size and competence, and gave regular concerts. Schubert's early orchestral works, including the first six symphonies, were probably all played under Hatwig's leadership.

Hauer, Josef (b. 1802). Doctor, violinist, music lover, and collector of first editions. He had attended the *Konvikt* later than Schubert and recalled playing orchestral works of the composer, whom he knew personally from about 1825. He played second violin in the first (private) performance of the D minor String Quartet D810 in Jan. 1826.

Hellmesberger, Joseph (1828–93). Viennese violinist, conductor, and Kapellmeister. Director and conductor of the *Gesellschaft der Musikfreunde* orchestra 1851–9, and founder and leader of the Hellmesberger Quarter 1841–91. His many first public performances included Schubert's C major String Quintet D956 (Nov. 1850), the G major String Quartet D887 (Dec. 1850), and the *Quartettsatz* D703 (March 1867), and led to the publication of the scores of these and other of Schubert's great chamber works.

Henikstein, Josef von (1768–1838). Merchant, musician, patron and member of the Philharmonic Society. Schubert was a regular attender at his salon in 1822/23.

Hofmann, August Heinrich, von Fallersleben (1798–1874). Poet and folklorist. He visited Vienna in the summer of 1827 with the intention of making Schubert's acquaintance, but found the experience disillusioning.

Hofmann, Georg Ernst von (1771–1845). Librettist at the Kärntnertor theatre. He wrote the book for *Die Zwillingsbrüder* and for *Die Zauberharfe*. Both were adaptations from a French original.

Hölty, Ludwig Christoph (1748–76). German poet. Founder member of a group of young writers at Göttingen university called the *Hainbund*, followers of the new poetic movement associated with Klopstock. Schubert set twenty-three of his poems in 1815 and 1816.

Holz, Karl (1798–1858). Violinist. He played in Schuppanzigh's quartet, and took part in first performances of Schubert's A minor Quartet and the Octet for strings and wind. He also played in Schubert's only public concert on 26 March 1828, and claimed to have arranged a performance of Beethoven's C sharp minor Quartet for Schubert on his deathbed.

Holzapfel, Anton (1792–1868). A student at the *Konvikt*, senior by some years to Schubert, but who seems to have been a close associate of the composer in the years 1813–16. In his memoirs, written for Luib in 1858, he speaks of Schubert's love of poetry, and of the Therese Grob affair. It was Holzapfel who awakened Schubert's interest in Ossian, by lending him an old and tattered translation of the prose poems. He followed a successful career as a lawyer.

Hönig, Anna (Netti) (1803–88). Daughter of a barrister. The ups and downs of her love affair with Schwind were a source of some amusement in the circle. She was a devout Catholic, whose high standards Schwind found it difficult to live up to. The engagement was finally announced in March 1828, only to be broken off in October of the following year. In 1832 she married Ferdinand von Mayerhofer (q.v.) and after his death went into a convent.

Huber, Josef (1794–1870). 'Tall Huber' was a popular member of the circle, though something of a butt, because of his ungainly size and general clumsiness. Schubert shared lodgings with him in 1823–4. He came from Lower Austria, and became an accountant in the War Department.

Hummel, Johann Nepomuk (1778–1837). German pianist and composer. He had a wide international reputation as a virtuoso and as a composer. He came to Vienna with his pupil Ferdinand Hiller in March 1827 to make his peace with Beethoven, and met Schubert and Vogl at Frau von Lászny's. The meeting made a great impression on Schubert, who intended dedicating his last three piano sonatas to Hummel.

Hüttenbrenner, The family came from Graz. Anselm (1794–1868) came to Vienna in 1815 as a law student, and studied composition with Salieri. He and Schubert were close associates over the next few years, and corresponded when Anselm was absent from Vienna. Josef (1796–1882) arrived at the end of 1818, as Anselm's permanent residence in Vienna ended, became an enthusiast for Schubert's music, and appointed himself a kind of business manager and secretary for him. Two other brothers, Andreas and Heinrich (who had ambitions as a poet), also figure briefly in the records. Schubert showed scant regard for Josef, though he seems to have been genuinely attached to Anselm. The part played by the brothers in the disappearance of the 'Unfinished' Symphony is well known.

Jacobi, Johann Georg (1740–1814). German poet and philosopher. Schubert set seven of his poems in August and September 1816.

Jenger, Johann Baptist (1793–1856). Jenger was a founder member and secretary of the Styrian Philharmonic Society, based at Graz, and a good pianist. In April

1823 he took the lead in the award of the Society's Diploma of Honour to Schubert. At the end of 1824 he moved to Vienna to take up a post in the War Office, and frequently appeared as soloist and as accompanist at the Philharmonic Society concerts and at private performances of Schubert's works. He masterminded the visit to Graz in September 1827, and tried without success to arrange a return visit.

Kanne, Friedrich August (1778–1833). Editor of the *Allgemeine musikalische Zeitung* of Vienna 1821–4, and probable author of appreciative notices of Schubert's work published therein. He was also a composer.

Kenner, Josef (1794–1868). Entered the public service after leaving the *Konvikt*, where he was a fellow student with Schubert. His reminiscences, written for Luib in 1858, are noteworthy for the most damning and outspoken attack on the role played by Schober in Schubert's life. Kenner blamed Schober for the permissive habits which led to the composer's chronic illness.

Kiesewetter, Irene (1811–1872). She displayed her gifts as a pianist very early, and was especially fond of accompanying Schubert songs. Schubert wrote the music for a cantata (D936) especially written to celebrate Irene's recovery from a serious illness in December 1827. Like *Der Tanz* (D826), it was an occasional piece intended for a private performance at one of the Kiesewetters' musical parties, and was accompanied by two pianos, probably played by Schubert himself and Jenger. In 1832 Irene married Anton Prokesch (q.v.), the stepson of Julius Schneller (q.v.).

Kiesewetter, Raphael Georg (1773–1850). Father of the preceding. Vice President of the Philharmonic Society 1825–43, singer, flautist, and musicologist. He was one of the first musicians to campaign for the cause of early music. The concerts held regularly at his house were attended by most of the musical establishment, including Schubert, and Jenger, who presided often at the piano. Kiesewetter was an official in the War Office.

Klopstock, Friedrich Gottlieb (1724–1803). German poet and dramatist. His Odes (1771) strongly influenced the early Romantics, and made an impression on Schubert, who wrote a poem in imitation of them while still at school. The thirteen Klopstock settings belong to 1815 and 1816.

Koller, Josefine von (1801–1874). Daughter of the iron merchant Josef von Koller at Steyr. According to Stadler, Schubert wrote a piano sonata for her during his holiday in Steyr in 1819, presumably the one in A major (D664). She married Franz Krackowizer, a head steward, in 1828. She was a regular performer at the Schubertiads held at Steyr.

Köppen, Peter Johann (1793–1864). Academic of Russian birth and German extraction, who visited Vienna 1822 to 1823 as companion to Alexis von Beresin (q.v.). His unpublished diary gives a fascinating glimpse of fashionable salon society in Vienna at the time, and of Schubert's part in it.

Korner, Philipp (1761–1831). He sang tenor in the choir of the Imperial Chapel, and acted as choirmaster in Schubert's day. He also taught singing.

Körner, Theodor (1791–1813). Poet and dramatist. He was appointed resident poet at the Burg Theatre in 1811. Spaun introduced him to Schubert after a performance of Gluck's *Iphigénie en Tauride*; at supper afterwards they all enthused over the singing of Vogl and Anna Milder, who sang the principal roles. Körner volunteered for service in the wars of liberation and died of wounds after a skirmish at Gladebach, 26 August 1813. His war poems, published posthumously, made a great impression. Schubert set several of his poems in 1815.

Kosegarten, Ludwig Theobul (1758–1818). German poet. Schubert set twenty of his poems, June to September 1815; the best of them show a predictive vein of Romantic feeling.

Kotzebue, August von (1761–1819). The most prolific and popular dramatist of his day. Schubert's two juvenile operas, *Der Spiegelritter* and *Des Teufels Lust-schloss*, were based on two of his plays. Kotzebue's absolutist sympathies made him highly suspect in liberal circles. His assassination in 1819 by a young student led to a general crackdown on student political activities, not least in Vienna.

Kreissle von Hellborn, Heinrich (1812–1869). Viennese lawyer and official, Schubert's first biographer. He was a good musician, and a director of the Philharmonic Society. He took over the biographical material collected by Luib (q.v.) in the 1850s, and produced a short biography in 1861. This was extended to a full-length book in 1865. An English translation by Arthur Duke Coleridge was published in London in 1869. Kreissle married a sister of Marie Wagner, who knew Schubert well and has left us moving accounts of the deep impression made by his songs on contemporary audiences. He wrote at a time when many of Schubert's friends and associates were still alive, and his book, though anecdotal and loosely organized by modern standards, is still an invaluable source.

Kreutzer, Konradin (1780–1849). German composer, whose operas and *Singspiele* enjoyed popular success in Vienna during Schubert's lifetime. He was appointed deputy conductor at the Kärntnertor theatre in 1825. Spaun recalled how Schubert expressed his warm admiration for Kreutzer's 'Wanderlieder', nine songs to texts by Uhland.

Kriehuber, Joseph (1801–1876). Celebrated painter and lithographer, who specialized in portraits and produced fine likenesses of many of Schubert's friends and patrons. He was personally acquainted with Schubert, although his two Schubert portraits were made only after the composer's death and published by Diabelli in 1846.

Kupelwieser, Josef (1791–1866). Secretary of the Court Theatre 1821–3, he wrote the libretto for Schubert's projected grand opera *Fierabras*, which was abandoned after the failure of *Euryanthe*. His later career as a theatre manager took him to Graz, and finally to the Josefstadt theatre in Vienna.

Kupelwieser, Leopold (1796–1862). Brother of the above. Austrian artist, Professor of Fine Art at the Academy in Vienna from 1836. Kupelwieser emerges first as a member of the Schubert circle at the Atzenbrugg 'feasts', 1820–3. His portrait sketches of members of the circle, and water-colours of life at Atzenbrugg, are the most important of the contemporary iconographical records. In November 1823 he left Vienna to accompany Beresin (q.v.) on his Italian tour, and did not return to Vienna till 1825. The letters of his betrothed, Johanna Lutz, during his absence provide a valuable insight into the life of the circle at the time. In September 1826 he and Johanna were married, and thereafter we hear little of them in the records of the circle.

Lablache, Luigi (1794–1858). Italian bass singer. He came to Vienna in 1824 and became a leading member of Barbaja's company. He seems to have thought highly of Schubert, who dedicated his Three Songs for Bass Voice, Op. 83, to him.

Lachner, Franz Paul (1803–90). Composer and conductor. He took up the post of organist at the Lutheran church in Vienna in December 1823. A pupil of Sechter and Abbé Stadler, he became assistant conductor at the Kärntnertor in 1827 and chief conductor in 1829. He was closely associated with Schubert, and did his best to promote his chamber music and, so far as he was able, his stage pieces. He went to the Munich opera in 1836, and did his most important work there.

Lanner, Josef (1801–43). Viennese dance composer and violinist. His quintet became famous in the 1820s for its playing at the 'Partridge' tavern, where Schubert must often have heard it.

Lászny, Katharina von, née Buchwieser (*c.*1789–1828). Opera singer. She was on the staff of the Kärntnertor 1809–17. She held open house for musical friends, and Schubert and Vogl were frequent visitors. Schubert dedicated to her a book of songs (Op. 36) and the *Divertissement à l'hongroise.* She was twice married, and was rumoured to have a long list of other lovers.

Leidesdorf, Maximilian Josef (1787–1840). He was the active partner in the publishing house of Sauer & Leidesdorf, founded 1822. After breaking with Diabelli, Schubert made an agreement with Leidesdorf towards the end of 1822 to provide songs for two years in return for 480 florins AC. The association lasted till the end of the composer's life.

Leitner, Karl Gottfried von (1800–90). Poet and teacher of Graz. Schubert was introduced to his work in 1822, and returned to it in the autumn of 1827, on the recommendation of Marie Pachler (q.v.).

Lewy, Josef Rudolf (1802–1881). Hornist. He and his brother, Eduard Constantin Lewy (b.1796), were among the first virtuosi of the new valve horns. Schubert's *Nachtgesang im Walde* for male-voice quartet with accompaniment of four horns, was written for Josef Lewy's concert on 22 April 1827. Lewy played the solo horn part in 'Auf dem Strom' at Schubert's own concert on 26 March 1828.

Liebenberg, Emanuel Karl von (1796–1856). Pianist and patron of the arts. He was a pupil of Liszt, and commissioned the 'Wanderer' Fantasie, Op. 15.

Linke, Josef (1783–1837). Cellist. He played in the orchestra of the Court Theatre, and was a member of the Schuppanzigh quartet.

Luib, Ferdinand (b. 1811). Civil servant, editor of the Vienna *AmZ*, and musicologist. In 1857 and 1858 he collected material for a biography of Schubert, which he later passed on to Kreissle. He had also inherited the material collected by Fuchs. It is reasonable to assume, therefore, that Kreissle had access to all the existing material when writing his biography, except of course what had been deliberately destroyed, and what had not yet come to light.

Lutz, Johanna (1803–83). A cousin of Leopold Sonnleithner, and member of an artistic family. She married Leopold Kupelwieser in 1826, and Schubert played for dancing at her wedding. The correspondence between her and her betrothed in 1823 to 1825, during his absence in Rome, is of great interest.

Manns, Sir August (1825–1907). German-born conductor, who moved to London in 1854 and took over as director of the newly formed Crystal Palace orchestra. With the help and encouragement of George Grove (q.v.), secretary of the Crystal Palace Company, he quickly enlarged the orchestra and made its regular Saturday concerts the most enterprising and professional concert series in London. Manns gave the world premières of Schubert's first three symphonies at the Crystal Palace, and also the symphonic sketch in E major/minor of 1821 in the realization of J. F. Barnett (May 1883). In Feb./March 1881 he conducted all eight Schubert symphonies in consecutive weeks and in chronological order.

Matthisson, Friedrich von (1761–1831). German poet. His verses were widely read and admired in Schubert's day, and he was among the first of his contemporaries to attract the composer's concentrated attention. The Matthisson songs are not among Schubert's greatest, but they represent an important stage in his development.

Mayerhofer, Ferdinand von (1798–1869). One of Schubert's schoolfellows at the *Konvikt*, and an active member of the circle in the 1820s. He became a surveyor in military service. He had literary interests, and collaborated with Bauernfeld in the translations made for the Vienna Shakespeare. After breaking off his own engagement, he married Anna Hönig, Schwind's early love.

Mayrhofer, Johann (1787–1836). Poet. He came from Steyr, studied law in Vienna, and seems to have maintained himself by teaching till *c.*1820, when he became an official in the Censorship Office. He was introduced to Schubert by Spaun in 1814. From 1816 to 1821 he and Schubert were close associates and friends. They lived in the same rooms for two years from the autumn of 1818, and Mayrhofer's influence on Schubert's development as a songwriter in these years can hardly be overestimated. Mayrhofer's neo-classicism, and his deep commitment to Romantic *Sehnsucht*, was an important source of that poetic sense of *Wehmut* so characteristic of Schubert's greatest work. Mayrhofer's melancholic temperament and misanthropic outlook ultimately got the better of him in 1836, when he committed suicide.

Mayssen, Josef (1790–1860). Schoolmaster and choirmaster at Hernals, near Vienna, and one of Ferdinand Schubert's closest friends. Some of Schubert's minor liturgical pieces were written for performance at Hernals church. Mayssen joined Schubert and Ferdinand on their walking expedition to Eisenstadt in October 1828.

Milder, Pauline Anna (1785–1838). Opera singer. Born in Vienna, she studied under Salieri and Tomaselli and made her debut in 1803. She was the first Leonore in Beethoven's *Fidelio* (1805). Schubert's enthusiasm for her as an artist was first kindled by her performance in Gluck's *Iphigénie en Tauride*, while he was still at school. In later years they corresponded, and Schubert wrote his second Suleika song for her, as well as 'Der Hirt auf dem Felsen' (October 1828). She remained in Berlin as prima donna till 1829, and in that year sang in Mendelssohn's famous revival of Bach's *St. Matthew Passion*. Her last public appearance was in 1836.

Mohn, Ludwig (1797–1857). Painter, and a prominent member of the circle till about 1824. He was a regular attender at Atzenbrugg, and he hosted the reading parties in the autumn and winter of 1823/24. His etching, 'Game of Ball at Atzenbrugg', is well known.

Mosel, Ignaz Franz von (1772–1844). Official in the Lord High Steward's office, Secretary to Count Moritz Dietrichstein, and an influential supporter of Schubert's music. The four Goethe songs of Op. 3 were dedicated to him.

Mozart, Wolfgang Amadeus (1791–1844). Youngest son of the composer. in June 1820 he was present at the first performance of *Die Zwillingsbrüder*, and he may possibly have met Schubert then, for in 1825 they exchanged greetings through Spaun, then living in Lemberg, where the young Mozart was musical director. He also met Jenger at Graz in July 1820.

Müller, Sophie (1803–30). Popular star of the Burg Theatre, where she specialized in juvenile roles. She lived alone with her father in the village of Hietzing. She was an enthusiastic admirer of Schubert's songs, and he and Vogl were frequent visitors at her house. Her diary records many of these visits in 1825 and 1826, usually with a note of the songs sung.

Müller, Wenzel (1759–1835). Kapellmeister at the Leopoldstadt Theatre, and highly successful composer of operettas. Schubert much enjoyed his farce with music, *Herr Josef und Frau Baberl*, in May 1826.

Müller, Wilhelm (1794–1827). German poet, publicist and man of letters, of Dessau. Like Schubert, he was interested both in music and in poetry, and saw his verses as pretexts for songs. His song cycle, *Die schöne Müllerin*, took shape first as a kind of party game played by a group of intellectuals in Berlin. He was an enthusiast for Greek independence, and had strong liberal principles. His early death, in somewhat mysterious circumstances, has never been fully explained, but contemporary gossip about a political intrigue has never been substantiated.

Nestroy, Johann (1801–62). Viennese satirist and playwright, singer and member of the circle. He was a scholar at the *Konvikt* (1810–13), studied law, then entered on a career as a bass singer. In 1821 and 1822 he performed several times in Schubert partsongs. After a spell at Amsterdam and another at Brünn, he moved to Graz in 1826, where he began to discover his true vocation, first as a comic actor, and then as a dramatist.

Neumann, Johann Philipp (1774–1849). Professor of physics, liberal theologian, with literary ambitions. He was a champion of the liberal reforms of Joseph II, and a believer in eighteenth-century rational deism. In 1820 he wrote the libretto of *Sakuntala*, one of Schubert's many abortive operatic projects, based on an Indian tale by Kalidasa. He was also responsible for the text of the German Mass, a series of hymns to be sung by the congregation during the celebration, for which Schubert wrote music in 1827. Its use for liturgical purposes was forbidden till well on in the nineteenth century.

Ottenwalt, Anton (1789–1845). Official of Linz, and member of the circle. Schubert and he were acquainted, long before they met in 1819, through Spaun. Schubert set a poem of his, 'Der Knabe in der Wiege', in 1817. He married Spaun's sister Marie in November 1819. Whenever Schubert and Vogl visited Linz, Schubertiads were held at his house.

Pachler, Karl (1789–1850). Brewer and barrister, of Graz, and local patron of the arts.

Pachler, Marie, née Koschak (1794–1855). Wife of the above. A brilliant pianist, she captivated Beethoven when they met in 1817. She kept open house for visiting artists, and hosted the visit of Schubert and Jenger in September 1827. Schubert dedicated his four songs, Op. 106, to her.

Paumgartner, Sylvester (1764–1841). Mining engineer, cellist, and local patron of the arts at Steyr. During Schubert's stay in Steyr in 1819 he commissioned the Piano Quintet in A (the 'Trout').

Pennauer, Anton (*c.* 1784–1837). Music publisher of Vienna. Began publishing in 1822, and opened his music shop in July 1825. His association with Schubert lasted from 1825 to 1827, over which period he published nine opus numbers.

Pettenkoffer, Anton von (1788–1834). Merchant and landowner, of Vienna. Concerts and receptions were held in his fine apartment in the Bauernmarkt.

When Otto Hatwig withdrew from the leadership of the orchestral society to which Schubert belonged, Pettenkoffer put his fine salon at the disposal of the group. Rehearsals and concerts were held there from 1818 to 1820, when the arrangement came to an end.

Pichler, Karoline (1769–1843). Author and literary hostess. Few of her sixty surviving volumes are read today, except perhaps her memoirs, which reflect the intellectual and artistic life of the age. Her salon in Vienna was the resort of the intelligentsia, and visitors from abroad. Schubert was a frequent visitor, especially during the successful years, 1821 and 1822, and his music was often played there.

Pinterics, Karl (d.1831). Private secretary to Prince Pálffy, he sang bass, played the piano, cut silhouettes, and collected engravings and music manuscripts. An early admirer of Schubert's work, he made a large collection of his songs in manuscript, over 500 of them, which was acquired by Josef Witteczek after his death. He was acquainted both with Beethoven and with Schubert, and was said to have been the only one to oppose the suggestion that Schubert should seek instruction from Sechter in counterpoint, when the plan was mooted in 1824.

Platen-Hallermunde, August, Count (1796–1835). German poet and dramatist. His mockery of Romantic extravagances in his plays made him enemies, and his homosexuality hindered his professional advancement, at a time when homosexuality was almost politically suspect. From 1826 he lived in Italy. Among Platen's closest admirers was Franz Bruchmann (q.v.), who met Platen in Erlangen and introduced Schubert to the poet's work. Despite Bruchmann's enthusiastic advocacy, Schubert set only two of Platen's poems, but both are emotionally charged.

Probst, Heinrich Albert (1791–1846). His music publishing house was founded in Leipzig in 1823. Correspondence with Schubert was conducted through Artaria, his Vienna agent. Schubert's first approach, in August 1826, led nowhere. Contact was resumed in February 1828, and eventually Probst did publish the E flat Piano Trio, Op. 100.

Prokesch, Anton (1795–1876). Stepson of Julius Schneller (q.v.). As a young lieutenant, he was closely associated with Schubert in 1822, both as a tavern companion and as a regular visitor at fashionable salons. He left some interesting observations on the composer. In 1832 he married Irene von Kiesewetter (q.v.).

Pyrker, Johann Ladislaus (1772–1847). Poet, playwright, and liberal churchman. Hungarian by birth, he became Patriarch of Venice in 1820, and about this time met Schubert at Matthäus von Collin's. In August 1825 the two met again as guests at Gastein. Schubert was deeply impressed by Pyrker's Romantic view of Nature as the immanent spirit of God, and treasured the memory of this meeting as one of the great experiences of his life. In Gastein also he set two of Pyrker's poems, 'Die Allmacht' and 'Das Heimweh'.

Randhartinger, Benedict (1802–93). He became a choirboy of the Imperial Chapel in the autumn of 1812, filling one of the vacancies left by the retirement of Schubert and others. He became secretary to Count Széchényi, and remained in touch with Schubert, though he was never one of the inner circle of the composer's friends. His later reminiscences are anecdotal and unreliable.

Rellstab, Ludwig (1799–1860). German poet, novelist and journalist. He does not appear to have met Schubert, though he was in Vienna in 1825 and met

Beethoven. It seems to be true that the poems he sent in manuscript to Beethoven, in the hope that the master would set them, were passed on to Schubert, either by Beethoven himself or by Schindler, and were the source for the Rellstab songs embodied in the collection *Schwanengesang*.

Richter, Johann Paul (1763–1825). German Romantic novelist, universally known by his pseudonym, Jean Paul. He was at Erlangen in August 1823, where he may well have met Bruchmann. In 1817 Mayrhofer included extracts from Jean Paul in his short-lived anthology, *Contributions to the Education of Youth*. He and Schubert never met, though the novelist was a great admirer of Schubert's songs. According to his nephew, R. O. Spazier, he asked for 'Erlkönig' to be played to him in the last days of his life.

Rieder, Johann. Schoolmaster and choirmaster in the Währing suburb, and a close friend of Schubert's brother Ferdinand. He performed several of Schubert's liturgical works, including possibly the A flat Mass.

Rieder, Wilhelm August (1796–1880). Painter, member of the circle, and brother of the above. His three-quarter length water-colour of the composer, executed in May 1825, is the best contemporary portrait, and became popular even in Schubert's lifetime. It was engraved by Passini in 1825, and lithographed by Rieder himself in 1828.

Rinna, Ernst von (1793–1837). Court physician. He attended Schubert during the last year of his life, but had to hand over the case to Vering (q.v.) in the final phase because of his own illness. He wrote a book on cures and spas, and was a strong advocate of fresh air and exercise.

Rochlitz, Johann Friedrich (1769–1842). German novelist, poet and journalist, of Leipzig. He met Schubert in 1822 while on a visit to Vienna, and formed a high opinion of his work. Schubert's settings of two Rochlitz texts, Op. 81, were dedicated to the author. In November 1827 Rochlitz wrote to the composer suggesting that he should set the long poem 'Der erste Ton' (The First Sound), but Schubert, possibly because he was heavily engaged with the E flat Piano Trio and other works, sent a temporizing reply.

Rückert, Friedrich (1788–1866). German Romantic poet. He was closely associated with the Vienna orientalist Hammer-Purgstall, who was well known to Bruchmann and other members of the circle. Perhaps through this connection Schubert turned to his poetry in 1822. The five Rückert settings belong to 1822/23, and represent Schubert's art as a songwriter at its best.

Ruzicka, Wenzel (1757–1823). Viola player and court organist. He also taught piano and organ at the *Konvikt*, and established the student orchestra there. For a year or so he gave the young Schubert lessons, but soon decided that he could do no more to help his gifted pupil, and handed him over to Salieri in the summer of 1812.

Salieri, Antonio (1750–1825). Italian composer. He was taken to Vienna as a youth of sixteen and spent the rest of his life in the service of the Viennese court. As a young man he was the friend and colleague of Gassman, Gluck, and Metastasio, and in his maturity Beethoven, Schubert, Liszt, and Hummel were among his pupils. He was thus a link between the great figures of the eighteenth century and the nineteenth. He was Court Kapellmeister in Vienna from 1788 to 1824. Schubert was his pupil from 1812 to the end of 1816, and contributed to the celebrations to mark the fiftieth anniversary of his arrival in the city.

Salis-Seewis, Johann Gaudenz von (1762–1834). Swiss poet and official. He was almost exactly contemporary with Matthisson, and had something of the same popular appeal. Schubert's Salis settings, mainly strophic, belong to 1816 and 1817.

Schaeffer, August von (1790–1865). Medical doctor, who attended Schubert in 1823 and 1824. Schubert kept in touch with him by correspondence even when away on holiday. In 1824 Bernhardt (q.v.) took over the case.

Schechner, Nanette (Anne) (1806–60). Opera singer. She sang in the chorus at the Munich opera at the age of fifteen. After moving to Vienna she made her successful debut there in Weigl's *Die Schweizerfamilie* in May 1826. The circle was highly impressed, and Schubert thought she would do nicely for the opera he and Bauernfeld planned to do together (*Der Graf von Gleichen*). A few months later, however, according to Schindler, she was involved in the operatic audition staged at the Kärntnertor theatre, which ended in a public quarrel between her and Schubert. The details of Schindler's account are dubious, to say the least, though it seems probable that some such event occurred.

Schindler, Anton Felix (1795–1864). German musician and biographer. He gave up the practice of law in favour of music, and from 1820 acted as Beethoven's secretary and representative. His biographical work is marred by his self-importance, and by a cavalier attitude towards the facts. However, his reminiscences of Schubert are full of interest, and include a valuable early chronological catalogue of his works.

Schlechta, Franz Xaver von (1796–1875). After attending the seminary at Kremsmünster he became a pupil at the *Konvikt*, and there met Schubert. He was a loyal friend and devoted admirer of the composer's music, took part in the performance of the *Prometheus* cantata in 1816, wrote a congratulatory poem about it, and lived to write a commemorative epitaph after Schubert's death. Schubert set five of his poems, including 'Des Sängers Habe' and 'Fischerweise'. He had a distinguished career in the public service.

Schlegel, August Wilhelm von (1767–1845). Romantic poet, philosopher, and publicist. Translator of Shakespeare. Schubert wrote nine songs to his texts.

Schlegel, Karl Wilhelm Friedrich von (1772–1829). Brother of the above. German Romantic poet and essayist. He moved to Vienna in 1808 with his wife Dorothea Veit, and became the leader of a group of writers and artists there with Romantic ideas. It is not clear that Schubert ever met him, but he was certainly influenced by his ideas, and set sixteen of his poems, most of them from the sequence *Abendröte* (Sunsets).

Schneller, Julius Franz (1777–1833). Liberal historian and philosopher. Spaun was his pupil at Linz, where he was professor of history. He moved to Graz in 1806, and was a close friend of the Pachlers and of Jenger (q.v.); but his liberal political views made him unacceptable to the authorities, and he was forced to leave Graz. In 1826 he published (under the pseudonym of Julius Velox!) a congratulatory poem on Schubert's songs.

Schober, Franz von (1796–1882). Schober's restless temperament and dilettante attitude led him into a variety of occupations after Schubert's death. He went to Hungary as companion and steward to various noble families, and for a time acted as Liszt's secretary. In 1856, at the age of sixty, he married Thekla von Gumpert, who edited a kind of early teenage magazine for girls; but the marriage ended in disaster eight years later. He never found time in his long life to write down his memories of Schubert in any orderly way.

Schönstein, Karl von (1797–1876). Baritone singer, public official, and member of the circle. Schubert met him in 1818 at Zseliz. He was a close friend of the Esterházy family, and acted as the representative of the Count in Vienna. A sensitive and devoted interpreter of Schubert's songs, he was especially famous for his performance of the song cycle *Die schöne Müllerin*, which Schubert dedicated to him. His contributions to the Schubert biographical literature are important.

Schubert, Ferdinand Lukas (1794–1859). Married for the second time in 1832, he became director of the teachers' training school in 1851. It is said that, dealing with so many children, he sometimes failed to recognize his own when he met them in the street. Ferdinand sold most of his Schubert manuscripts to Diabelli, but reserved the symphonies and continued to try to interest publishers in them during the 1830s. He also collaborated with Alois Fuchs in the preparation of a thematic catalogue of his brother's works.

Schubert, Franz, of Dresden (1768–1827). Double bass player and composer in the service of the Dresden court. He it was who angrily repudiated any responsibility for 'Erlkönig', which the publisher Härtel had sent to him by mistake. His son is remembered as the composer of *L'Abeille* (The Bee), still sometimes attributed to Schubert.

Schubert, Franz, of Graz, whom the composer met in 1827, was a cellist.

Schubert, Ignaz (1785–1844). Succeeded his father as headmaster of the Rossau school in 1830.

Schumann, Robert (1810–1856). The German composer, already a great admirer of Schubert, visited Vienna in the winter of 1838/9, where he visited the composer's brother Ferdinand and was amazed to find large quantities of manuscripts remaining, even after so many had been sold to Diabelli (q.v.). He wrote: 'The sight of these riches filled me with joy; where to begin, where to leave off'. He arranged for the first performance of the 'Great' C major Symphony, which took place under Mendelssohn in Leipzig, March 1839. Schumann was also a publicist for Schubert, writing enthusiastically about his works in the columns of his *Neue Zeitschrift für Musik*.

Schuppanzigh, Ignaz (1776–1830). Austrian violinist. His famous quartet was schooled by Haydn himself, became the vehicle for Beethoven's genius, and launched Schubert's chamber works in public. After the destruction by fire of the Razumovsky palace in 1814 Schuppanzigh moved to Russia. Schubert met him on his return to Vienna in 1823. The A minor String Quartet, of which Schuppanzigh gave the first public performance, was dedicated to him.

Schwind, Moritz von (1804–71). His later career as a painter was distinguished; he was noted for his imaginative treatment of fairy tales and myths. He remained devoted to Schubert's memory, and to his music, for the rest of his life. His masterpiece, the 'Schubert Evening at Josef von Spaun's', was never finished, but it survives as a magnificent sketch. In later years he violently opposed the new music of Liszt and Wagner, and quarrelled openly with Schober.

Sechter, Simon (1788–1867). Austrian composer, organist, and theorist. Born in Bohemia, he served for many years as music teacher at the Blind Institute in Vienna. He became assistant to the court organist in 1824 and succeeded

Voříšek as principal court organist in 1825. The fugue subject on the letters of Schubert's name, which he wrote down at the end of the one and only lesson he gave to the composer, he later published in the form of a complete commemorative fugue.

Seidl, Johann Gabriel (1804–75). Viennese poet, journalist, and civil servant. Schubert's eleven songs to his texts all belong to the last three years of his life.

Senn, Johann Chrysostomus (1792–1857). Born in the Tyrol, he was a passionate supporter of Tyrolese independence. He lost his place at the *Konvikt* as the result of a row with the authorities over the punishment of a fellow student. After the police raid on his rooms in March 1820 he was kept in prison without charges being brought against him, and then banished to his homeland. He served later as an officer in the army, but died poor and friendless.

Slawjk, Josef (1806–1833). Bohemian violinist, who came to Vienna in 1826. Schubert wrote for him the Rondo in B minor and the Fantasie in C, which he performed with his compatriot Bocklet (q.v.). The Fantasie received its first performance at Slavjk's recital in February 1828, making little impression, despite Slavjk's reputation as a virtuoso.

Sonnleithner, Leopold (1797–1873). Like his father Ignaz (1770–1831), he had a distinguished career as a barrister, and played a leading part in the affairs of the Philharmonic Society. His uncle Josef (1766–1835), secretary of the court theatres 1804 to 1814, masterminded the formation of the Philharmonic Society in 1812/13. Leopold, who shared his uncle's interest in musical history, left illuminating articles on the musical life of Vienna in Schubert's day. Though he used his considerable power and influence to further Schubert's interests during his lifetime, he was never a member of the inner circle of the composer's friends.

Spaun, Josef von (1788–1865). Government official. Founder of the Schubert circle. He remained devoted to the memory of the composer till the end of his life. He inherited Witteczek's collection of Schubert's papers and manuscripts and bequeathed it, augmented by his own collection, to the Philharmonic Society.

Spendou, Josef (1757–1840). Liberal churchman, inspector of schools, and patron of the Schubert family. He was founder and governor of the Orphanage at which Ferdinand Schubert taught from about 1809 onward. Several of Schubert's works were probably performed there, and Schubert wrote a congratulatory cantata in honour of Spendou (D472) for performance at the concert to celebrate the twentieth anniversary of the foundation of the orphanage.

Stadler, Albert (1794–1888). He attended the *Konvikt* from 1812 to 1817, and during this period was in close contact with Schubert. From 1817 to 1820 he was employed in the district administration at Steyr, his birthplace, and in 1821 moved to Linz. He maintained contact with the composer until the 1820s, and saw him on his occasional visits to Upper Austria. His manuscript collection of Schubert's songs, an important source for the songs of 1814 to 1817, is now in the university library at Lund in Sweden.

Streinsberg, Josef Ludwig von (1798–1862). Another member of the circle who first met Schubert at the *Konvikt*. A man of strong political views, he was involved in the police raid on Senn's rooms in March 1820. Shortly afterward he moved to Linz, but returned to Vienna in 1824. In January 1826 he married Bruchmann's sister Isabella. Both he and his wife converted to Catholicism.

Széchényi, Louis, Count (1781–1855). A Hungarian by birth, he was chief steward to the Archduchess Sophie, and a prominent member of the Philharmonic Society. Schubert's Op. 7, consisting of three songs (two by Széchényi himself), was dedicated to him.

Teltscher, Josef (1801–37). Painter and portraitist, member of the circle. The well-known lithograph of Schubert was made in 1826. In 1829 he moved to Graz, where for some time he lived with Josef Hüttenbrenner. His delightful coloured drawing of Jenger, Schubert and Anselm Hüttenbrenner is frequently reproduced. According to Josef Hüttenbrenner, Schindler took Schubert, Teltscher and the two Hüttenbrenners to see Beethoven on his deathbed, and Teltscher made a sketch of the dying composer. Teltscher's portrait sketch of Karoline Esterházy, for many years in the possession of Schönstein, was bequeathed to Schwind, who incorporated it in his 'Schubert Evening at Josef von Spaun's'. He was drowned while bathing in the harbour of Piraeus near Athens.

Tietze, Ludwig (1797–1850). Tenor. From 1822 he took part regularly in performances of Schubert's partsongs at Philharmonic Society concerts and elsewhere. He also appeared at Schubert's own concert in March 1828. Later he moved to Graz, and according to Josef Hüttenbrenner opposed the idea of doing a Requiem Mass for the dead composer, on the grounds that he was 'a good song-writer but not a great composer'.

Traweger, Eduard (1820–1909). Knew Schubert as a child in Gmunden and remembered him with great affection, preserving the composer's memory into the present century.

Traweger, Ferdinand (1787–1832). Merchant and music patron, of Gmunden. Father of the above. Schubert and Vogl were his guests during the holiday tour of 1825. But Schubert had met Traweger before, possibly in 1819 or 1823. He ran a male-voice choir in Gmunden, and was especially keen on Schubert's partsongs. In 1828 he sent a warm invitation to the composer to return to Gmunden.

Troyer, Ferdinand Count (1780–1851). Chief steward of the Archduke Rudolph. A good clarinettist, he commissioned the Octet for wind and strings (D803), and the first performance was given at his house in the spring of 1824.

Unger, Johann Karl (1771–1836). Professor of History at the Theresian Academy in Vienna, writer, poet, and amateur singer. He was a close friend of Karl Esterházy, to whom he recommended Schubert as a music tutor. He wrote the words of the partsong for male voices, 'Die Nachtigall' (D724).

Unger, Karoline (1803–77). Austrian contralto. Daughter of the preceding. She made her debut in Vienna in February 1821, in a German version of *Così fan tutte*. Schubert was paid fifty florins for coaching her in her part. She took part also in the first performance of Beethoven's Ninth Symphony; it was she who turned the deaf composer round, so that he could see the applause of the audience. She retired from the stage in 1843.

Vering, Josef von (1793–1862). Medical doctor, who attended Schubert during the last days of his life. He was a specialist in the treatment of venereal disease.

Vogl, Johann Michael (1768–1840). Baritone. He continued to sing Schubert songs in public and private until he was over seventy. His annotated copies, now in the archive of the Philharmonic Society, contain numerous vocal ornaments which give a lively idea of his manner of performance. His wife, Kunigunde Rosa, retired to Steyr and survived him for many years.

Voříšek, Jan Vaclav (alias **Worzischek,** Johann Hugo) (1791–1825). Bohemian composer. A pupil of Tomášek, he moved to Vienna *c.* 1818 and became conductor of the Philharmonic Society. He took part in the salon concerts at Ignaz Sonnleithner's, where he met Schubert. He became assistant court organist in 1822, and principal court organist in 1823. He was the first exponent in Vienna of the short piano piece in ternary form, which Tomášek had pioneered under such titles as impromptu, rhapsody, and eclogue, and his influence on Schubert's piano music, and particularly on the *Moments Musicaux* and the Impromptus, has not been fully realized.

Walcher, Ferdinand (1799–1873). Member of the circle, and a close friend of Schubert during the last years of his life. He had a fine high baritone voice. On his departure for Venice in May 1827 Schubert gave him the autograph of the C minor Allegretto (D915), inscribed 'To my dear friend Walcher'.

Watteroth, Heinrich Josef (1756–1819). Professor of Law and political science in the University of Vienna, and a music lover. Musical parties were held at his house, in which both Witteczek and Spaun (q.v.) lived as tenants in 1816. Brought up as a Catholic, he became a rationalist; he was not popular with the authorities, but was regarded with respect and affection by the student community because of his radical views. Schubert's first commission was the music for the cantata *Prometheus*, written in his honour, and first performed on his nameday on 24 July 1816. Spaun, Sonnleithner, Stadler, Schlechta, and other members of the circle were all his pupils.

Weigl, Josef (1766–1846). German composer. Court Theatre conductor in Vienna. He was a pupil of Salieri, and wrote operas in both German and Italian. His greatest successes were operettas in the German *Singspiel* tradition, like *Das Waisenhaus* (The Orphanage) and *Die Schweizerfamilie* (The Swiss Family), which strongly influenced Schubert's own early operas.

Weigl, Thaddäus (1776–1844). Composer and publisher, brother of the preceding. He founded his own publishing house in Vienna in 1803, and in 1826–8 published a number of Schubert songs and piano music in six opus numbers.

Weintridt, Vincentius (1778–1849). Professor of Theology. Because of his rationalist views he was relieved of his appointment in 1820. Among his disciples were Schwind and Bauernfeld. It was at one of his parties in January 1822 that Bauernfeld first met Schubert. He retired to Retz, some sixty miles from Vienna, where a grand Schubertiad was held in April 1825.

Weissenwolf, Johann Nepomuk, Count (1779–1855). He lived at the castle of Steyregg, five miles from Linz, with his wife Sophie, Countess Breuner, who was a contralto. They were members of the Linz Philharmonic Society and enthusiastic Schubertians. Schubert and Vogl paid them several visits during their 1825 tour, and Schubert dedicated his songs from Scott's *The Lady of the Lake* (Op. 52) to the Countess Weissenwolf.

Willemer, Marianne von (1784–1860). Adopted daughter, and later third wife, of the banker J. J. Willemer. Her attachment to Goethe led to their collaboration on the *West-östlicher Divan* (1819). She was the real author of the two *Suleika* poems which Schubert set, though her authorship was not publicly acknowledged.

Witteczek, Josef Wilhelm (1787–1859). Doctor of Law and conveyancer. He made Schubert's acquaintance through Spaun, and became an enthusiastic admirer of his music. In 1819 he married Watteroth's daughter Wilhelmine. After

Schubert's death he continued to hold Schubertiads at his house, collected fair copies of his songs, and first editions of all those published posthumously. He also purchased in 1831 the collection of Schubert songs made by Pinterics (q.v.). This vast store of Schubert MSS was an important source for the first collected edition at the end of the century. He bequeathed it to Spaun, who left it to the Philharmonic Society.

Zumsteeg, Johann Rudolf (1760–1802). He was a cellist in the Stuttgart court orchestra, and a composer of operas, instrumental music and songs. His name is especially associated with the extended ballad, influenced by the loose episodic structure of the cantata, with alternating passages of arioso and recitative, and descriptive interludes on the piano. He wrote 300 or more lieder and ballads, which were highly regarded in their day. Schubert was much attracted by this attempt to combine lyrical and dramatic elements in a long composition, and his earliest songs of 1811 were closely modelled on Zumsteeg's work. A primitive system of leitmotifs is sometimes to be found in Zumsteeg, but the effective unification of the Romantic ballad, as in 'Erlkönig', had to wait for Schubert.

Appendix D

Select bibliography

The enormous surge of interest in Schubert's work during the last ten years is reflected in the many new entries in this bibliography, including important articles from journals, some of which will, no doubt, be expanded into books in the fullness of time. Where this process has occurred recently, the original articles have been deleted from the bibliography. Otherwise there are few deletions from the first edition, as it was felt that pioneering studies often have a value of their own, as well as being a part of the fascinating story of Schubert's reception history. The fact that books listed are almost exclusively either in English or German reflects to a large extent the current strength of Schubert scholarship in Britain, America, Austria, and Germany.

BASIC SOURCES

Brahms, Mandyczewski et al. (eds.), *Franz Schubert's Werke. Kritisch durchgesehene Gesammtausgabe* (Leipzig, 1884–97, Breitkopf & Härtel). Complete works in 41 volumes. Reprinted in 19 volumes (New York, 1965–9, Dover).

Dürr, Walther, Feil, Arnold et al. (eds.), *Franz Schubert: Neue Ausgabe sämtlicher Werke* (Kassel, 1968– , Bärenreiter). New revised edition of complete works in eight series, including fragments and variants, nearing completion.

Deutsch, Otto Erich, *Schubert: Thematic Catalogue of all his Works in Chronological Order* (London, 1951).

—— *Franz Schubert Thematisches Verzeichnis seiner Werke in chronologischer Folge* (Kassel, 1978). Revised and enlarged edition of above, issued as part of the *Neue Ausgabe*. Where numbers differ from the original English edition, it is referred to as D2 in the main text. Appendix B follows the new Deutsch catalogue.

—— *Werkverzeichnis 'Der kleine Deutsch'* (Kassel, 1983). Compact, paperback version of above, but without musical incipits.

—— *Schubert: A Documentary Biography*, trans. Eric Blom (London, 1946).

—— *Schubert: Die Dokumente seines Lebens* (Kassel, 1964). Revised and enlarged German edition of above.

—— *Schubert: Memoirs by his Friends* (London, 1958).

—— *Schubert: Die Erinnerungen seiner Freunde* (Leipzig, 1957). Original German edition of above.

Hilmar, Ernst, *Verzeichnis der Schubert-Handschriften in der Musiksammlung der Wiener Stadt- und Landesbibliothek*. Catalogus Musikus vol. 8 (Kassel, 1978).

Waidelich, Till (ed.), *Franz Schubert. Dokumente 1817–1830. Erster Teil* (Tutzing, 1993). The first part of this new edition of documents contains contemporary programmes, reviews, concert announcements, obituaries, etc.

ICONOGRAPHY

Deutsch, Otto Erich, *Franz Schubert: Sein Leben in Bildern* (Munich, 1913).
Hilmar, Ernst, *Schubert* (Graz, 1989).
—— 'Zur Schubert-Ikonographie: eine unbekannte Aquarell-Miniatur', in *Brille* 5 (June 1990), p. 42.
—— 'Neues zur Schubert-Ikonographie', in *Brille* 7 (June 1991), pp. 42–4.
—— and Brusatti, Otto, *Franz Schubert. Gedenkausstellung 1978* (Vienna, 1978). Illustrated catalogue of 1978 exhibition.
Klein, Rudolf, *Schubert-Stätten* (Vienna, 1972).
Litschauer, Walburga, 'Unbekanntes zur Schubert-Ikonographie', in *Brille* 6 (Jan. 1991), pp. 56–65.
Orel, Alfred, *Franz Schubert 1797–1828, sein Leben in Bildern* (Leipzig, 1939).
Steblin, Rita, 'Schwinds Porträtskizze Schubert am Klavier', in *Brille* 10 (Jan. 1993), pp. 45–52.
—— 'Schubert und der Maler Josef Teltscher', in *Brille* 11 (June 1993), pp. 118–32.
—— 'Friedrich Lieders Schubert-Porträt von 1827', in *Brille* 12, pp. 92–100.

SOCIAL AND CULTURAL BACKGROUND

Barea, Ilse, *Vienna, Legend and Reality* (London, 1966).
Biba, Otto, 'Schubert's Position in Viennese Musical Life', in *NCM* 3/2 (Nov. 1979), pp. 106–13.
Brion, Marcel, *Daily Life in the Vienna of Mozart and Schubert*, trans. Jean Stewart (London, 1961).
Englander, Richard, 'The Struggle between German and Italian Opera at the time of Weber', in *MQ* 31 (1945), pp. 479ff.
Gal, Hans, *The Golden Age of Vienna* (London, 1948).
Hanslick, Eduard, *Geschichte des Concertwesens in Wien* (2 vols.; Vienna, 1869), r/p 1971, Gregg International).
Hanson, Alice, *Musical Life in Biedermeier Vienna* (Cambridge, 1985).
Hilmar, Ernst, *Franz Schubert in his Time*, trans. Pauly (Portland, 1985).
Kobald, Karl, *Franz Schubert and his Times*, trans. Marshall (London, 1928).
Morrow, Mary Sue, *Concert Life in Haydn's Vienna* (New York, 1989).
Musulin, Stella, *Vienna in the Age of Metternich* (London, 1975).
Yates, W. E., 'Cultural Life in Early Nineteenth-Century Vienna', in *Forum for Modern Language Studies* 13/2 (April, 1977).

CRITICAL BIOGRAPHY

Brown, Maurice, *Schubert, A Critical Biography* (London, 1958).
—— *Essays on Schubert* (London/New York, 1966).
—— and Sams, Eric, *The New Grove Schubert* (London, 1983).

Dahms, Walter, *Schubert* (Stuttgart, 1918).

Dürr, Walther, 'Schubert and Johann Michael Vogl: A Reappraisal', in *NCM* 3 (Nov. 1979), pp. 126–40.

Eder, Gabriele, 'Schubert and Caroline Esterházy', in *Brille* 11 (June 1993), pp. 6–20.

Einstein, Alfred, *Schubert*, trans. David Ascoli (London, 1951).

Gal, Hans, *Franz Schubert and the Essence of Melody* (London, 1974).

Gramit, David, 'Constructing a Victorian Schubert: Music, Biography and Cultural Values', in *NCM* 17 (Summer 1993), pp. 65–78.

Grove, Sir George, Dictionary article of 1882, reprinted in *Beethoven, Schubert, Mendelssohn* (London, 1951), pp. 121–251.

Heuberger, Richard, *Franz Schubert* (Berlin, 1901/1920).

Kerner, D., 'Was wissen wir von Franz Schuberts letzter Krankheit?', in *Medizinische Welt* 29 (1978), pp. 1824–9.

Kreissle von Hellborn, Heinrich, *The Life of Franz Schubert*, trans. A. D. Coleridge (2 vols; London, 1869; r/p New York, 1972).

Massin, Brigitte, *Schubert* (Paris, 1978).

Mies, Paul, *Franz Schubert* (Leipzig, 1954).

Porhansl, Lucia, 'Auf Schuberts Spuren in der *Ludlamshöhle*', in *Brille* 7 (June 1991), pp. 53–78.

Reed, John, *Schubert, The Final Years* (London, 1972).

—— 'Schubert's Reception History in Nineteenth Century England', in *Schubert: The Cambridge Companion*, ed. Gibbs (Cambridge, forthcoming).

Sams, Eric, 'Schubert's Illness Re-examined', in *MT* 121 (1980), p. 15f.

Schumann, Robert, *Music and Musicians*, trans. F. Ritter (2 vols.; London 1877, 1880).

Solomon, Maynard, 'Franz Schubert and the Peacocks of Benvenuto Cellini', in *NCM* 12 (Spring 1989), pp. 193–206.

Winter, Robert, 'Whose Schubert?', in *NCM* 17 (Summer 1993), pp. 94–101.

SONGS

Armitage-Smith, J., 'Schubert's *Winterreise* Part I: Sources of the Musical Text', in *MQ* 60 (1974), pp. 20–36.

Baumann, Cecilia, *Wilhelm Muller. The Poet of the Schubert Song Cycles* (Univ. of Pennsylvania, 1981).

Brown, Maurice, *Schubert's Songs* (BBC Music Guide, 1967).

Capell, Richard, *Schubert's Songs* (London, 1928; r/p 1973).

Feil, Arnold, *Franz Schubert: Die schöne Müllerin; Winterreise* (Stuttgart, 1975). Trans. Ann Sherwin (Portland, 1988).

Fischer-Dieskau, Dietrich, *Auf den Spuren der Schubert-Lieder* (Wiesbaden, 1971). Trans. Kenneth Whitton as *Schubert, A Biographical Study of his Songs* (London, 1976).

Friedländer, Max, *Das deutsche Lied im 18. Jahrhundert* (3 vols.; Stuttgart/Berlin, 1908; r/p 1970, Georg Olms Verlag).

Georgiades, Thrasybulos, *Schubert, Musik und Lyrik* (Gottingen, 1967).

Goldschmidt, Harry, 'Welches war die ursprüngliche Reihenfolge in Schuberts Heine-Liedern?', in *Deutsches Jahrbuch der Musikwissenschaft für 1972* (1974), pp. 52–62.

Hirsch, Marjorie Wing, *Schubert's Dramatic Lieder* (Cambridge, 1993).

Hoorickx, Reinhard van, 'A Schubert Song rediscovered', in *MT* (1980), pp. 97–8.

Kramer, Richard, *Distant Cycles. Schubert and the Conceiving of Song* (Chicago/London, 1994).

McKay, Elizabeth Norman, 'Schubert's *Winterreise* reconsidered', in *MR* 38 (May, 1977), pp. 94–100.

Moore, Gerald, *The Schubert Song Cycles* (London, 1975).

Porter, E. G., *Schubert's Song Technique* (London, 1961).

Reed, John, *The Schubert Song Companion* (Manchester, 1985).

Schnapper, Edith, *Die Gesänge des jungen Schubert* (Bern, 1937).

Schochow, M. and L., *Franz Schubert, Die Texte seiner einstimmig komponierten Lieder und ihre Dichter* (Hildesheim, 1974).

Smeed, J. W., *German Song and its Poetry 1740–1900* (London, 1987).

Stein, Jack, *Poem and Music in the German Lied* (Cambridge, Mass., 1971).

Sternfeld, F. W., *Goethe and Music* (New York, 1954).

Wigmore, Richard, *Schubert. The Complete Song Texts* with English translations (London, 1988).

Youens, Susan, *Retracing a Winter's Journey. Schubert's Winterreise* (Ithaca/London, 1991).

—— *Schubert: Die schöne Müllerin* (Cambridge, 1992).

—— *Schubert's Poets and the Making of the Lieder* (Cambridge, 1996).

—— (ed.), *Winterreise: The Autograph Score* (New York, 1989). Facsimile and introduction.

PIANO WORKS

Brendel, Alfred, 'Schubert's Piano Sonatas 1822–28', in *Musical Thoughts and Afterthoughts* (London, 1976), pp. 57–74.

—— 'Schubert's Last Piano Sonatas', in *Music Sounded Out* (London, 1990), pp. 72–141.

Brown, Maurice, 'The Dance-Music Manuscripts', in *Essays on Schubert* (London, 1966), pp. 217–43.

Chusid, Martin, 'A Suggested Redating for Schubert's Piano Sonata in E flat, op. 122', in *Schubert-Kongress Wien 1978* (Graz, 1979), pp. 37–44.

Dale, Kathleen, 'The Piano Music', in *Schubert: A Symposium* (London, 1946), pp. 111–48.

Hilmar, Ernst (ed.), *Franz Schubert. Drei grosse Sonaten für das Pianoforte* (Tutzing, 1987). Facsimile of early versions of D958–60.

Költzsch, H., *Franz Schubert in seinen Klaviersonaten* (Leipzig, 1927).

Krause, Andreas, *Schuberts Klaviersonaten. Bemerkungen zu Form, Gattung und Ästhetik* (Kassel, 1992).

Newman, W. S., *The Sonata since Beethoven* (Chapel Hill, 1969), chap. 7.

Radcliffe, Philip, *Schubert Piano Sonatas* (BBC Music Guide, 1967).

Sams, Eric, 'Schubert's Piano Duets', in *MT* 117 (1976), pp. 120–1.

Weekly, Dallas, and Arganbright, Nancy, *Schubert's Music for Piano Four-Hands* (Pro-Am Music Resources Inc., 1990).

STAGE WORKS

Branscombe, Peter, 'Schubert and his Librettists', in *MT* 99 (1978), p. 943.
—— 'Schubert and the Melodrama', in *Schubert Studies* (Cambridge, 1982), pp. 105–41.
Hyatt King, A., 'Music for the Stage', in *Schubert: A Symposium* (London, 1946), pp. 198–216.
McKay, Elizabeth Norman, 'Schubert as a Composer of Operas', in *Schubert Studies* (Cambridge, 1982), pp. 85–104.
—— *Franz Schubert's Music for the Theatre* (Tutzing, 1991).
Waidelich, Till, 'Die Weimarer Uraufführung von "Alfonso und Estrella" unter Franz Liszt', in *Brille* 6 (Jan. 1991), pp. 5–21.

LITURGICAL WORKS

Biba, Otto, 'Kirchenmusikalische Praxis zu Schuberts Zeit', in *Franz Schubert. Jahre der Krise 1818–1823* (Kassel, 1985), pp. 113–20.
Brown, Maurice, 'Schubert's Settings of the Salve Regina', in *ML* 37 (1956), pp. 234ff.
Dickinson, A. E. F., 'The Choral Music', in *Schubert: A Symposium* (London, 1946), pp. 217–37.
Dürr, Walther, 'Dona Nobis Pacem. Gedanken zu Schuberts späten Messen', in *Zeichen-Setzung* (Kassel, 1992), pp. 83–100.
Fischer, Kurt von, 'Bemerkungen zu Schuberts As-dur-Messe', in *Franz Schubert. Jahre der Krise 1818–1823* (Kassel, 1985), pp. 121–8.
Hoorickx, Reinhard van, 'Textänderungen in Schuberts Messen', in *Schubert-Kongress Wien 1978* (Graz, 1979), pp. 249–55.
—— 'Schubert and the Bible', in *MT* 119 (Nov. 1978), pp. 953–5.

ORCHESTRAL WORKS

Brown, Maurice, *Schubert Symphonies* (BBC Music Guide, 1970).
Carner, Mosco, 'The Orchestral Music', in *Schubert: A Symposium* (London, 1946), pp. 17–87.
Newbould, Brian, *Schubert and the Symphony. A New Perspective* (London, 1992).
—— *Franz Schubert: Symphony No. 7 in E (D729)*. Study score of Newbould's realization (Hull, 1992).
Tovey, Sir Donald, *Essays in Musical Analysis* (London, 1936–9).
Dvořák, Antonín, 'Franz Schubert', in *The Century Magazine* 48 (New York, 1894), p. 341.
Griffel, L. M., 'A Reappraisal of Schubert's Methods of Composition', in *MQ* 63 (1977), p. 186.
Jacobson, Daniel and Glendening, Andrew, 'Schuberts D936A: eine sinfonische Hommage an Beethoven?', in *Brille* 15 (June 1995), pp. 113–26.
Langevin, Paul-Gilbert, 'Franz Schubert et la Symphonie', in *La Revue Musicale* (Paris, 1982), pp. 355–7.
Reed, John, 'The Gastein Symphony Reconsidered', in *ML* 40 (1959), p. 341.
—— 'How the "Great" C major was written', in *ML* 56 (1975), p. 18.

CHAMBER WORKS

Badura-Skoda, Eva, 'The Chronology of Schubert's Piano Trios', in *Schubert Studies* (Cambridge, 1982), pp. 277–96.

Black, Brian, 'Die Entwicklung der Sonatenform in Schuberts frühen Streichquartetten', in *Brille* 9 (June 1992), pp. 104–12.

Chusid, Martin, 'Schubert's Cyclic Compositions of 1824', in *Acta Musicologica* 36 (1964), pp. 37–45.

Dahlhaus, Carl, 'Formprobleme in Schuberts frühen Streichquartetten', in *Schubert-Kongress Wien 1978* (Graz, 1979), pp. 191–8.

Westrup, Sir Jack, *Schubert Chamber Music* (BBC Music Guide, 1969).

—— 'The Chamber Music', in *Schubert: A Symposium* (London, 1946), pp. 88–110.

STYLE

Blom, Eric, 'His Favourite Device', in *ML* 9 (1928). Reprinted in *Classics Major and Minor* (London, 1958).

Cone, Edward T., 'Schubert's Promissory Note', in *NCM* 5/3 (Fall 1981), pp. 233–41.

Domokos, Maria, 'Über die ungarischen Charakteristiken des "Divertissement à l'Hongroise" (D818)', in *Brille* 11 (June 1993), pp. 53–64.

Gramit, David, 'Schubert and the Biedermeier': The Aesthetics of Johann Mayrhofer's *Heliopolis*', in *ML* 74/3 (August 1993).

Hinrichsen, Hans-Joachim, '*Gerüstklänge*: Verwandte Prinzipien formbildender Harmonik bei Schubert und Liszt', in *Brille* 11 (June 1993), pp. 91–106.

Kerman, Joseph, 'A Romantic Detail in Schubert's *Schwanengesang*', in *MQ* 48 (1962), pp. 36–49.

Kramer, Richard, 'Gradus ad Parnassum: Beethoven, Schubert, and the Romance of Counterpoint', in *NCM* 11 (Fall 1987), pp. 107–20.

Macdonald, Hugh, 'Schubert's Volcanic Temper', in *MT* 119 (Nov. 1979), pp. 949–52.

Newman, W. S., 'Freedom of Tempo in Schubert's Instrumental Music', in *MQ* 61 (1975), pp. 528ff.

Pritchard, T. C. L., 'The Schubert Idiom', in *Schubert: A Symposium* (London, 1946), pp. 238–57.

Spohr, Mathias, 'Wie kommt der "Tristan-Akkord" in Schubert's *Zauberharfe?*' in *Brille* 9 (June 1992), pp. 139–47.

Tovey, Sir Donald, 'Tonality', in *ML* 9 (1928), p. 341.

Wischusen, Mary, '*Die Zauberharfe* und Schuberts reifer Instrumentalstil', in *Brille* 13 (June 1994), pp. 85–102.

SYMPOSIA

[Collections of essays, conference proceedings, etc., generally of a specialized nature. Some important essays are referred to under the relevant section earlier in the Bibliography.]

Abraham, Gerald (ed.), *Schubert: A Symposium* (London, 1946). Slightly dated, but an important landmark at the time of its publication, this volume contains an essay on 'Schubert the Man' by O. E. Deutsch, and studies of various aspects of Schubert's work, each by a different author.

Adelhold, Werner, Dürr, Walther, and Litschauer, Walburga (eds.), *Franz Schubert. Jahre der Krise 1818–1823* (Kassel, 1985). Report of a Symposium held in Kassel from 30 September to 1 October 1982, dedicated to Arnold Feil for his 60th birthday in 1985. After an introductory essay on Schubert's 'Wanderjahre' by Walther Dürr, eleven essays explore works of this period and place them in historical context. In German.

Badura-Skoda, Eva and Branscombe, Peter (eds.), *Schubert Studies. Problems of Style and Chronology* (Cambridge, 1982). An important collection of studies by leading Schubertian scholars on specific topics. The longest contribution is an essay, 'Paper studies and the future of Schubert research', by Robert Winter, pointing to an objective method of dating works.

Brusatti, Otto (ed.), *Schubert-Kongress Wien 1978*. Bericht (Graz, 1979). Report of a Conference held in Vienna from 4 to 10 June 1978, organized by the Österreichische Gesellschaft für Musikwissenschaft, to mark the 150th anniversary of Schubert's death. Thirty-two summaries of papers, mainly in German.

Frisch, Walter (ed.), *Schubert: Critical and Analytical Studies* (Lincoln/London, 1986). A collection of specialized essays about Schubert's technique, with particular reference to song-writing. Contributors include Lawrence Kramer, T. G. Georgiades, Joseph Kerman, Anthony Newcomb, and Frisch himself.

Grasberger, Franz and Wessely, Othmar (eds.), *Schubert-Studien. Festgabe der Österreichischen Akademie der Wissenschaften zum Schubert-Jahr 1978* (Vienna, 1978). Eleven interesting articles in German about aspects of Schubert's life and works, concluding with Ignaz Weinmann's survey of the Schubert collection in Seitenstetten Abbey.

Index

Alexander I, Emperor of Russia 124
Alsergrund 168, 176
Anschütz, Heinrich 165, 180
Artaria & Co. 111, 128, 132–3, 136, 165
Atzenbrugg 79, 98, 100, 116
Augustiner Church 16, 181

Bach, Johann Sebastian 5, 100
(Bad) Gastein 120, 122, 128
Badura-Skoda, Paul 59
Barbaja, Domenico 74, 75, 91, 129, 165
Barnett, john xv
Bauernfeld, Eduard von xiii, 53, 60, 79, 115,
    127–8, 129–30, 137, 138, 140–1, 146–7,
    158, 163, 165–6, 179, 180
Baumberg songs 29
Beethoven, Ludwig van xi, xii, 8, 16, 18, 19,
    20, 22, 28, 38, 39, 40, 46, 49, 50, 51, 55,
    56, 58, 59, 73, 74, 76, 77–8, 81, 89, 92,
    95, 101, 105, 109, 110–11, 118, 121, 122,
    128, 130, 132, 134, 135, 142–3, 144, 145,
    149, 157, 160, 161, 162, 167, 168, 169,
    172, 174, 176, 179, 181
Berchtold, Anton Count 111
Beresin, Alexis von 77, 98
Berg, Isak Albert 154
Bergmann, Johann 71
Berlin 74, 80, 95, 177
Bernhardt, J. (Dr) 99, 100
Bertrand, Friedrich 28
Biba, Otto 127
Bobrik, Friedrich 28
Bocklet, Karl Maria von 123, 159, 160
Bogner, Ferdinand 108
Bogner's coffee house 137, 158
Bohemia 11
Brahms, Johannes 69, 164, 168
Breitkopf und Härtel 39, 132
Brendel, Alfred 173
Breslau 92, 98, 108, 127, 144
Breuning, Gerhard von 179
British Library 91
Brown, Maurice J. E. 152
Browning, Robert 174
Bruchmann, Franz von 65, 67, 80, 82–4,
    98–9, 116, 126

Bruchmann songs 82
Bruchmann, Justina 99, 116
Bruckner, Anton 176
Budapest 158
Bürger, Gottfried August 26
Burney, Charles 144
Byron, Alfred Lord 142

Calderón, de la Barca 91
Capell, Richard 181
Cappi und Diabelli 78
Castelli, Ignaz Franz 90
'Castle of Eisenstadt' Inn 140, 143
Cherubini, Luigi 74
Chézy, Helmina von 93, 94, 150, 177
Chusid, Martin 51
Cibber, Colley 126
Claudius songs 23, 34–6, 54, 70, 82
Clodi, Therese 119
Collin, Matthäus von 69, 82
Congress of Vienna 15, 17
Cooper, Fenimore 179
Craigher, Jakob 126
Crystal Palace Orchestra xv
Czech Republic 1

Debussy, Achille-Claude 171
Derffel, Josef 79, 137
Dessau 95
Deutsch, Otto Erich xi, xii, 14, 19, 75, 90,
    170, 180
Diabelli, Anton 31, 43, 46, 81, 124, 132, 137,
    159, 164, 169, 173
Dietrichstein, Moritz Count 69, 71
Dilettanten Gesellschaft (Amateurs' Society)
    76
Dittersdorf, Karl Ditters von 24
Doblhoff, Anton 67
Doppler, Joseph 16
Dräxler, Philipp 21
Dreschler, Josef 138
Dresden 74, 80, 90, 93
Dumba, Nicolaus xv
Duport, Louis Antoine 129
Dvořák, Antonin 1

Index

Ebenzweier Castle 119, 124
Eckel, Franz 4
Eisenstadt 175
Einstein, Alfred 149
Enderes, Karl 115, 137
Enk, Karl 158
Erlangen 83
Esch, Karl 115
Esterházy, Karl Count 57, 58, 60, 96, 98
Esterházy, Karoline Countess 57, 60, 101, 141, 159
Esterházy, Marie Countess 57, 101
Esterházy, Rosine Countess 101
Eybler, Josef 128, 167

Fallersleben, August Heinrich Hoffman von 144
Faust (Goethe) 19
Feil, Arnold 142
Feuchtersleben, Ernst von 153
Fink, Gottfried Wilhelm 159
Fiske, Roger 32
Fouqué, la Motte 101
Franck, César 86
Frankl, Ludwig 140
Franz I, Emperor of Austria 11, 15, 72, 81, 166
Friedländer, Max 28
Frischling, Franz 16
Fröhlich, Anna 71, 146, 162, 179, 181
Fröhlich, Josefine 162, 179, 181
Fuchs, Alois 154
Führer, Robert 43

Gahy, Josef von 120, 137, 158
Gassmann, Florian Leopold 8
Gastein (see Bad Gastein)
Gesellschaft der Musikfreunde (see Philharmonic Society of Vienna)
Geymüller, Barbara Baroness 86
Glendening, Andrew 178
Gluck, Christoph Willibald 8, 9, 10, 22, 73, 80
Gmunden 118, 119, 120, 128, 130
Goethe, Johann Wolfgang von 5, 23, 26, 28, 29, 31, 47, 49, 69, 86, 95, 105, 110, 126, 129, 136–7, 159, 174
Goethe songs 19, 22, 23, 29, 34, 55, 65, 66, 70, 81, 84, 147
Gosmar, Louise 146
Graz 21, 63, 87, 138, 143, 149, 150, 153, 157, 165
'Green Anchor' Inn 137, 140
Grétry, André 8
Grillparzer, Franz 63, 138, 162, 181
Grinzing 144
Grob, Heinrich 16
Grob, Therese 16, 19, 22, 24, 43, 71, 169

Gross, Karl 115, 179
Grünwedel, Gusti 140
Gundelhof 70
Gymnich, August von 70
Gyrowetz, Adalbert 49

Hallé, (Sir) Charles xv, 39, 135, 173
Hallmark, Rufus 161
Hammer-Purgstall, Josef von 69
Handel, Georg Frideric 162
Hanslick, Eduard 91
Harmonicon, The, of London 78, 126, 156
Harold, Edmund von 31
Hartmann, Franz von 137, 140, 158
Hartmann, Fritz von 137, 140
Haslinger, Tobias 132, 141, 145, 147, 150, 170
Hatwig, Otto 16, 25, 39, 70
Haydn, Franz Joseph xi, 13, 16, 37, 40, 46, 56, 57, 89, 144, 168, 175
Heine, Heinrich 159
Heine songs 83, 163, 169–71, 177
Hellmesberger Quartet 132
Henikstein, Josef von 77
Herbeck, Johann 88, 91, 147
Herder, Johann Gottfried von 5, 31, 150
Hernals 81, 176, 179
Hiller, Ferdinand 143–4
Hilmar, Ernst 84
Himmelpfortgrund 2, 178
Hoffmann, August Heinrich (*see* Fallersleben)
Hofmann, Georg von 60, 61, 63
Holmes, Edward 144
Hölty songs 23, 29–30, 33–4
Holzapfel, Anton 3, 17, 31, 79
Holzer, Michael 3
Hönig, Anna (Netti) 114, 130, 157, 165
Huber, Josef 72
Hummel, Johann Nepomuk 143–4, 145, 171, 173
Hutchings, Arthur xii
Hüttenbrenner, Anselm xii, 17, 21, 22, 61, 63, 87–8, 143, 163
Hüttenbrenner, Heinrich 63
Hüttenbrenner, Josef 47, 63, 70, 77–8, 80, 87–8

Immerman, Karl 159
Imperial and Royal Chapel 166
Imperial and Royal Orphanage 22
Imperial Riding School 15, 18
Internationales Franz Schubert Institut (IFSI) xvi

Jacobi songs 23, 34
Jacobson, Daniel 178
Jaëll, Edward 56

Jäger, Franz 63
Jahn, Otto xi
Janáček, Leos 1
Jean Paul (pseudonym of Johann Paul
    Richter) 57
Jenger, Johann Baptist xii, 138, 149, 160,
    163, 165
Joachim, Joseph 111
Josefstadt theatre 152
Joseph II, Emperor 2, 22, 40, 73

Kalkbrenner, Friedrich Wilhelm 133
Karlsruhe 92
Kärntnertor theatre 10, 52, 60, 63, 70, 71, 75,
    79, 80, 91, 129, 132, 150, 152, 165, 177
Kenner, Josef 17, 28, 64
Kiesewetter, Raphael Georg 15, 113
Kleist, Heinrich von 158
Klenke, Louise von 150
Klopstock songs 19, 23, 28, 30–1, 43
Klosterneuburg 79
Koller, Josef von 64
Koller, Josefine von 64
Konvikt (Imperial and Royal Seminary) 3–4,
    5, 8, 9, 11, 12, 16, 17
Köppen, Peter Johann 77, 78, 98
Korner, Philipp 3
Körner, Theodor 29–30, 47, 49
Kosegarten songs 19, 30, 113
Kotzebue, August von 10, 11, 18, 67
Kozeluch, Johann Antonin 24
Kreissle von Hellborn, Heinrich 21, 47, 60,
    90, 92, 114, 152, 153, 181
Kremsmünster 20, 64, 119, 120
Kreutzer, Conradin 91
Kuffner, Christoff 168
Kupelwieser, Josef 91, 92, 93, 149
Kupelwieser, Leopold 79, 91, 98, 99–100,
    105, 116, 127, 138

Lachner, Franz 132, 152, 162, 163, 179–80
'Lady of the Lake' songs 118, 119, 123–4,
    128
Laibach 23
'Lamento' topos 5
Landon, Christa 176
Lang, Dr Innocenz 3, 12
Lappe, Karl 114
Lászny, Katharina von 111, 144
Leidesdorf, Maximilian Josef 81, 94, 113, 149
Leipzig 26, 116, 118, 126, 132, 159
Leipzig, battle of 11
Leipzig Gewandhaus 134
Leitermayer, Michael 168
Leitner songs 150–1
Lemberg 118, 128, 179
Leningrad 77

Leopoldstadt 1
Lewy, Josef 146, 160
Liebenburg, Emanuel Karl 86
Liechtental 3, 8, 13, 14, 16, 40, 41, 166
Linke, Josef 159
Linz 4, 64, 66, 79, 90, 98, 118, 119, 120, 130,
    137, 158
Liszt, Franz 86, 87, 176
London xv, 39, 126, 135, 143, 173
'Ludlam's Cave' Society 138
Luib, Ferdinand xii, 78
Lutz, Johanna 99, 116, 127, 138

McClary, Susan xvi
Macpherson, James 31
Mahler, Gustav 89
Mainz 147, 159
Manchester 39, 135
Mandyczewski, Eusebius xv
Mann, Thomas 175
Männergesang-Verein of Vienna xiii, 176
Manns, (Sir) August xv, 39
Margereten suburb 180
Matthisson songs 18, 23, 27–8, 76
Mayerhofer, Ferdinand von 129, 137
Mayrhofer, Johann xvi, 11, 20, 24, 34, 47,
    53, 56, 57, 58, 59–60, 66, 71, 82, 130,
    140, 166, 174, 180
Mayrhofer songs 53–4, 65, 70, 71, 110,
    131
Mayseder, Josef 16
Mayssen, Josef 81, 176
Mendelssohn, Felix xii, 4, 111, 132, 134
Metastasio, Pietro 9, 52
Metternich, Clemens Prince 105
Meyerbeer, Giacomo 74, 149
Milder-Hauptmann, Pauline Anna 80, 177
Mohn, Ludwig 80, 98
Moravia 1
Moscheles, Ignaz 132
Mosel, Ignaz Franz Hofrat von 15, 69, 71,
    80, 90, 129
Mottl, Felix 92
Mozart, Wolfgang Amadeus xi, 4, 12, 13, 22,
    34, 37, 39, 42, 43–4, 45–6, 49, 56, 73, 76,
    77, 89, 100, 105, 144, 145
Müller, Wilhelm 53, 95, 141, 177
Munich 74, 158, 165
Musical Times xv

Nägeli, Hans Georg 132
Napoleon I, Emperor 7, 11
Neefe, Hermann 61
Neudorf 1
Neumann, Emilie 93–4
Neumann, Johann Philipp 69, 146, 166
Neumarkt 120

Index

Newbould, Brian 88, 178
Niemeyer, August Hermann 67
Nikolaus I Emperor of Russia 124
Novalis songs 65–6, 110
Novello, Vincent 40

Ossian songs 19, 23, 28–9, 31–3
Ottenwwalt, Anton 118, 119, 120

Pachler, Faust 157
Pachler, Karl 149, 150, 157
Pachler, Marie 138, 149, 150, 157, 163
Paganini, Nicolo 163
Paisiello, Giovanni 95
Paris 55, 126, 171
Passini, Johann 127
Paumgartner, Sylvester 64
Pennauer, Anton 115, 118, 124, 135
Pergolesi, Giovanni Battista 5, 43
Peters, Karl of Leipzig 77
Pettenkoffer, Anton von 70
Philharmonic Society of London 142–3
Philharmonic Society (*Gesellschaft der
    Musikfreunde*) of Vienna xii, xiii, 15,
    56, 57, 71, 75, 108, 113, 120, 121, 127,
    132, 134, 145, 146, 152–3, 160, 162
Piarist order 3
Piazza, Lucca 61
Pichler, Karoline 69, 77, 78
Pinterics, Karl 176
Platen-Hallemunde, August Count xvi, 82,
    83–4
Pöckelhofer, 'Pepi' 58–9
Pohl, Carl Ferdinand xi
Poissl, Johann von 75
Prague 43
Pratobevera, Adolf von 139
Probst, Heinrich, of Leipzig 126, 132–3, 156,
    159, 162, 163, 170, 171–2, 173
Prokesch, Anton 78–9
Purcell, Henry 5
Pyrker, Ladislaus 40, 69, 120, 166

Racek, Fritz 69, 142
Raimund, Ferdinand 138
Ratz, Erwin 59
'Red Cross' Inn 178
Reichardt, Johann Friedrich 28
Reichstadt, Duke of 82
Reil, Friedrich 146, 168
Reissmann, August 44
Rellstab songs 143, 145, 160–1, 163, 169–70
Rieder, Johann 176
Rieder, Wilhelm August 127
Riepl, Franz 115
Ries, Ferdinand 132
Rinna, Dr Ernst 169, 175, 179

Rochlitz, Johann Friedrich 26, 145
Roller, Anton 61
Romberg, Andreas Jakob 76
Rome 98
Roner, Franziska 159
Rossau 57, 58, 69, 72, 86, 100, 112, 114
Rossini, Gioachino Antonio 55, 63, 74, 75,
    127, 144, 157, 168
Rössler, Eduard 158
Royal College of Music 88, 135
Rückert songs 82, 83, 156
Rudolf, Archduke 109
Ruzicka, Wenzel 4, 8, 12, 17, 20

St Anna, Normal School of 12, 14
St Florian 118, 119
St Pölten 75
Salieri, Anton 3, 4, 8–9, 11, 12, 13, 16, 17, 18,
    21, 22, 23, 41, 49, 52, 71, 80, 128, 176
Salis-Seewis songs 23, 34
Salzburg 120
Sanssouci, Anna 60
Sauer und Leidesdorf 95, 96, 111, 148
Säulengasse 2, 4, 14, 15, 18
Schäffer, August von 100
Schechner, Nanette 130
Scheidel, Josef 56
Schelling, Friedrich Wilhelm 83
Schellmann, Dr Albert 64
Schiller, Franz Ferdinand von 119
Schiller songs 6, 23, 26, 28, 30, 34, 55, 66,
    105, 110
Schindler, Anton 17, 78, 130, 143, 161, 169
Schlechta, Franz von 53, 61, 64, 115, 136
Schlegel, August Wilhelm von 65, 137
Schlegel, Friedrich von 65, 71, 159
Schmidt of Lübeck 34, 53
Schmidtlein, Eduard 83
Schnabel, Walter 173
Schneider, Eduard 67
Schneider, Friedrich Johann 75
Schober, Franz von xii, 20, 24, 50, 52, 53, 58,
    64, 72, 74, 75, 79, 80, 82, 92, 93, 94, 98,
    99, 105, 108, 112, 114–15, 116, 127, 128,
    130, 137, 140, 141, 143, 151, 158, 159,
    166, 179
Schönstein, Karl von 59, 60, 96, 101, 112, 179
Schott of Mainz 147, 159–60, 162, 171
Schreiber, Alois 58
Schubert, Anna née Kleyenböck (stepmother)
    8
Schubert, Anna (sister-in-law, wife to
    Ferdinand) 179
Schubert, Elisabeth née Vietz (mother) 1, 8
Schubert, Ferdinand (brother) 2, 3, 22, 38,
    43, 56, 58, 59, 96, 101, 116, 119, 120,
    150, 169, 176, 178, 179, 180–1

Schubert, Franz Peter
LIFE
Beethoven, relations with 78, 145, 161–2
cause of death 179–80
diaries, notes, and poems 22, 25, 80, 90, 105, 112
illness 90, 93, 99–100, 114, 128, 157, 165, 169
income 14, 57, 63, 69–70, 80–1, 101, 124, 128, 160, 165
letters 7–8, 58, 59, 100, 105, 118, 119, 150, 157, 162–3, 166, 171–2, 179
lodgings 59–60, 86, 112, 114, 169
Philharmonic Society, relations with 56, 75–6, 77, 127, 134–5
public concert 160–2
reading parties 79–80, 98, 112, 158–9, 165
religious beliefs 3, 39–40, 166
reputation 63, 69–70, 76, 77–8, 126–7, 128, 144–5
reviews 61, 76, 115, 118, 126, 159
Romantic feeling and philosophy 34–6, 53
salons and private 'academies' 15, 16, 17, 77, 79
Schubert circle 3–4, 20–1, 60, 64, 79, 98, 112, 115–16, 127–8, 137–8, 165–6
Schubert 'family orchestra' 16, 25, 39, 70
Schubert societies and associations xv–xvi
Schubertiads 72, 90, 99, 112, 114, 115, 119, 137, 159
WORKS
Piano solo
Sonata in E major (1815) 50
Sonata in C major (1815) 50
Sonata 'in mixed keys' (1816) 50
Sonata in A minor (1817) 51, 173
Sonata in A flat (1817) 51
Sonata in E minor (1817) 51
Sonata in D flat (1817) 51, 135
Sonata in B major (1817) 51
Sonata in F minor (1818) 59
Sonata in A major (1819) 64
Sonata in A minor (1823) 97, 172
Sonata in C major ('Reliquie') 116, 135
Sonata in A minor (1825) 116–18
Sonata in D major 51, 120, 122–3, 128, 133
Sonata in E flat (1826) 51, 135–6
Sonata in G major (1826) 132, 135–6, 137, 145
Sonata in C minor (1828) 145, 171–4
Sonata in A major (1828) 145, 171–4
Sonata in B flat (1828) xiii, 145, 171–4
Adagio in D flat (?1818) 59
'Air Russe' 94, 148
Allegretto in C minor 148
Deutsche (Six) (1824) 112

Fantasie in C (the 'Wanderer') 4–5, 86, 87, 89, 97, 156
Fantasie in C minor (1811) 4
Fantasie in C (fragment) 84
Fugue in C major (fragment) 5
'Grazer Walzer' (1827) 150
'Grazer Galopp' (1827) 150
Hungarian Melody in B minor 111
Impromptus opus 90: 140, 145, 147, 171
Impromptus opus 142: 140, 147–8, 160, 162, 171
Klavierstücke, Drei (1828) 163–4
Klavierstück in C minor (?1827) 148, 177–8
Moments Musicaux 113, 147, 148–9, 171
'Plaintes d'un Troubadour' 113
Rondo in E major (1817) 51
Valses Nobles 145
Waltz, 'Trauer' 78
Piano duet
Allegro in A minor (*Lebensstürme*) 145, 164–5
Divertissement à l'hongroise 111, 128, 144
Fantasie in G (1810) 4
Fantasie in G minor (1811) 4
Fantasie in C minor (1813) 5, 156
Fantasie in F minor (1828) 157, 159, 160, 163
4 *Ländler* (1824) 112
Grand Marches (Six) 111, 115, 118
Grande Marche Funèbre in C minor 124
Grande Marche Héroique in A minor 124
March in G (1827) 157
Marches Caractéristiques, Deux, in C 124
Marches Militaires, Trois 59
Polonaisen, Vier 59
Polonaisen, Sechs 124
Rondo in D (1818) 57
Grand Rondo in A (1828) 165
Sonata in B flat 59
Sonata in C major ('Grand Duo') 110–11, 172
Sonata in E minor (?1826) 124
Introduction and Variations on an Original Theme 59
Variations on a French Song in E minor 59, 77, 78
Variations on an Original Theme in A flat 111, 115, 118, 159
Orchestral
Symphony No. 1 in D 12, 37–8
Symphony No. 2 in B flat 18, 19, 37–8
Symphony No. 3 in D 19, 37–8
Symphony No. 4 in C minor ('Tragic') 38–9, 55, 89, 172
Symphony No. 5 in B flat 25, 39
Symphony No. 6 in C 55
Symphony in B minor ('Unfinished') xiii, 55, 82, 86, 87–9, 97, 122, 177

Index

Schubert, Franz Peter (*cont.*):
 WORKS (*cont.*):
  Orchestral (*cont.*):
  Symphony No. 7 in C major (the 'Great')
   38, 44, 55, 71, 77, 88, 89, 118, 120–2,
   133–5, 172, 177
  Symphonic sketch in D (?1811) 5
  Symphonic sketch in D (1818) 57, 177
  Symphonic sketch in D (?1821) 88
  Symphonic sketch in E (1821) 88, 177
  Symphonic sketch in D (1828) 18, 177–8
  Overture for strings in C minor (1811) 5,
   16
  Overture in D 'in the Italian style' 55, 88
  Overture in C major 'in the Italian style' 56
  Overture in E minor (1819) 76
  Rosamunde Overture 55–6, 62, 94
  Sechs Menuette for wind band (1811) 5
  Five Menuets, six trios, and five *Deutsche*
   for strings 16
  Concerto in D for violin and orchestra 46
  Polonaise for violin and orchestra 52
  Adagio and Rondo in A for violin and
   strings 46
 Chamber music
  String Quartet in mixed keys 12, 172
  String Quartet in D (?1811) 12
  String Quartet in C major (1812) 5, 12
  String Quartet in B flat (1812–13) 12–15
  String Quartet in C major (1813) 12, 44
  String Quartet in D (1813) 12
  String Quartet in B flat (1813) 12–13, 173
  String Quartet in E flat (1813) 44
  String Quartet in B flat (1814) 20, 44
  String Quartet in G minor (1815) 19, 45
  String Quartet in E (1816) 45–6
  String Quartet in C minor (*Quartettsatz*)
   38, 44, 71, 97
  String Quartet in A minor (1824) 100,
   105–7, 112, 130
  String Quartet in D minor ('Death and the
   Maiden') (1824) xiii, 108, 112, 130, 131,
   159
  String Quartet in G major (1826) 100,
   130–2, 134, 159–60, 160, 173
  Quintet for piano and strings (the 'Trout')
   64–5, 108, 153
  String Quintet in C (1828) 44, 139, 145,
   169, 171, 173, 174
  Octet in F for strings and woodwind
   (1824) 100, 109, 132
  Adagio and Rondo for piano quartet 46
  Piano Trio in B flat xiii, 140, 144, 152–3, 177
  Adagio in E flat for piano trio ('Notturno')
   152
  Piano Trio in E flat xv, 126, 140, 145, 151,
   152, 153, 154–6, 159, 162, 171–2

Sonata for violin and piano in D 46
Sonata for violin and piano in A minor 46
Sonata for violin and piano in G minor 46
Sonata for violin and piano in A (1817) 44,
 52
Rondo in B minor for violin and piano
 (1826) 136, 137, 156
Fantasie in C for violin and piano (1827)
 157, 159, 160
Variations for flute and piano (1824) 108
Arpeggione sonata (1824) 112
Stage works
 Adrast 66–7
 Alfonso und Estrella 74–5, 80, 81, 86, 90,
  91, 94, 112, 130, 150
 Claudine von Villa Bella 19, 47, 49, 56
 Das Zauberglöckchen 73, 81
 Der Graf von Gleichen 130, 146–7, 179
 Der Hochzeitsbraten 151–2, 160, 165
 Der Spiegelritter 10, 11
 Der vierjährige Posten 47–9
 Des Teufels Lustschloss 18
 Die Advokaten 152
 Die Freunde von Salamanka 47, 49, 109
 Die Verschworenen (*Der häusliche Krieg*)
  90–1
 Die Zauberharfe 61–3, 71, 88, 94, 147
 Die Zwillingsbrüder 60–1, 63
 Fernando 19, 47, 49
 Fierabras 90, 91–2, 94, 163
 Rosamunde (incidental music) 33, 73, 88,
  93–4, 101, 108, 148, 149
 Rudiger 90
 Sakuntala 69, 146
Liturgical and religious Works
 Mass No. 1 in F 15, 16, 18, 40
 Mass No. 2 in G 32, 41, 43
 Mass No. 3 in B flat 41
 Mass No. 4 in C 41, 43
 Mass No. 5 in A flat 72, 166–7
 Mass No. 6 in E flat 72, 145, 166–8, 171,
  172
 Auguste jam coelestium 43
 Benedictus for Mass in C (1828) 169
 Deutsche Messe 146
 Glaube, Hoffnung und Liebe 168
 Hymnus an den heiligen Geist 169, 176
 Intende Voci 176
 Kyrie in D minor (1812) 13
 Kyrie in B flat (1813) 13
 Kyrie in D minor (1813) 13
 Kyrie in F (1813) 13
 Lazarus 67, 147
 Magnificat 43
 Psalm 92: 168–9
 Salve Regina (1815) 43
 Salve Regina D379 (1816) 43

266

Salve Regina D386 (1816) 43
Salve Regina (1819) 43
Stabat Mater (1815) 43
Stabat Mater (1816) (German version to
  Klopstock's text) 43, 64
Tantum ergo (1816) 43
Tantum ergo (1821) 81
Tantum ergo (1822) 81
Tantum ergo (1828) 176
Trauermesse (*Deutsches Requiem*) 59
Cantatas
Am Geburtstage des Kaisers 81
Mirjams Siegesgesang 145, 162
Prometheus 21, 24, 63
Salieri, cantata in honour of 21
Spendou, cantata in honour of 22
Vogl's birthday, cantata in honour of 64
Wer ist gross? 18
Songs and partsongs
Abendröte 65, 95
'Abendstern' 110
'Abschied' (Rellstab) 170
'Abschied von der Erde' (melodrama) 139,
  172
'Abschied von einem Freunde' 55
'Amalia' 22
'Am Flusse' 84
'Am Meer' 171
'Am See' (Mayrhofer) 19
'Am See' (Bruchmann) 82
'Am Strome' (Mayrhofer) 54
'Andenken' 28
'An den Mond' (Hölty) 30
'An den Mond' (Goethe) (1) 29
'An den Mond' (Goethe) (2) 66
'An den Mond in einer Herbstnacht' 57
'An die Entfernte' 84
'An die Geliebte' 35
'An die Laute' 145
'An die Nachtigall' (Claudius) 35–6, 82,
  131
'An die Nachtigall' (Hölty) 30
'An die Türen will ich schleichen' 34
'An Silvia' 137
'Aufenthalt' 170
'Auf dem Strom' (Rellstab) 160
'Auf der Donau' 54
'Auflösung' 110, 131
'Ave Maria' (Ellen's third song) 119
'Cronnan' 32
'Das Abendrot' 58
'Das Dörfchen' TTBB 70, 71, 75–6
'Das Fischermädchen' 170
'Das Heimweh' (Pyrker) 120
'Das Lied im Grünen' 146
'Das Rosenband' 31
'Dass sie hier gewesen' 84

'Dem Unendlichen' 31
'Der Atlas' 171
'Der blinde Knabe' 126
'Der Blumenbrief' 58
'Der Doppelgänger' 88, 170, 171
'Der Einsame' 114
'Der Geistertanz' 28
'Der Gott und die Bajadere' 29
'Der Hirt auf dem Felsen' 177
'Der Jüngling und der Tod' 55
'Der Jüngling am Bache' 9, 26–7
'Der Leidende' 33, 88
'Der Leiermann' 34, 142
'Der Lindenbaum' 141
'Der Musensohn' 84, 89
'Der Schatzgräber' 29
'Der Sieg' 110
'Der Tod und das Mädchen' 35, 54, 108
'Der Unglückliche' 81
'Der Vatermörder' 6, 7, 29
'Der Wachtelschlag' 126
'Der Wanderer' (Schmidt of Lübeck) 34–5,
  70, 76, 77, 87
'Der Wanderer an den Mond' 136, 145
'Der Wegweiser' 148
'Der Winterabend' 151
'Der zürnenden Diana' 71
'Der Zwerg' 6, 82, 88
'Des Fischers Liebesglück' 151
'Des Sängers Habe' 53, 115
'Des Tages Weihe' SATB 84–6
Didone Abbandonata (recitative and aria
  from) 52
'Die Allmacht' 31, 120, 122
'Die Allmacht' SATB 122
'Die Betende' 147
'Die Erscheinung' 30, 113
'Die Forelle' 30, 55, 64
'Die Gebüsche' 65, 131
'Die Götter Griechenlands' 66
'Die junge Nonne' 126
'Die liebe Farbe' 95
'Die Liebe hat gelogen' 83–4
'Die Mondnacht' 30
'Die Nacht' 32
'Die Nachtigall' TTBB 70
'Die Nebensonnen' 142
'Die Post' 142
Die schöne Müllerin 94–6, 142, 170
'Die Stadt' 171
'Die Sterne' 151
'Die Sternennächte' 66
'Die Taubenpost' 170, 177
'Dithyrambe' 110
'Drang in die Ferne' 150
'Du bist die Ruh' 84
'Du liebst mich nicht' 83–4

Index

Schubert, Franz Peter (*cont.*):
WORKS (*cont.*):
Songs and partsongs (*cont.*):
  'Edward' 150
  'Eifersucht und Stolz' 94
  'Einsamkeit' (Mayrhofer) 58, 95
  'Einsamkeit' (Müller) 141
  'Erlafsee' 56
  'Erlkönig' 6, 20, 23, 29, 34, 70, 75, 91
  'Erstarrung' 123
  'Erster Verlust' 29
  'Ewige Liebe' TTBB 115
  'Fischerweise' 136
  'Flucht' TTBB 115
  'Frühlingssehnsucht' 163, 170
  'Frühlingstraum' 142
  'Ganymede' 55
  'Gebet' SATB 101
  'Gebet während der Schlacht' 29
  'Geheimes' 81
  'Geheimnis' 25
  'Geist der Liebe' TTBB 76, 81
  'Gesang der Geister über den Wassern'
    TTBB/TTBB strings 70, 71
  'Gesang der Norna' (D831) 115
  Glaube, Hoffnung und Liebe 168
  'Gondelfahrer' 110
  'Gott in der Natur' SSAA 84
  'Grab und Mond' TTBB 137
  'Grablied für die Mutter' 88
  'Grenzen der Menschheit' 81
  'Gretchen am Spinnrade' 19, 23, 26, 28
  'Gruppe aus dem Tartarus' 55
  'Hagars Klage' 6, 28
  'Hänflings Liebeswerbung' 55
  'Heidenröslein' 29, 131
  'Heimliches Lieben' 150
  'Heiss mich nicht reden' 82
  Heliopolis 82, 95
  'Herbst' 163
  'Hymnen an die Nacht' 66
  'Ihr Bild' 171
  'Im Abendrot' 114
  'Im Freien' 136
  'Im Frühling' 123–4, 146, 173
  'Im Haine' 89
  'Im Walde' (Schlegel) 71
  'Im Walde' (Schulze) 123
  'In der Ferne' 170
  'Ins stille Land' 33, 136
  'Klaglied' 26
  'Kolmas Klage' 31–2, 33
  'Kriegers Ahnung' 170
  'Lachen und Weinen' 84, 89
  'Laura am Klavier' 34
  'Lebensmut' (Rellstab) 163
  'Lebensmut' (Schulze) 123

  'Lebenstraum' 4
  'Leichenfantasie' 6, 26
  'Liebesbotschaft' 163, 170
  'Liebesrausch' 29–30
  'Liebhaber in allen Gestalten' 55
  'Lied der Anne Lyle' 115
  'Litanei auf das Fest Aller Seelen' 34
  'Lodas Gespenst' 32
  'Marie' 66
  'Mein' 95
  'Memnon' 53
  Mondenschein TTBBB 162, 171
  'Mut' 123
  'Nachtgesang' 30
  'Nachtgesang im Walde' TTBB 4 horns
    146
  'Nachthelle' TTBB tenor solo 137
  'Nachtstück' 66
  'Nacht und Träume' 82
  'Nachtviolen' 82
  'Nähe des Geliebten' 29
  'Nur wer die Sehnsucht kennt' 33, 136
  'Orpheus' 34
  'Pause' 96
  'Pilgerweise' 172
  Prometheus 66
  Psalm 23 SSAA 71, 179
  'Rastlose Liebe' 22
  'Schäfers Klagelied' 63
  Schlachtlied TTBB 160
  'Schlaflied' 53
  'Schwanengesang' (Senn) 84
  Schwanengesang (Song cycle) 170
  'Schwestergruss' 82
  'Sehnsucht' (Schiller) 70, 81
  'Sehnsucht' (Seidl) 136
  'Sei mir gegrüsst' 156
  'Selige Welt' 84
  'Seligkeit' 33–4
  'Shilruk und Vinvela' 32
  'So lasst mich scheinen' 82, 172
  Ständchen (Grillparzer) SSAA (also TTBB)
    146, 160
  'Ständchen' (Shakespeare) 137
  'Ständchen' (Rellstab) 170
  'Stimme der Liebe' (Matthisson) 34, 131
  'Suleika I' 81, 88
  'Suleika II' 110
  'Szene aus *Faust*' 19
  'Täuschung' 142
  Tiefes Leid 123
  'Todesmusik' 131
  'Totengräbers Heimweh' 116
  'Totengräber-Weise' 136
  'Tränenregen' 95–6
  'Trockne Blumen' 95, 96, 108
  'Trost, an Elisa' 28

'Ungeduld' 95
'Versunken' 81
'Vor meiner Wiege' 151
'Wandrers Nachtlied II' 82, 84
'Wasserflut' 123
'Wehmut' 82
'Wehmut' TTBB 115
'Wer sich der Einsamkeit ergibt' 34
'Wiegenlied' (Seidl) 136
'Willkommen und Abschied' 84
Winterreise 34, 123, 136, 140, 141–32, 145, 147, 151, 152, 162, 170, 177
'Wohin?' 95
'Wonne der Wehmut' 147

Schubert, Franz Theodor (father) 1, 2, 7, 8, 13, 57
Schubert, Ignaz (brother) 1, 2, 3, 8, 40, 58
Schubert, Josefa (stepsister) 179
Schubert, Karl (uncle) 1
Schulze songs 123–4, 146, 170
Schumann, Robert 26, 110, 116, 134, 147, 173
Schuppanzigh, Ignaz 159, 160
Schuppanzigh Quartet 108, 152
Schwind, Moritz von xii, 79, 94, 98, 99, 105, 108, 114–16, 127, 130, 137, 138, 143, 158, 165
Scott (Sir) Walter 92, 115, 118, 123, 124, 126
Scott songs 115, 123–4
Sechter, Simon 41, 166, 176–7, 179
Seidl, Johann Gabriel 100, 112, 136, 137, 145, 170
Senn, Johann 17, 67, 69, 82, 84
Shakespeare, William 79, 137
Silbert, Johann Petrus 65
Silesia 1
Slawjk, Josef 136, 156, 159
Smetana, Bedřich 147
Solomon, Maynard xvi, 60
Sonnleithner, Ignaz von 15, 63, 70, 113
Sonnleithner, Josef von 70
Sonnleithner, Leopold von xii, 8, 21, 61, 63, 70, 71, 76, 80, 81, 134, 146, 152, 154, 166
Spaun, Josef von 4, 5, 7, 9, 13, 17, 20, 21, 23, 31, 52, 55, 57, 64, 69, 79, 86, 87, 89, 98, 118, 128, 137, 141, 143, 158, 159, 166, 179, 181
Spendou, Josef 22, 23, 40, 166
Spontini, Gasparo 74
Staatsbibliothek, Berlin 23
Stadler, Albert 17, 47, 64, 78, 79
Stadler, Maximilian (Abbé) 144
Staufer, Johann Georg 112
Steblin, Rita xvi
Steyr 64, 92, 116, 118, 119, 120
Steyregg Castle 119, 120, 124

Storck, Adam 124
Strauss, Richard 26, 168, 171
Streinsberg, Josef 67
Styrian Music Society 87, 88, 138
Sulzer, Salomon 169
Széchényi, Ludwig Count von 70

Tchaikovsky, Pyotr 89
Thayer A.W. xi
Theater an der Wien 61, 93, 112
Therese Grob collection 24
Theresian Academy 81
Tieck, Ludwig 158–9
Tietze, Ludwig 160
Tomášek, Václav Jan 113, 147
Tovey, (Sir) Donald 110
Traweger, Ferdinand 119
Treitschke, Georg 63
Troyer, Ferdinand Count 109
Tyrol 69

Umlauff, Johann Karl 75
Unger, Karl 57
Unger, Karoline 71
Uz songs 23, 34

Vering, Josef von 179, 180
Vienna xvi, 1, 3, 4, 7, 8, 15, 17, 20, 21, 23, 47, 49, 50, 53, 55, 57, 59–60, 63, 64, 69, 70, 74, 75, 76, 77, 93, 94, 98, 100, 101, 105, 112, 114, 118, 119, 120, 126, 128, 132, 133, 134, 136, 143, 144, 147, 150, 154, 169
Vienna City Library 69, 130, 147
Vienna Schubet Society 177
Vienna General Hospital 93
Vogl, Johann Michael 52–3, 55, 60, 63, 64, 70, 73, 80, 90, 92, 98, 115, 118, 119, 120, 130, 137, 138, 143, 160, 166, 177
Vogl, Kunigunde, née Rosa 130
Voříšek, Jan 113, 128, 147

Währing 132, 137, 143, 165, 180
Walcher, Ferdinand 137, 148
Watteroth, Heinrich Josef, Professor 20, 114
Watteroth, Hermann 25
Watteroth, Wilhelmine 20
Weber, Carl Maria von 74, 75, 80, 90, 91, 92, 93, 94, 112, 128, 132
Weigl, Josef 9, 49, 63, 75, 90, 129
Weigl, Thaddäus 124, 128
Weimar 23, 80, 143
Weintridt, Vincentius 79, 115
Weissenwolf, Karl Count 119
Weissenwolf, Sophie Countess 119
Wesley, Samuel 40
Whistling, Karl Friedrich 116

Index

Whitehead A.N. xi
Wieden suburb 169, 180
Willfort, Manfred 154
Winter, Peter 8
Wipplingerstrasse 59–60
Wisgrill, Johann 179
Witteczek, Josef 20–1, 114, 115

Wolf, Hugo 168, 171

Zechenter, Johann 67
Zuckmantel 1
Zumsteeg, Johann Rudolf 5–6, 9, 26, 28, 171
Zseliz 56, 57, 58, 59, 60, 78, 96, 98, 100, 101,
   105, 110, 11

270